Patterns of Fashion

The cut and construction of clothes for men and women c1560–1620

Written and illustrated by
Janet Arnold

Contents

ISBN 0 333 38284 6

First published 1985 by
MACMILLAN LONDON LIMITED
4 Little Essex Street London WC2R 3LF
and Basingstoke

Associated companies in Auckland, Delhi, Dublin, Gaborone, Hamburg, Harare, Hong Kong, Johannesburg, Kuala Lumpur, Lagos, Manzini, Melbourne, Mexico City, Nairobi, New York, Singapore and Tokyo

Reprinted 1987

Designed by Janet Arnold
Typeset by Wyvern Typesetting Limited, Bristol
Printed in Hong Kong

Photographic acknowledgements

Most of the photographs in this book were taken by the author, with the unstinting help of private owners and the staff of art galleries, museums and costume collections. Each source is acknowledged beside the photograph. Plates 56, 58 and 59 are reproduced by Gracious Permission of Her Majesty the Queen.

The following are reproduced by kind permission of their owners and from their own or museum photographs: British Library, 40; The Duke of Buccleuch and Queensberry, KT (photo Tom Scott) 326; Dulwich College Gallery, 138; Germanisches Nationalmuseum, Nürnberg, 249, 302; GLC, Ranger's House, Blackheath, 139, 200, 365; Gripsholm Slott, 90, 94, 96; Ipswich Museums and Art Galleries, 361; Kunsthistorisches Museum, Vienna, 72, 211, 245; Lippisches Landesmusem, Detmold, 297; Los Angeles County Museum of Art, 123, 124; Monasterio de las Descalzas Reales, Madrid, 71; Museo Lázaro-Galdiano, Madrid, 32, 333; Museum of London, 109, 112; National Gallery of Scotland, 115; National Museet, Copenhagen, 351, 352; National Portrait Gallery, London, 35, 39, 55, 57, 112, 173, 190, 283, 332, 346; National Trust, Hardwick Hall (photo Courtauld Institute) 66; Nordiska Museet, Stockholm, 272, 274; Norton Simon Foundation, Pasadena, 60; Prado Museum, Madrid, 19, 70, 107, 254, 284, 285; Royal Shakespeare Company (Photo Joe Cocks) 382; Lord Sackville, Knole (Photo Courtauld Institute) 69; Schloss Schwerin, 73, 93, 310; Staatliche Museen Preussischer Kulturbesitz, Berlin–Dahlem, 49; Stichting Historische Verzamelingen van het Huis Oranje-Nassau, 187; Tate Gallery, 349; Uffizi Gallery, Florence, 287; Victoria and Albert Museum (Crown Copyright) 153, 154, 179, 191, 192, 218, 252, 253, 362, 363, 364.

Patterns, drawings and photographs taken from original specimens
+ indicates burial clothes

1. +1562. Suit. Satin doublet with paned trunk-hose in velvet and satin, worn by Don Garzia de'Medici. *Palazzo Pitti, Florence*. pattern, page 54, drawings, page 53, photographs 74–9 on pages 14–15.

2. +1562. Velvet bonnet worn by Don Garzia de'Medici. *Palazzo Pitti, Florence*. pattern, page 56, drawing, page 55, photographs 80–2 on page 15.

3. +1574. Satin doublet worn by Cosimo I de'Medici. *Palazzo Pitti, Florence*. pattern, page 56, drawing, page 55, photographs 83–7 on page 15.

4. +1567. Suit. Velvet doublet with pluderhose in velvet and silk, worn by Svante Sture. *Upsala Cathedral*. pattern, page 58, drawings, pages 57 and 59, photographs 88–92 on page 16.

5. +1567. Suit. Velvet doublet with pluderhose in velvet and silk, worn by Erik Sture. *Upsala Cathedral*. pattern, page 61, drawings pages 60 and 62, photographs 94–5 on page 17.

6. +1567. Suit. Leather doublet with pluderhose in velvet and wool camlet, worn by Nils Sture. *Upsala Cathedral*. pattern, pages 64, 65 and 68, and drawings, pages 63, 66 and 67, photographs 96 and 99–106 on pages 17–18.

7. c1560. Youth's pinked and cut leather jerkin. *Museum of London*. pattern, page 68, drawings, page 69, photographs 109–14 on page 19.

8. c1560. Red satin doublet. *Hever Castle, Kent*. pattern, page 71, drawings, page 70, photographs 117–121 on page 20.

9. c1620. Jerkin in green and gold brocatelle. *Los Angeles County Museum of Art*. pattern, page 71, drawings, page 70, photographs 123–4 on page 20.

10. c1595–1610. Embroidered leather doublet. *Stibbert Museum, Florence*. pattern, page 73, drawings, page 72, photographs 125 and 127–130 on page 21.

11. c1595–1605. Youth's doublet in cut and uncut velvet. *Kostuummuseum, The Hague*. pattern, page 73, drawings, page 72, photographs 132–7 on pages 21–2.

12. c1600–5. Suit. Doublet and trunk hose with canions, in dark mulberry uncut velvet on a voided satin ground. *Grimsthorpe and Drummond Castle Trust Ltd, on loan to the Victoria and Albert Museum, London*. pattern, page 75, drawings pages 74, 76 and 77, photographs 140–4 on pages 22–3.

13. c1605–10. Cut and pinked green satin doublet with padded peascod belly. *Germanisches Nationalmuseum, Nürnberg*. pattern, page 79, drawings, page 78, photographs 146–52 on pages 23–4.

14. c1590–1600. Jerkin in black satin, cut and decorated with couched cord to resemble interlaced strapwork. *Hessisches Landesmuseum, Darmstadt*. pattern, page 79, drawings, page 80, photographs 155–8 on page 24.

15. c1610. Padded doublet of shot silk. *Germanisches Nationalmuseum, Nürnberg*. pattern, page 81, drawings, page 80, photographs 159–64 on page 25.

16. c1610. Youth's padded leather doublet, probably for fencing. *Germanisches Nationalmuseum, Nürnberg*. pattern, page 83, drawings, page 82, photographs 166–8 on page 25.

17. c1610. Youth's padded leather doublet, probably for fencing. *Royal Scottish Museum, Edinburgh*. pattern, page 83, drawings, page 82, photographs 169–72 on page 26.

18. c1615–20. Doublet in pinked satin. *Hessisches Landesmuseum, Darmstadt*. pattern, page 85, drawings, page 84, photographs 174–8 on page 26.

19. c1615–20. Silk doublet. *Lord Middleton Collection, Museum of Costume and Textiles, Nottingham*. pattern, page 85, drawing, page 84, photographs 181–4 on page 27.

20. c1615–25. Doublet in pinked satin. *Bayerisches Nationalmuseum, Munich*. pattern, page 87, drawing, page 86, photographs 185–6 on page 28.

21. 1615–20. Breeches or venetians in striped velvet. *Germanisches Nationalmuseum, Nürnberg*. pattern, page 87, drawing, page 86, photographs 188–9 on page 28.

22. 1618. Suit. Doublet and trunk-hose with canions, in slashed and pinked satin, worn by Sir Richard (?) Cotton. *Victoria and Albert Museum, London*. pattern, page 89, drawing, page 88, photographs 191–7 on pages 28–9.

23. c1615–20. Suit. Doublet and trunk-hose in satin with applied leather cut in a decorative pattern. *Museo Parmigianino, Reggio Emilia*. pattern, page 91, drawings, pages 90 and 92, photographs 202–10 on page 30.

24. +1567. Bonnet of thick felt with tufted wool pile. *Upsala Cathedral*. pattern, page 93, photographs 212–17 on page 31.

25. c1565–1600. High crowned felt hat with tufted silk pile. *Germanisches Nationalmuseum, Nürnberg*. pattern, page 93, photographs 220–5 on page 32.

Introduction and Acknowledgements

This is the first book in a series on the cut and construction of clothes for both men and women, covering periods of varying length between the Middle Ages and the twentieth century, related to portraits and other visual sources. It is a continuation of the work started in my two introductory volumes of *Patterns of Fashion*, which dealt only with women's clothes. The format of the series has been governed by the need to convey information in the form of flat pattern diagrams.

The careful study of individual items of clothing and tailoring techniques can help textile conservators and archaeologists piecing together fragments from excavations. It can also assist art historians working with heavily restored paintings. Unfortunately detailed records of cleaning and restoration were not kept in the past and sometimes much of the original top layer of paint has been removed. Traces of textile designs, constructional features, braid and other trimmings may often be detected and aid in identifying the subject of a picture as well as helping to date it.

The book is also a practical guide to cutting period costumes. It is not intended to be a complete history of fashion between c1560 and 1620 and should be used with the books and articles listed on pages 127–8. I hope it will prove useful to students of any age with an interest in the history of dress and the tailor's craft, for people who find making model dolls and dressing them in period costume an enjoyable hobby and for those working in the amateur and professional theatre.

Few complete garments of any type survive from the sixteenth and early seventeenth centuries and almost all are fragile to the point of disintegration. Sometimes this is due to exposure to strong light or iron mordant in black dye slowly rotting the cloth. In other cases the clothes were heavily worn originally, then used again for fancy dress in the nineteenth century, when perspiration did further damage. The garments described and illustrated in these pages do not give a representative survey of the fashions between c1560 and 1620 – they are simply a large number of those still in existence dating from this period, which spans the reigns of Elizabeth I and James I in England. These clothes are the work of the tailor: the work of the seamstress – shirts, smocks, ruffs and other neckwear – will appear in the next volume.

My original intention was to make reconstructions and give pattern diagrams of styles which had not survived, based on clothes depicted in portraits, to fill in the gaps. However, after collecting together material on surviving specimens – patterns, drawings and photographs – it became apparent that there was already as much as could be printed in one volume at a price which would make it readily available to students. It seemed more useful to print this information as it stood, within the limits of available space, than wait to prepare a larger volume, which would have been extremely expensive. The reconstructions will be included in a later volume covering the cut and construction of clothes from c1300 to 1600, overlapping with this book, together with material which I hope to include from the Elizabeth Day McCormick collection at Boston Museum of Fine Arts, the Historisches Museum in Dresden and the Metropolitan Museum, New York. Unfortunately I was unable to study in these collections when I visited them as all the items were packed away while storerooms were being redecorated and new cupboards built.

Seven of the patterns here have already been published in articles in *Costume, Waffen-und Kostümkunde* and *The Burlington Magazine*, but have been included to make the survey as complete as possible. I would like to thank the editors of these journals, Dr Ann Saunders, Dr Leonie von Wilckens and Mr Neil MacGregor for kindly allowing me to use them again. I have referred to gold and silver thread throughout. As George Wingfield Digby points out in *Elizabethan Embroidery*, '... more accurately gold thread is always silver gilt, but it seems unnecessary to insist on this rather colourless expression in every case.' Most gold (or silver gilt) and silver thread consists of a thin strip of metal wound round a silk or linen core. Strips and wires of silver gilt and silver metal are also used.'

Taking patterns and making detailed drawings to show constructional features is a time-consuming occupation. Many of the garments are so fragile that they can hardly be touched. In some cases fabrics and decorations have almost disintegrated and it has taken many hours to sort out their original appearance in a drawing. The whole project has been undertaken with the generous aid of a Leverhulme Fellowship in the Department of Drama and Theatre Studies at Royal Holloway College, University of London. Some of the research was started over ten years ago at the West Surrey College of Art and Design, Farnham, with the help of a Winston Churchill Travelling Fellowship for three months in 1973. This enabled me to visit a large number of art galleries and museums in France, Germany, Italy, Spain and Sweden.

I would like to thank the Directors, Curators and Assistants of the museums, art galleries and costume collections which I visited while compiling the material for this book for all their kindness and help. I am also very grateful to the staffs of the British Library, the National Art Library at the Victoria and Albert Museum and the Westminster and Bristol Central Reference Libraries for their assistance. I have received encouragement and help from many people: in some cases this has ranged from carrying cups of tea up numerous flights of stairs and steadying my position on chairs and stepladders while taking photographs of inaccessible tombs and portraits, to interesting discussions on various aspects of sixteenth- and early seventeenth-century clothing. There is not enough space to mention everyone but I would particularly like to thank Dr Ellen Anderson, Miss Jane Apple, Lord Astor, Dr J.W. Bell, Miss Gunnel Berggrén, Dr Ingrid Bergman, Miss Anna Borggren, Professor George Brandt, Dr Mary Westerman Bulgarella, the late Dr Lionel Butler, Miss Pamela Clabburn, Miss Gudrun Ekstrand, Dr Inger Estham, Mr Jeremy Farrell, Miss Annemarie Fearnley, Mrs Karen Finch OBE, Mr Christopher Foley, Dr Hanne Frøsig, the late Professor Girri Guilio, Mrs Janet Haigh, Miss Zillah Halls, Dr Wilhelm Hansen, Miss Avril Hart, Miss Wendy Hefford, Dr Carl B. Heller, Mrs Jean Hunnisett, Mrs Millie Jaffé, Dr Mary de Jong, Mr John Kerslake, Miss Santina M. Levey, Mr Bo Lönnqvist, Miss Susie Mayor, Miss Ella McLeod, Mr and Mrs Michael Morgan, Dr Sigrid Müller-Christensen, Mrs Anne W. Murray, Miss Monica Murray, Mr Revel Oddy, Dr Kirsten Aschengreen Piacenti, Miss Judith Prendergast, Mrs Susan Ranson, Miss Natalie Rothstein, Mrs Thessy Schoenholzer, Mr Ken Smalley, Miss Kay Staniland, Miss Anneliese Streiter, Miss Pilar Tomás, Mrs Inger Lavesson-Ulfeby, Mrs Winifred Underwood, Dr Angela Völker, Miss Erika Weiland, Miss Norma Whittard, Miss Margit Wikland, Dr Leonie von Wilckens, Miss Lorraine Williams, Miss Sarah Wimbush and Professor Katharine Worth. Finally I would like to thank my mother and Mr Ian Robinson and Mr Robert Updegraff at Macmillan.

The Art and Craft of the Tailor

By the mid-sixteenth century the foundations of the cut and craft of tailoring, as we know it today, had been laid. All over Western Europe from the thirteenth century onwards tailors, like other craftsmen in towns, had slowly grouped themselves together into various guilds and fraternities to protect their interests. They laid down rules for conditions and length of apprenticeships, thus ensuring that certain standards were reached before a tailor could become a Master of his craft.

Records of the Merchant Taylors' Company in London have been preserved but there are no diagrams of patterns to show the clothes that tailors made. In south Germany and Austria a few tailors' masterpiece books have survived and some of the pattern diagrams have been published by Ingeborg Petraschek-Heim. The Biblioteca Querini-Stampalia in Venice has a book of designs with a few cutting diagrams which belonged to an unknown Milanese tailor. Included in it are tents, banners, beds and costumes for tournaments. The examples of civilian costume include men's suits and gowns from the mid-1550s, women's gowns from the 1550s to the 1580s, loose gowns for doctors and learned men and liveries of the German fashion with heavily slashed doublets and pluderhose: the latter were worn by servants of the Count Anguissola and have been dated to 1548 by Rosita Levi-Pisetzky.

Our best information on pattern shapes to link with surviving specimens comes from the early books on tailoring, which are all of Spanish origin. In 1580 the first edition of *Libro de Geometria, pratica y traça* by Juan de Alcega was printed in Madrid. This was followed by Diego de Freyle's *Geometria, y traça para el oficio de los sastres*, printed in Seville in 1588. The second edition of Alcega's book appeared in 1589 and in 1618 Francisco de la Rocha Burguen produced *Geometria, y traça perteneciente al oficio de sastres*, which was printed in Valencia. One further book, *Geometria y trazas pertenecientes al oficio de sastres* by Martin Anduxar, was published in Madrid in 1640 but this is just outside the period covered here.

Until the late seventeenth century tailors made clothes for both men and women, often specializing in some particular area such as farthingales or jerkins. Linen smocks, shirts, ruffs, other neckwear and items of this kind were made by seamstresses. Tailoring seems to have been an exclusively masculine craft in the sixteenth century but Cunnington notes that the Overseers of an Essex parish in 1603 ordered that: '. . . none shall set any man tailor or woman tailor (being single persons) to work in their houses, nor otherwise, so long as there is any tailor a married man in the parish that can and will do the same work.' (*Essex Review*, Sept. 1953.) This may have been an early example of women making clothes for their own sex, a development which occurs in the third quarter of the seventeenth century in both France and England.

There is much documentary material on two English tailors, Walter Fyshe and William Jones, who made clothes for Queen Elizabeth I between 1559 and 1603. A detailed study of their work is given in my book *Queen Elizabeth's Wardrobe Unlock'd*, together with an account of the farthingale makers, embroiderers, hosiers, cappers and other craftsmen working closely with them. The very brief descriptions of the tailor's work and tools of his craft given here are based on that research and will enable a better understanding of the detailed studies of garments which follow.

The tailor required little equipment: a clear working area, a table for cutting out, chalk or soap for marking the cloth, strips of parchment or paper to take his measures, a yard-stick, an ell measure, a pair of shears, an iron, cutters for decorative pinking, pins, needles and thread, linen for toiles and paper for his patterns. In a lively scene with a tailor in *The Taming of the Shrew* Shakespeare also mentions a thimble.

Fynes Moryson in his *Itinerary*, written between 1606 and 1617, describes some Irish women sitting down by the fire 'with crossed legges like Taylers' and this was the traditional position for sewing, carried on into the twentieth century. Jost Amman shows an apprentice or journeyman sitting in this way on a wide bench by a window for good light in his illustration of a tailor's shop in Nürnberg in 1568 (Fig. 1) from his book *Eygentliche Beschreibung Aller Stände auff Erden*, popularly known as the *Ständebuch* or *Book of Trades*. The verse accompanying the woodcut describes the tailor making 'military tents, cloth for jousts and tourneys, Italian and French style, garments of silk and satin for courtiers and ladies, of wool for common folk'.

The tailor is cutting out with a large pair of shears, the small scraps left over being thrown into the box under the table. By the late seventeenth century these scraps and larger pieces of cloth appropriated by the tailor as his perquisites were described as 'cabbage'. The term may have derived from the word 'carbage'. The *Oxford English Dictionary* shows that in 1648 Herrick used both 'garbage' and 'carbage' apparently for 'shreds and patches used as padding'. 'Cabbage' in the sense of a tailor's perquisite is in use by the 1660s and thereafter is also used as a cant word for private theft. This definition is given in *A Dictionary of the Vulgar Tongue* printed in 1811: 'Cabbage . . . Cloth, stuff or silk purloined by taylors from their employers which they deposit in a place called hell, or their eye; from the first, when taxed with their knavery, they equivocally swear that if they have taken any they may find in hell; or alluding to the second, protest that what they have over and above is not more than they could put in their eye'. This slang term is becoming increasingly rare and may, perhaps, be confined to the South of England in the London area. Mr Nelson, a retired tailor

living in Edinburgh, who had worked in Scotland for most of his life, wrote in April 1979: '. . . it is over sixty years since I heard that word cabbage'. The note on the translation of Alcega's *Libro de Geometria, pratica y traça*, published in 1979, gives 'cabbage' as a modern technical term, the translation for 'medios'. However, Alcega was describing the left-over pieces from which facings and trimmings are cut, not the tailors' perquisites.

Amman's tailor has a yard-stick on the table beside him. At the back of the room hangs a pair of pluderhose, full baggy breeches with long panes of the type which the tailor is wearing, and a woman's gown with full pleated skirt. The pleats are being set permanently, held in position by horizontal bands with a weight beneath. These pleated skirts are a peculiarly German/Swiss fashion (Fig. 2) and persisted into the twentieth century in German folk dress. Examples may be seen in the Germanisches Nationalmuseum, Nürnberg, and are illustrated in *Deutsche Trachten* by Margarete Baur-Heinhold (c1939). The horizontal bands around the pleated skirts in the woodcut resembling hoops have led some people to think that it is a farthingale, but this is not so.

The woodcut of the furrier's workshop in Nürnberg (Fig. 3) from Amman's book has a verse accompanying it. This explains that the furrier 'makes and lines coats, cloaks, hoods and other garments with such furs as sable, marten, lynx, ermine, polecat, wolf and fox and from goatskins'. Working with fur was a separate craft from tailoring and although three women's gowns hanging on the rail in the workshop may be of woollen cloth, sent by the tailor for fur linings to be put in, it is possible that they are garments made completely by the furrier from skin with the fur facing inwards. Bo Lönnqvist has recorded a 'skinnkjortel', a kirtle made of lambskin, dating from the eighteenth century, in the National

1 2 3

1. The Tailor *from* Ständebuch *by Jost Amman and Hans Sachs, 1568. The woodcut shows a tailor's workshop in Nürnberg. Private collection.*

2. Nürnberg matron in festive attire *from* Di Gli Habiti Antichi et Moderni di Diverse Parti del Mondo *by Cesare Vecellio, 1590. The woodcut shows a full pleated skirt of the type seen in Fig. 1. Private collection.*

3. The Furrier *from* Ständebuch *by Jost Amman and Hans Sachs, 1568. The woodcut shows a furrier's workshop in Nürnberg. Private collection.*

Museum of Finland. This is cut in a similar way and would have been warm to wear, with the curly fleece facing the body.

The Italian tailor in Moroni's portrait (Fig. 4) painted at about the same time as Amman prepared his woodcuts, has shears in hand, ready to cut the cloth on pattern lines marked out with some white substance, either chalk or soap. Tailors' chalk is mentioned by Cennini in *Il Libro dell'Arte* written in 1437. He describes drawing on black or blue cloth for hangings: 'You cannot draw with charcoal. Take tailors' chalk, and make little pieces of it neatly, just as you do with charcoal; and put them into a goosefeather quill, of whatever size is required'. Alcega refers to the use of 'xabon' in his *Libro de Geometria, pratica y traça* and white soap is still used by tailors as well as chalk. On white silks the tailor might have used charcoal and on velvet 'a pen, with either ink or tempered white lead' as Cennini describes for embroidery designs. Alternatively he might have trace-tacked the pattern pieces, outlining each shape with thread.

Unfortunately Alcega does not give instructions for taking body measurements but to judge from his pattern diagrams they must have been fairly basic

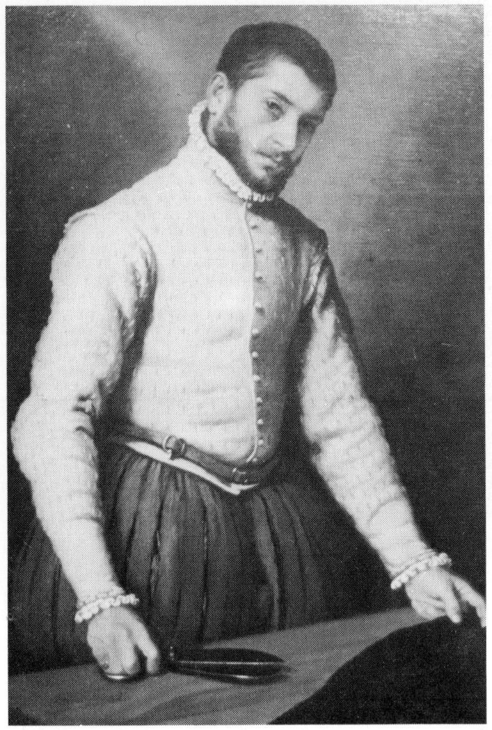

4

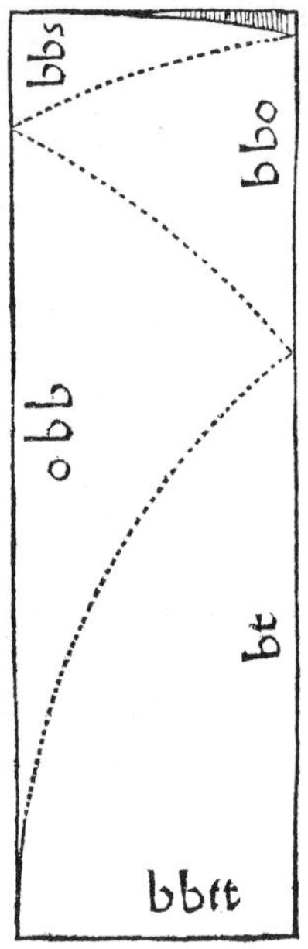

5

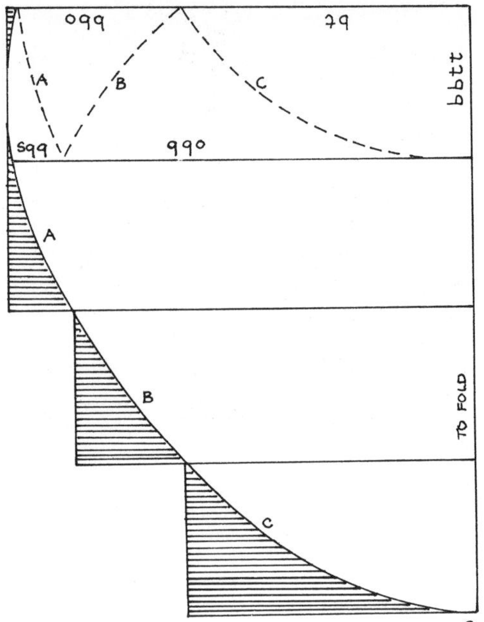

6

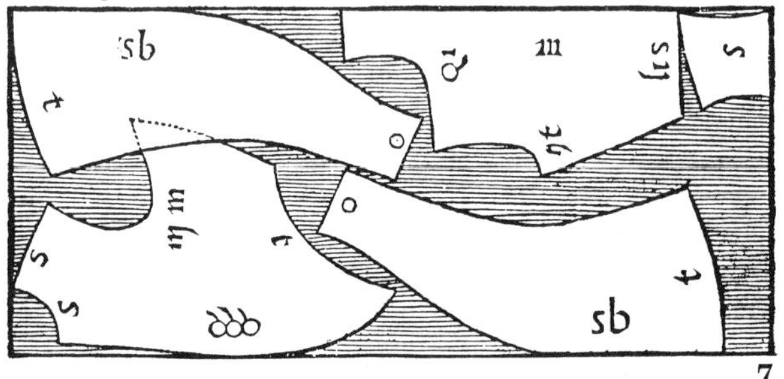

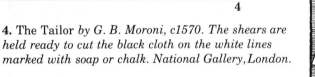

7

4. The Tailor *by G. B. Moroni, c1570. The shears are held ready to cut the black cloth on the white lines marked with soap or chalk. National Gallery, London.*

5. *Manto de seda para muger: mantle of silk for a woman, f.74, from* Libro de Geometria, pratica y traça, *by Juan de Alcega, 1589. Victoria and Albert Museum, London.*

6. *Diagram to show the arrangement of lengths of silk to form the mantle or veil given in Fig. 5.*

7. *Jubon de seda per otra traça a seda abierta: another pattern for a silk doublet from open silk, f. 13v from* Libro de Geometria, pratica y traça, *by Juan de Alcega, 1589. Victoria and Albert Museum, London.*

From left to right: doublet front (below), upper side of two-piece sleeve (above), doublet back (above), underside of sleeve (below), front collar (above).

and the finer points of fitting would have been dealt with on the client. Indeed for a 'manto de seda para muger' (Fig. 5), a woman's silk mantle which would have been described as a veil in England as it falls from the wearer's head, he gives the instruction that the material should first be thrown over the head of the lady for whom it is intended and the required length marked with soap. Here $14\frac{1}{2}$ Castilian baras (13 yards $10\frac{1}{2}$ inches) cut into four lengths of silk, $\frac{2}{3}$ bara wide (22 inches), are joined together along the selvedges, with instructions for shaping to decrease the size, giving a semi-elliptical shape (Fig. 6). The curves are shown on the fabric in Fig. 5. Alcega writes that the fourth length should be sewn on to the mantle and rounded out on the wearer, thus levelling the hemline. He then points out that if the instructions are followed carefully it is possible to cut out the mantle without using another mantle as a guide. This practice of using another garment as a pattern continued into the nineteenth century; Mrs Cory in *The Art of Dressmaking* (1849) gave 'Industrious Daughters of Tradesmen' and 'Persons of Little Means' these instructions for the first stage in cutting a bodice pattern: 'Supposing the reader to have no idea of cutting the first pattern, she is requested to take the body of an old dress and pick it to pieces.' Alcega suggested $2\frac{1}{6}$ Castilian baras ($71\frac{1}{2}$ inches) as the required length for the mantle at the front and $2\frac{2}{3}$ baras (88 inches) at the back. The Castilian bara, a measure equal to 33 inches (83.8 cm), is discussed on page 124.

Tape measures were not invented until the early nineteenth century but Garsault describes a strip of paper notched on the edge for each separate body measurement of the individual client in *L'Art du Tailleur*, printed in 1769. The same system was followed in the sixteenth century, when 'parchement for Meazures', which would have lasted much longer than paper, was supplied for the Office of Revels. The tailor would have kept these notched strips for all his customers rather than writing measurements down in a book. He used a measuring stick to check the lengths of cloth and to draw out his patterns. Shakespeare mentions a mete-yard in *The Taming of the Shrew* and 'Thre brazell mett yerdes and thre brazell mett elles' were delivered to the Wardrobe of Robes in 1578 with another 'sixe mett elles and yerdes of woode' in 1583: the term 'met yard' was still in use in England in the nineteenth century, defined in Whitby's *Glossary* of 1876 as a measuring rod. Measurements of ell and yard varied in each country and are discussed in some detail on page 124.

The tailor's patterns may have been drawn out on stiff paper or kept as flat buckram shapes. We know that 'Two Bundells of lardge browne paper' entered the Office of the Wardrobe of Robes in 1581. It can only be conjectured but it is possible that this paper was intended for Walter Fyshe to prepare patterns taken from the buckram and canvas toiles he made for the Queen and her ladies. Using the measurements on his parchment strip, the tailor would draw out the pattern shapes on these inexpensive linen materials, which might afterwards be used for interlining the garment, if not preserved as a permanent pattern to be adjusted for other clients. A paper pattern traced off from this would keep its shape better than linen, which might eventually stretch on the cut edges. After cutting the pieces out and tacking them together, the toile would be fitted and any necessary alterations made. Presumably similar methods were used for men's clothes.

There are many examples of these pattern toiles among the accounts of the Wardrobe of Robes in the third quarter of the sixteenth century. A selection is given in my book *Queen Elizabeth's Wardrobe Unlock'd* to show the range of materials and variety of garments. Two examples, 'for makinge of a pattron for a Gowne of buckeram being sent into Fraunce' in 1577 and 'for making of Two pattrones of buckeram thone for a frenche gowne thother for a Petycoate sent into Fraunce' in 1580, would seem to have solved the problem of getting ready-made gowns from France for Queen Elizabeth. These toiles were probably sent as a guide to size for the ambassadors and others who purchased gowns for her; a parchment measurement strip may have been sent on previous occasions and not been entirely successful.

After the fitting the toile would have been unpicked, the pieces pressed and all the seam lines carefully marked out. The pieces of buckram, or brown paper patterns traced from them, were then laid on velvet, satin, cloth of gold, cloth of silver, damask, wool camlet or whatever was to be used for the garment – matching the grain lines, keeping the pile running in the same direction and balancing any woven designs, while arranging the shapes to waste as little material as possible. This was not always an easy task as different fabrics came in a variety of lengths from the weavers and in several widths from selvedge to selvedge. Alcega's book must have been most warmly welcomed by Spanish tailors as he gives economical layouts for each pattern on silk and cloth of varying widths.

When the flat pattern shapes had been marked with tacking threads or drawn out with tailor's chalk, soap or fine brush or pen, the uncut length was passed to the embroiderer to be stretched taut on a frame for any embroidery to be carried out. On its return the garment was cut out and made up with suitable linings and interlinings. Examples of different garments with a wide variety of linings are given in *Queen Elizabeth's Wardrobe Unlock'd*, while drawings and photographs of the clothes studied in detail which follow show not only linings and interlinings but also pad-stitching, back-stitching and various types of padding, including cotton wool.

The pattern shapes are our main concern here: those of surviving garments recorded in detail on pages 53–123 may be compared with both Alcega's and Burguen's diagrams, which showed tailors how to lay out their patterns economically on various widths of cloth. Rare copies of both these Spanish tailors' cutting books are preserved in the National Art Library at the Victoria and Albert Museum but they are very fragile and will not stand excessive handling. Some of Alcega's pattern diagrams given here may be studied with the Spanish text in the 1979 facsimile of the second edition of his book *Libro de Geometria, practica y traça*, printed in Madrid in 1589. The large pattern diagrams are beautifully reproduced but the translation is not entirely accurate in some places, perhaps because the editors may not have understood how the shapes would appear when made up and no visual references to portraits and surviving garments are given.

Similar pattern shapes to those for a man's doublet in Alcega's book (Fig. 7) may be seen in the doublets worn by Don Garzia de'Medici in 1562 and Cosimo I de'Medici in 1574 (pages 53–6). These have the back collar cut in one with the doublet but made a little lower. Both have one-piece sleeves. The Hever Castle doublet, dating from c1560 (page 71) shows a more pronounced curve at the centre front and a two-piece sleeve. The slightly old-fashioned uncut velvet suit of c1600–5 (pages 74–5) shows similar shapes to Alcega's pattern but the two-piece sleeves are a little wider at the wrists and have the later development of a curved upper back seam. There are skirts and wings as well. Alcega gives two layouts for his doublet, the first on silk folded lengthwise and the second (Fig. 7) on the open width, which takes 3 Castilian baras (2 yards 27 inches) of silk $\frac{2}{3}$ bara (22 inches) wide. He points out that if the doublet is to be quilted ('pespuntado') it should be cut longer than the pattern as the stitching may take up to three extra finger's breadths ('dedos') in length, but that it shrinks very

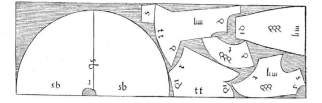

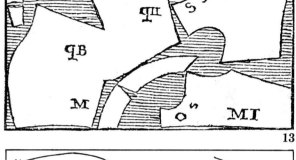
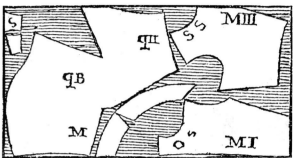

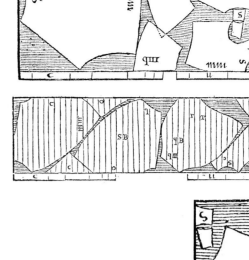

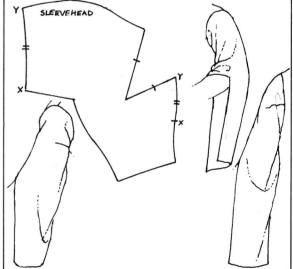

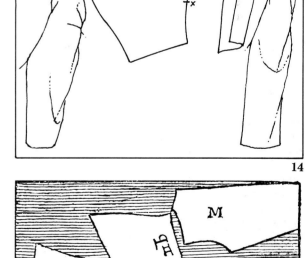

8. *Capa y ropilla de pano: a cloak and cassock of cloth, f.26 from* Libro de Geometria, pratica y traça, *by Alcega, 1589. Victoria and Albert Museum, London.*

From left to right: half of a circular cloak, hood (below), front collar (Above), back of cassock (above), front skirts (centre), front of cassock (below), sleeve (above).

9. *Ein Hispanischer hofsuncker: A Spanish nobleman on horseback, from* Diversarum Gentium Armatura Equestris *by Abraham de Bruyn, 1577. British Library.*

10. *Itali mercatoris habitus: An Italian merchant's dress, from* Omnium Poene Gentium Imagines *by Abraham de Bruyn, 1577. British Library.*

11. *Ropilla y calçon de seda: cassock and breeches of silk, f.147 from* Geometria, y traça, *by Francisco de la Rocha Burguen, 1618. Victoria and Albert Museum, London*

From left to right: back breeches, front skirts (above), back skirts (below), cassock back with collar cut in one (above), front collar (small pieces), cassock front (below), round sleeve, front breeches.

12. *Calçon de seda, ropilla y jubon al sesgo: breeches, cassock and doublet of silk on the bias, f.146 from* Geometria, y traça, *by Burguen, 1618. Victoria and Albert Museum, London.*

From left to right: back of breeches, piecing for back breeches (below), piecing for front breeches (above), front of breeches, round sleeve of cassock, skirts of doublet (above), doublet back (below), doublet front (below), back skirts of cassock (above), cassock front (below), front collar of doublet (above),

little in the width. The Hever doublet (pages 70–1) shows several rows of quilting.

Alcega's cloak and cassock pattern shapes (Fig. 8) are shown laid out on a 3⅛ Castilian baras (2 yards 32½ inches) length of cloth, 2 baras (66 inches) wide, folded along the bottom edge with selvedges at the top. This is a full circular cloak of the type from the Germanisches Nationalmuseum (page 95). The hood to the right of the cloak is also cut with the centre back to the fold. The curved shapes, at the right side, are joined together, bringing the sloping sides to meet. The resulting long hood, decorated with braid and buttons down the sloping seam at the centre back, is shown in Fig. 9 worn by a Spanish nobleman on horseback. The cloak has a rich lining.

front skirts of cassock (above), cassock back (below), front collar of cassock (above), two-piece sleeve of doublet.

13. *Jubon de seda de hombre con manga de armar: man's doublet of silk with hanging sleeve, from* Geometria, y traça, *by Burguen, 1618. Victoria and Albert Museum, London.*

From left to right: front collar pieces (above), sleeve, back skirts, front skirts, doublet back (below), doublet front (above).

14. *Drawings to show the sleeve in Figs. 13 and 15 when assembled.*

15. *Jubon de seda de muger con manga de armar: woman's doublet of silk with hanging sleeve, from* Geometria, y traça, *by Burguen, 1618. Victoria and Albert Museum, London.*

From left to right: sleeve, doublet front, doublet back (above), small pieces for back and front collar.

The same type of hooded cloak, but without the buttons, is worn by an Italian merchant (Fig. 10). Alcega's cassock ('ropilla') follows the same lines as his jerkin ('sayo'), except that the jerkin has completely separate skirts. The cassock has the collar and back skirts cut in one with the body of the garment. The front waist points downwards, following the line of a peascod belly, and the curved skirts are joined to it. The straight sleeve narrows towards the wrist. The cassock was semi-fitting and intended for wear over a doublet, probably for extra warmth when riding.

Alcega does not give any patterns for breeches but Burguen's layout for a cassock and breeches of silk (Fig. 11) gives shapes which may be compared

with a slightly narrower pair of velvet breeches of c1615–20 from the Germanisches Nationalmuseum (pages 86–7). The cassock ('ropilla') has skirts joined at both front and back waist. It shows the later fashion of a shorter waist and less of a curve at the centre front than Alcega's pattern. Cassock and breeches take 6½ Castilian baras (5 yards 34½ inches) of 22-inch-wide silk.

A pair of breeches, cassock and doublet are shown in another of Burguen's layouts (Fig. 12). The breeches and cassock are similar to those in Fig. 11, while the doublet, with its skirts cut in one piece, may be compared with the leather doublet of c1560 from the Museum of London (pages 68–9). Although Burguen's book was published in 1618, the pattern shapes of earlier styles are still seen: Spanish fashions changed slowly and even during the second half of the seventeenth century the rigid styles worn at the Spanish Court hark back to the end of the sixteenth century. This layout is of particular interest as it shows the pattern pieces laid on the bias grain of the cloth. This would give a chevron effect at centre front and back if using a striped material. The suit takes 9¼ Castilian baras (6 yards 9¼ inches) of silk 22 inches wide.

Burguen gives an interesting sleeve with another doublet for a man (Fig. 13). It is described as a 'manga de armar', a type of short hanging sleeve from the elbow. It appears in portraits and engravings but the drawings (Fig. 14) explain more clearly how it was put together, as the rough diagram is slightly out of proportion. The garment takes 2¾ Castilian baras (2 yards 18¾ inches) of 22-inch-wide silk. The same sleeve is given with a woman's silk doublet (Fig. 15) where the waist curves down steeply to a point at the front. The garment takes 2⅛ Castilian baras, less 3 dedos (1 yard 32 1/16 inches) of silk 22 inches wide.

SLEEVEHEAD

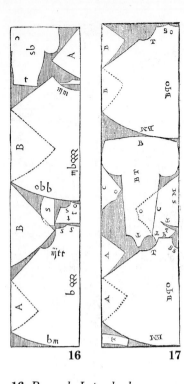

16 **17**

18

19

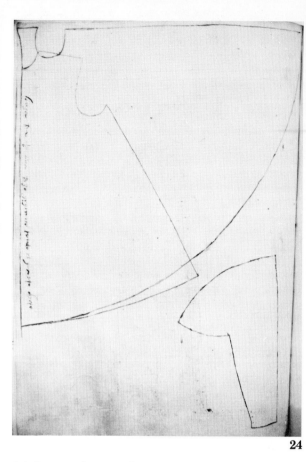

20

24

16. *Ropa de Letrado de pano: a learned man's gown of cloth, f. 49 from* Libro de Geometria, pratica y traça, *by Alcega, 1589. Victoria and Albert Museum.*
From top to bottom: sleeve (left), piecing for front, narrow back yoke, back, piecing for back (left), piecing for sleeve (centre), hood, front.

17. *Gauan de pano: gown of cloth, f.95 from* Geometria, y traça, *by Burguen, 1618. Victoria and Albert Museum, London.*
From top to bottom: piecing for back (left), back, sleeve, piecing for hood (left), hood, piecing for front (left), front.

18. *Drawings to show hood and sleeve in Fig. 17 when assembled.*

19. *Catherine of Austria, Queen of Portugal, by Antonio Mor, 1552. She wears a sleeve of the same shape as that in Fig. 16 and a gown as in Fig. 41. Prado, Madrid.*

20. *A man aged thirty-five wearing a red velvet doublet, the front bordered with satin, with four rows of stitching beside it and sleeves of the type in Fig. 16. Painting by an unknown Middle Rhenish artist, 1567. Germanisches Nationalmuseum, Nürnberg.*

21. Femina honesta Genevensis: dress of a respectable woman of Geneva, *from* Habitus Praecipuorum Populorum *by Hans Weigel and Jost Amman, 1577. Germanisches Nationalmuseum, Nürnberg.*

22. *Learned man in a black gown, c1570, f.87 from a Milanese tailor's album, c1555–80. MS. Classe VIII, Cod.1° Biblioteca Querini-Stampalia, Venice.*

23. *Learned man in a black gown, c1570, f.86 from a Milanese tailor's album, c1555–80. Biblioteca Querini-Stampalia, Venice.*

24. *Pattern diagram for gown in Fig. 22, c1570, f.86v from a Milanese tailor's album, c1555–80. Biblioteca Querini-Stampalia, Venice.*

A learned man's gown ('ropa de letrado') appears in Alcega's treatise with layouts for both cloth and silk (Fig. 16). It takes 4½ Castilian baras (4 yards 4½ inches) of cloth 2 baras (66 inches) wide. It has an interesting sleeve with the fullness springing out on each side under the arm. A gown with a similar sleeve appears in Burguen's book (Fig. 17). Here it has less of a curve on the arm and comes down to a point over the hand instead of being cut straight across at the wrist. When made up the seam is put towards the back of the armhole and the top of the sleeve forms a large puff which falls down over the lower part of the arm in a deep fold, giving the effect of a separate puffed sleeve (Fig. 18). This is seen earlier in the sixteenth century as a fashionable style for both men and women (Figs. 19–21) but, as given by both Alcega and Burguen, it has crystallized into this form worn by learned men. Burguen's pattern takes 4 Castilian baras (3 yards 24 inches) of cloth 66 inches wide.

A Milanese tailor's album shows how similar gowns would have appeared when made up (Figs. 22–3). His patterns show sleeves with fullness given under the arms but here the shape is that of an underarm gusset cut in one with the sleeve (Figs. 24–5). In Fig. 24 the back collar is cut in one with the gown and a deep scoop is made for the shoulder seam. The latter is attached to the front shoulder so that the long straight seam at the top of the pattern hangs from shoulder to hem. This gives a very full semi-circular back which hangs in soft folds. There is no scye, or armhole scoop, at the back and the straight edge is used. The sleeve is cut to a fold on the straight edge. The pattern in Fig. 25 is similar to Alcega's (Fig. 16) with the back gathered or pleated to a small yoke. The front turns back with a deep collar which lies over the yoke and the top of the sleeve is slashed (Fig. 23).

Alcega gives a woman's doublet pattern with two layouts, the first on silk folded lengthwise and the second (Fig. 26) on the open width. This takes 2½ Castilian baras (2 yards 10½ inches) of 22-inch-wide silk. He points out that, as for a man's doublet, it must be cut a little longer than the measurements given if it is to be quilted. The back collar is shown in one with the doublet but it might be cut

21

22

23

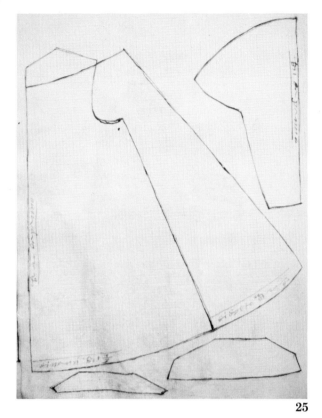

25. *Pattern diagram for gown in Fig. 23, c1570, f.85v from a Milanese tailor's album, c1555–80. Biblioteca Querini-Stampalia, Venice.*

26. *Jubon de muger a seda abierta: woman's doublet from open silk, f.14v from Libro de Geometria, pratica y traça, by Alcega, 1589. Victoria and Albert Museum, London.*

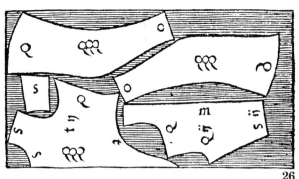

27. *Verdugado de seda para muger: farthingale of silk for a woman, f.67 from Libro de Geometria, pratica y traça, by Alcega, 1589. Victoria and Albert Museum, London.*

From left to right: front (marked A), back (marked B), gores for front and back.

28. *Drawings to show the farthingale in Fig. 27 when assembled. It is possible that the gown in Fig. 30 is open over a farthingale with 25 narrow hoops of bents, spirally bound.*

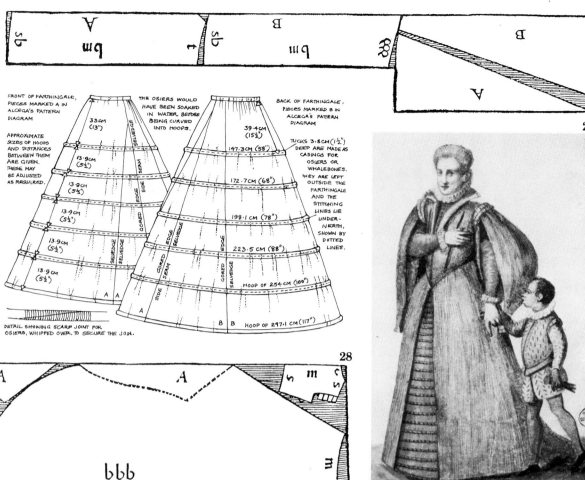

29. *Saya y cuera de pano con manga redonda: skirt and bodice with round sleeves, of cloth, f.63 from Libro de Geometria, pratica y traça, by Alcega, 1589.*

From left to right: front skirt, front bodice (above), round sleeve, piecing for back skirt (above), trained back skirt, back bodice.

30. *A lady in a blue velvet gown with round sleeves, c1580, f.103 from a Milanese tailor's album, c1555–80. Biblioteca Querini-Stampalia, Venice.*

separately if desired. Indeed Alcega advises doing so, taking off a little at the back neckline to avoid wrinkles across the back neck. The slight scoop to the neckline gives a better fit. Alcega writes that many experienced tailors think that a woman's collar should be cut in this way at the back and that it would not be considered a fault as many did it intentionally. The back neck wrinkles slightly on several of the surviving men's doublets and jerkins described later in this book. The leather jerkin from the Museum of London (pages 68–9) has a mass of fine pinking at the back neck to make the leather more supple but, in spite of this, there is a deep wrinkle across it.

The pattern diagram of a Spanish farthingale, a petticoat held out with hoops of osiers, bents or whalebones which supported the skirts in a stiff cone shape, is given by Alcega (Fig. 27). It takes 6 Castilian baras (5 yards 18 inches) of silk 22 inches wide, but no indication of the number of hoops is given. As apparently no farthingales have survived from the sixteenth century, the complete instructions are given here:

'To cut this farthingale in silk, fold the fabric in half lengthwise. From the left, the front (piece A) and then the back (piece B) are cut from a double layer. The rest of the silk should be spread out and doubled full width to intercut the gores (cuchillas). Note that the front gores (A) are joined straight to straight grain and the back gores (B) are joined bias to straight grain, so that there will be no bias together on the side seams and they will not drop. The front of this farthingale has more at the hem than the back. The silk left over may be used for a hem. The farthingale is 1½ baras long (49½ inches) and the width round the hem slightly more than thirteen handspans (palmos), which in my opinion is full enough for this farthingale, but if more fullness is required, it can be added to this pattern.'

This practice of putting the flared side of a gore to the straight grain is a subtle way of avoiding two bias edges on a side seam which would eventually stretch and drop. A good example may be seen in a linen smock embroidered in pink silk at the Museum of London, dating from about 1600. When worn by a woman just over 152 cm (5 ft) in height,

the farthingale is long enough to allow about 25.4 cm (10 inches) for making tucks to act as casings for six or more hoops (Fig. 28). These tucks may have been tacked up over the ready-made hoops rather than attempting to thread osiers through them. Allowing a handspan of about 22.8 cm (9 inches), the hem measures approximately 114.3 cm (117 inches). When Alcega writes that the front 'has more at the hem than the back' he probably means that as both front and back have been cut to the same length the front will need to be taken up a little to clear the feet. The silk left over could be used later as a replacement for a worn-out hem. The waist may have been gathered into a band, opening at both sides, or turned over to make a casing for a drawstring.

Alcega gives pattern diagrams of some petticoats or skirts ('saya') with 'a jerkin, a little cassocke such as women use in Spain' as Minsheu translates 'sayuélo'; others are with a 'cuera', translated by Minsheu as 'a Spanish leather jerkin'. The latter is a bodice which has apparently taken its name from the leather from which it was once made. The

shapes of 'sayuélo' and 'cuera' are almost identical, with tabbed shoulder wings in the armholes. The example given in Fig. 29 is arranged so that the pile or nap ('pelo abaxo') runs downwards throughout. The garment takes 5⅛ Castilian baras (4 yards 31 inches) of cloth, 66 inches wide. 'Manga redonda' is translated as 'puffed sleeve' in the facsimile edition of Alcega's book. It is, however, a round sleeve and the shape may also be seen in a velvet gown from the Victoria and Albert Museum (pages 122–3). The style is familiar from many Spanish portraits (Fig. 32) and was described in England as a Spanish sleeve. It is folded in half with both curved edges stitched together hanging at the back. The straight edges at the front are always slit open, as Alcega describes with another diagram, on f.65v in his book.

The round, or Spanish, sleeve appears in the Milanese tailor's album (Fig. 30) with a gown opening at the front and deeply slashed on the chest to reveal another bodice beneath. Descriptions of some of Queen Elizabeth's gowns refer to 'double bodies' and this style, slashed on the chest with

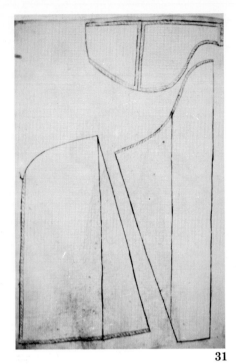

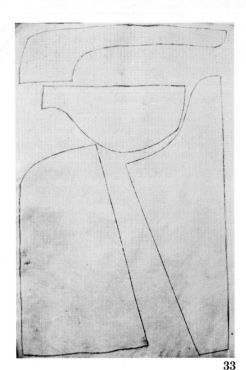

31

32

33

34

35

31. *Pattern diagram for gown in Fig. 30, c1580, f.94v from a Milanese tailor's album, c1555–80. Biblioteca Querini-Stampalia, Venice.*

From left to right: front skirt, back skirt (upside down), round sleeve (above).

32. *Anne of Austria, Queen of Philip II of Spain, wearing round sleeves slit across at elbow level and caught with decorative ribbon bows and aglets. These sleeves are similar to those in Fig. 31. Painting by Sanchez Coello, c1570–5. Museo Lázaro-Galdiano, Madrid.*

33. *Pattern diagram for gown in Fig. 34, c1580, f.103 from a Milanese tailor's album, c1555–80. Biblioteca Querini-Stampalia, Venice.*

From left to right: front skirt, back skirt (upside down), long hanging sleeve (top), under-sleeve (centre).

34. *Gown with trained skirt and hanging sleeves c1580, f.102 from a Milanese tailor's album, c1555–80. Biblioteca Querini-Stampalia, Venice.*

35. *Queen Elizabeth I, the 'Darnley' portrait by an unknown artist, c1580. National Portrait Gallery.*

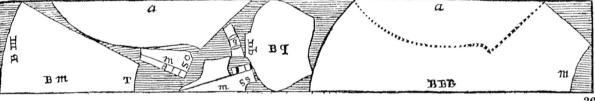

36

36. *Saya grande lanilla para muger: woman's woollen gown with a large skirt, f.181 from Geometria, y traça, by Burguen, 1618. Victoria and Albert Museum, London.*

From left to right: front skirt, piecing for back skirt (above), back bodice (below), front bodice, collar pieces (centre), round sleeve, back skirt. The tabbed wings are shown attached to the armholes.

another bodice below, appears in woodcuts of clothes worn by gentlewomen in Verona, Brescia and other cities of Lombardy, in Vecellio's *Di Gli antichi et moderni di Diverse Parti del Mondo*, printed in 1590. Half the pattern shape of the sleeve is shown (Fig. 31). There are lines of braid round the edges and two across the centre, where the sleeve is often slashed and tied with large ribbon points and aglets in Spanish portraits (Fig. 32). The skirt is curved down at the front, joined to the bodice, unlike Alcega's pattern. In the latter the front skirt seems to lie underneath the pointed bodice, reaching to the waist, the two garments apparently made separately, a method used during the 1840s and 1850s. The trained back skirt is shown upside down and the joins needed for narrow silks are indicated on both front and back.

Similar skirt shapes are seen in another pattern from the Milanese tailor's album (Fig. 33) but the sleeve here is slightly narrower. In this example the curved seam runs down the outside of the arm to give fullness and is worn under a long hanging sleeve (Fig. 34). The 'Darnley' portrait of Queen

Elizabeth shows a similar sleeve with braid decorating the curved seam on the outside (Fig. 35).

Women's bodices were not shaped with waist darts until the nineteenth century and underarm darts even later, although a fish might be taken across the centre front seam on the bust line for a riding habit in the eighteenth century. In the late sixteenth and early seventeenth centuries tailors controlled unsightly bulges with a rigid 'pair of bodies' or corset, stiffened with bents or whalebone (pages 112–13). Shaping for a gown was given with a curved front seam, sloping side seams or curved side back seams. The bust was pushed up to fill a low square neckline or, as a last resort, a very plump woman would wear a loose gown over a waistless kirtle (see page 109). Burguen shows lines on front and back bodice patterns (Fig. 36) which would have allowed for slight shaping beneath lines of braid. Pfalzgräfin Dorothea Maria's gown shows similar lines (pages 115–16). The skirt has a shorter train than that in Fig. 36. The gown takes 12¾ Castilian baras (11 yards 24¾ inches) of woollen cloth, 66 inches wide.

The low-cut bodice in Fig. 37 is similar to that worn by Eleanora of Toledo (pages 102–4). Minsheu translates 'vasquina' as 'a woman's petticoat or kirtle'. As kirtles in the Wardrobe Accounts for Queen Elizabeth have bodices, the latter would appear to be the correct term. Alcega refolds the wide woollen cloth so that there are folds on both edges and the selvedges meet in the centre. He thus avoids piecings on one side of the skirt and both front and back of the bodice are to the fold as well. The instructions do not say where the kirtle should open. It could have been laced at the back or fastened edge to edge with hooks and eyes at the front. The kirtle takes 2 Castilian baras (1 yard 30 inches) of cloth 66 inches wide.

One style of bodice with an arched square neckline, opening at the front, is seen in many French and English portraits. A good example is given in Fig. 39, worn by Queen Elizabeth: the opening, bordered with narrow padded rolls of velvet, can be seen clearly below her hand, running up behind the Phoenix jewel. This superbly cut gown may have been influenced by an unknown

French tailor's work. Although Queen Elizabeth employed only two tailors to make her clothes during her reign – Walter Fyshe from 1558 to 1582 and William Jones from 1582 onwards – an attempt to get another tailor was made in 1567. Sir William Cecil wrote early in that year to Sir Henry Norris, Ambassador at Paris:

'The Queen's Majesty would fain have a tailor that had skill to make her apparel both after the Italian and French manner, and she thinketh that you might use some means to obtain some one that serveth the French Queen, without mentioning any manner of request in our queen's majesty's name. First cause your lady to get such a one.'

No French tailor's name appears in the warrants for the Wardrobe of Robes so apparently this was beyond the Ambassador's ingenuity to contrive. The secret of Italian and French cut was conveyed to England in the form of ready-made gowns 'brought out of France', recorded in the warrants for the Wardrobe of Robes when alterations were made. The arrangement of the embroidery on the gown in Fig. 39 shows that the body was cut without side seams with all the shaping at the centre front (Fig. 38). This pattern was made from Alcega's kirtle body in Fig. 37, placing the side seams together and drawing round front and back as one piece. The arrangement of embroidery is given. The front of the bodice is slightly more arched at the neck and less pointed at the waist than Alcega's pattern. The side seam is indicated by the dotted line. The sleeve shape is conjectured partly from the pattern of the embroidery in the portrait and partly from the sleeve worn by Don Garzia de'Medici (page 54). It would have been supported by a linen roll padded with cotton wool beneath the sleevehead. The style is worn by a Parisian woman in Fig. 40.

Alcega and Burguen give a variety of women's loose gowns following the lines of those for men. 'Loose gown', a term appearing in the Inventory of the Wardrobe of Robes prepared in 1600, seems to be a descriptive term for overgowns worn with kirtles; they may also be described as 'nightgowns' and 'Flanders gowns'. The Spanish tailors' books show that these gowns might fall loosely from shoulders to hem at both front and back with unshaped, gored side seams (Fig. 41), a style seen earlier in Holbein's portrait of the Duchess of Milan, painted in about 1538. Alcega's pattern has a round sleeve and would have been similar to the gown worn by a Neapolitan matron in Fig. 42 when made up. Here the round sleeve is seen from the front, the wearer's arm passing through the opening. The front fastens with clasps in a similar way to that in Fig. 19, where the Queen of Portugal is too plump for her gown to hang straight down below the waist. A longer gown of similar cut from the Milanese tailor's album (Fig. 43) shows a variation of style with short slashed sleeves and long narrow hanging sleeves behind.

Burguen gives a similar pattern for a gown with unshaped, gored side seams and hanging round sleeves, worn over a doublet with a two-piece sleeve and petticoat (Fig. 44). The garments are made of linsey-woolsey, a fabric with linen warp and woollen weft. They take 4½ Castilian baras (4 yards 19½ inches) of cloth 1⅝ baras (60½ inches) wide. The gown is slightly shorter than the petticoat and would be similar in appearance to that in Fig. 45 when made up. The Genoese lady in Fig. 46 wears a gown of similar cut, with short padded sleeves, almost shoulder rolls, instead of hanging round sleeves. Her kirtle follows the lines of Alcega's pattern in Fig. 37.

Alternatively, a loose gown might be semi-fitted, shaped in at the front waist, with unshaped, gored side seams at the back (Fig. 47). The centre back seam has been sloped in a little from hem to neck to fit smoothly over the shoulders. Burguen's gown has a round sleeve and would have resembled that worn by the noblewoman of Lombardy in Fig. 48. The latter has long slashes over the chest, a style described as 'the Italian fashion' in England. Burguen's pattern could have been slashed in the

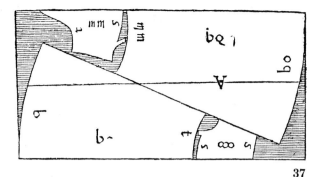

37

CENTRE FRONT OPENING

CENTRE BACK BODICE TO FOLD

THE SLEEVEHEAD IS GATHERED IN 'RUFFS', OR CARTRIDGE-PLEATED, TO FIT THE ARMHOLE AND A PADDED ROLL PUT BENEATH TO HOLD THE SHAPE.

THIS MARK MEETS CENTRE SHOULDER

SCALE

1:1 CM

1:1 INCH

38

37. Vasquina y cuerpo baxo de raxa para muger: woman's kirtle with a low-cut bodice of cloth rash, f.60 from Libro de Geometria, pratica y traça, *by Alcega, 1589. Victoria and Albert Museum, London.*

From left to right: front skirt (below), front bodice (above), back skirt (above), back bodice (below).

38. Conjectured pattern shapes of bodice and sleeve in Fig. 39.

39. Queen Elizabeth I, the 'Phoenix' portrait, attributed to Nicholas Hilliard, c1575. National Portrait Gallery, London.

40. Femina Parisiensis: A Parisian woman, from Omnium Poene Gentium Habitus, *by Abraham de Bruyn, 1581. British Library.*

39

40

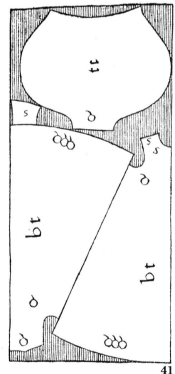

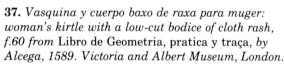

41

42

43

41. Ropa de pano para muger: woman's cloth gown, f.68 from Libro de Geometria, pratica y traça, *by Alcega, 1589. Victoria and Albert Museum, London.*

From top to bottom: round sleeve, collar piece (left), back (left), front (right). Other collar pieces and wings are cut from remnants left over.

42. Neapolitan matron, from Di Gli Habiti Antichi, *by Cesare Vecellio, 1590. Private collection.*

43. Woman in a loose gown, c1570–80, f.100 from a Milanese tailor's album, c1555–80. Biblioteca Querini-Stampalia, Venice.

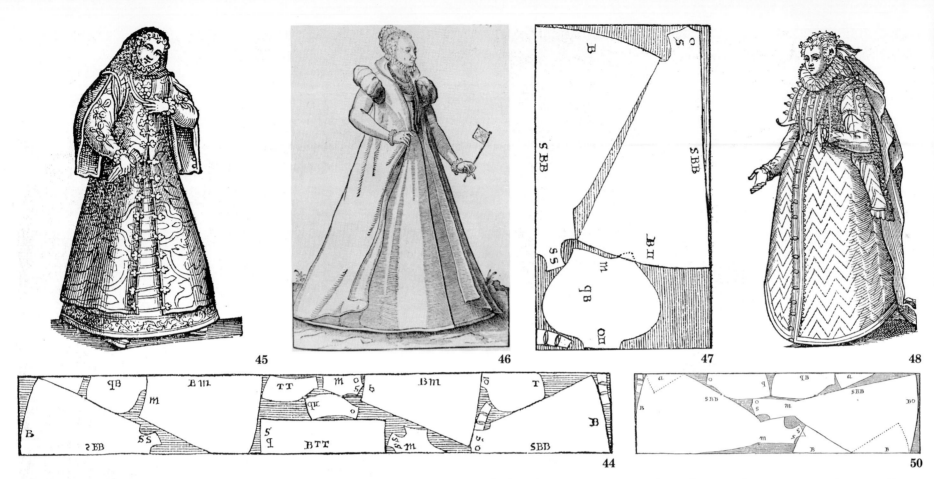

45 **46** **47** **48**

44 **50** **49**

44. *Ropa, vasquina, jubon y escapulario de estamena: gown, petticoat, doublet and hood or shoulder cape of linsey-woolsey, f.175 from Geometria, y traça, by Burguen, 1618. Victoria and Albert Museum, London.*

From left to right: gown front, piecing for petticoat (above), half of gown sleeve, petticoat back, two-piece doublet sleeve, back doublet (above), hood or shoulder cape (below), front doublet (below), forepart of petticoat (above), half of gown sleeve (above), collar pieces of doublet, back of gown (below), collar pieces of gown.

45. Noble matron of Milan and other places in Lombardy, *from Di Gli Habiti Antichi by Cesare Vecellio, 1590. The woodcut shows a loose gown fastening at the front, with doublet and petticoat beneath. These clothes are similar in style to those given in the pattern diagram in Fig. 44, with the exception of the hanging sleeve, which appears to be cut in the same way as that in Fig. 15.*

46. *Nobilis Femina Genuensis: Noblewoman of Genoa, from Habitus Praecipuorum Populorum by Hans Weigel and Jost Amman, 1577. Germanisches Nationalmuseum, Nürnberg.*

47. *Ropa de vayeta de muger: woman's gown of baize or fine frieze, f.168 from Geometria, y traça, by Burguen, 1618. Victoria and Albert Museum, London.*

From top to bottom: gown front (left), gown back (right), sleeve, collar pieces.

48. Dress worn by chief noblewoman of Lombardy, *from Di Gli Habiti Antichi by Cesare Vecellio, 1590. The woodcut shows the gown slashed on the breast in a similar way to that in Fig. 49.*

49. *Margaret of Parma wearing a semi-fitted gown with shaping on the side seam at the front. Painting by Antonio Mor, c1562. Gemäldegalerie, Staatliche Museen Preussicher Kulturbesitz, Berlin–Dahlem.*

50. *Galerilla de raxa para muger: woman's fitted gown of cloth rash, f.169 from Geometria, y traça, by Burguen, 1618. Victoria and Albert Museum, London.*

From left to right: collar pieces (above), front of gown, two-piece sleeve (above), back of gown, piecing for back of gown (below), piecing for front of gown (above).

same way. Mor's portrait of Margaret of Parma (Fig. 49) shows a similar black satin gown with an alternative sleeve style, revealing a carnation silk kirtle beneath the slashes and front opening.

The gown might be fitted at the waist on both front, back and side seams (Fig. 50). Burguen's pattern gives straight sleeves, fitting closely at the wrist, with it. It takes 4$\frac{11}{12}$ Castilian baras (4 yards 18$\frac{1}{4}$ inches) of fine cloth rash 1$\frac{5}{8}$ baras (60$\frac{1}{2}$ inches) wide. Florio defines 'saetta' as 'a kind of fine serge or rash' in his *World of Wordes* in 1598. A Neapolitan noblewoman's gown is cut in this way, falling open below the waist (Fig. 51). It is made with hanging round sleeves.

No tailor's pattern diagrams of the flounced skirts worn over French, or drum-shaped, farthingales

seem to have survived but this is not surprising. Although apparently complicated, these skirts were simply loom widths of material joined together down the selvedges, sloped slightly at the front and pleated or gathered to fit the waist (see page 117). No French farthingales appear to have survived either but a contemporary engraving (Fig. 52) shows the 'Hausse-cul: a French vardingale or (more properly) the kind of roll used by such women, as weare (or are to weare) no Vardingales' as described by Randle Cotgrave in his *Dictionarie of the French and English Tongues* printed in 1611. Made of fustian or linen, padded with cotton wool with extra stiffening of bents, wire or whalebone, they were also described as 'bum rowls' by Ben Jonson in *The Poetaster.*

A watercolour drawing of the 'Entrée des Esperducattes' shows dancers wearing French farthingale frames (Fig. 53). They are following Jacqueline, Fairy of the Mad People, in the Ballet des Fées des Forêts de Saint Germain, presented at the Louvre in Paris, on 11 February 1625. Many noblemen at Court and King Louis XIII himself took part in it. The 'Esperducattes' are 'those who are difficult to deceive' and here six male dancers mock the deception practised by women wearing farthingales, revealing the framework beneath on the left. All the dancers wear green bodices decorated with white braid, white scarves and full black sleeves. The farthingale frames are black, probably made of taffeta, and the casings holding whalebones or bents may be seen clearly. The black

skirts, probably of taffeta or satin, are carefully arranged in even pleats from the waist to the edge of the farthingale, falling loosely below.

Skirts fall smoothly over padded rolls standing out evenly round the hips during the 1580s. It seems likely that the flounce recorded in so many paintings of the 1590s and after evolved from a loose tuck made to shorten the skirt front when worn over a half roll. This stood out at back and sides and was described as a semi-circled farthingale by Falstaff in Shakespeare's *The Merry Wives of Windsor*. A skirt made to hang over a complete roll would have to be tucked up for several inches at the front if the other style of roll was worn instead (Fig. 54). The carefully arranged flounce slowly evolved from this loose tuck, probably

52

53

51. Femina Nobilis Neapolitana: Neapolitan noblewoman, *from* Habitus Praecipuorum Populorum *by Hans Weigel and Jost Amman, 1577. Germanisches Nationalmuseum, Nürnberg.*

to disguise the pronounced ridge made by whalebones, osiers or bents on the circumference of the wide drum-shaped farthingale (Fig. 55). Some of the flounces may have been cut separately, but in all the portraits I have been able to examine closely, they have been made by pinning the skirt to the farthingale frame and then stroking the fullness down from the waist in soft pleats (Figs. 56–7).

A later development in the arrangement of the flounce was to pin above and below the edge to form a ruffle around the circumference of the farthingale (Figs. 58–9). In some cases the material was arranged in a tuck first of all, then pulled up with two or three rows of large gathering stitches, before being pinned to the farthingale (Fig. 350). This gives a neat, evenly pleated surface. The evidence for the gathering threads still remains in the form of stitch holes through the pink silk lining of the skirt on page 117. One particularly attractive red velvet petticoat, with a semi-transparent covering of *mezza mandolina,* a type of netting, has the flounce apparently secured with red ribbon points tied in bows (Fig. 60). These are probably hiding pins beneath.

54

55

56

National Portrait Gallery, London.

52. *French farthingales, one being arranged on the wearer. The stitching lines for casings to hold bents or whalebone are clearly shown. Engraving with verses in French and Dutch, c1590. Private collection.*

53. *Costumes for a ballet at the French Court, showing French farthingales stiffened with bents or whalebone, giving the drum shape to the skirt. Watercolour drawing, 1625. Bibliothèque Nationale, Paris.*

54. *Mrs Ralph Sheldon wearing a black silk damask gown with big sleeves, either bombasted or 'borne out with whalebones' over a kirtle of light brown and pale grey silk, woven in a pattern of acorns, roses and other flowers, with silver metal thread in the weft. The skirt, supported with a half roll, is caught up with a tuck at the front. Painting by an unknown artist, English School, c1593–5. Private collection.*

55. *Queen Elizabeth I, the 'Ditchley' portrait by Marcus Gheeraerts the Younger, c1592–5. The flounce is formed by carefully pleating the material.*

56. *Anne of Denmark, attributed to Marcus Gheeraerts the Younger, 1614. This flounce gives the impression that it was cut separately but in fact the skirt opens all the way down the front. Two of the buttons which fasten it may be seen below the ropes of pearls. The silk is folded in a deep tuck and pinned to the farthingale. The creases may be seen clearly by her left cuff. Royal Collection, London. Reproduced by Gracious Permission of Her Majesty the Queen.*

57

58

60

61

62

59

57. *Lady Throgmorton wearing a doublet and matching petticoat of silk, embroidered with a linear design of bunches of grapes and vine leaves. The material is loosely pleated into a flounce over the*

semi-circled farthingale. Dents appear in the pleats where the silk is caught with pins underneath. Painting by an unknown English artist, c1600. Present whereabouts unknown.

58. Elizabeth of Brunswick, *attributed to Jacob van Doort, 1609. The flounce is pinned in a pronounced ruffle at the edge of the farthingale. Royal Collection, London. Reproduced by Gracious Permission of Her Majesty the Queen.*

59. *Detail of the pinned flounce in Fig. 58.*

60. *Unknown lady wearing a white silk doublet with red ribbon points at the waist and a red velvet petticoat with a fine silk covering of* mezza mandolina, *a type of netting, in a design of cobwebs. The flounce is arranged with red ribbon points at the edge, probably hiding pins below. Portrait attributed to Marcus Gheeraerts the Younger, c1605–10. Norton Simon Foundation, Pasadena, California.*

61. *Kneeling effigy of Christian, daughter of Edward, Lord Bruce of Kinloss, Master of the Rolls. Monument of alabaster and marble, gilded and painted, 1610. Rolls Chapel, London.*

62. *Back view of effigy in Fig. 61 taken at eye level.*

The farthingale was worn at a slight angle, tilting up at the back. A girl, possessed of an evil spirit in 1597, called out to it: 'My lad, I will have a French farthingale, it shall be finer than thine; I will have it low before and high behind and broad on either side that I may laye mine arms upon it' (Harrison, *Elizabethan Journals*). The effigy of Christian, the daughter of Edward, Lord Bruce of Kinloss, Master of the Rolls, shows the tilt from various angles (Figs. 61–4). Her mother and Lady Cavendish wear the flounce hanging down over a small padded roll (Figs. 65–6). This alternative style was less cumbersome than the large farthingale. Indeed, at the marriage of Princess Elizabeth to Count Frederick, Elector Palatine of the Rhine, in 1613, John Chamberlain wrote to Alice Carleton that: '. . . no lady or gentlewoman should be admitted to any of the sights with a farthingale, which was to gain more room, and I hope may serve to make them quite left off in time.' This foreshadows the slow decline of the farthingale after about 1617 in England. The fashion lasted longer in France. Elizabeth Suckling wears another variation of this more moderate style over a padded roll: the deep tuck taken round the skirt at hip level, which would have been pinned to the edge of a drum-shaped farthingale by a more fashionable woman, is left hanging downwards (Fig. 67). Martha Suckling

wears her skirt tightly gathered in cartridge pleats at the waist, with the tuck pinned to the edge of a small drum-shaped farthingale (Fig. 68).

The arrangement of the skirt worn over a French farthingale was left to the wearer and her servant, who folded and pinned the flounce to suit the size of padded rolls or frame as required. The tailor simply joined the breadths of material together, making the skirt as long as his customer required, with the correct waist measurement. He might also have put in the gathering threads for the style in Fig. 350.

The waistline rose slightly above the natural level between 1616 and 1618, retaining the pointed shape in front. In 1619 the rise was more pronounced and by 1621 the waistline was immediately underneath the bust, often straight round without a point (Fig. 69). Many tailors must have pressed the creases from pinned flounces to re-use these skirts for the new fashion. There would have been plenty of material from the depth of the farthingale and flounce for the length from raised waist level to feet. Several portraits dating from about 1620 show patterned silks woven in the early 1600s which have been used again.

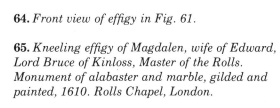

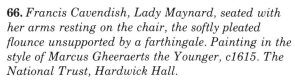

63. *Side view of effigy in Fig. 61.*

64. *Front view of effigy in Fig. 61.*

65. *Kneeling effigy of Magdalen, wife of Edward, Lord Bruce of Kinloss, Master of the Rolls. Monument of alabaster and marble, gilded and painted, 1610. Rolls Chapel, London.*

66. *Francis Cavendish, Lady Maynard, seated with her arms resting on the chair, the softly pleated flounce unsupported by a farthingale. Painting in the style of Marcus Gheeraerts the Younger, c1615. The National Trust, Hardwick Hall.*

67. *Kneeling effigy of Elizabeth Suckling, the first wife of Robert Suckling, with her daughters. Monument erected in 1611. St Andrew's Church, Norwich.*

68. *Recumbent effigy of Martha, wife of Sir John Suckling, Treasurer to James I. Monument dated 1613. St Andrew's Church, Norwich.*

69. *Martha Cranfield, Countess of Monmouth, wearing a gown made of silk with a woven pattern of slips of flowers. The silk is slightly stiff for the raised waist level and may be of an earlier date than the portrait. Painting by Daniel Mytens, c1620. Lord Sackville, Knole.*

63

65

68

64

66

67

69

Portraits and other Visual Sources with Photographs of Original Garments showing Stitching, Fabrics and Trimmings

The details of stitching, fabrics, interlinings, braids and embroidery which follow should be considered in conjunction with the drawings, descriptions and patterns given on pages 53–123. They have been printed in this separate section for quick visual reference to early sewing techniques for textile conservators. Photographs are sufficient to give a clear idea of the original appearance of several garments and contemporary portraits show how they were worn, together with appropriate accessories and hair styles. In those cases where drawings are not needed, longer descriptions have been given with the photographs to link with the pattern diagrams.

Related portraits are printed among the groups of photographs recording each piece of clothing to enable art historians to see at a glance how painters interpreted what they saw: the surface textures given by slashing and pinking, braids, embroidery and woven fabrics. They will also help costume designers to understand how the rich, icon-like effect of sixteenth- and early seventeenth-century portraits was given by different fabrics – silk, linen and wool, with linings, interlinings and cotton padding – and by a variety of tailoring techniques. Wardrobe staff in theatres will be able to translate and adapt the information for practical use.

Men's suits, doublets and hose, or breeches

'We . . . are never content except wee have sundry sutes of apparel one divers from an other, so as our Presses crack withall, our Cofers burst, and our backs sweat with the cariage thereof: we must have one sute for the forenoone, another for ye afternoone, one for the day, another for the night, one for the worke day, another for the holieday, one for sommer, another for winter one of the newe fashion, an other of the olde, one of this colour, another of that, one cutte, an other whole, one laced, another without, one of golde, and other of silver, one of silkes and velvets, and another of clothe with more difference and varietie than I can expresse.'

(Phillip Stubbes, *The Anatomie of Abuses*, 1583)

70. *Prince Carlos wearing a pink satin suit, pinked diagonally between rows of couched gold metal cord. Over this is a dark mulberry velvet cloak lined with lynx. The black velvet bonnet, worn at an angle, is decorated with jewels and a white feather. The clothes in this portrait are similar to those worn by Don Garzia de'Medici (Fig. 74 and page 53). Painting by Sanchez Coello, c1556. Prado, Madrid.*

71. *The white satin doublet is decorated with diagonal lines of couched yellow silk braid, possibly with some metal threads, and pinked on the straight*

70

75

74

grain between them. It may be compared with that worn by Erik Sture where the braid is applied in an alternative diagonal arrangement (Fig. 94). The doublet is slightly padded at the front. The cod-piece is similar to that worn by Don Garzia de'Medici (Fig. 76). Short canions may just be seen below the trunk-hose. Portrait of King Don Sebastian of Portugal by Cristoforo Morales, 1565. Monasterio de las Descalzas Reales, Madrid.

72. *The white silk doublet is decorated with couched cord in a similar way to that in Fig. 70, but shows the later development of padded peascod belly. The trunk-hose are slightly shorter and more rigidly*

padded, the fashionable line of the early 1570s. Portrait of Erzherzog Wenzel by Sanchez Coello c1571. Kunsthistorisches Museum, Vienna.

73. *Velvet doublet and trunk-hose trimmed with couched cord, a cloak with sleeves worn on top. Portrait of Herzog Johann Albrecht zu Mecklenburg by Peter von Boeckel, 1574. Schloss Schwerin.*

74. *Fragments of the suit worn by Don Garzia de'Medici when he was buried in 1562. The satin doublet and velvet panes of the trunk-hose are decorated with couched gold metal cord. The sleeves are stored separately. Palazzo Pitti, Florence.*

75. *Detail of silk points with metal aglets which are still threaded through eyelet holes in the waistband of the trunk-hose in Fig. 74.*

76. *Detail of cod-piece which closes the front of the trunk-hose in Fig. 74. Originally it was padded with crimson satin and small puffs were pulled out between the slashes. The doublet front is still attached to the trunk-hose with a ribbon point.*

71

72

73

76

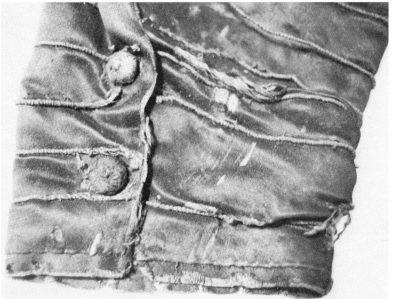

77

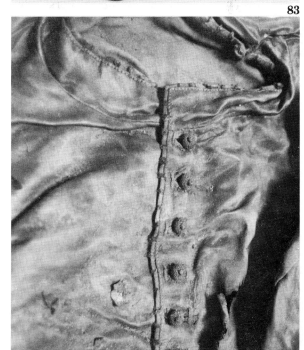

78

79

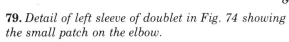

80

81

82

83

84

77. *Detail of the velvet panes of the trunk-hose in Fig. 74, which are lined with silk and interlined with linen, most of which has disintegrated into a fine powder. The ends of the trunk-hose are gathered into cartridge pleats with silk thread. The edges of the panes are not turned under. The raw edges are oversewn with fine gold cord for a decorative finish. This is made of three plied threads of metal strip wrapped round yellow silk cores. One piece has started to unravel in this detail.*

78. *Detail of sleeve end of doublet in Fig. 74. The doubled strip of bias satin is snipped at the edge. The buttons have wooden bases, worked over with silk.*

79. *Detail of left sleeve of doublet in Fig. 74 showing the small patch on the elbow.*

80. *Black velvet bonnet worn by Don Garzia de'Medici when he was buried in 1562. The pile is disintegrating. Similar bonnets may be seen in Figs. 70 and 71. Palazzo Pitti, Florence.*

81. *Detail from Fig. 82 showing bonnet crown pleated to fit the brim.*

82. *Underside of black velvet bonnet worn by Don Garzia de'Medici showing brim and silk lining.*

83. *Fragments of red satin doublet, now discoloured, together with fragments of black velvet bonnet and the silk laces and tassels from the mantle of the Grand Master of the Order of St Stephen worn by Cosimo I de'Medici when he was buried in 1574 (page 55). Palazzo Pitti, Florence.*

84. *Detail of doublet front in Fig. 83 showing the even stitching holding the strip of satin snipped on the edge for decoration. The buttons are made of silk worked over wooden bases.*

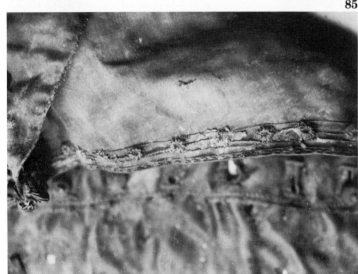

85

90

91

88

87

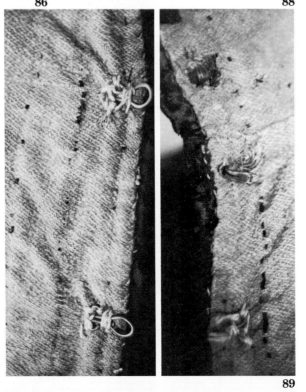

89

92

85. *Detail of mantle laces and tassels in Fig. 83. The two devices holding the cords together, which slide up and down, are worked in silk. The back of the cod-piece and silk binding strips from the waistband lie above the mantle laces. Palazzo Pitti, Florence.*

86. *Detail inside bottom edge of doublet in Fig. 83. Originally there was a linen tape for reinforcement. The line of tacking stitches held it in position while the eyelet holes were worked in silk.*

87. *Detail of Fig. 83 showing a ribbon point still tied through the bottom pair of holes in the doublet front and a pair of eyelet holes in the fragments of the waistband of the hose or breeches. The latter are worked over metal rings for reinforcement.*

88. *Black velvet suit worn by Svante Sture when he was murdered in 1567 (page 57). Doublet and pluderhose are decorated with pinked guards. Puffs of greenish-grey silk are pulled out between the panes. Upsala Cathedral.*

89. *The doublet in Fig. 88 is lined with reddish-brown fustian and fastens with hooks and eyes. Stitches in black silk from the decorative guards may be seen inside the doublet, beside the metal eyes on the left front.*

90. *Svante Sture wears a suit with embroidered guards or borders. Painting by an unknown artist, c1567. Gripsholm Slott.*

91. *Details of the white linen strip with pairs of worked eyelet holes inside the waist of the doublet in Fig. 88. Points were tied through these holes to others in the waistband of the pluderhose.*

92. *Detail from pluderhose in Fig. 88 with one of the silk puffs at the bottom of the leg pulled out to reveal the stay tape of chamois leather to which the silk is stitched.*

93

95

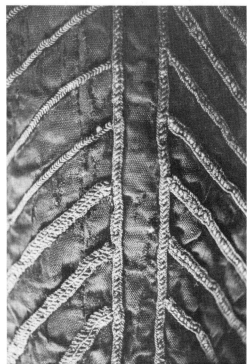

97

98

99

94

96

93. *Black velvet cloak with doublet, cloak lining and pluderhose panes in golden-yellow silk, possibly with gold thread in the weft, embroidered with black silk. Yellow silk damask is pulled out between the panes in a similar way to Svante Sture's suit (Fig. 88 and page 57). Portrait of Herzog Ulrich zu Mecklenburg by Peter van Boeckel, 1573. Schloss Schwerin.*

94. *Erik Sture wears the suit in which he was murdered in 1567 (page 60). It is trimmed with*

golden yellow braid. *Painting by an unknown artist, c1567. Gripsholm Slott.*

95. *Detail of three widths of braid used on the left sleeve of Erik Sture's doublet in Fig. 94. Upsala Cathedral.*

96. *Nils Sture wears a black velvet slashed jerkin trimmed with braid over a doublet with plain black sleeves. The panes of the trunk-hose are also trimmed with braid. Painting by an unknown artist, c1567. Gripsholm Slott.*

97. *A German soldier wearing similar pluderhose to those worn by Erik Sture (page 60). The slashed jerkin worn by the standard bearer is probably made of leather. From* Omnium Poene Gentium Imagines *by Abraham de Bruyn, 1577. Germanisches Nationalmuseum, Nürnberg.*

98. *A German soldier* (Landsknecht) *showing the back view of a pair of pluderhose. They fit tightly over the buttocks. German woodcut, 1559. Private collection.*

99. *Detail of the black velvet panes, trimmed with black wool braid fringed on both edges, from the pluderhose Nils Sture was wearing when he was murdered in 1567 (page 63). Upsala Cathedral.*

100. *Side view of velvet pane in Fig. 99 to show the brown fustian lining. The cut edges of the velvet are waxed to prevent fraying and held down with catch stitch.*

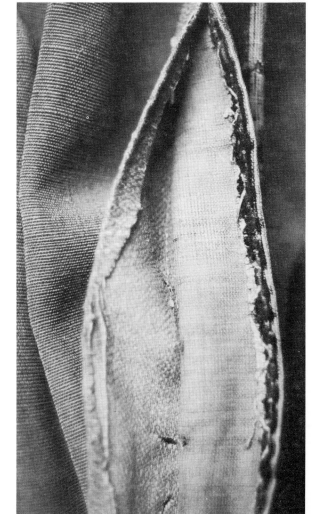

100

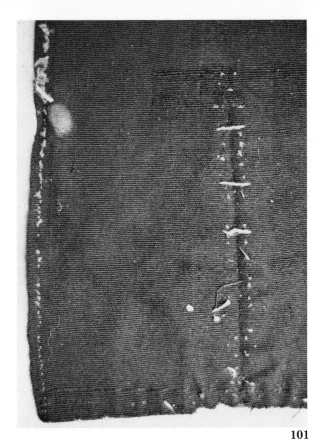

101

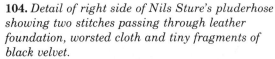

103

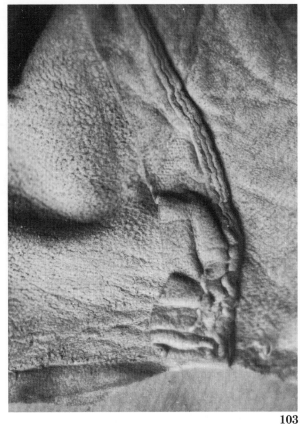

105

106

106. *Collar of Nils Sture's leather doublet (page 63), showing marks of pad-stitching on the right side.*

107. *Emperor Maximilian II wearing a slashed leather jerkin. Painting by Antonio Mor, 1550. Prado, Madrid.*

108. *A traveller wearing pluderhose with looped panes below the waist and puffs on the cod-piece. The slashed leather jerkin is similar to a surviving specimen (Figs. 109–14 and page 69). Beneath the jerkin is a plain doublet similar to that worn by Nils Sture (page 63). Woodcut by Jost Amman, c1570. Victoria and Albert Museum, London.*

101. *Detail of one panel of the worsted cloth in Nils Sture's pluderhose, showing the back stitches and running stitches remaining by the selvedges. On the right is one of the long darts made inside each puff at the bottom of the leg. The large stitches here are tacking stitches which have not been removed. Weaving faults may be seen in the material at the end of the dart. Upsala Cathedral.*

102. *One of the puffs in Nils Sture's pluderhose pulled inside out to show the stay tape of coarse black wool to which the worsted cloth is stitched.*

Tacking threads may be seen in the seam in the centre of the picture.

103. *Detail of leg seam in the leather foundation breeches of Nils Sture's pluderhose, with inset strip of leather for reinforcement.*

104. *Detail of right side of Nils Sture's pluderhose showing two stitches passing through leather foundation, worsted cloth and tiny fragments of black velvet.*

105. *Detail of linen thread stitches in seam of narrow panels at centre back of Nils Sture's pluderhose. Fustian and leather are sewn together, with strips of leather acting as stay tapes and for reinforcement.*

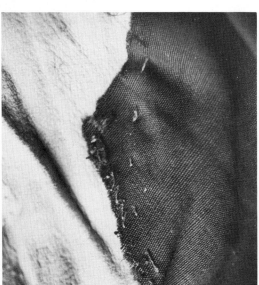

102

104

107

108

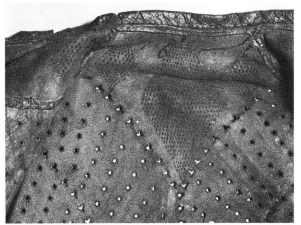

109. *Detail of youth's leather jerkin which fastens with pewter buttons imitating wooden ones worked over with silk. The seams are joined with strips of leather placed between them, hammered flat. This method protects the stitching from being rubbed. c1560. Museum of London.*

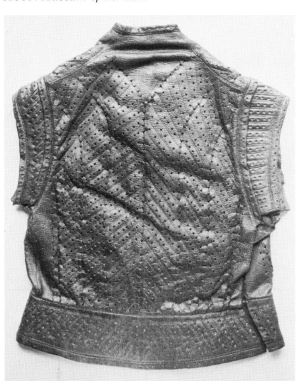

110. *Back view of youth's leather jerkin in Fig. 109, showing pinking of hearts and stars between lines of scoring.*

111. *Detail of back neck of jerkin in Fig. 109. Three diamond shapes of fine pinking make the leather more supple.*

112. *Inside back of neck of jerkin in Fig. 109 to show the three diamond shapes of fine pinking more clearly and the reverse side of the strips of leather inset in the seams.*

113. *Detail of wing of jerkin in Fig. 109.*

114. *Inside the front of the jerkin in Fig. 109. The waist seam is reinforced at the edge with an extra piece of leather for a pair of punched eyelet holes. The skirts of the jerkin are lined with leather. The button shanks are passed through punched holes and secured with a long strip of leather inside the front of the jerkin. Traces of silk and stitching remain from a lining probably put in during the nineteenth century for the jerkin to be put on display.*

115. *Back view of doublet similar in shape to that in Fig. 117. Detail from* The Adoration of the Kings *by Jacopo Bassano, c1550. National Gallery of Scotland, Edinburgh.*

116. *Front view of ivory and brown striped silk doublet worn by a hunter similar in shape to that in Fig. 117. Detail from fresco by Paolo Veronese, c1560. Villa Maser, Treviso.*

117

118

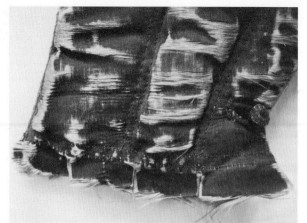

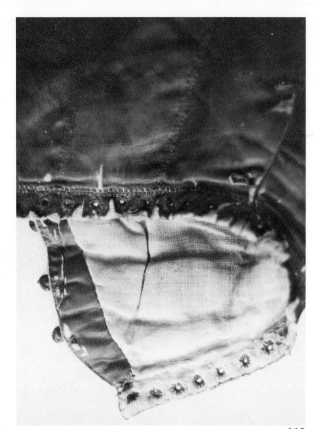

119

120

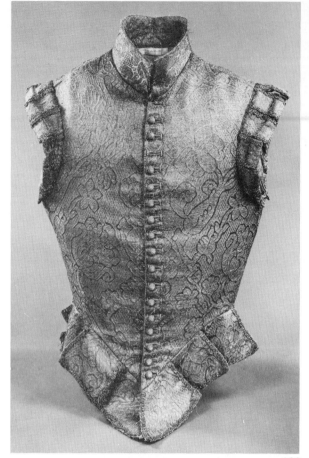

121

122

123

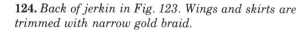

124

117. *Doublet in rich red satin, changing to crimson in some lights, lined with white linen and lightly padded with cotton wool. This may be an arming doublet, c1560. Lord Astor, Hever Castle, Kent.*

118. *Detail of hook at neck on left front of doublet in Fig. 117. The hole in the linen lining reveals the heavier linen interlining.*

119. *Detail of eyelet holes and double row of stitching at waist of doublet in Fig. 117.*

120. *Detail of buttons and buttonholes at front of doublet in Fig. 117.*

121. *Detail of double row stitching at end of sleeve of doublet in Fig. 117. The snipped edge gives a decorative finish.*

122. *Henry, Prince of Wales, wears a fashionably unbuttoned jerkin with cord loop buttonholes on the left front. It is similar in style to that in Fig. 123. The doublet wings may be seen beneath the jerkin wings. Painting by Robert Peake, c1610. National Portrait Gallery, London.*

123. *Jerkin on pages 70–1 in green silk brocatelle with additional weft threads of gold strip wrapped round a silk core. It was cut to lie open at the front and would have resembled the jerkin in Fig. 122 in wear, c1620. Los Angeles County Museum of Art.*

124. *Back of jerkin in Fig. 123. Wings and skirts are trimmed with narrow gold braid.*

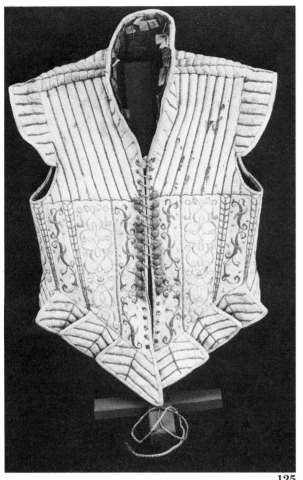

125

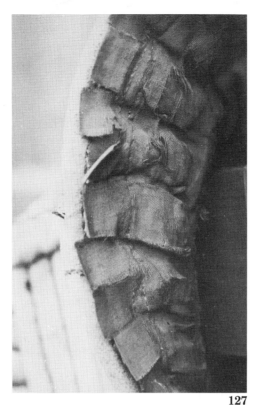

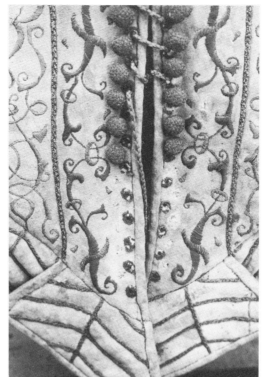
127

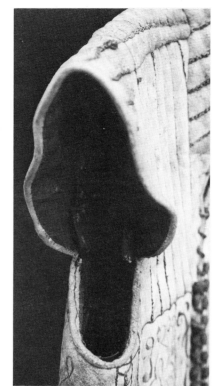
128

129

131

125. *Padded leather doublet embroidered with yellow silk and silver metal thread, c1595–1610. Stibbert Museum, Florence.*

126. *Padded and embroidered leather doublet similar to that in Fig. 125 but with sleeves and a padded peascod belly. It fastens with lacing by the double row of buttons at the front and is closed below, opening at the side back seams, c1585–95. Metropolitan Museum of Art, New York.*

127. *Detail of neck of doublet in Fig. 125, showing the brown silk lining cut in pickadil. Two lines of stitching may be seen below the cuts.*

128. *Detail of front of doublet in Fig. 125. The bottom ten buttons are missing and the worked eyelet holes for lacing may be seen more easily.*

129. *Detail of armhole of doublet in Fig. 125 showing lacing strip for attaching sleeves stitched inside.*

130. *Detail of back neck of doublet in Fig. 125, showing horizontal join and three small decorative tufts of yellow ochre silk at the bottom of the rows of padding. Originally the tufts may have been larger, but the silk has worn away.*

131. *Cesare Colonna, aged seven, wearing a doublet similar in style to that in Fig. 132 but with a padded peascod belly. Detail from a painting of the Colonna family by Scipio Pulzone, 1581. Galleria Colonna, Rome.*

126

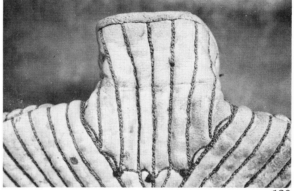
130

132

133

132. *Youth's doublet in green cut and uncut velvet on a voided ivory silk ground. It fastens in a similar way to the doublet in Fig. 125 with lacing under buttons at the front, c1595–1605. Nederlands Kostuummuseum, The Hague.*

133. *Detail of fabric used for doublet in Fig. 132, showing the areas of long cut pile resembling the frayed edges of slashed silk. The yellow silk braid is 6 mm (¼") wide. It is enriched with silver metal thread.*

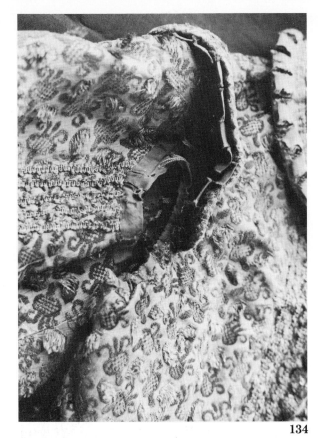

134. *Detail of armhole of doublet in Fig. 132. There are strips of silk with worked eyelet holes for points round both top of sleeve and armhole. Nederlands Kostuummuseum, The Hague.*

135. *Back of doublet in Fig. 132.*

136. *Detail of left side back seam of doublet in Fig. 132, showing lacing at the top, under the arms.*

137. *Detail of lacing strip inside waist of doublet in Fig. 132.*

138. *King James I wearing a suit with a doublet slightly padded at the front, similar to that in Fig. 140. The paned trunk-hose are padded into a smooth shape, c1604. Dulwich Picture Gallery, London.*

139. *Edward Sackville, 4th Earl of Dorset, wearing a suit with full trunk-hose, similar in shape to those on pages 74–7 (Figs. 140 and 144). Painting attributed to William Larkin, c1613. The Suffolk Collection, Ranger's House, Blackheath, GLC.*

140. *Suit in mulberry uncut velvet on a voided satin ground, open to show the padded lining (pages 74–7), c1600–5. Grimsthorpe and Drummond Castle Trust Ltd, on loan to the Victoria and Albert Museum, London.*

135

137

140

138

139

141

143

145

148

141. *Detail of collar in Fig. 140, showing striped wool pad-stitched over two layers of linen and another layer of wool. The collar is lined with purple-brown silk, which is disintegrating, and a modern cotton lining has been stitched on top to protect it.*

142. *Detail of wing, showing two braids used for suit in Fig. 140, purple-brown silk and gold thread on the left, yellow silk and gold thread on the right.*

143. *Detail of mulberry uncut velvet on a voided satin ground used for suit in Fig. 140.*

144. *Detail of trunk-hose in Fig. 140, showing the long darts and canions.*

145. *An unknown man wearing a satin doublet with padded front similar to that on page 78 and in Fig. 146 but with the natural waist level. Painting by Frans Pourbus the Younger, 1600. Groeninge Museum, Bruges.*

146. *Back of doublet in green satin with slightly raised waist level, decoratively pinked and cut in an interlocking design, c1605–10. Germanisches Nationalmuseum, Nürnberg.*

147. *Detail of wing from the doublet in Fig. 146.*

148. *Detail of buttons in worked silk over wooden bases on the left front of the doublet in Fig. 146.*

149. *Detail of pinking on the doublet in Fig. 146.*

146

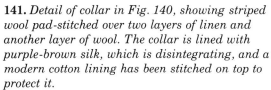

142

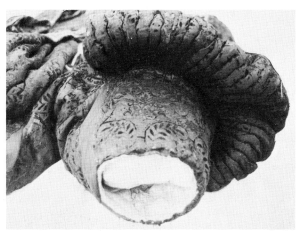

144

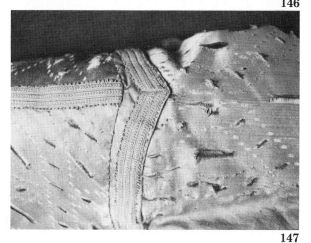

147

149

150

151

152

150. *Detail of buttonholes inside collar on left front of doublet in Fig. 146. Germanisches Nationalmuseum.*

151. *Metal eye stitched to lacing strip inside waist of doublet in Fig. 146. A selvedge cut from the satin is used to neaten the seam just above the eyelet holes. Hooks and eyes are the new method of supporting the breeches and soon replace points.*

153

154

155

156

152. *Waist strip lifted to show the eye made of coiled wire in Fig. 151.*

153. *Doublet made of interlaced strips of embroidered silk imitating strapwork. Miniature, possibly of the Earl of Essex, by Nicholas Hilliard, c1585–90. Victoria and Albert Museum, London.*

154. *The gown worn by Queen Elizabeth I is made of interlaced strips of embroidered silk with sets of four pearls in the spaces between the intersections. Miniature by Nicholas Hilliard, c1595–1600. Victoria and Albert Museum, Ham House.*

155. *Front of jerkin made of panels of black satin decorated with a pattern of interlaced bands of couched cord simulating strapwork. The satin is disintegrating and the jerkin has been bound round the edges to conserve the shape, c1590–1600. Hessisches Landesmuseum, Darmstadt.*

157

158

156. *Detail of shaped tab from skirts of jerkin in Fig. 155. Black silk was originally placed over the blue linen lining to back the embroidery but this has almost completely disintegrated.*

157. *Back of jerkin in Fig. 155.*

158. *Detail of embroidery carried out in couched black silk cords on black satin for the jerkin in Fig. 155.*

159

160

159. *Front of padded green shot silk taffeta doublet, pinked for decoration, c1610. Germanisches Nationalmuseum, Nürnberg.*

160. *Back of doublet in Fig. 159.*

161. *Detail of front of doublet in Fig. 159 showing eyelet holes at waist, buttons and buttonholes and decorative braid.*

162. *Side view of buttons in Fig. 161. They have wooden bases with silk worked over the top and linen shanks.*

163. *Detail of padding inside right front of doublet in Fig. 159.*

164. *Detail of linen lacing strip with worked eyelet holes in linen thread shown in Fig. 163.*

165. *Two men wearing padded doublets for fencing practice. Woodcut from* Ein new Künstliches Fechtbuch im Rappier, *by Michael Hundt, 1611. Germanisches Nationalmuseum, Nürnberg.*

166. *Detail of neck of doublet on page 82, showing the collar cut in one with the back, c1610. Germanisches Nationalmuseum, Nürnberg.*

167. *Detail of tightly packed cotton wool padding and linen stitching in sleeve seam of doublet in Fig. 166.*

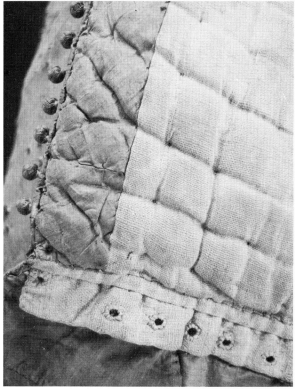

163

168. *Detail of buttonholes, worked eyelet holes at waist and braid trimming on skirts of doublet in Fig. 166.*

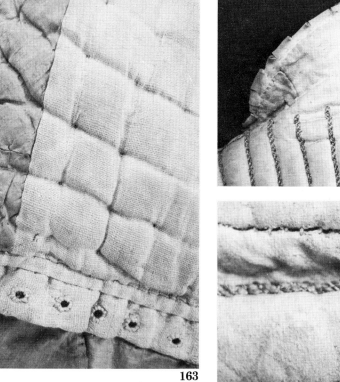

166

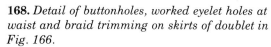

167

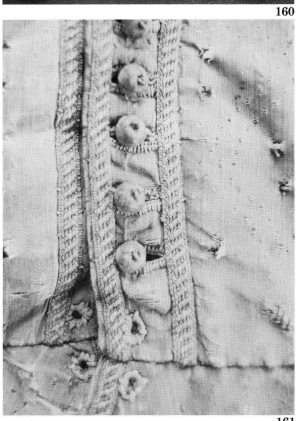

161

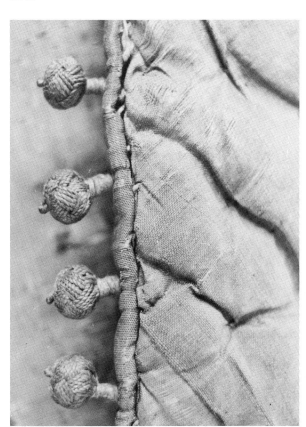

162

164

165

168

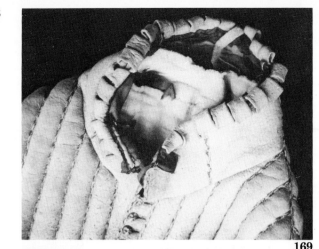

169

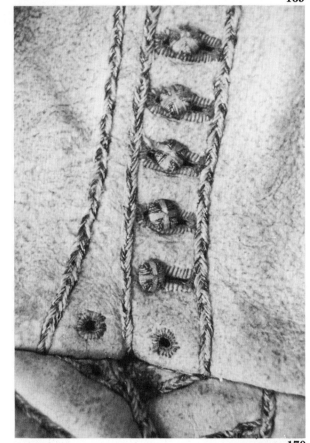

170

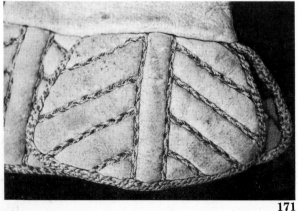

171

172

173

174

175

176

169. *Detail of collar with border cut in pickadil from doublet on page 82, c1610. Royal Scottish Museum, Edinburgh.*

170. *Detail of buttons, buttonholes and worked eyelet holes at front waist of the doublet in Fig. 169.*

171. *Detail of braid trimming skirts of doublet in Fig. 169.*

172. *Cotton wool wadding laid between linen interlining and green silk lining of the skirts of the doublet in Fig. 169.*

173. *Charles I when Prince of Wales, wearing a suit of red silk woven with a stylized design of sprays of leaves and flowers, slashed diagonally between the motifs. The doublet is similar in shape to that in Fig. 174. Painting attributed to A. van Blijenberch, c1615. National Portrait Gallery, London.*

174. *Detail of deep reddish-plum satin doublet on page 84, pinked between the lines of stone-coloured silk braid trimming. It is lined with white linen and the collar is stiffened with one or two layers of coarse linen. The collar lining of stone and black shot taffeta has almost disintegrated, c1615–20. Hessisches Landesmuseum, Darmstadt.*

175. *Left front of doublet in Fig. 174 turned back to show the pad-stitching in white linen thread on the black coarsely woven linen belly-piece, which is attached to the white linen lining. The interlining of black linen can be seen beside the buttonholes.*

176. *Detail of pad-stitching in Fig. 175 beside the stone and black shot silk taffeta which faces the front and covers the edge of the belly-piece.*

177. *Detail of braid loop sewn to the belly-piece inside left front of doublet in Fig. 174. This is tied to the loop on the opposite side to hold the fronts together while the buttons are fastened. The stitching from the lines of braid may be seen beneath the shot black and stone silk lining which is disintegrating.*

178. *Detail of sleeve of doublet in Fig. 174, showing pleated strip of black and stone shot silk taffeta at wrist. The buttons are of stone-coloured silk worked over wooden foundations. The buttonholes are worked in matching stone silk.*

179. *Richard Sackville, 3rd Earl of Dorset, wearing a doublet similar in construction to that in Fig. 180. Miniature by Isaac Oliver, 1616. Victoria and Albert Museum, London.*

180. *Doublet of patterned ivory silk with thin silver strip in the weft on page 84. It would originally have had wings and braid trimming as in Fig. 179, c1615–20. Lord Middleton Collection, Museum of Costume and Textiles, Nottingham.*

181. *Back view of doublet in Fig. 180. The sleeves were moved slightly from their original position when the wings were taken out. All the braid covering the seams has been removed, but tufts of yellow silk remain to show its original position covering the seams and bordering the skirt tabs.*

182. *Inside right front of doublet in Fig. 180, showing the layers of linen used to stiffen the front beneath the disintegrating pink silk lining. The interlining of dark brown wool with pad-stitching in linen thread gives a smoother line over shoulders and chest.*

183. *Detail of inside right front of doublet in Fig. 180, showing one of the pair of lacing tabs on top of the belly-piece. A lace would have been tied through the worked eyelet holes to hold the stiffened fronts together while the buttons were fastened. The worked*

eyelet holes in the skirts were for points to attach the trunk-hose, or breeches.

184. *The left front of the doublet in Fig. 180 is made separately from the belly-piece, so that the buttonholes are sufficiently pliable for the buttons to be fastened. The belly-piece is attached to the pink silk lining. Several layers of linen are pad-stitched together to make the belly-piece stiff.*

177

180

181

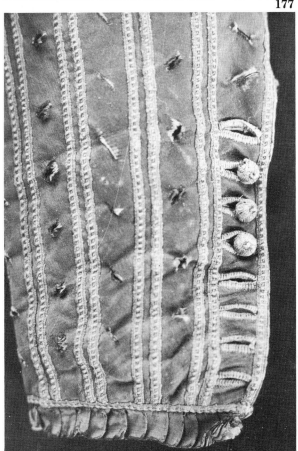

178

179

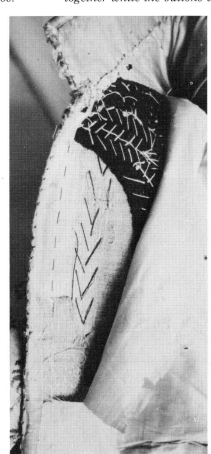

182

183

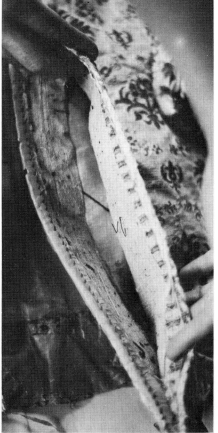

184

28

185

191

187

188

192

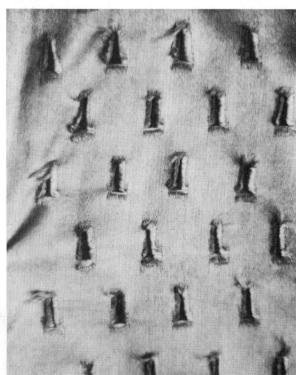

186

189

190

185. *Detail of front of tan satin doublet on page 86 showing very narrow shoulder wings, c1615–25. Bayerisches Nationalmuseum, Munich.*

186. *Detail of pinking on doublet in Fig. 185.*

187. *Prince Maurits of Nassau wearing doublet and breeches similar in shape to those on pages 86–7 (Figs. 185–6 and 188–9). Paintings by Adriaan van der Venne, c1616–17. Stichting Historische Verzamelingen van het Huis Oranje–Nassau.*

188. *Detail of cut velvet with broad stripes of patterned cut and uncut velvet now disintegrating, used for the breeches on page 86, c1615–20. Germanisches Nationalmuseum, Nürnberg.*

189. *Detail of hook to secure breeches on page 86 to eyes inside doublet waist. Black silk braid, now disintegrating, binds the top of the waistband. The large stitches were put in early in the present century to help hold the fragments of velvet together.*

190. *Sir Richard (?) Cotton wearing the satin suit in Fig. 191, which is now in the Victoria and Albert Museum. Painting by Daniel Mytens, 1618. Present whereabouts unknown.*

191. *Pale stone satin suit, pinked and slashed for decoration, revealing a layer of blue silk over white silk, 1618. Until 1938 this was kept at Etwall Hall, Derbyshire, the seat of the Cotton family. Victoria and Albert Museum, London.*

192. *Side view of suit in Fig. 191, which is now so fragile that it can no longer be put on display.*

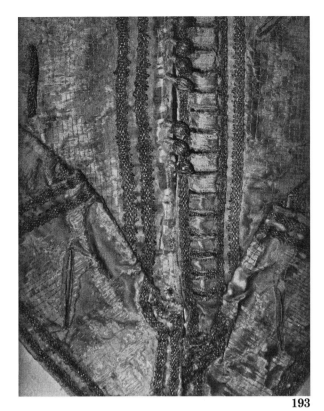

193

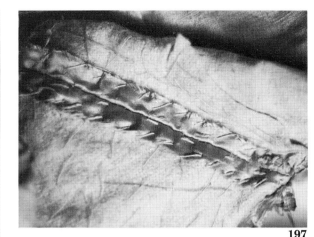

195

197

199

193. *Detail of front of doublet in Fig. 191. The disintegrating surface is held together with couched threads. The silk thread in the buttonholes has almost disappeared but the stitch holes remain.*

194. *Detail of buttons in Fig. 193 with wooden bases worked over with silk and metal threads.*

194

196

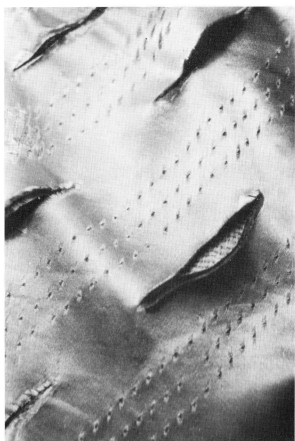

198

195. *Detail of pinking and slashing on the breeches in Fig. 191. The layer of white wool, open weave and springy in texture, which provides the padding may be seen beneath the satin.*

196. *Detail of belly-piece for doublet in Fig. 191, made of layers of linen pad-stitched together, possibly with three whalebones inside but these can only be felt, not seen. The green shot silk lining has almost disintegrated but the small lacing tab remains for a lace to tie across and hold the two sides of the front together while fastening the buttons.*

197. *Detail of left shoulder seam inside doublet in Fig. 191, showing the layer of wool pad-stitched with linen thread to the linen interlining to keep the chest and shoulders smooth.*

198. *Sir Rowland Cotton wearing similar trunk-hose to those in Fig. 191 but with longer canions. Alabaster tomb, after a design by Inigo Jones, commemorating Lady Cotton who died in 1606, c1610–15. Parish Church of St Chad, Norton-in-Hales, Shropshire.*

199. *The trunk-hose in Fig. 198 from another angle. Sir Rowland wears armour over his suit. He died in 1634 but apparently had his effigy carved not long after that of his wife.*

200. *Richard Sackville, 3rd Earl of Dorset, wears a white cloth of silver doublet embroidered with stylized slips of honeysuckle in black satin and gold metal thread. His trunk-hose are of black silk grosgrain, cut to show the lining of white cloth of silver and embroidered with black satin and gold metal thread in a similar design to that of the doublet. The suit is similar in shape to that worn by Sir Richard (?) Cotton. Painting attributed to William Larkin, 1613. Suffolk Collection, Ranger's House, Blackheath. GLC.*

200

30

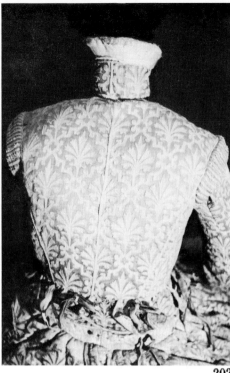

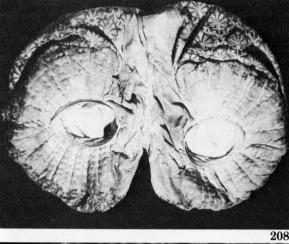

201

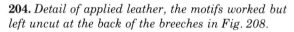

202

204

205

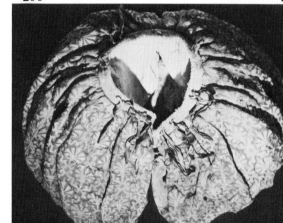

206

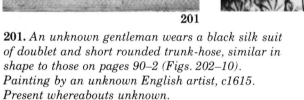

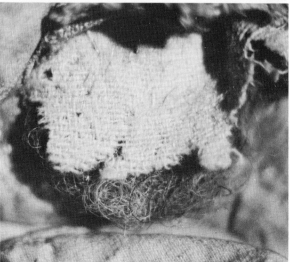

207

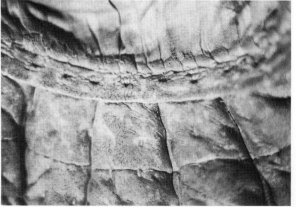

208

209

210

203

201. *An unknown gentleman wears a black silk suit of doublet and short rounded trunk-hose, similar in shape to those on pages 90–2 (Figs. 202–10). Painting by an unknown English artist, c1615. Present whereabouts unknown.*

202. *Back of doublet of suit on pages 90–2, showing the stylized design of gillyflowers, or carnations, in applied cream leather with a suede finish on red satin. The trunk-hose waistband may be seen below the skirts of the doublet, with one ribbon point still threaded through a pair of eyelet holes, c1615–20. Museo Parmigianino, Reggio Emilia.*

203. *Detail of front of doublet in Fig. 202. The applied leather motifs are stitched in pale pink silk thread. The buttonholes are worked in creamy yellow silk.*

204. *Detail of applied leather, the motifs worked but left uncut at the back of the breeches in Fig. 208.*

205. *Points made of strips of satin, the edges turned in once and stitched, with metal aglets. They are tied through eyelet holes worked in the skirts of the doublet in Fig. 202.*

206. *Trunk-hose for suit in Fig. 202, viewed from above, with satin points threaded through pairs of eyelet holes in the waistband.*

207. *Fragment of wool interlining and horsehair padding holding out the trunk-hose in Fig. 206.*

208. *Underside of trunk-hose in Fig. 206, from the back, with long darts to shape them, the fullness caught into narrow leg bands.*

209. *The linen stitching from the horsehair padding and wool interlining comes through the leather to the right side. The leather is pieced.*

210. *Eyelet holes are worked in the leg bands in Fig. 209 to attach the nether stocks, or stockings, with points. The linen lining is gathered to fit the leg band.*

Bonnets and hats

A few examples of headwear have been included here, although these were the work of other craftsmen, not tailors. The sewing techniques used by cappers and hatters are of interest for comparison with those of the tailors.

'Wherefore to begin first with their Hattes. Sometimes they weare them sharp on the crowne, peaking up like a sphere, or shafte of a steeple, standing a quarter of a yard above the crown of their heads, some more, some lesse, as please the phantasies of their mindes. Othersome be flat, and broad on the crowne, like the battlements of a house. An other sort have round crownes, sometimes with one kinde of bande, sometime with an other, nowe black, now white, now russet, now red, now greene, now yellow, now this, nowe that, never content with one colour, or fashion two dayes on ende. . . . Some are of silke, some of velvet, some of taffetie, some of sarcenet, some of wooll, and which is more curious, some of a certaine kind of fine haire, far fetched and deare bought you may bee sure . . . he is no account or estimation amongst men, if hee have not a velvet, or a taffetie Hatte, and that must be pincked and cunningly carved of the beste fashion . . . of late there is a new fashion of wearing their Hattes sprung up amongst them, which they father upon the Frenchman, namely to weare them without bandes. . . . An other sort (as phantasticall as the rest) are content with no kind of Hatt, without a great bunche of feathers of diverse and sundrie colours, peaking on toppe of their heades, not unlyke (I dare not say) Cockscombes.'

(Phillip Stubbes, *The Anatomie of Abuses*, 1583)

211

212

213

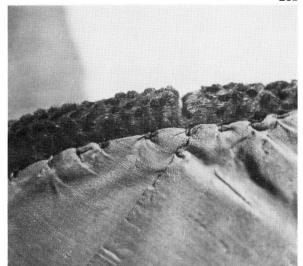

214

215

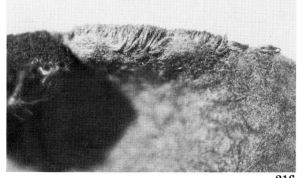

216

217

218

211. *King Charles IX of France wears a bonnet which appears to be made in the same way as the fragments of that in Fig. 212, but probably with a silk pile, like the hat in Fig. 220. Painting by François Clouet, 1561. Kunsthistorisches Museum, Vienna.*

212. *Fragments of top of bonnet on page 93, stored with the Sture clothes in an iron chest in Upsala Cathedral by Svante Sture's widow, 1567. Upsala Cathedral.*

213. *Upper side of pink silk taffeta brim lining of bonnet in Fig. 212 with some fragments of felt and Rya wool remaining. Dr Inger Estham suggests that this may be an example of a 'Ryahatt', which appears in contemporary Swedish accounts. 'Rya' wool is the top fleece from the Rya sheep. It is very shiny and hard in texture.*

214. *Detail of underside of brim of bonnet in Fig. 213, showing the pink silk lining stitched with silk thread to the felt foundation of the bonnet. The tufts of Rya wool have almost worn away.*

215. *Detail of curved area at edge of bonnet crown in Fig. 212. Dr Inger Estham says that early Swedish bedspreads were made with Rya wool, using a knotting technique identical to Ghiordes knotting in oriental carpets but with longer tufts. The bedspreads were silky in appearance, not as soft as* cashmere, and springy to touch. The word 'Rya' was first used for the wool and later the knotting technique. The thick pile of Rya wool here is tightly packed and resembles moss.

216. *Detail of side of curved piece of felt in Fig. 215, showing the tufts of Rya wool.*

217. *The tufts of Rya wool in Fig. 216 worked in rows.*

218. *An unknown woman, probably a London merchant's wife, wearing a hat which may be of velvet but is similar in shape and texture to that in Fig. 220. Miniature by Nicholas Hilliard, 1602. Victoria and Albert Museum, London.*

219

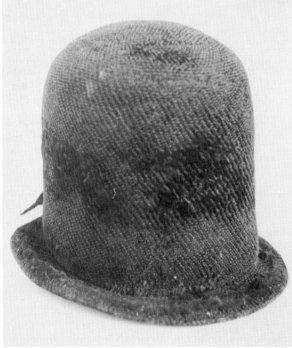

220

221

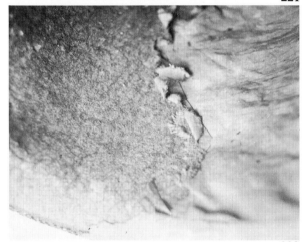

222

223

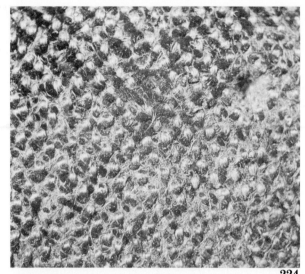

224

225

226

227

219. *An unknown man wearing a hat of the type in Fig. 220, with a silk or wool pile. This would apparently have been termed a 'thrummed' hat in England, described by Linthicum as 'a felt hat so made as to leave projecting ends of threads upon the surface to form a pile or nap'. Portrait attributed to Corneille de Lyon, c1560. Louvre, Paris.*

220. *High crowned hat on page 93, with felt base and silk pile. The pile has worn away in many places, making it easier to see how the hat was made, c1560–1600. Gift of Prince of Schwarzburg in 1877. Germanisches Nationalmuseum, Nürnberg.*

221. *Inside hat in Fig. 220 showing the felt base, interlining of coarsely woven linen and lining of black silk, which is in a very fragile state. The*

feathers were put on in the nineteenth century, probably to replace an original ostrich feather which had disintegrated.

222. *Large areas of both linen interlining and black silk lining are missing. This detail from Fig. 221 shows felt (on the left) and some linen protruding beneath the fragments of silk.*

223. *Detail of top of hat in Fig. 220, to show how the pile is formed by black six-strand plied silk, without much twist, worked in even rows round the crown.*

224. *Detail of Fig. 223. The black silk pile has worn away.*

225. *Detail of side of hat in Fig. 220, showing some of the remaining black silk pile.*

226. Calator et honorarius puer Nobilis Germani: *Noble German youth acting as honorary attendant, wearing a morion helmet, or possibly a felt morion hat similar to that in Fig. 227. From* Diversarum Gentium Armatura Equestris *by Abraham de Bruyn, 1577. British Library.*

227. *Morion hat on page 93, of felt covered with black velvet, from which most of the pile has disintegrated, embroidered with couched gold metal thread, c1600. Gift of Prince of Schwarzburg in 1877. Germanisches Nationalmuseum, Nürnberg.*

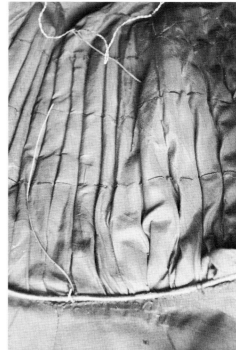

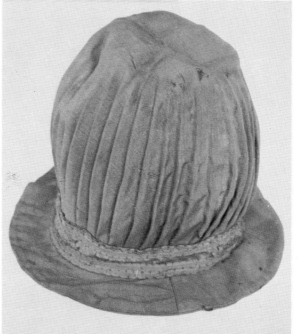

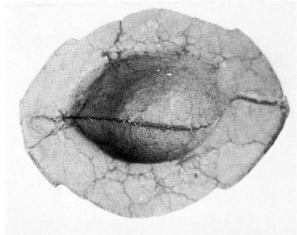

228

230

233

231

232

234

235

229

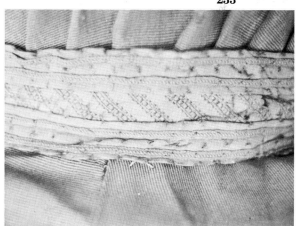

228. *Detail of embroidery from Fig. 227. The hat is similar to one which belonged to Herzog Moritz von Sachsen–Lauenburg, with the date 1599 incorporated into the embroidery. The latter is preserved in the Niedersächsische Landesgalerie, Hanover, and is illustrated in* Kostüme des 16. und 17. Jahrhunderts *by Eva Nienholdt.*

229. *The hat in Fig. 227 is moulded from thick felt. The crest is pinched together and stitched through at the base, over the top of the head, with white linen thread. The stitches may be seen in this detail.*

230. *Detail of embroidery on brim at front of morion hat in Fig. 227. Some of the velvet has disintegrated, revealing the felt beneath.*

231. Princeps sive Dominus Belgae: *The chief or ruler of the Belgians, from* Diversarum Gentium Armatura Equestris *by Abraham de Bruyn, 1577. British Library.*

232. *Hat on page 94 made of a pleated circle of brown corded silk which probably originally had a foundation of pasted paper or felt (Fig. 235). Apparently this was removed for some reason and a wire framework put in instead, probably in the eighteenth century. c1575–1600. Purchased in 1896 from Mr Forrer in Strasbourg. Germanisches Nationalmuseum, Nürnberg.*

233. *Detail inside hat in Fig. 232, showing the* brown silk lining and fragments of the wire frame. Four rows of brown silk gathering threads are pulled up to form forty-three loose pleats.

234. *Detail of hatband from Fig. 232, in brown silk with a woven stripe cut on the bias, bordered with bias strips of brown silk decorated with tablet-woven braid.*

235. *Hat made of a circle of black cut and uncut patterned velvet pleated down over a hard foundation in a similar way to those in Figs. 236 and 237, c1580–1600. Museum of London.*

34

236. *Sir William Cecil wearing a hat of pinked satin pleated over a felt or pasted paper foundation, similar to those in Figs. 232, 235 and 237. The silhouette reveals the fraying edges. Painting by an unknown English artist, 1586. Present whereabouts unknown.*

237. *Hat on page 94 made of a pleated circle of rich pink velvet, now faded to pale beige/pink in places, with a foundation of felt. There are two lines of stitching to hold the pleats, c1600–10. Purchased in 1871 from Mr Pickert in Nürnberg. Germanisches Nationalmuseum, Nürnberg.*

238. *The crown and brim of the hat in Fig. 237 are lined with brilliant pink silk.*

239. *Detail of upper side of hat brim in Fig. 237, showing the outline of a cord decoration, which has been removed, remaining imprinted in the velvet.*

240. *Detail of a tear in the silk lining the hat brim in Fig. 238, revealing the layer of linen covering the felt.*

241. *Leather hat, possibly worn by a page, on page 94. It is embroidered with ivory silk and couched silver metal thread, c1600–10. Purchased in 1898 from Mr Böhler, an art dealer in Munich. Germanisches Nationalmuseum, Nürnberg.*

242. *Inside the hat in Fig. 241 showing silk lining, which seems to be glued to the layer of linen covering the felt beneath the leather. Rows of stitching may be seen through the silk.*

243. *Detail of padded leather hatband from Fig. 241. This shell shape at the back is made over a*

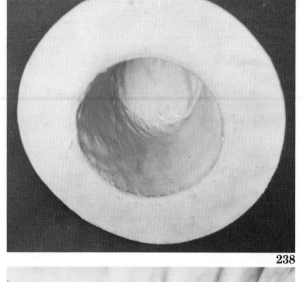

236

parchment base, padded with hair, and may have held a feather.

244. *Leather hat of a similar design to that in Fig. 241, c1600–10. Others may be seen at the Museum of London, the Deutsches Ledermuseum, Offenbach, and the Stibbert Museum, Florence. Museo Parmigianino, Reggio Emilia.*

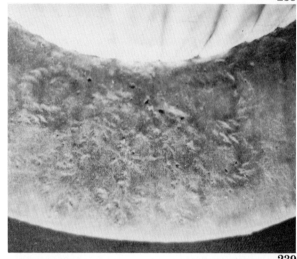

238

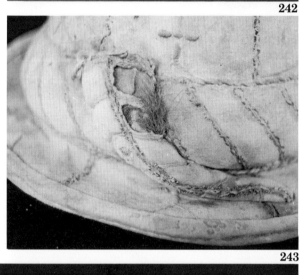

242

239

243

237

240

241

244

Cloaks and loose gowns

'They have clokes there also in nothing discrepante from the rest, of dyverse and sundry colors, white, red, tawnie, black, greene, yellowe, russet, purple, violet, and infynite other colors: some of cloth, silk, velvet, taffetie and such like, wherof some be of the Spanish, French and Dutch fashion. Some short, scarsely reachinge to the gyrdlestead, or waist, some to the knee, and othersome traylinge upon the ground (almost) liker gownes, than clokes. These clokes must be garded, laced and thorowly faced: and sometimes so lyned, as the inner side standeth almost in as much as the outside: some have sleeves, othersome have none, some have hoodes to pull over the head, some have none, some are hanged with points and tassels of gold, silver, or silk, some without all this. But how soever it be, the day hath bene, when one might have bought him two clokes for lesse than now he can have one of these clokes made for, they have such store of workmanship bestowed upon them.'
(Phillip Stubbes, *The Anatomie of Abuses*, 1583)

245. *Charles IX, King of France, wears a black velvet cloak with similar couched gold metal cord embroidery to that in Fig. 249. Portrait by François Clouet, c1568. Kunsthistorisches Museum, Vienna.*

246. *A short satin cloak reaching to just below the waist, lined with light crimson velvet, is worn over the shoulders. Ball for the Wedding of the Duc de Joyeuse, School of Clouet, c1581–2. Louvre, Paris.*

247. *Hispanici vestitus & habitus varii. Hispanus: Various Spanish clothes and appearance. A Spaniard wearing a cloak with a rich border similar to those in Figs. 252 and 253. From Habitus Praecipuorum Populorum by Hans Weigel and Jost Amman, 1577. Germanisches Nationalmuseum, Nürnberg.*

248. *Detail of embroidery on the cloak in Fig. 249. The braid gives the appearance of an uncut fringe.*

249. *Crimson velvet compass cloak on page 95, cut in a full circle, slightly longer than that in Fig. 245. It is embroidered with couched gold and silver metal cord and the edges are bordered with a thick braid of crimson silk and gold metal thread. The cloak is lined with natural linen, c1560–80. Purchased in 1898 from Mr Böhler, an art dealer in Munich. Germanisches Nationalmuseum, Nürnberg.*

250. *Detail of embroidery in Fig. 251 showing the couched blue linen cord, wrapped with acid-yellow silk, outlining the applied satin shapes. The French knots are in blue and pink silk.*

251. *Short cloak on page 95 in red satin with an applied design of acid-yellow satin, giving the effect of gold. The lining is of natural linen. It is said to have been worn by a fool or perhaps a dwarf at the Ansbach court, c1600–20. Provenance unknown. Germanisches Nationalmuseum, Nürnberg.*

245

247

249

248

250

246

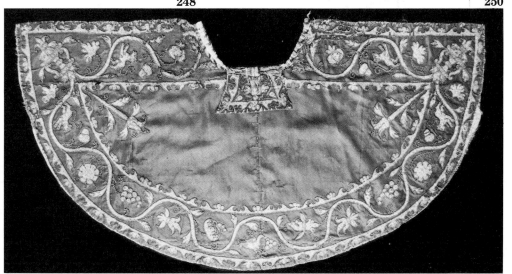
251

36

252. *Cloak (page 96) in deep red cut velvet with a voided palmate pattern on a cream satin ground. This is probably 'branched' velvet. Dion's wish in the play* Philaster, *that 'moths will branch their velvets', explains the term. The cloak is cut in ten panels with the pile running in both directions. Alcega was aware of the need to arrange pattern pieces carefully on cloth with a nap so that they would all lie in the same direction (Geometria, pratica y traça, f.67v). In this case the tailor seems to have cut the cloak from an old garment, probably a skirt, dating from the early sixteenth century and luckily the pile stands almost upright. The applied decoration of yellow satin is enriched with couched cream and green silk cord. The cloak is lined with saffron-yellow linen. Probably Spanish, c1560–90. Purchased in 1904 from a London dealer. Victoria and Albert Museum, London.*

253. *Semi-circular cloak (page 96) in rich red satin with a linear design in couched gold metal thread on collar and hem, and panels of heavier embroidery of laid and couched metal thread with coloured silks in long and short satin stitches on the front edges. It is lined with deep pink or red linen, now faded. Probably Spanish, c1580–1600. Purchased in 1901 from a Paris dealer. Victoria and Albert Museum, London.*

254. *A short semi-circular cloak, the collar and hem decorated with couched cord, is slung casually over the left shoulder. It is of a similar length to that in Fig. 253. Detail from* Las Ciencias y las Artes *by Adrian van Stalbent, c1615. Prado, Madrid.*

255. *A long semi-circular cloak embroidered over the shoulders, with two lines of braid round the hem, is worn falling off the left shoulder. Two men at the back are wearing loose coats with sleeves hanging down at front and back. These are mandilions 'worn to colley westonward'. The Valois tapestries, c1575. Uffizi, Florence.*

256. Nobilis Anglus: *An English nobleman on horseback wearing a long cloak, probably made of woollen cloth, which seems to have a double layer over the shoulders. It is trimmed with lines of cord radiating from the neck. From* Diversarum Gentium Armatura Equestris *by Abraham de Bruyn, 1577. British Library.*

257. Eques Hispanus: *A Spanish Rider wearing a cloak with a double layer over the shoulders, the hood pushed back. It is decorated with radiating lines of embroidery. From* Diversarum Gentium Armatura Equestris *by Abraham de Bruyn, 1576. Germanisches Nationalmuseum, Nürnberg.*

252

253

254

255

Ein Hofiuncker in Engeland.   Nobilis Anglus   30

256

Eques Hispanus.   Ein Hispanische Reuter   19

257

258. Eques Hispanus: *A Spanish Rider wearing a cloak with a double layer over the shoulders. The hood is pulled over the head and a protective flap, to cover the nose and mouth for warmth, tied to it at the side. Engraving from* Diversarum Gentium Armatura Equestris *by Abraham de Bruyn, 1577. British Library.*

259. *Short, semi-circular ivory woollen cloak on page 97, embroidered with dark brown wool in a linear design. The hood is decorated with woollen tufts, c1570–80. Purchased in 1903 from Mr Böhler, an art dealer in Munich. Germanisches Nationalmuseum, Nürnberg.*

260. *The join in the cloth may be seen clearly inside the cloak shown in Fig. 259. The front edges, the front of the hood and the flaps are oversewn with brown wool in what seems to be crossed buttonhole stitch. The hood is lined with the same woollen cloth and is rather bulky.*

261. *The woollen cloth in Fig. 259 has a twill weave and is heavily milled. The couched embroidery is carried out in brown wool. Tassels of brown wool are placed at the points of the radiating design where they meet the border.*

262. *Short semi-circular palest aquamarine satin cloak on page 97, embroidered in a radiating design with yellow silk, couched cord and French knots. It is slashed between the embroidered areas. The satin has faded to oyster colour. The collar is missing. c1610–20. Victoria and Albert Museum, London.*

263. *Detail of embroidery at hem of cloak in Fig. 262. Cord is used for the outlines with satin stitch and French knots for fillings. The satin stitch is padded in some places.*

264. *Detail of slashed acid-yellow silk lining of cloak in Fig. 262.*

258

261

263

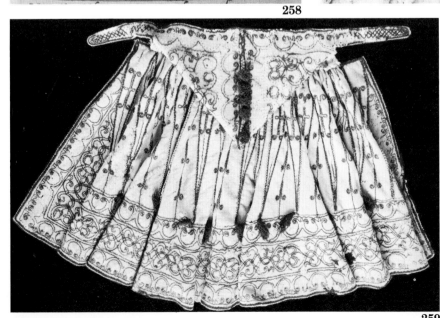

259

262

264

265

267

268

265. *Detail of top of sleeve and wing from rich mulberry satin loose gown on pages 98–9. Each of the tabs forming the wing is bordered with a strip of bias satin. A similar strip of bias satin is set into the sleeve seam. c1600–10. The National Trust, Hardwick Hall, Derbyshire.*

266. Edward, Lord Bruce of Kinloss, Master of the Rolls, *wears a loose gown similar to that in Fig. 267, with what appears to be a shag lining. Monument of alabaster and marble, gilded and painted, 1610. Rolls Chapel, London.*

267. *Loose gown of rich purple silk damask on pages 98, 100, lined with grey silk shag, by tradition worn by Sir Francis Verney. 1605–15. Sir Ralph Verney, Claydon House (The National Trust), near Aylesbury.*

268 and 268A. *Detail of buttons and braid in Fig. 267, made with purple silk and gold thread.*

269. *The back of the gown in Fig. 267 is gathered up and joined to the collar. Two stay tapes of green silk are stitched to the armholes to hold the back pleats in position. Another strip of green silk covers the neck and shoulder seam.*

270. *Detail of hanging sleeve in Fig. 267, showing the front unfastened. The braid trimming on the side seam simulates a pocket opening but the buttons are purely decorative.*

271. *Detail of back neck and gathering across shoulder of gown in Fig. 267.*

268a

270

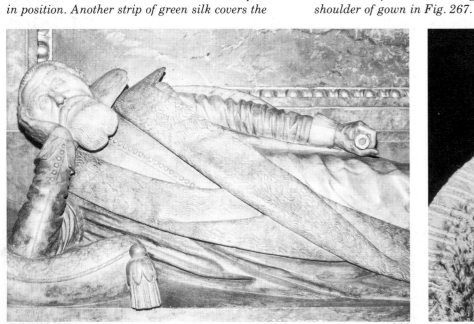

266

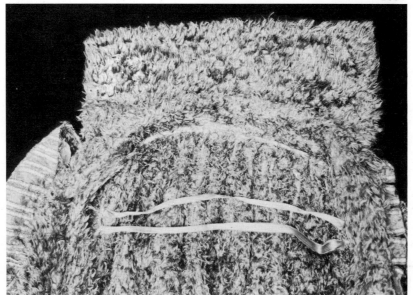

269

271

Women's Doublets, Jackets, Foreparts, Gowns and Loose Gowns

Five hours ago I set a dozen maids to attire a boy like a nice gentlewoman; but there is such doing with their looking glasses, pinning, unpinning, setting, unsetting, formings and conformings, painting blew veins and cheeks; such stir with sticks and combs, cascanets, dressings, purls, falls, squares, busks, bodies, scarfs, necklaces, carcanets, rebatoes, borders, tires, fans, palisadoes, puffs, ruffs, cuffs, muffs, pusles, fusles, partlets, frislets, bandlets, fillets, crosslets, pendulets, amulets, annulets, bracelets, and so many lets [hindrances] that yet she is scarce dressed to the girdle; and now there's such a calling for fardingales, kirtles, busk-points, shoe ties, etc., that seven pedlars' shops — nay all Stourbridge Fair — will scarce furnish her: a ship is sooner rigged by far, than a gentlewoman made ready.

(Thomas Tomkis, *Lingua or the Combat of the Tongues*, 1607)

272. *Detail of back of girl's loose gown on pages 101–2, showing the areas of crushed velvet where braid or lace trimmings have been removed. c1600–10. Nordiska Museet, Stockholm.*

273. *Detail of hook and eye at hem of gown in Fig. 272. The eye has had the ends pushed inside the gown. They are similar to those in Figs. 89, 278, 368 and 369.*

274. *Detail of silk in Fig. 272, showing cut velvet design on uncut ground.*

275. *Pair of red satin sleeves, crimson in some lights, decorated with horizontal rows of white silk back-stitching (page 101). Between them are sets of three lines of pinking, approximately 1.5 mm ($\frac{1}{16}$") long, which score the red silk warp threads and leave the pale beige weft threads beneath to shine through like gold spots. These rows of pinking are uneven, perhaps the work of an apprentice. c1580–1600.*

Purchased from Mr Böhler, an art dealer in Munich. Germanisches Nationalmuseum, Nürnberg.

276. *Detail of lines of pinking and stitching on left sleeve in Fig. 275. The buttonholes are worked in white silk, now disintegrating, with square ends worked later in beige silk by a different hand. The buttons are 13 mm ($\frac{1}{2}$") in diameter, made with a flat wooden base covered with matching satin, with a circle of buttonhole stitch and a little knob on top, worked in beige silk matching the weft threads in the satin. The shanks are of linen thread, 5 mm ($\frac{3}{16}$") long. Two folded strips of satin, cut on straight grain and snipped on the edge for decoration, are stitched to the end of the sleeve.*

277. *Inside the wrist in Fig. 276, showing reverse side of rows of pinking and stitching. In a few places on each sleeve part of a row of pinking has been missed out. On the underside of the left sleeve one complete row is missing. The pinks vary between 1.5 mm ($\frac{1}{16}$") and 5 mm ($\frac{3}{16}$") apart.*

278. *The sleeves in Fig. 275 are padded. The white linen lining is cut to the same shape as the satin, cotton wool is laid on top, then an interlining of blue linen. These three layers are quilted together, single*

small stitches showing on the white linen about 25 mm (1") apart, large diagonal ones on the blue linen. This can just be seen at the bottom of the right sleeve where some stitching has come undone. The padded sleeve lining is made separately, then placed inside the satin sleeve and caught to the front seams with stitches in white linen thread. At the back seam the layers of linen and padding are caught to the satin on one side, then the other is hemmed down on top. The sleevehead is bound with a straight band of matching satin, 6 mm ($\frac{1}{4}$") finished width on both sides, hemmed down with rather large stitches. Six hooks were originally sewn to this binding inside each sleeve. Three remain on the right sleeve, with tufts of thread and one modern replacement. Two remain on the left sleeve, with tufts of thread and three modern replacements.*

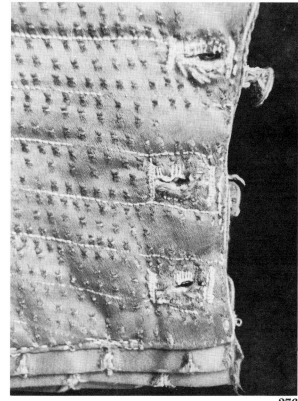

276

277

273

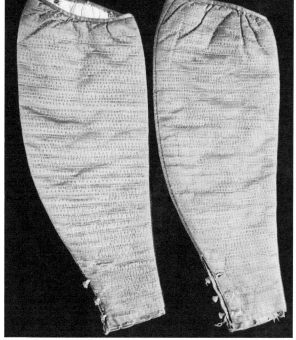

275

272

274

278

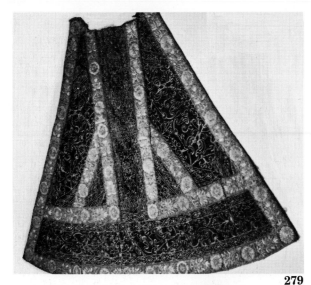

279

280

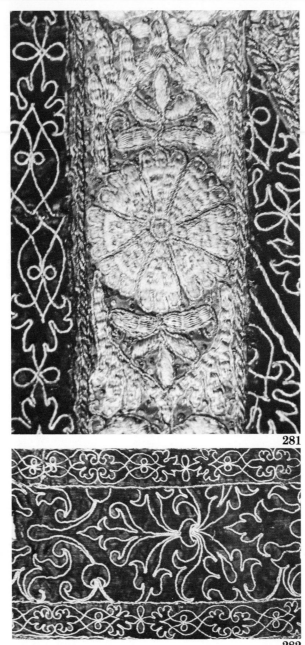

281

282

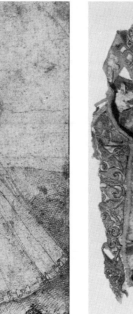

283

286

284

285

287

279. *Green velvet forepart on page 101, embroidered with fine gold metal cord, which would have filled in the front of a gown worn over a Spanish farthingale. It is similar in design to that in Fig. 318 and in shape to Fig. 283. The guards are worked in polychrome silks, silver and gold thread. c1575–85. Museo Parmigianino, Reggio Emilia.*

280. *The curving lines of the embroidery indicate that the green velvet used for the forepart in Fig. 279 was probably taken from an old cloak similar in style to those in Figs. 246–7, probably dating from c1560–70.*

281. *Detail of guard on forepart in Fig. 279, embroidered on beige silk in bright pink, blue and yellow silk (now faded) with couched silver and gold metal threads and cord.*

282. *Detail of couched fine gold metal cord on green velvet forepart in Fig. 279.*

283. *Queen Elizabeth I or a lady-in-waiting wearing one of her gowns with a richly embroidered forepart for Hilliard to draw. The sleeve rolls are decorated with bows of ribbon and she wears full linen sleeves beneath them. Drawing by Nicholas Hilliard, c1588. Victoria and Albert Museum, London.*

284. *Isabella of Portugal, wife of Emperor Charles V, wearing a gown similar in style to that worn by Eleanora of Toledo in her grave in 1562 (pages 102–4 and Figs. 286, 288–91) except that the skirt opens at the front to reveal a forepart. Posthumous statue by Pompe, 1564. Prado, Madrid.*

285. *Back of statue in Fig. 284, showing sleeves tied in, with puffs of the smock pulled through over the shoulders for decoration. The pattern of the rich cut velvet, probably with additional metal threads in the weft and areas of looped metal threads, is clearly defined. This would have been stiff to make up and there are no pleats at the waist.*

286. *Back of Eleanora of Toledo's satin bodice from the gown in which she was buried (pages 102–4). Beneath it are fragments of her red velvet bodice or 'bodies' which fastened at the front with hooks and eyes. 1562. Palazzo Pitti, Florence.*

287. *Maria de'Medici wearing a green velvet gown with a similar arrangement of embroidery to that of her mother's gown (pages 102–4, Fig. 286). Jewelled buttons on the sleeves are fastened to loop buttonholes on the shoulder straps and puffs of the smock are pulled through the gaps between them. The square of the smock, embroidered with gold thread and black silk, may be seen immediately above the square neckline of the gown, covered with a pleated, semi-transparent silk partlet. Portrait by Agnolo Bronzino c1555–7. Uffizi, Florence.*

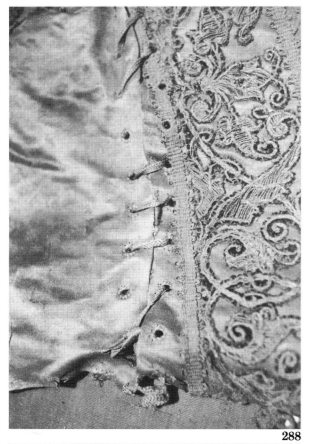

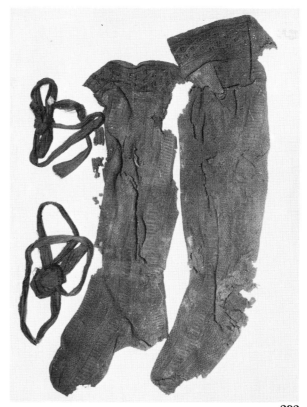

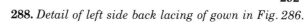

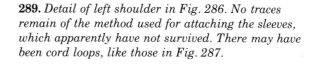

288

290

292

293

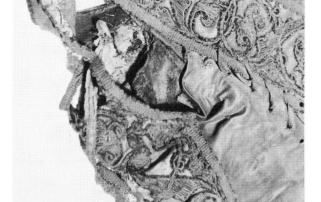

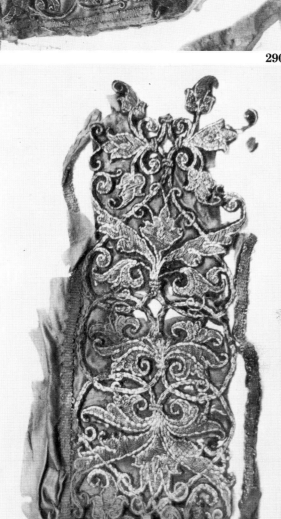

288. Detail of left side back lacing of gown in Fig. 286.

289. Detail of left shoulder in Fig. 286. No traces remain of the method used for attaching the sleeves, which apparently have not survived. There may have been cord loops, like those in Fig. 287.

290. Detail of hem of Eleanora of Toledo's gown on pages 102–4. It has been faced with a bias strip of matching satin snipped on the edge for decoration, which helps to support the embroidered guards.

291. Detail of embroidery in Fig. 290, carried out in couched gold metal thread and cord on a brown velvet ground, probably originally black, but now discoloured. This has been cut away to reveal the satin beneath. The guards may have been used first on a black velvet gown.

292. Knitted red silk stockings and silk garters worn by Eleanora of Toledo, probably crimson, but now discoloured, 1562. Palazzo Pitti, Florence.

293. Detail of tops of knitted stockings in Fig. 292.

294. Detail of foot of stocking in Fig. 292. There is a decorative woven border round the edge of the garter, which is still tied up.

295. Isabella, aged three years, wearing a gown laced on both back side seams in the same way as that in Figs. 286,8. The Colonna Family, painting by Scipione Pulzone, 1581. Palazzo Colonna, Rome.

289

291

294

295

296

298

299

301

297

296. *A little girl wearing a gown similar to that in Fig. 297 but without hanging sleeves. Portrait by an unknown Dutch painter, c1600. Present whereabouts unknown.*

297. *Velvet gown on pages 105–6 worn by Gräfin Katharina zur Lippe when she was buried, aged six, in 1600. Lippisches Landesmuseum, Detmold.*

298. *Detail of shoulder roll on gown in Fig. 297. Wooden buttons worked over with silk and gold metal thread are used for decoration.*

299. *Detail of deep sandy golden brown cut velvet on a voided ground of soft old-gold silk, used for gown in Fig. 297. This may originally have been dark brown on ivory.*

300. *Detail of gold and silver metal bobbin lace used to decorate the hem of the gown in Fig. 297. It is mounted on modern silk.*

301. *Detail of couched gold and silver twisted cord embroidery on dark sage-green velvet under-sleeve in Fig. 297, now faded. This material has probably been taken from an earlier gown.*

302. *Lady at the virginals wearing a black doublet similar to that on page 107, with white linen sleeves and a pink skirt. Gouache from the Stammbuch of Anton Weihenmayer, who lived in Lauingen, near Augsburg, 1586. Germanisches Nationalmuseum, Nürnberg.*

300

302

303. *Detail of doublet in Fig. 302 showing the chevron arrangement of black braid and the large sleeve rolls. The lady probably lived in or near Augsburg.*

304. *Detail of right shoulder roll from black embroidered doublet on pages 106–8. The linen padding and layer of felt stitched over it may be seen in places through the rotten velvet. The strip with*

worked eyelet holes for lacing in the sleeves is placed just inside the armhole. c1585. Germanisches Nationalmuseum, Nürnberg.

305. *One of the best-preserved silk and cotton tufts at front of right shoulder roll of doublet in Fig. 304.*

306. *Detail of embroidery on left back skirts of doublet in Fig. 304.*

307. *Back view of collar from black embroidered doublet in Fig. 304, showing the coarse linen interlining and padding of hemp and wool mixture.*

308. *Detail of buttons from doublet in Fig. 304, made of knotted cotton worked over a firm core, covered with black velvet. A web of knotted black silk is worked over the top. There is a line of back-stitching on the front edge to prevent stretching.*

309. *Inside lower part of doublet in Fig. 304, showing lines of stitching for whalebones and strips with worked eyelet holes which enabled the two fronts to be pulled together before fastening buttons.*

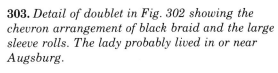

303

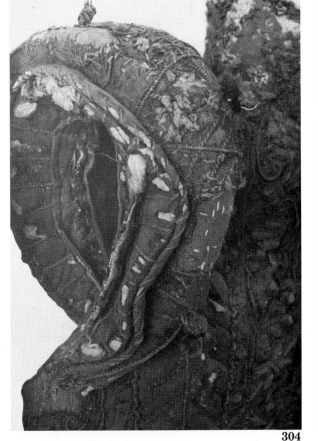
304

305

307

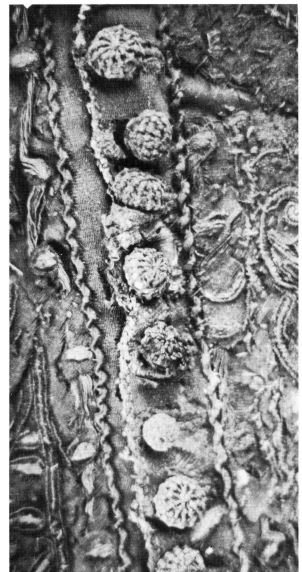
308

306

309

310

311

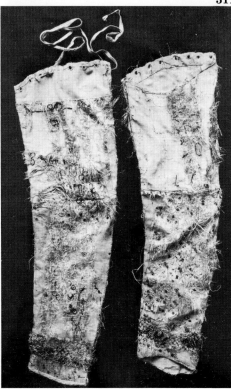

312

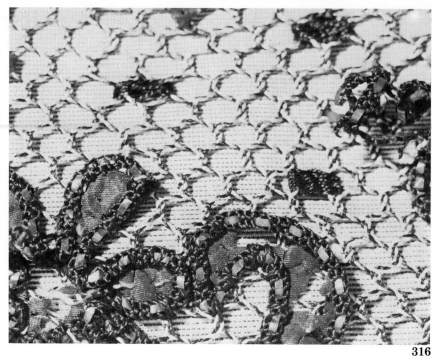

313

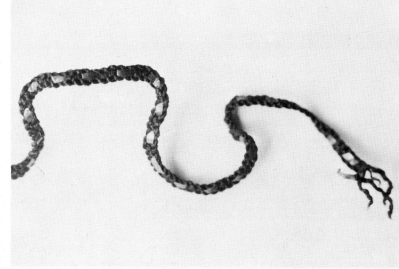

316

314

315

317

310. *Anna Sophia, Herzogin zu Mecklenburg, wears a loose gown of black velvet with padded short sleeves over a yellow silk kirtle. The kirtle hem is trimmed with what seems to be a border of yellow and white silk patterned with double-headed eagles, set with six large enamelled gold jewels. The same motifs are used between the jewels at the front. Gown and kirtle are similar to those in Figs. 311 and 321. Painting attributed to Peter van Boeckel, 1574. Schloss Schwerin.*

311. *Kirtle on pages 109–10 in ivory silk, lined with linen, hanging from the shoulders without a waist seam, fastening at the back with lacing through worked eyelet holes. c1570–80. Germanisches Nationalmuseum, Nürnberg.*

312. *Detachable sleeves belonging to kirtle in Fig. 311. They are attached to the armhole with lacing through worked eyelet holes.*

313. *Detail of ivory silk embroidered with black silk, decorated with spangles, used for the front panel of the kirtle in Fig. 311.*

314. *Detail of embroidered bobbin net panel decorating the hem of the kirtle in Fig. 311.*

315. *Detail of ivory silk with additional silver metal strip in the weft used for the kirtle in Fig. 311. This is probably the 'silver chamblet/camlet' found in contemporary English accounts. It would seem that camlet was the name for a ribbed material which could be made from silk or a combination of fibres including silk, worsted, camel's hair and mohair in the sixteenth and early seventeenth centuries.*

316. *Detail of embroidery in Fig. 314: applied black silk motifs, outlined with black silk braid, enriched with metal strip.*

317. *Fragment of black silk braid in Fig. 316.*

318

321

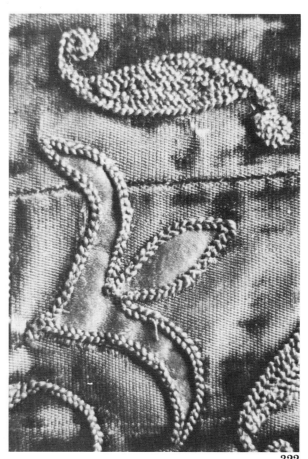

322

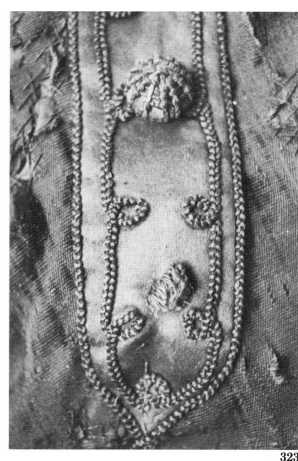

323

318. Primariae mulieris ornatus inter Belgas: *Richly dressed lady of the first rank among the Belgians wearing a loose gown similar to that on pages 111–12 (Fig. 321). From* Omnium Poene Gentium Habitus *by Abraham de Bruyn, 1581. Germanisches Nationalmuseum, Nürnberg.*

319. *Anne, wife of Alexander Denton, wearing a loose gown caught in at the waist with a girdle, lying on her cloak with the collar falling over the pillow. Effigy on tomb, 1576. Hereford Cathedral.*

320. *Detail of short padded sleeve from Anne Denton's gown in Fig. 319. It is similar to that in Fig. 321.*

321. *Detail from black velvet gown on pages 111–12, decorated with black satin guards, outlined with black silk cord. The sleeves are padded with horsehair over a linen foundation held out with whalebones and decorated with black satin buttons covered with knotted black silk cord. c1570–80. Germanisches Nationalmuseum, Nürnberg.*

322. *Almost all the black silk pile has disintegrated from the velvet of the gown in Fig. 321.*

323. *Detail of applied satin decoration outlined with rows of black silk cord from the gown in Fig. 321. One button is missing.*

324. *The front of the gown in Fig. 321 fastens at the top with 'froggings' made of looped and twisted black silk cord and buttons to match those on the sleeves. Some of the buttons are missing. The buttons and loops at the bottom of the gown are purely for decoration.*

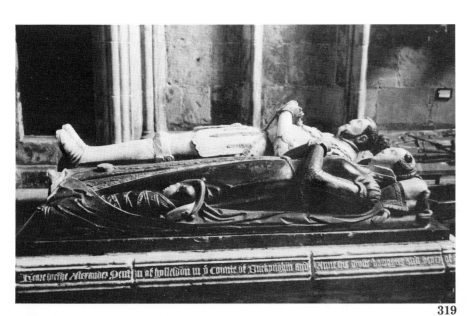

319

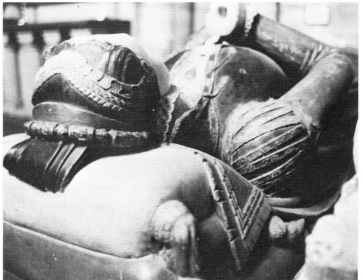

320

324

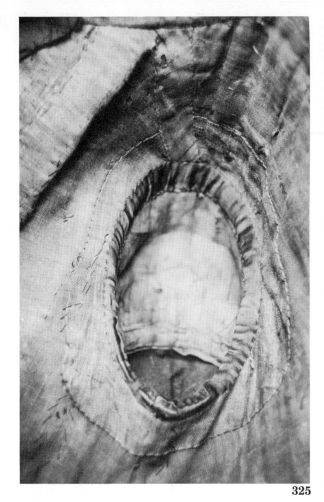

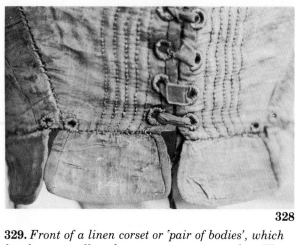

325

328

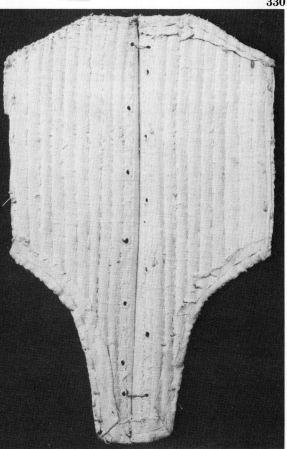

330

329. *Front of a linen corset or 'pair of bodies', which has been cut off, perhaps to use as a stomacher. The bents are held in position by rows of stitching, with two whalebones put across them for extra stiffening. Early seventeenth century or provincial eighteenth century. Rocamora Collection, Barcelona.*

330. *Detail of bents, the reedy stems of grasses grown on sand dunes, in Fig. 329. They are arranged in bunches of about twenty and held between the two layers of linen by the lines of stitching.*

331. *Upper side of corset front in Fig. 329, showing the raw edges of the binding. This would originally have been covered with silk.*

325. *Inside the gown in Fig. 321, showing the strips of linen facing the shoulder seams and round the armhole, with the black satin binding strip over the armhole seam.*

326. *Elizabeth Vernon, Countess of Southampton, wears a pink silk 'pair of bodies' or corset with rows of stitching to hold whalebones or bents for stiffening. It laces at the centre front. c1600. The Duke of Buccleuch and Queensberry, KT, Boughton House, Northants.*

327. *'Pair of bodies' or corset of ivory silk worn by Pfalzgräfin Dorothea Sabina von Neuberg (page 113). The linen lining and whalebones have all disintegrated in the grave but the lines of silk stitching remain. A pair of eyelet holes for attaching a wooden busk are worked at the bottom of the casing at the front. One ribbon point remains in the pair of eyelet holes at the side for attaching the farthingale. 1598. Bayerisches Nationalmuseum, Munich.*

328. *Detail of back of corset in Fig. 327. The eyelet holes for lacing up the centre back are worked over metal rings for reinforcement. Both sides of the back opening and the edges of the tabbed skirts are bound with ribbon.*

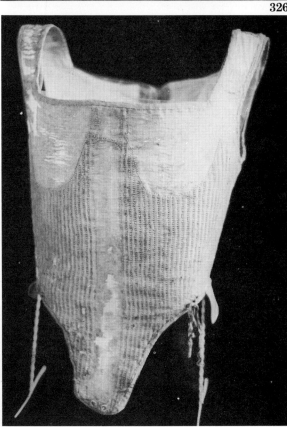

327

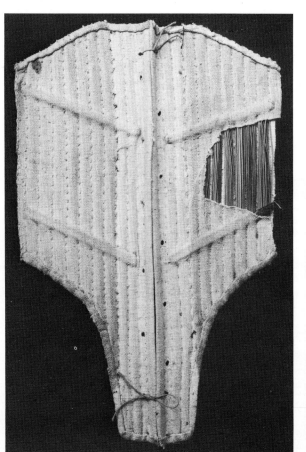

329

331

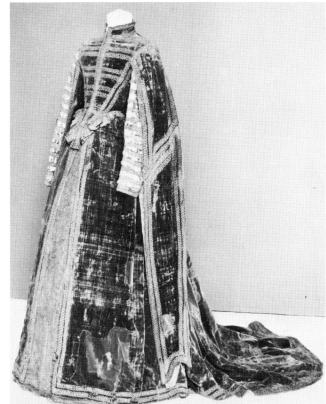

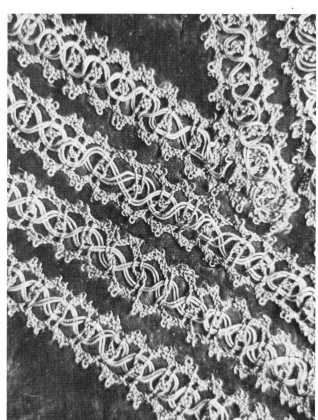

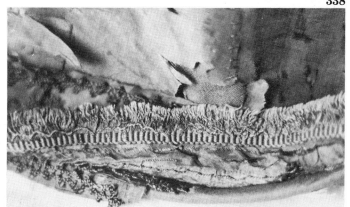

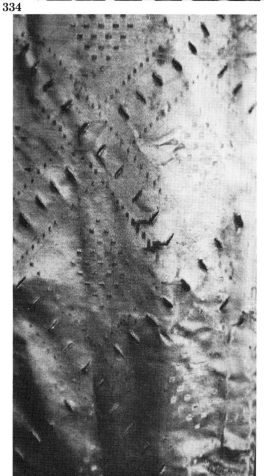

332. Bianca Capelle wearing under-sleeves similar to those in Fig. 334, with rows of vertical cuts divided by double lines of braid. Portrait by Agnolo Bronzino, c1570. Present whereabouts unknown.

333. Unknown girl, perhaps Infanta Catalina Micaela, daughter of Philip II of Spain, wearing a red velvet gown, the bodice trimmed with rows of braid in a similar way to that in Fig. 334. Painting by Sanchez Coello, c1580–5. Museo Lázaro Galdiano, Madrid.

334. Rich russet velvet gown worn by Pfalzgräfin Dorothea Sabina von Neuberg, with a petticoat of soft green silk (pages 113–14), 1598. Bayerisches Nationalmuseum, Munich.

335. Detail of scored, pinked and cut yellow satin lining of the hanging sleeves in Fig. 334. The pinks measure less than 3 mm (⅛″) in some cases.

336. Detail of golden-yellow satin under-sleeve from gown in Fig. 334. The rows of vertical cuts are caught back and stitched. Strips of tarnished metal bobbin lace are stitched between them.

337. Detail of gold and silver metal bobbin lace trimming the velvet gown in Fig. 334.

338. Detail of tarnished metal bobbin lace at the hem of the green silk petticoat in Fig. 334.

339. The silk fringe on the petticoat in Fig. 338 is from a braid sewn on the hem beneath. This would have taken the wear from the folded edge. Woollen 'brush braid' was used in the 1860s for the same purpose.

340

342

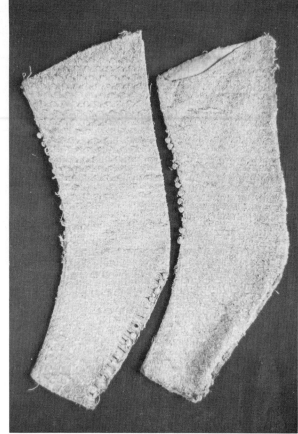

343

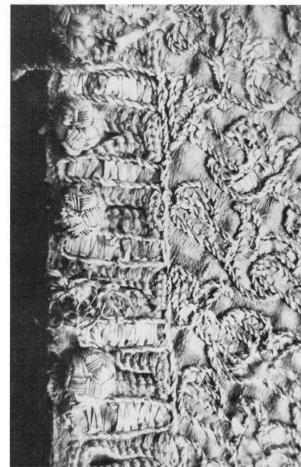

345

340. *Cut and uncut patterned velvet gown on pages 115–16 worn by Pfalzgräfin Dorothea Maria von Sulzbach. The deep shoulder wings are trimmed with silk braid. The cut is similar to gowns in the Spanish tailors' books (Fig. 36). Italian velvet of 1620s or early 1630s, worn in the grave, 1639. Bayerisches Nationalmuseum, Munich.*

341. *The gown in Fig. 340 is decorated with silk braid.*

342. *Cut and uncut velvet simulating strapwork in dark brown and sandy beige used for gown in Fig. 340, now faded and disintegrating.*

343. *Pair of sleeves on page 115 in soft pale golden-brown satin, embroidered with silver strip outlined with metal thread of silver strip wrapped round a yellow silk core. They are lined with matching silk, opening at the front on the upper arm with buttons and loops of braided silver thread and from wrist to elbow with worked buttonholes. Some of the buttons are missing. c1600–10. Germanisches National-museum, Nürnberg.*

344. *Detail of couched silver metal thread and silver strip embroidery on sleeves in Fig. 343.*

345. *Detail of buttonholes worked in brown silk and buttons 8 mm ($\frac{5}{16}$″) in diameter, made of silver metal thread with a silk core worked over a wooden base, at wrist of sleeve in Fig. 343.*

346. *Mary Cornwallis wearing a black velvet gown open at the front to reveal a forepart embroidered with a linear design similar to that in Fig. 347. Portrait by George Gower, c1585. Manchester City Art Gallery.*

341

344

346

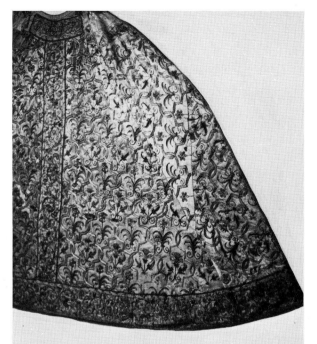

347

348

351

349

347. *Forepart on page 115, in ivory printed, or stamped, satin. This was carried out with hot irons in a decorative pattern of geometric flowers and leaf shapes. The interlocking pattern of the embroidery is similar to the layout of an Elizabethan knot garden. The guards at the centre front and round the hem are of ivory linen and the embroidery is coarser in execution than the rest. The whole forepart is backed with pale pink linen with a double layer beneath the hem which may have been put on in the eighteenth century. It was probably made in the early 1580s and extra pieces were added at the sides in the late 1580s or early 1590s to accommodate the wider farthingale. c1580–95. Museo Parmigianino, Reggio Emilia.*

348. *The embroidery inside the interlocking shapes in Fig. 347 is carried out in shades of pink, yellow and white. The gillyflowers, or pinks, have bright blue leaves and the other flowers have green and yellow ones. All the shapes are outlined with gold metal thread couched with yellow silk in most places and with red on the front area. The embroidery on the guards is in blue-, green-, yellow- and tan-coloured silks, with couched gold metal thread.*

349. *Anne Wortley, Lady Morton, wears a rich plum silk gown, embroidered with gold metal thread, with a pinned flounce to hide the edge of the farthingale frame. The arrangement of embroidery is similar to that on the black satin petticoat in Fig. 351. Painting by Paul van Somer, c1615. Tate Gallery, London.*

350. *Detail of flounce, pulled up with gathering threads and carefully pinned, worn by Queen Anna Cathrine, wife of King Christian IV of Denmark. Painting by Peter Isaacsz, c1620. Rosenborg Slot, Copenhagen.*

351. *Pinked black satin petticoat, or skirt, lined with bright pink silk (page 117). It is embroidered with pink and turquoise silk and black beads. The waist would probably have been cartridge pleated originally but is now arranged in flat pleats. c1615–20. Nationalmuseet, Copenhagen.*

350

352. *Detail of petticoat in Fig. 351, showing the pinked satin, which is now disintegrating. It has been covered with fine black crêpeline to protect it. The embroidery of satin stitch, couched cords and French knots is enriched with black shiny beads. The narrow bands of embroidery are outlined with couched cords, turquoise between pink, contrasting with pink between turquoise for the wide bands.*

352

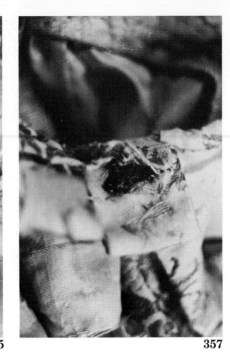

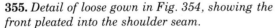

355

357

359

360

354. *Kneeling effigy of Magdalen, wife of Edward Lord Bruce of Kinloss, Master of the Rolls. She wears a loose gown gathered across the back in a similar way to that worn by Sir Francis Verney (Fig. 271). Monument of alabaster and marble, gilded and painted, 1610. Rolls Chapel, London.*

357. *Fragment of silver spangled bobbin lace, mounted on rich salmon-pink corded silk ribbon trimming the loose gown in Fig. 356. This originally decorated seams, front edges, tabbed wings and collar, but was removed long ago, probably for use on another gown.*

360. *The foundation yoke of the gown in Fig. 356 is made of ivory fustian and saffron-yellow linen pad-stitched together. Tiny stitches show on the fustian layer.*

353. *An unknown lady aged twenty-three, wearing a loose gown which apparently could be fastened at the front with buttons and loops. It is open, with the fronts pushed back, making folds by the arms. This was an alternative style to the gown with fronts cut away, as in the examples on pages 118–23. Painting by unknown artist, 1617. Present source unknown.*

355. *Detail of loose gown in Fig. 354, showing the front pleated into the shoulder seam.*

356. *Detail of shoulder and wing of loose gown on pages 118–19. The silk is pleated at the back and mounted on a stiffened linen yoke piece. c1610–20. Victoria and Albert Museum, London.*

358. *Detail of woven motif in polychrome silks from Fig. 359.*

359. *Ivory silk with woven pattern, slashed diagonally between the motifs, used for the gown in Fig. 356. The silk is pieced in several places and the gown has probably been cut from an old petticoat.*

361. *Lady Dorothy Manners wears a short-waisted jacket in woven patterned silk, similar in length to that in Fig. 367, and a loose gown of the same type as that on pages 118–19, with the addition of hanging sleeves. The silk is slashed to match the petticoat. c1615–20. Painting attributed to William Larkin. Ipswich Museums and Art Galleries.*

354

356

358

361

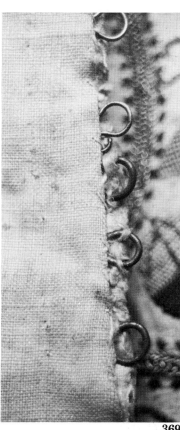

362

364

366

368

369

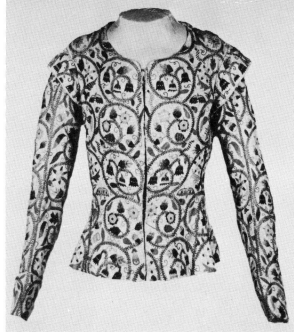

363

365

367

364. *Back of jacket in Fig. 362. The gussets give shaping to accommodate the fullness of the skirt over the hips, worn without a farthingale.*

365. *White linen jacket, embroidered in polychrome silks and gold metal thread, fastening at the front with ribbons. The waist is a little above the natural level but not as high as Margaret Laton's waist in Fig. 363. c1618–20. Museum of Costume, Bath.*

366. *Lady Dorothy Cary wears an embroidered jacket similar to that in Figs. 362,4, fastening with red ribbons over an embroidered petticoat without a farthingale. c1615. The Suffolk Collection, Ranger's House, Blackheath, GLC.*

367. *White linen jacket on pages 120–1, embroidered in polychrome silks and gold metal thread. It is of particular interest as the same embroidery motifs have been used as those in Fig. 365, but the arrangement has been changed and different coloured silks employed. It is slightly longer waisted and fastens edge to edge at the front with hooks and eyes. c1615–18. Burrell Collection, Glasgow.*

368. *Hooks fastening the jacket in Fig. 367. The three at the top of the picture are original but the two at the bottom were probably put on later to replace some which were missing.*

369. *Eyes fastening the jacket in Fig. 367. Three at the bottom are original but two at the top of the picture were probably put on later with the hooks.*

362. *White linen jacket on page 121, embroidered with polychrome silks, tiny spangles and gold metal thread, trimmed with gold metal bobbin lace with large spangles hanging from the points. It apparently*

363. *Margaret Laton, wife of the Keeper of the Jewel House, wears the embroidered linen jacket, fastening*

fastened with five pairs of pink silk ribbon bows at the front, as in Fig. 366, but these were removed, probably when the jacket was worn in 1620. c1610–15. Private collection, on loan to the Victoria and Albert Museum, London.

invisibly at the front with hooks and eyes, in Figs. 362,4. The jacket was made around 1610–15, but the petticoat is worn over it giving the raised waist level fashionable around 1619–22. Portrait and jacket have been kept together in the same family. Painting attributed to Marcus Gheeraerts the Younger, c1620. Private collection, on loan to the Victoria and Albert Museum, London.

370

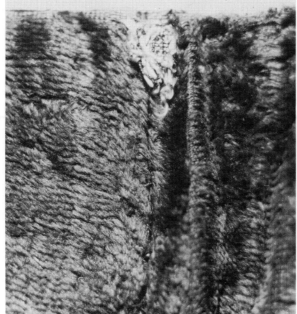

372

375

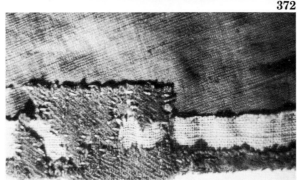

373

green twill-weave wool put over it. Much of this has been eaten by moth.

374. An unknown woman aged thirty-five, wearing a loose gown with pinked linings to the hanging sleeves similar to those in Fig. 378. Painting attributed to Marcus Gheeraerts the Younger, 1620. Present whereabouts unknown.

375. Pleats on right back, wing and part of hanging sleeve of girl's loose gown in cut and uncut dark mulberry-coloured velvet on pages 122–3. Tufts of yellow silk remain to show original position of silver bobbin lace and spangles. c1610–20. Victoria and Albert Museum, London.

376. The gown in Fig. 375 is mounted on a foundation yoke of pink silk interlined with black stiffened linen canvas or buckram, and lightly padded over the shoulders with a thin layer of wool. Rows of pad-stitching hold the layers together and tiny stitches may be seen in the silk.

377. Detail of front of gown in Fig. 375, interfaced with black stiffened linen canvas or buckram. The selvedge of the velvet is caught down over it and a strip of pink silk is stitched on top to form a facing.

378. The round, or Spanish, hanging sleeves of the gown in Fig. 375 are lined with pinked pink silk. An apprentice may have carried out the pinking as one row is missing.

370. Shoulder and wing of girl's olive-green silk plush loose gown on pages 120–1, mounted on a stiffened yoke. Almost all the silver braid trimmings have been removed, probably to use on another gown. c1610–20. Victoria and Albert Museum, London.

371. The vents in the side seams of the gown in Fig. 370 are faced with olive-green wool with a twill weave.

372. Detail of remaining fragment of silver braid trimming the gown in Fig. 370.

373. The hem of the gown in Fig. 370 is stiffened with coarse white linen and a false hem of olive-

371

374

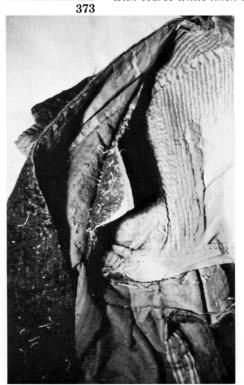

376

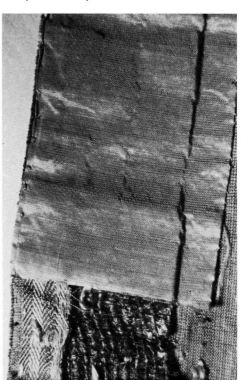

377

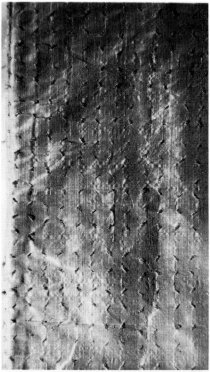

378

Drawing and Patterns taken from Original Garments dating from c1560 to 1620
+ indicates burial clothes

+1562 Palazzo Pitti, Florence

1A. A suit, consisting of doublet and paned trunk-hose, worn by Don Garzia, the fourth son of Eleanora of Toledo and Cosimo I de'Medici, who died of malaria at the age of fifteen in 1562. He was buried wearing this suit in the Sagrestia Vecchia of San Lorenzo in Florence. In 1791 all the Medici coffins, except those in the marble tombs, were removed to the subterranean vaults of the Capella di Principe of San Lorenzo. It was not until 1857 that the coffins were opened and in the intervening years twenty-two of them had been violated. An article initialled G.S.P., 'Esumazione e Ricognizione delle Ceneri dei Principe Medicei fatta nell'anno 1857' printed in *Archivo Storico Italiano* in 1888, attempts to identify the various bodies and gives descriptions of the clothes at this time. Don Grazia's satin doublet, now reddish brown, was described as 'raso rosso' and may originally have been light crimson. It is striped horizontally with couched cord made of three plied threads of gold strip wrapped round a silk core. These metal threads are now tarnished. There is a small patch in yellow satin (probably faded from crimson) on the left sleeve, which shows that the suit had been worn before being used for the burial (Fig. 79). It may have been made in 1560 or 1561. The doublet was originally lined with linen but almost all of this disintegrated with the decomposing body and only a few tiny fragments are left. The drawing shows how the suit would originally have appeared, complete with buttons, as only those on the wrist have survived.

1B. The dark crimson velvet paned trunk-hose are lined with lighter crimson satin, much of which has rotted away. The remainder is discoloured. The velvet panes are interlined with linen, a few fragments of which remain, and are backed with light crimson silk, now discoloured: the velvet is decorated with horizontal lines of couched gold cord and the raw edges are oversewn with similar cord on the edges of each pane (Fig. 77). The front closes with a velvet cod-piece, made like a folded pouch, decorated with couched gold cord and cut to reveal the crimson satin lining which pads it out. The panes are gathered in tight cartridge pleats at waist and leg; although most of the stitching and both leg bands have disintegrated, the folds of velvet may still be seen and much of the waistband remains. Pairs of eyelet holes are worked in the waistband to correspond with similar pairs in the lower edge of the doublet. Ribbon points, or laces, were threaded through those opposite pairs of holes and knotted in a row of loops or bows around the waist. This was known as 'trussing the points'. The points here are of silk ribbon with metal aglets, or tags, at the ends.

1A

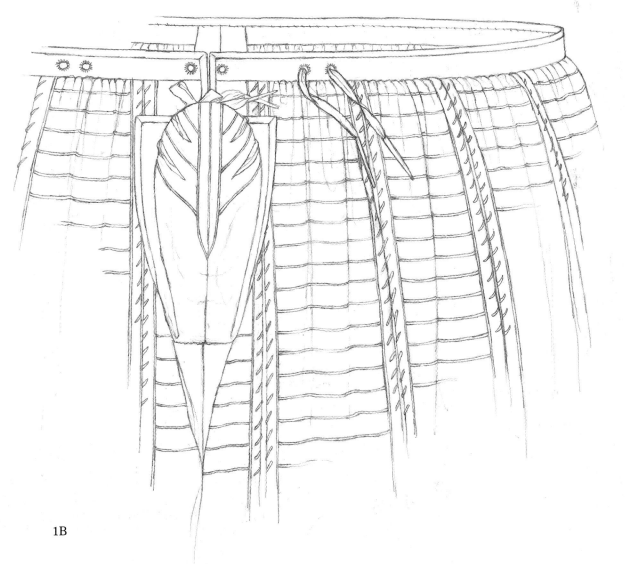

1B

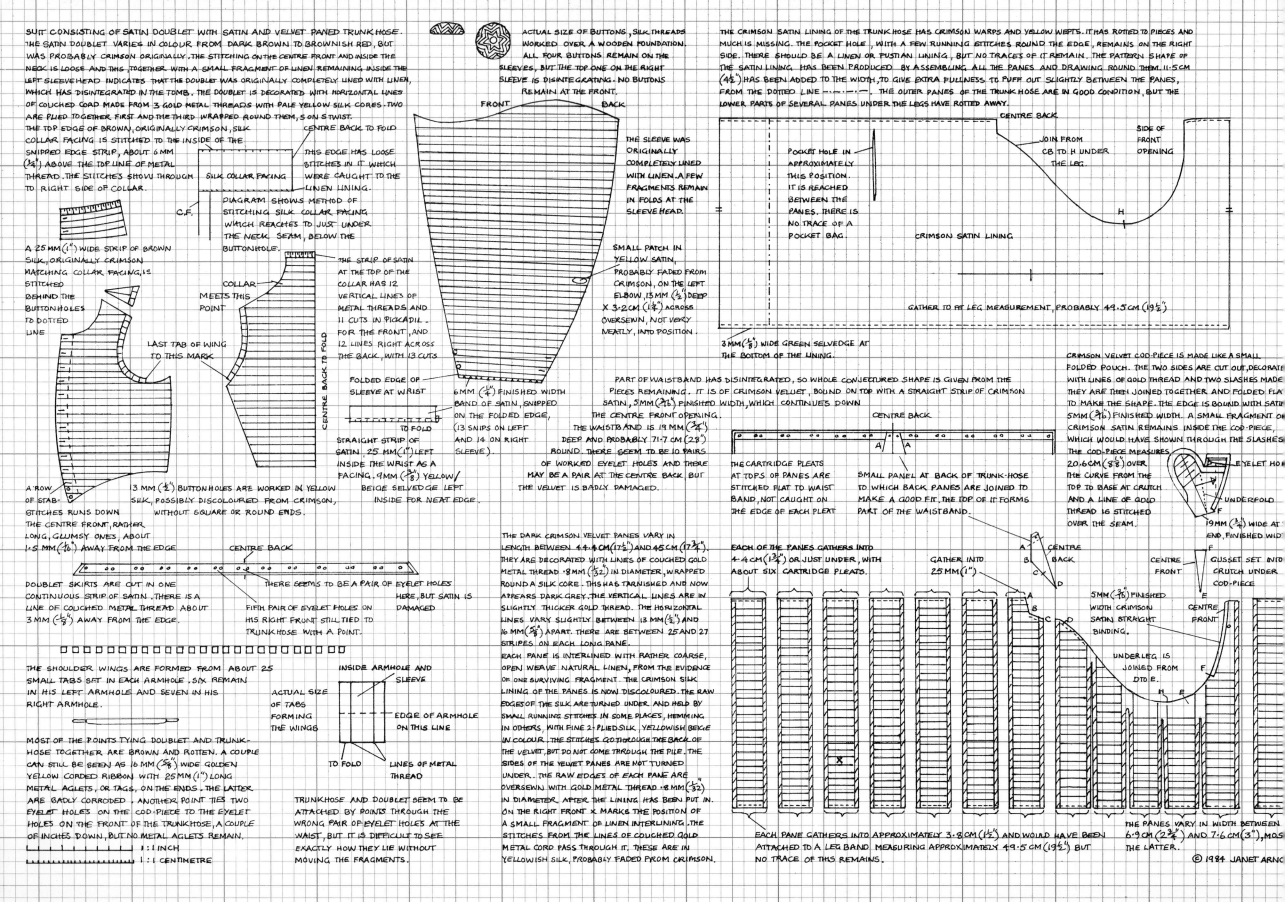

1. †1562 DOUBLET AND PANED TRUNKHOSE WORN BY DON GARZIA DE' MEDICI PALAZZO PITTI, FLORENCE

SUIT CONSISTING OF SATIN DOUBLET WITH SATIN AND VELVET PANED TRUNK HOSE. THE SATIN DOUBLET VARIES IN COLOUR FROM DARK BROWN TO BROWNISH RED, BUT WAS PROBABLY CRIMSON ORIGINALLY. THE STITCHING ON THE CENTRE FRONT AND INSIDE THE NECK IS LOOSE AND THIS, TOGETHER WITH A SMALL FRAGMENT OF LINEN REMAINING INSIDE THE LEFT SLEEVEHEAD INDICATES THAT THE DOUBLET WAS ORIGINALLY COMPLETELY LINED WITH LINEN, WHICH HAS DISINTEGRATED IN THE TOMB. THE DOUBLET IS DECORATED WITH HORIZONTAL LINES OF COUCHED CORD MADE FROM 3 GOLD METAL THREADS WITH PALE YELLOW SILK CORES. TWO ARE PLIED TOGETHER FIRST AND THE THIRD WRAPPED ROUND THEM, S ON S TWIST.

THE TOP EDGE OF BROWN, ORIGINALLY CRIMSON, SILK COLLAR FACING IS STITCHED TO THE INSIDE OF THE SNIPPED EDGE STRIP, ABOUT 6 MM ($\frac{1}{4}$") ABOVE THE TOP LINE OF METAL THREAD. THE STITCHES SHOW THROUGH TO RIGHT SIDE OF COLLAR.

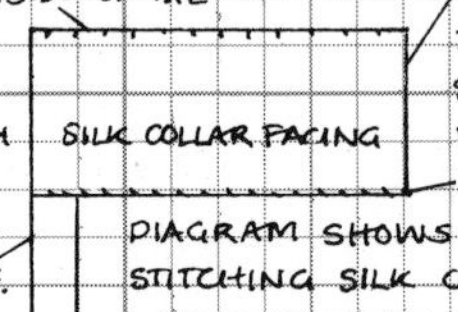
CENTRE BACK TO FOLD
SILK COLLAR FACING
C.F.
THIS EDGE HAS LOOSE STITCHES IN IT WHICH WERE CAUGHT TO THE LINEN LINING.

DIAGRAM SHOWS METHOD OF STITCHING SILK COLLAR FACING WHICH REACHES TO JUST UNDER THE NECK SEAM, BELOW THE BUTTONHOLE.

ACTUAL SIZE OF BUTTONS, SILK THREADS WORKED OVER A WOODEN FOUNDATION. ALL FOUR BUTTONS REMAIN ON THE SLEEVES, BUT THE TOP ONE ON THE RIGHT SLEEVE IS DISINTEGRATING. NO BUTTONS REMAIN AT THE FRONT.

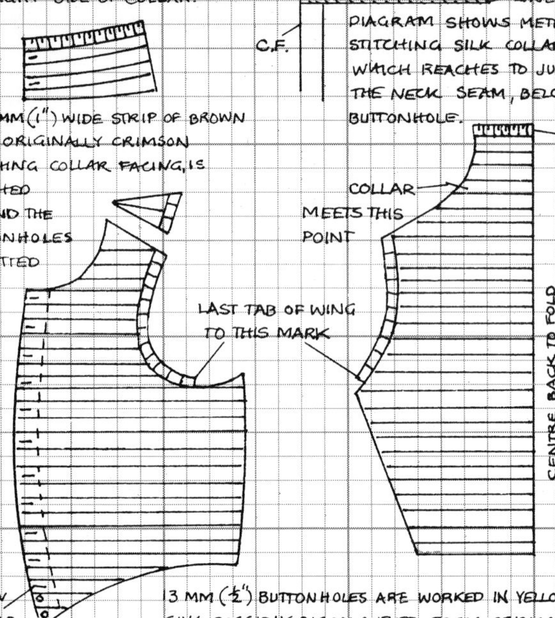
A 25 MM (1") WIDE STRIP OF BROWN SILK, ORIGINALLY CRIMSON MATCHING COLLAR FACING, IS STITCHED BEHIND THE BUTTONHOLES TO DOTTED LINE
COLLAR MEETS THIS POINT
LAST TAB OF WING TO THIS MARK
THE STRIP OF SATIN AT THE TOP OF THE COLLAR HAS 12 VERTICAL LINES OF METAL THREADS AND 11 CUTS IN PICKADIL. FOR THE FRONT, AND 12 LINES RIGHT ACROSS THE BACK, WITH 13 CUTS
CENTRE BACK TO FOLD
A ROW OF STAB-STITCHES RUNS DOWN THE CENTRE FRONT, RATHER LONG, CLUMSY ONES, ABOUT 1.5 MM ($\frac{1}{16}$") AWAY FROM THE EDGE
13 MM ($\frac{1}{2}$") BUTTONHOLES ARE WORKED IN YELLOW SILK, POSSIBLY DISCOLOURED FROM CRIMSON, WITHOUT SQUARE OR ROUND ENDS.

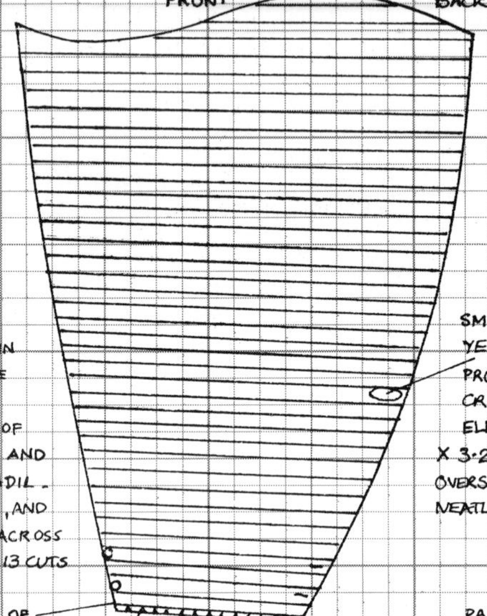
FRONT
BACK
THE SLEEVE WAS ORIGINALLY COMPLETELY LINED WITH LINEN. A FEW FRAGMENTS REMAIN IN FOLDS AT THE SLEEVE HEAD.
SMALL PATCH IN YELLOW SATIN, PROBABLY FADED FROM CRIMSON, ON THE LEFT ELBOW, 13 MM ($\frac{1}{2}$") DEEP X 3·2 CM ($1\frac{1}{4}$") ACROSS OVERSEWN, NOT VERY NEATLY, INTO POSITION.
FOLDED EDGE OF SLEEVE AT WRIST
6 MM ($\frac{1}{4}$") FINISHED WIDTH BAND OF SATIN, SNIPPED ON THE FOLDED EDGE, (13 SNIPS ON LEFT AND 14 ON RIGHT SLEEVE).

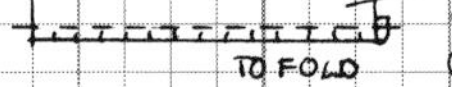
TO FOLD

STRAIGHT STRIP OF SATIN 25 MM (1") LEFT INSIDE THE WRIST AS A FACING. 9 MM ($\frac{3}{8}$") YELLOW/BEIGE SELVEDGE LEFT INSIDE FOR NEAT EDGE.

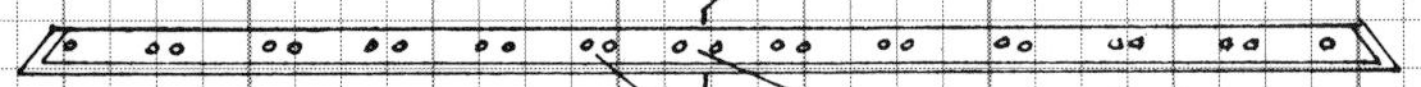
CENTRE BACK
THERE SEEMS TO BE A PAIR OF EYELET HOLES HERE, BUT SATIN IS DAMAGED
FIFTH PAIR OF EYELET HOLES ON HIS RIGHT FRONT STILL TIED TO TRUNKHOSE WITH A POINT.

DOUBLET SKIRTS ARE CUT IN ONE CONTINUOUS STRIP OF SATIN. THERE IS A LINE OF COUCHED METAL THREAD ABOUT 3 MM ($\frac{1}{8}$") AWAY FROM THE EDGE.

THE SHOULDER WINGS ARE FORMED FROM ABOUT 25 SMALL TABS SET IN EACH ARMHOLE. SIX REMAIN IN HIS LEFT ARMHOLE AND SEVEN IN HIS RIGHT ARMHOLE.

ACTUAL SIZE OF TABS FORMING THE WINGS

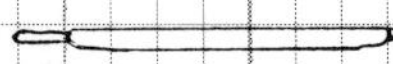

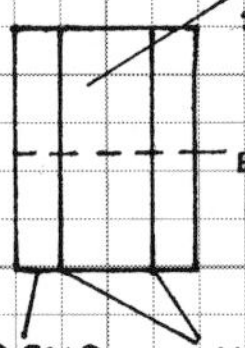
INSIDE ARMHOLE AND SLEEVE
EDGE OF ARMHOLE ON THIS LINE
TO FOLD
LINES OF METAL THREAD

MOST OF THE POINTS TYING DOUBLET AND TRUNK-HOSE TOGETHER ARE BROWN AND ROTTEN. A COUPLE CAN STILL BE SEEN AS 16 MM ($\frac{5}{8}$") WIDE GOLDEN YELLOW CORDED RIBBON WITH 25 MM (1") LONG METAL AGLETS, OR TAGS, ON THE ENDS. THE LATTER ARE BADLY CORRODED. ANOTHER POINT TIES TWO EYELET HOLES ON THE COD-PIECE TO THE EYELET HOLES ON THE FRONT OF THE TRUNKHOSE, A COUPLE OF INCHES DOWN, BUT NO METAL AGLETS REMAIN.

1:1 INCH

1:1 CENTIMETRE

TRUNKHOSE AND DOUBLET SEEM TO BE ATTACHED BY POINTS THROUGH THE WRONG PAIR OF EYELET HOLES AT THE WAIST, BUT IT IS DIFFICULT TO SEE EXACTLY HOW THEY LIE WITHOUT MOVING THE FRAGMENTS.

THE CRIMSON SATIN LINING OF THE TRUNK HOSE HAS CRIMSON WARPS AND YELLOW WEFTS. IT HAS ROTTED TO PIECES AND MUCH IS MISSING. THE POCKET HOLE, WITH A FEW RUNNING STITCHES ROUND THE EDGE, REMAINS ON THE RIGHT SIDE. THERE SHOULD BE A LINEN OR FUSTIAN LINING, BUT NO TRACES OF IT REMAIN. THE PATTERN SHAPE OF THE SATIN LINING HAS BEEN PRODUCED BY ASSEMBLING ALL THE PANES AND DRAWING ROUND THEM. 11·5 CM ($4\frac{1}{2}$") HAS BEEN ADDED TO THE WIDTH, TO GIVE EXTRA FULLNESS TO PUFF OUT SLIGHTLY BETWEEN THE PANES, FROM THE DOTTED LINE –·–·–·–. THE OUTER PANES OF THE TRUNK HOSE ARE IN GOOD CONDITION, BUT THE LOWER PARTS OF SEVERAL PANES UNDER THE LEGS HAVE ROTTED AWAY.

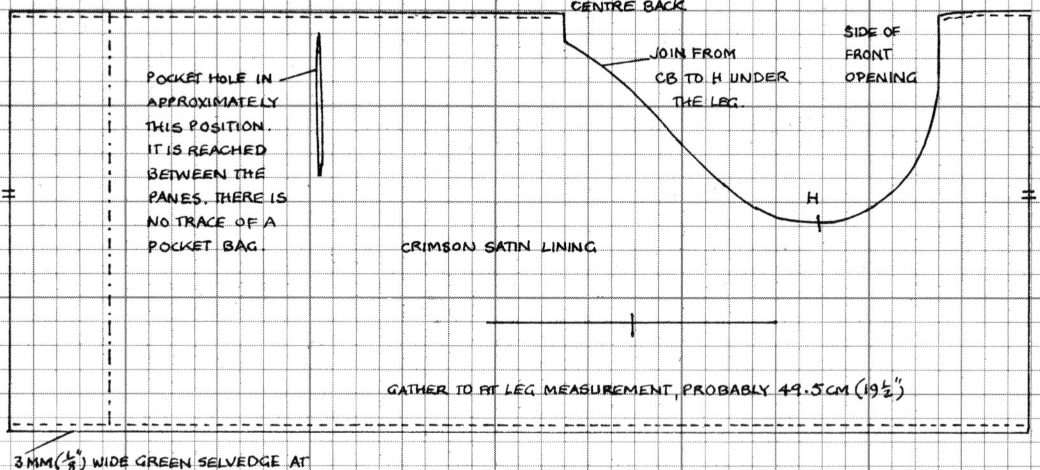
CENTRE BACK
POCKET HOLE IN APPROXIMATELY THIS POSITION. IT IS REACHED BETWEEN THE PANES. THERE IS NO TRACE OF A POCKET BAG.
JOIN FROM CB TO H UNDER THE LEG.
SIDE OF FRONT OPENING
H
CRIMSON SATIN LINING
GATHER TO FIT LEG MEASUREMENT, PROBABLY 49·5 CM ($19\frac{1}{2}$")

3 MM ($\frac{1}{8}$") WIDE GREEN SELVEDGE AT THE BOTTOM OF THE LINING.

PART OF WAISTBAND HAS DISINTEGRATED, SO WHOLE CONJECTURED SHAPE IS GIVEN FROM THE PIECES REMAINING. IT IS OF CRIMSON VELVET, BOUND ON TOP WITH A STRAIGHT STRIP OF CRIMSON SATIN, 5 MM ($\frac{3}{16}$") FINISHED WIDTH, WHICH CONTINUES DOWN THE CENTRE FRONT OPENING. THE WAISTBAND IS 19 MM ($\frac{3}{4}$") DEEP AND PROBABLY 71·7 CM (28") ROUND. THERE SEEM TO BE 10 PAIRS OF WORKED EYELET HOLES AND THERE MAY BE A PAIR AT THE CENTRE BACK BUT THE VELVET IS BADLY DAMAGED.

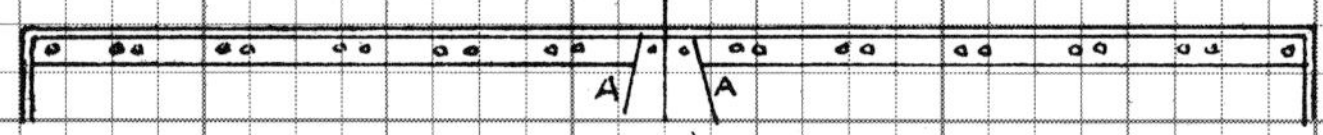
CENTRE BACK
A
A

THE CARTRIDGE PLEATS AT TOPS OF PANES ARE STITCHED FLAT TO WAIST BAND, NOT CAUGHT ON THE EDGE OF EACH PLEAT

SMALL PANEL AT BACK OF TRUNK-HOSE TO WHICH BACK PANES ARE JOINED TO MAKE A GOOD FIT. THE TOP OF IT FORMS PART OF THE WAISTBAND.

CRIMSON VELVET COD-PIECE IS MADE LIKE A SMALL FOLDED POUCH. THE TWO SIDES ARE CUT OUT, DECORATE WITH LINES OF GOLD THREAD AND TWO SLASHES MADE THEY ARE THEN JOINED TOGETHER AND FOLDED FLA TO MAKE THE SHAPE. THE EDGE IS BOUND WITH SATI 5MM ($\frac{3}{16}$") FINISHED WIDTH. A SMALL FRAGMENT O CRIMSON SATIN REMAINS INSIDE THE COD-PIECE, WHICH WOULD HAVE SHOWN THROUGH THE SLASHES THE COD-PIECE MEASURES 20.6 CM ($8\frac{1}{8}$") OVER THE CURVE FROM THE TOP TO BASE AT CRUTCH AND A LINE OF GOLD THREAD IS STITCHED OVER THE SEAM.

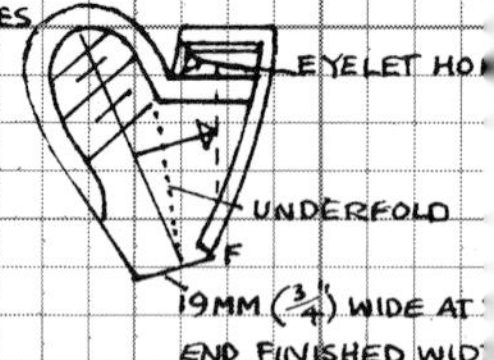
EYELET HO
UNDERFOLD
19MM ($\frac{3}{4}$") WIDE AT END, FINISHED WID

THE DARK CRIMSON VELVET PANES VARY IN LENGTH BETWEEN 44·4 CM ($17\frac{1}{2}$") AND 45 CM ($17\frac{3}{4}$"). THEY ARE DECORATED WITH LINES OF COUCHED GOLD METAL THREAD ·8 MM ($\frac{1}{32}$") IN DIAMETER, WRAPPED ROUND A SILK CORE. THIS HAS TARNISHED AND NOW APPEARS DARK GREY. THE VERTICAL LINES ARE IN SLIGHTLY THICKER GOLD THREAD. THE HORIZONTAL LINES VARY SLIGHTLY BETWEEN 13 MM ($\frac{1}{2}$") AND 16 MM ($\frac{5}{8}$") APART. THERE ARE BETWEEN 25 AND 27 STRIPES ON EACH LONG PANE.
EACH PANE IS INTERLINED WITH RATHER COARSE, OPEN WEAVE NATURAL LINEN, FROM THE EVIDENCE OF ONE SURVIVING FRAGMENT. THE CRIMSON SILK LINING OF THE PANES IS NOW DISCOLOURED. THE RAW EDGES OF THE SILK ARE TURNED UNDER AND HELD BY SMALL RUNNING STITCHES IN SOME PLACES, HEMMING IN OTHERS, WITH FINE 2-PLIED SILK, YELLOWISH BEIGE IN COLOUR. THE STITCHES GO THROUGH THE BACK OF THE VELVET, BUT DO NOT COME THROUGH THE PILE. THE SIDES OF THE VELVET PANES ARE NOT TURNED UNDER. THE RAW EDGES OF EACH PANE ARE OVERSEWN WITH GOLD METAL THREAD ·8 MM ($\frac{1}{32}$") IN DIAMETER AFTER THE LINING HAS BEEN PUT IN. ON THE RIGHT FRONT X MARKS THE POSITION OF A SMALL FRAGMENT OF LINEN INTERLINING. THE STITCHES FROM THE LINES OF COUCHED GOLD METAL CORD PASS THROUGH IT. THESE ARE IN YELLOWISH SILK, PROBABLY FADED FROM CRIMSON.

EACH OF THE PANES GATHERS INTO 4·4 CM ($1\frac{3}{4}$") OR JUST UNDER, WITH ABOUT SIX CARTRIDGE PLEATS.

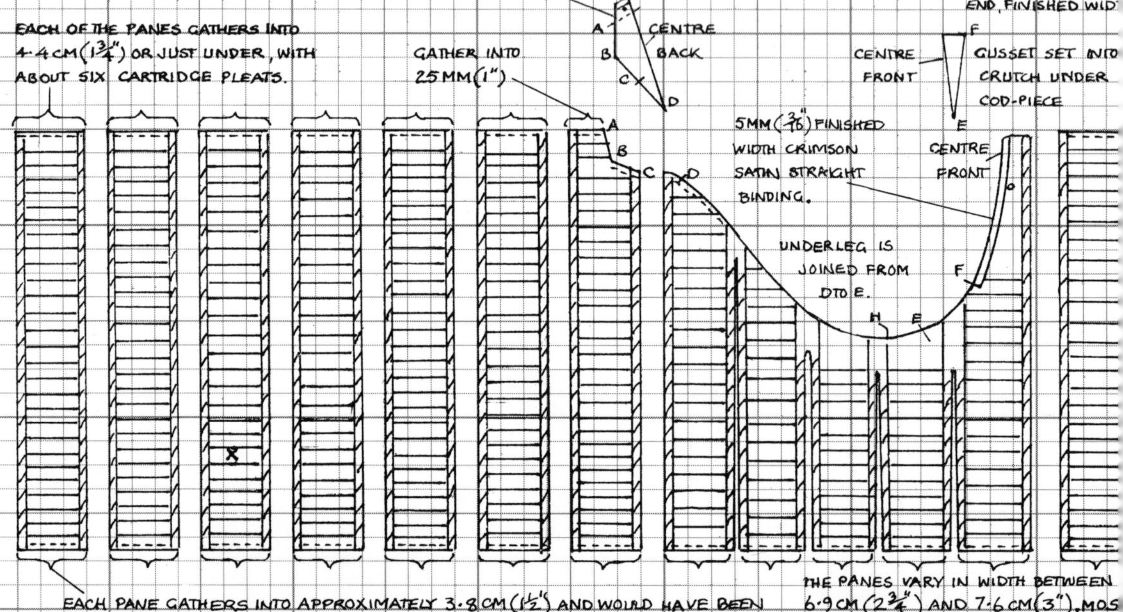
GATHER INTO 25 MM (1")
A
B
C
D
CENTRE BACK
CENTRE FRONT
E
F
GUSSET SET INTO CRUTCH UNDER COD-PIECE
5MM ($\frac{3}{16}$") FINISHED WIDTH CRIMSON SATIN STRAIGHT BINDING.
CENTRE FRONT
UNDERLEG IS JOINED FROM D TO E.
H
X

EACH PANE GATHERS INTO APPROXIMATELY 3·8 CM ($1\frac{1}{2}$") AND WOULD HAVE BEEN ATTACHED TO A LEG BAND MEASURING APPROXIMATELY 49·5 CM ($19\frac{1}{2}$") BUT NO TRACE OF THIS REMAINS.

THE PANES VARY IN WIDTH BETWEEN 6·9 CM ($2\frac{3}{4}$") AND 7·6 CM (3"), MOS THE LATTER.

+1562 Palazzo Pitti, Florence

2.   A black velvet bonnet, now faded to dark brown, worn by Don Garzia de'Medici, with the crimson satin and velvet suit just described, when he was buried in 1562. The flat round brim is made of two layers of velvet; there is apparently no stiffening but there may have been a layer of paper or linen between them originally. The crown is lined with black silk, now faded to dark brown, worked as one layer with the velvet. Thirty-nine evenly spaced dart tucks shape the crown to the brim (Fig. 81). Bonnets of this shape were fashionable all over Western Europe. They are seen in many portraits, trimmed with a small ostrich feather and a jewelled ornament, or worn with a narrow band of twisted cord round the brim, sometimes decorated with jewels. Twenty-two of the coffins had been robbed of their jewels long before they were opened in 1857, Don Garzia's among them: any jewels there might have been in the bonnet were removed at that time.

+1574 Palazzo Pitti, Florence

3A.   A doublet of light crimson satin, now discoloured to yellowish brown, worn by Cosimo I de'Medici, who died at the age of fifty-five, in 1574. The description of his clothes made in 1857 records a 'giobbone di raso rosso' – a red satin doublet – with cloth breeches of the same colour and a white silk mantle of the Grand Master of the Order of St Stephen, with mantle laces and tassels and emblazoned with its red Maltese cross. Settimanni's *Diario Fiorentino* describes Cosimo's burial in these clothes but the ruby cross, silver sceptre and other pieces of jewellery are missing. The cloth ('panno') breeches and white silk mantle have discoloured to yellowish brown and are in too many fragments to be handled at the present time but Dr Mary Westerman Bulgarella has identified the fragments of the Maltese cross during preliminary conservation work. The mantle laces, two thick silk cords with tassels, were arranged at the doublet waist, presumably in 1857 (Fig. 85). I recognized their similarity to those in the 'Coronation' portrait and miniature of Queen Elizabeth I of England, wearing the robes used for the ceremony in 1559. They have now been put with the mantle of the Grand Master of the Order of St Stephen. The doublet is too fragile to be turned over although the buttons are still intact and the pattern has been taken from what could be seen without moving the garment. It can be deduced that it would originally have been lined with linen from the evidence of a tiny fragment remaining inside the wrist facing on the left sleeve.

3B.   Only small fragments of wool and braid at the top of the trunk-hose remain with the doublet.

Other fragments of wool and silk have been preserved with Cosimo's silk mantle of the Grand Master of the Order of St Stephen but these are too fragile to be handled before conservation work begins. This drawing of the cod-piece was made from the silk braid trimming, which is complete, although the woollen fabric beneath has disintegrated. The satin backing and fragments of linen interlining remain, together with the silk binding strip at the top of the waistband and down the front opening. The silk point with metal aglets is still tied through the bottom two eyelet holes on the doublet and two eyelet holes on the fragments of the breeches' waistband. The latter are worked in silk over metal rings for reinforcement.

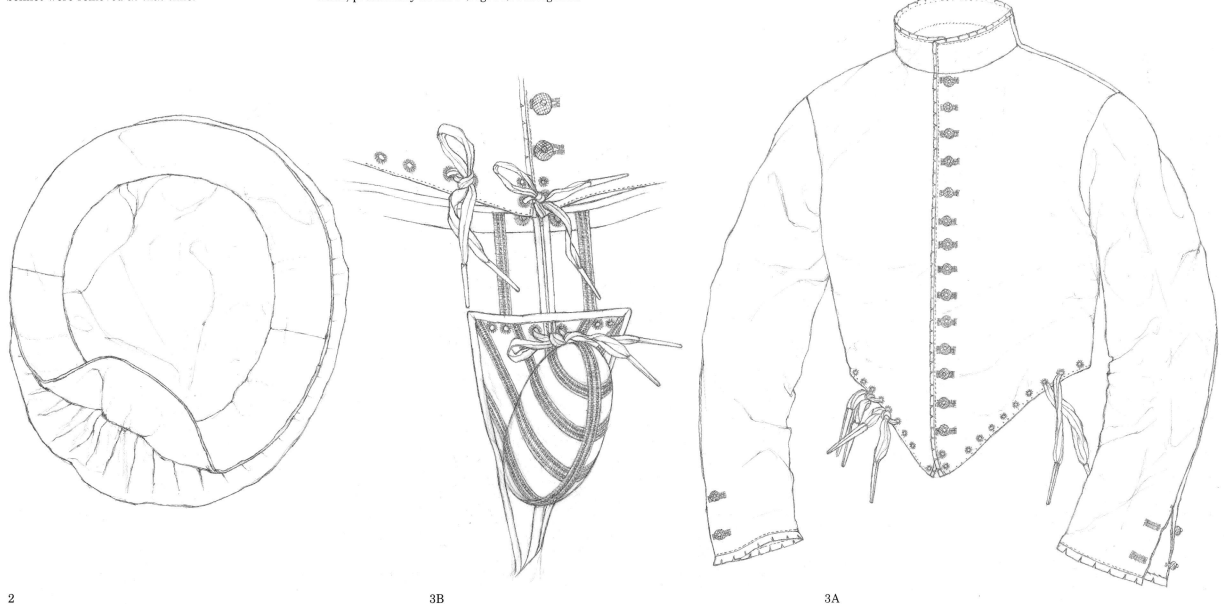

2

3B

3A

2. †1562 VELVET BONNET WORN BY DON GARZIA DE'MEDICI
PALAZZO PITTI, FLORENCE

A BONNET WITH A FLAT CROWN MADE OF DARK BROWN VELVET, LINED WITH DARK BROWN SILK TAFFETA, BOTH OF WHICH WERE PROBABLY BLACK ORIGINALLY. IT MEASURES 25·4 CM (10") X 26·6 CM (10½") ON THE EXTREME EDGES OF THE TOP OF THE CROWN, AND THE BRIM LIES JUST BENEATH IT.
THE BONNET MEASURES 50·8 CM (20") ROUND THE INSIDE OF THE BRIM, WHERE THE GATHERED VELVET CROWN IS STITCHED ON. IT WOULD PROBABLY HAVE BEEN WORN TILTED SIDEWAYS AND ORIGINALLY THE DARTS WOULD HAVE MADE THE VELVET STAND OUT IN THE WAY SEEN IN MANY PORTRAITS.

THE BRIM APPEARS TO HAVE BEEN MADE UP FIRST AND THE TOP SIDE ATTACHED TO THE DARTED EDGE OF THE CROWN. THE UNDERSIDE OF THE BRIM WAS THEN TURNED IN, ALLOWING FOR THE SEAM ROUND THE EDGE TO ROLL UNDER, AND THEN STITCHED DOWN.

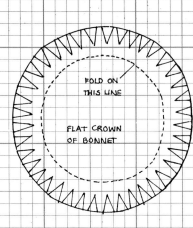

FOLD ON THIS LINE

FLAT CROWN OF BONNET

THE DARK BROWN SILK LINING IS CUT TO THE SAME SHAPE AS THE VELVET AND THE TWO LAYERS OF MATERIAL ARE WORKED AS ONE.

39 EVENLY SPACED DART TUCKS ARE MADE ROUND THE CIRCUMFERENCE OF THE BONNET, APPROXIMATELY 13MM (½") DEEP AND 4·4 CM (1¾") LONG.

ACTUAL SIZE OF DART TUCKS MADE ROUND CROWN OF BONNET

THE BRIM VARIES IN WIDTH BETWEEN 3·8 CM (1½") AND 4·4 CM (1¾").

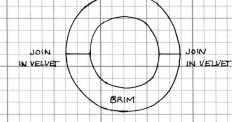

JOIN IN VELVET

JOIN IN VELVET

BRIM

THE BRIM IS CIRCULAR IN SHAPE, MADE OF TWO LAYERS OF VELVET. THERE IS APPARENTLY NO INTERLINING. THERE MAY HAVE BEEN A LAYER OF LINEN ORIGINALLY WHICH HAS DISINTEGRATED IN THE TOMB. THE TURNINGS ON THE OUTER EDGE MAKE THE SEAM RATHER THICK, AND THIS HELPS TO STIFFEN THE BRIM.

3 †1574 DOUBLET WORN BY COSIMO DE'MEDICI
PALAZZO PITTI, FLORENCE

DOUBLET IN WHAT WAS PROBABLY CRIMSON SATIN, NOW FADED UNEVENLY TO YELLOWISH BROWN. IT WOULD ORIGINALLY HAVE BEEN LINED WITH LINEN BUT THIS HAS COMPLETELY DISINTEGRATED. TRACES OF LINEN INTERLINING REMAIN INSIDE THE SATIN FACINGS AT THE WRIST. THERE WOULD HAVE BEEN A LINEN INTERLINING, PROBABLY STIFFENED FOR THE COLLAR AND BOTH FRONTS BENEATH THE SATIN FACING AS WELL.

THERE ARE 40 CUTS IN THE STRIP ROUND THE TOP OF THE COLLAR, VARYING BETWEEN 9MM (⅜") AND 13 MM (½") APART.

SIDE NECK

THE COLLAR IS JOINED TO THE FRONT NECK AND THE SEAM PRESSED OPEN. THE TURNINGS ARE 5MM (3⁄16") WIDE, AND ARE CAUGHT DOWN WITH SMALL RUNNING STITCHES IN FINE SILK.

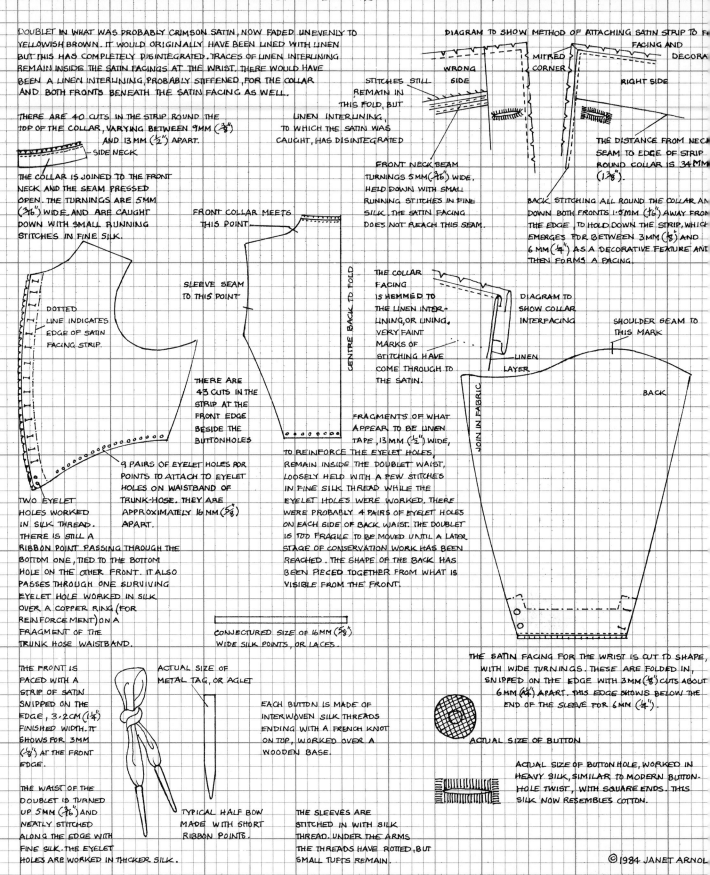

DOTTED LINE INDICATES EDGE OF SATIN FACING STRIP.

SLEEVE SEAM TO THIS POINT

FRONT COLLAR MEETS THIS POINT

THERE ARE 43 CUTS IN THE STRIP AT THE FRONT EDGE BESIDE THE BUTTONHOLES

TWO EYELET HOLES WORKED IN SILK THREAD. THERE IS STILL A RIBBON POINT PASSING THROUGH THE BOTTOM ONE, TIED TO THE BOTTOM HOLE ON THE OTHER FRONT. IT ALSO PASSES THROUGH ONE SURVIVING EYELET HOLE WORKED IN SILK OVER A COPPER RING (FOR REINFORCEMENT) ON A FRAGMENT OF THE TRUNK HOSE WAISTBAND.

9 PAIRS OF EYELET HOLES FOR POINTS TO ATTACH TO EYELET HOLES ON WAISTBAND OF TRUNK-HOSE. THEY ARE APPROXIMATELY 16 MM (⅝") APART.

CENTRE BACK TO FOLD

JOIN IN FABRIC

THE COLLAR FACING IS HEMMED TO THE LINEN INTER-LINING, OR LINING. VERY FAINT MARKS OF STITCHING HAVE COME THROUGH TO THE SATIN.

FRAGMENTS OF WHAT APPEAR TO BE LINEN TAPE, 13MM (½") WIDE, TO REINFORCE THE EYELET HOLES, REMAIN INSIDE THE DOUBLET WAIST, LOOSELY HELD WITH A FEW STITCHES IN FINE SILK THREAD WHILE THE EYELET HOLES WERE WORKED. THERE WERE PROBABLY 4 PAIRS OF EYELET HOLES ON EACH SIDE OF BACK WAIST. THE DOUBLET IS TOO FRAGILE TO BE MOVED UNTIL A LATER STAGE OF CONSERVATION WORK HAS BEEN REACHED. THE SHAPE OF THE BACK HAS BEEN PIECED TOGETHER FROM WHAT IS VISIBLE FROM THE FRONT.

DIAGRAM TO SHOW METHOD OF ATTACHING SATIN STRIP TO FACING AND

MITRED CORNER

WRONG SIDE

DECORA...

RIGHT SIDE

STITCHES STILL REMAIN IN THIS FOLD, BUT LINEN INTERLINING, TO WHICH THE SATIN WAS CAUGHT, HAS DISINTEGRATED

FRONT NECK SEAM TURNINGS 5MM (3⁄16") WIDE, HELD DOWN WITH SMALL RUNNING STITCHES IN FINE SILK, THE SATIN FACING DOES NOT REACH THIS SEAM.

THE DISTANCE FROM NECK SEAM TO EDGE OF STRIP ROUND COLLAR IS 34MM (1⅜")

BACK STITCHING ALL ROUND THE COLLAR AND DOWN BOTH FRONTS 1·5MM (1⁄16") AWAY FROM THE EDGE, TO HOLD DOWN THE STRIP, WHICH EMERGES FOR BETWEEN 3MM (⅛") AND 6 MM (¼") AS A DECORATIVE FEATURE AND THEN FORMS A FACING.

DIAGRAM TO SHOW COLLAR INTERFACING

SHOULDER SEAM TO THIS MARK

LINEN LAYER

BACK

THE SATIN FACING FOR THE WRIST IS CUT TO SHAPE, WITH WIDE TURNINGS. THESE ARE FOLDED IN, SNIPPED ON THE EDGE WITH 3MM (⅛") CUTS ABOUT 6 MM (¼") APART. THIS EDGE SHOWS BELOW THE END OF THE SLEEVE FOR 6MM (¼").

ACTUAL SIZE OF BUTTON

CONJECTURED SIZE OF 16MM (⅝") WIDE SILK POINTS, OR LACES.

THE FRONT IS FACED WITH A STRIP OF SATIN SNIPPED ON THE EDGE, 3·2CM (1¼") FINISHED WIDTH. IT SHOWS FOR 3MM (⅛") AT THE FRONT EDGE.

THE WAIST OF THE DOUBLET IS TURNED UP 5MM (3⁄16") AND NEATLY STITCHED ALONG THE EDGE WITH FINE SILK. THE EYELET HOLES ARE WORKED IN THICKER SILK.

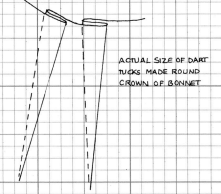

ACTUAL SIZE OF METAL TAG, OR AGLET

TYPICAL HALF BOW MADE WITH SHORT RIBBON POINTS.

EACH BUTTON IS MADE OF INTERWOVEN SILK THREADS ENDING WITH A FRENCH KNOT ON TOP, WORKED OVER A WOODEN BASE.

THE SLEEVES ARE STITCHED IN WITH SILK THREAD. UNDER THE ARMS THE THREADS HAVE ROTTED, BUT SMALL TUFTS REMAIN.

ACTUAL SIZE OF BUTTON HOLE, WORKED IN HEAVY SILK, SIMILAR TO MODERN BUTTON-HOLE TWIST, WITH SQUARE ENDS. THIS SILK NOW RESEMBLES COTTON.

1 : 1 INCH

1 : 1 CENTIMETRE

© 1984 JANET ARNOLD

4A. A black velvet suit, consisting of doublet and pluderhose, worn by Svante Sture when he was murdered at the age of fifty in Upsala Castle on 24 May 1567 with his two sons Erik and Nils, together with Abraham Stenbock and Ivar Ivarson, on the orders of Erik XIV of Sweden. Marta Leijonhufvud, his widow, put the clothes in which her husband and sons had been murdered into an iron chest, which was placed in Upsala Cathedral near their graves. The suits have been on display in the cathedral since 1744 and are now in a fragile condition (Fig. 88). In 1975 the suits were taken to the Riksantikvarieämbetet at the Historiska Museet in Stockholm for essential conservation work to be carried out under the direction of Dr Inger Estham.

4B. The doublet is trimmed with bias strips of black velvet, decorated with rows of cuts on the straight grain. These are arranged alternately in pairs and sets of three, with a space between. Each velvet strip is bordered with narrow bias strips of greenish-grey silk, of a similar texture and weight to modern silk paper taffeta, snipped at the edges. A black silk cord is placed in the centre of the velvet. Small pieces of extra material added at the side seams appear to be contemporary alterations by the tailor and suggest that Svante put on weight. The suit was probably not new in 1567 but could date from 1565 or even earlier.

4C. The end of the sleeve is decorated with a double band of bias-cut velvet trimming and below this, around the wrist, there is a narrow doubled strip of black velvet, snipped at the edge to form small tabs. This strip is cut from odd scraps of material on both straight and bias grain.

4A

4B

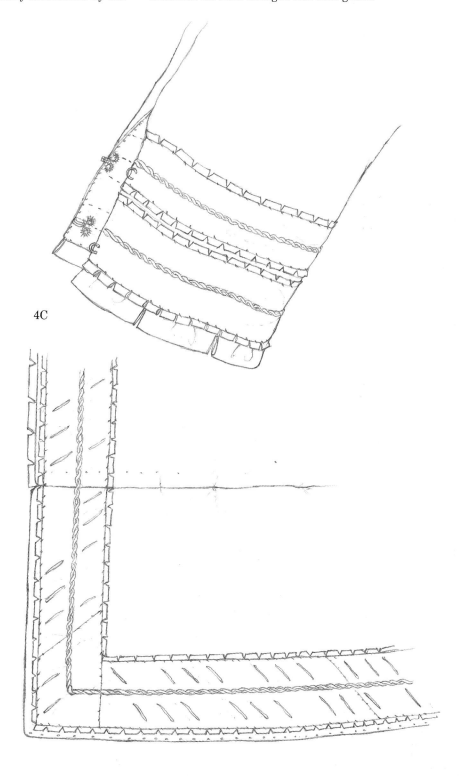

4C

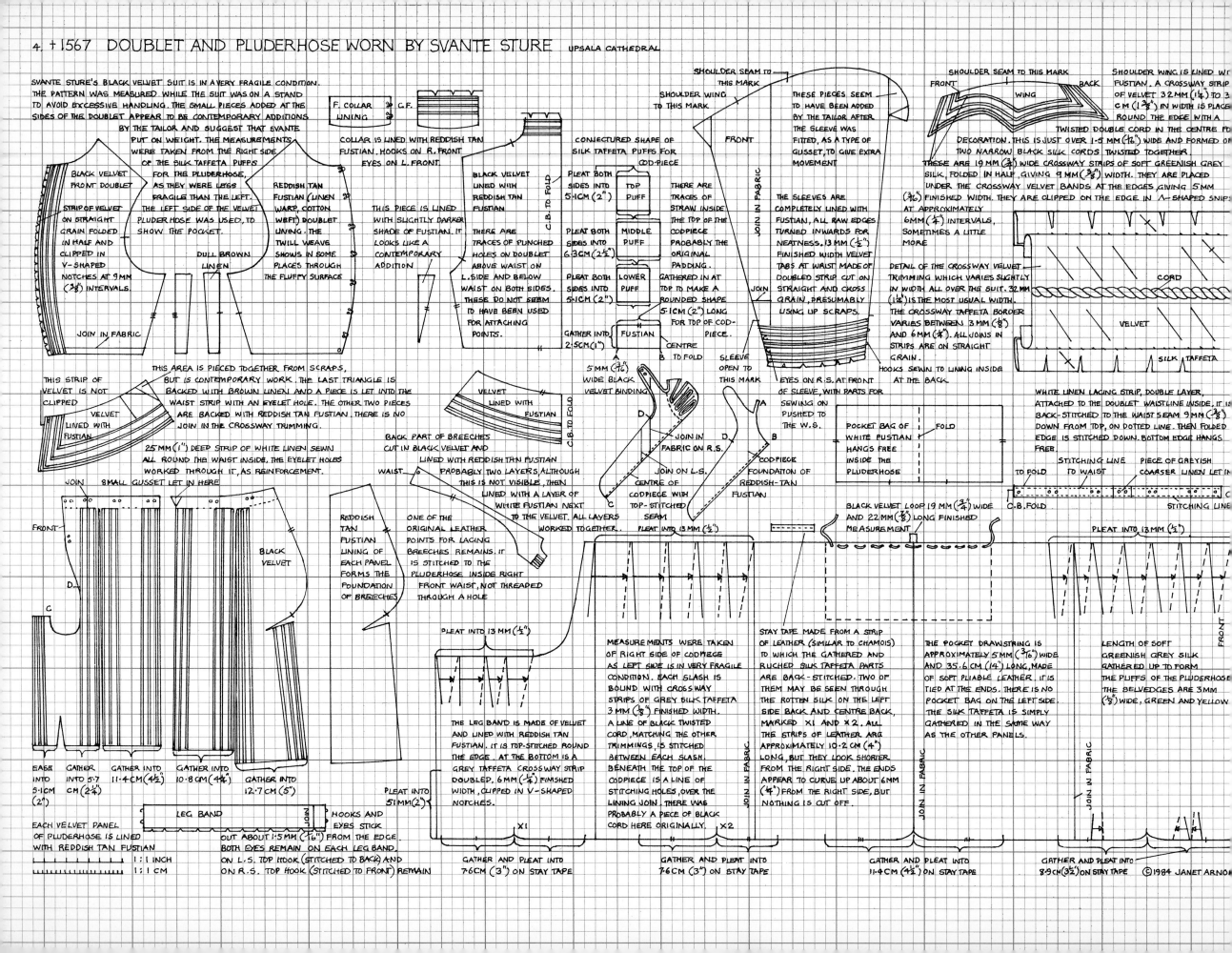

©1984 JANET ARNOLD

4D. The breeches are pluderhose, a variant of the trunk-hose style, particularly popular in Germany where the style originated. They may be seen in many woodcuts, engravings and paintings from the 1560s onwards. Trunk-hose were often paned, i.e. arranged with vertical strips of material hanging from waist to leg, parting to reveal the lining beneath and heavily padded or bombasted. Pluderhose were not bombasted and were probably more comfortable to wear than trunk-hose. They varied in length, the panes reaching to mid-thigh or to the more usual level above the knee and, in their most exaggerated form, to just below the knee.

Svante's pluderhose are of a moderate size, to suit an older man, not in the height of fashion. They are made with a reddish-tan fustian (linen warp, cotton weft) lining. The outer layer of velvet is cut to the same shape and the panes are trimmed with bias-cut velvet bands to match the doublet. A strip of white linen is sewn all round the waist inside as a reinforcement. Eyelet holes are worked through it for points, or laces, to attach the breeches to the doublet waist. The full puffs pulled out between the panes are made of greenish-grey silk, similar in texture and weight to modern silk paper taffeta. On the right side only a white fustian pocket bag is attached to the top of the silk and hangs free inside the pluderhose, with a leather drawstring to pull it up into loose folds.

4E. The front is caught together and the cod-piece tied up with narrow leather points, or laces, passing through pairs of eyelet holes. Here the cod-piece is shown untied. There are traces of straw inside the top of the cod-piece, probably the original padding.

4F. The silk puffs are arranged by joining the hemline in four large bags on both sides. Each one is gathered up on the join and stitched to a leather stay tape on the wrong side, as shown here. When the puffs are pulled through the panes they stand out at the hemline, supported along the lower edge by these small strips of leather (Fig. 92).

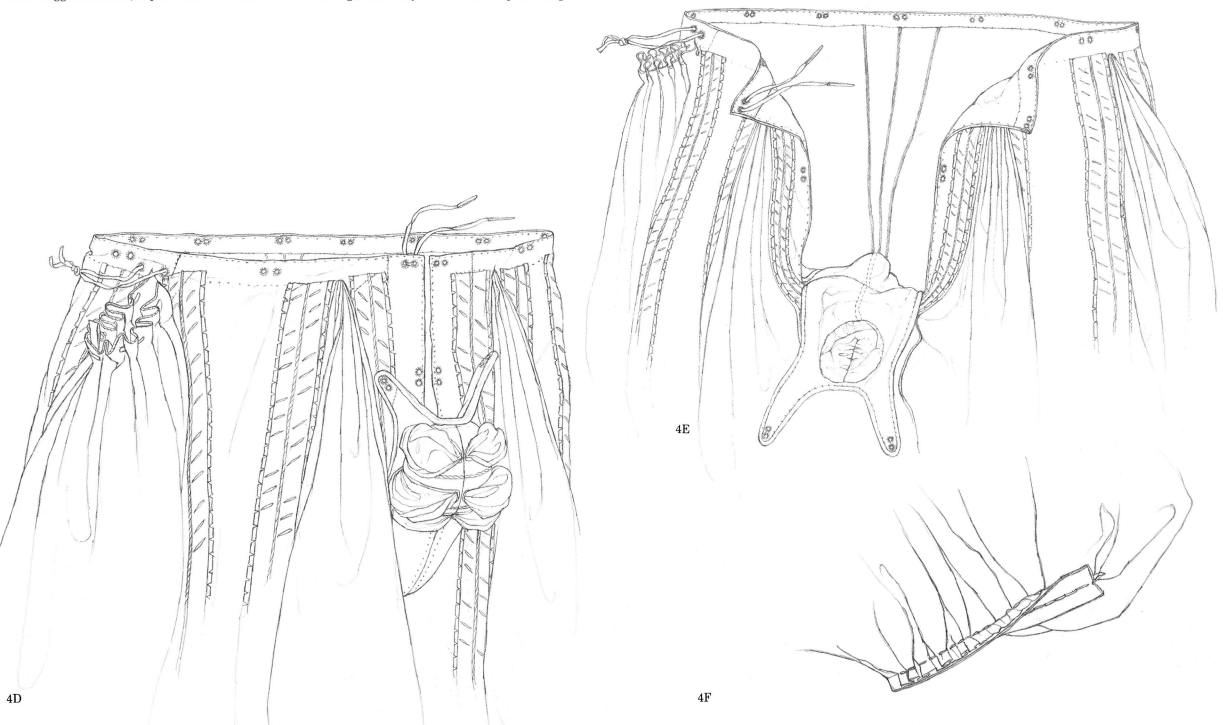

4D

4E

4F

60

5A. A black velvet suit worn by Erik Sture when he was murdered at the age of twenty-one in Upsala Castle on 24 May 1567 with his father Svante and brother Nils, whose suits are also described here. This is a more fashionable pair of pluderhose than those worn by Svante and the style is seen in many woodcuts, engravings and paintings from the 1560s onwards, usually worn by young men. Both moderate and exaggerated pluderhose were worn by all classes of society from the evidence of Jost Amman's woodcuts dating from 1568, which depict craftsmen, merchants and soldiers in Nürnberg. The fashion continued until the end of the century and may still be seen today in crystallized form in the uniforms worn by the Swiss Guards at the Vatican Palace in Rome. The style is particularly associated with the *Landesknechte*, the first German regular troops.

5B. The doublet is trimmed with narrow golden-yellow braid, now discoloured apart from one unfaded area on the right front. The arrangement of braid helped Miss Margit Wikland, who conserved this suit, to recognize that Erik Sture was wearing it in his portrait at Gripsholm (Fig. 94). The tailor apparently ran out of matching braid for the whole garment but carefully arranged three of slightly different widths to balance on both sides. The difference can only be seen on careful inspection. The doublet would have fitted closely and a small piece of black material has been let in at the back neck. This seems to date from conservation carried out in 1908 and is probably a replacement for a piece of velvet put in by the original tailor. Erik apparently put on weight and the suit was probably not new in 1567 but could date from 1565 or earlier. The linen lining is slightly larger than the doublet, so it was simply eased over the alteration. Pairs of eyelet holes are worked in the waist strip for points to attach the pluderhose. Shoulder wings were normally placed over sleeveheads at this time. This doublet may not have had them but it is also possible that they were removed as souvenirs by visitors to Upsala Cathedral after 1744 when the suits were put on display, 'hung well and in a seemly fashion'. The cupboard in which they were displayed did not have glass until the nineteenth century. The records show that some repair work was carried out on the suit in 1906, 1908 and probably earlier, in 1883, as well.

5A

5B

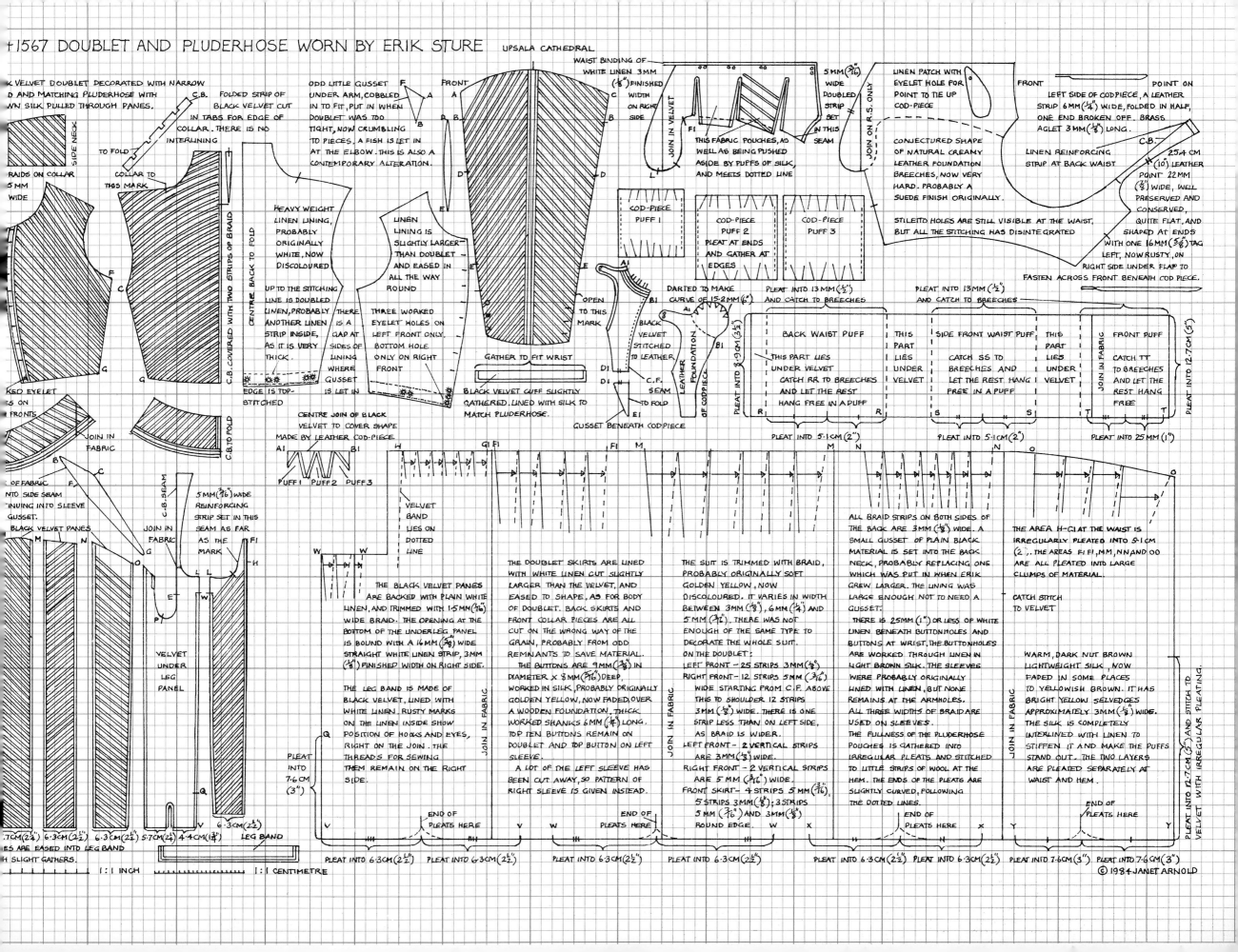

5C. The pluderhose fit snugly below the waist and the velvet panes hang from hip level. There are puffs of what may have been warm, dark brown silk, now faded to yellowish brown, round the waist, as well as the more exaggerated puffs pulled out between the long panes. The silk is similar in weight and texture to modern silk paper taffeta. Pairs of eyelet holes were punched with a stiletto through the leather foundation and layer of velvet at the waist, for points to attach the pluderhose to the doublet. All the stitching has disintegrated but the eyelet holes may still be seen. The front fastens with points and eyelet holes beneath the cod-piece, which is a separate flap lifted up to cover the front opening and tied with points; there is a linen patch to reinforce the eyelet holes on the front of the pluderhose, inside the leather foundation.

5D. The pluderhose are based on a leather foundation, possibly deer skin, which is now very hard. It probably resembled heavy chamois leather originally, soft, and flexible and comfortable to wear. It was very difficult to take a pattern – and the leather may have shrunk slightly – but a conjectured shape is given from the measurements which could be taken. There is a linen reinforcing strip at the back waist and the top of the whole waist is bound with linen, giving 3 mm ($\frac{1}{8}$″) finished width on the right side. The cod-piece is made with a leather foundation, covered with black velvet, trimmed with braid and puffs of silk. Some of the leather points for trussing the hose remain and are shown in the drawing. One, on the cod-piece, still retains one metal tag or aglet. All the others have disintegrated.

5E. The legs of the pluderhose are gathered into bands just below the knee. These originally fastened with hooks and eyes, which have since disappeared, but rusty marks and a few threads from stitching show their position. The velvet panes are decorated with strips of braid, the panes immediately under the legs being left plain. The large panels of dark brown silk, now faded to yellowish brown in some places, are completely backed with linen to stiffen the pluderhose and make the puffs stand out. The two layers are pleated separately at waist and hem. The fullness of each puff is gathered into irregular pleats and attached to woollen stay strips at the hem. There are four large pouches of silk, puffed out between the panes, for each leg.

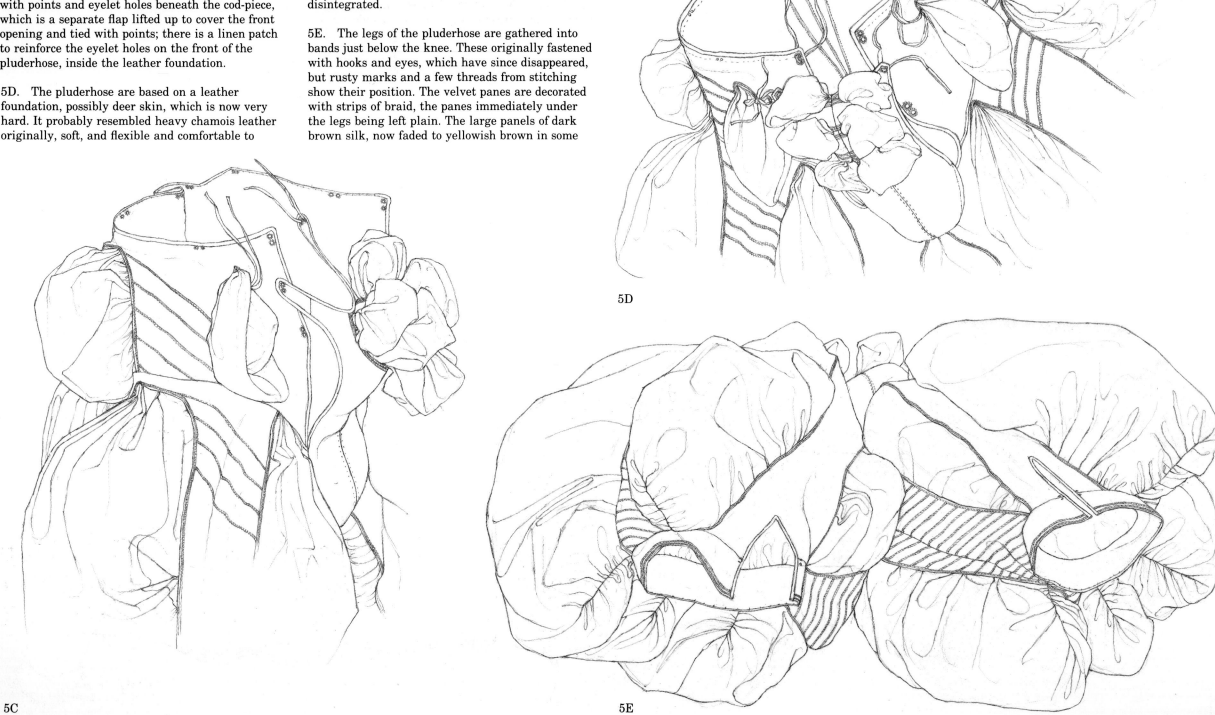

5C

5D

5E

6A.   A leather doublet and pair of black wool camlet pluderhose with velvet panes, worn by Nils Sture when he was murdered in Upsala Castle on 24 May 1567 with his father Svante and brother Erik, an example of warm, hard-wearing clothing suitable for travelling or hunting. Their silk and velvet suits are also described here. For some time it was thought that the heavy black worsted cloth was a nineteenth-century replacement for the original material, possibly silk, which had rotted away. The black cloth looked so fresh and uncreased that it was quite easy to see why it had been considered as such; it was similar to samples of single mohair camlet woven in the early 1790s and the cloth used for several eighteenth-century riding habits which I had examined. All these materials were hard to the touch, springy and uncrushable. It was most interesting to find, by the threads used to sew it, that the black cloth was the original of 1567.

6B.   The doublet is made of leather with a suede finish, which Dr Estham suggested might be elk. It may originally have been black. There are small areas, particularly inside the gathers on the strip sewn to the neck edge of the collar, which show that some kind of black pigment had been brushed on to the surface. C.H. Spiers records two painted doeskins for a pair of breeches in 1695 in his article 'Deer skin leathers and their use for costume', but comments that what exactly 'painted doeskin' was is obscure. It may be conjectured that the pigment was to render the skin more waterproof. At all events most of it has worn off the doublet, leaving the leather a pale creamy grey in colour outside and a soft cream colour inside. It is the general opinion that King Erik stabbed the young man before ordering the guards to kill the other prisoners. There are eleven cuts from a dagger or halberd through the doublet and the bloodstains remain as historical evidence of the murder. The doublet is plain, of simple cut with a high collar, skirts of medium depth and no shoulder wings. There are pocket flaps on each side at the front but only one pocket hole, on the right front. Originally there were twenty silver buttons, nineteen of which were still there in 1791. These are now missing, probably removed as 'souvenirs' when the suit was on open display in Upsala Cathedral.

6A

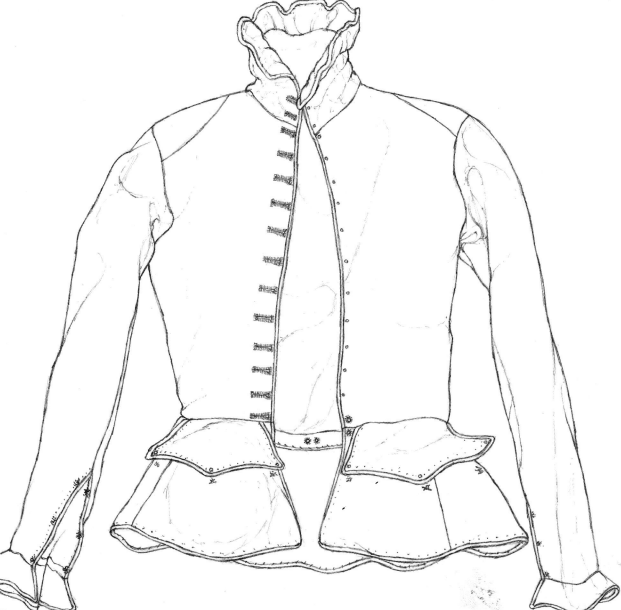

6B

6. †1567 PLUDERHOSE WORN BY NILS STURE   UPSALA CATHEDRAL

ROUND THE TOP OF THE LEATHER FOUNDATION BREECHES IS SEWN A 25MM (1") DEEP FOLDED BAND OF BROWN FUSTIAN (LINEN WARP, COTTON WEFT) 5·1CM (2") SINGLE WIDTH. THE FOLDED EDGE IS PLACED TO THE TOP OF THE BREECHES. THIS FOLD IS SEWN INTO THE FUSTIAN BINDING. THE FOLDS IN THE LONG PANES ARE STITCHED TO R.P, P.C AND C.A ON THE FUSTIAN STRIP APPROXIMATELY 6MM (¼") TO 13MM (½") DOWN FROM THE WAIST LEVEL.

THE WAIST PUFF IS FOLDED IN HALF LENGTHWISE, THE ENDS JOINED AND TURNED THROUGH, THEN A GATHERING THREAD FOR PULLING UP THE MATERIAL INTO CARTRIDGE PLEATS IS PUT INTO EACH LAYER SEPARATELY. THE LENGTH IS THEN PULLED UP TO THE CORRECT MEASUREMENT, 25·4 CM (10") AND THE EDGES CAUGHT TOGETHER WITH LARGE STITCHES. THE TOPS OF THE VELVET PANES ARE THEN LIFTED UP, ROUND THE PUFF, OVER IT AND TACKED TO THE TOP OF THE FUSTIAN STRIP AND LEATHER BREECHES.

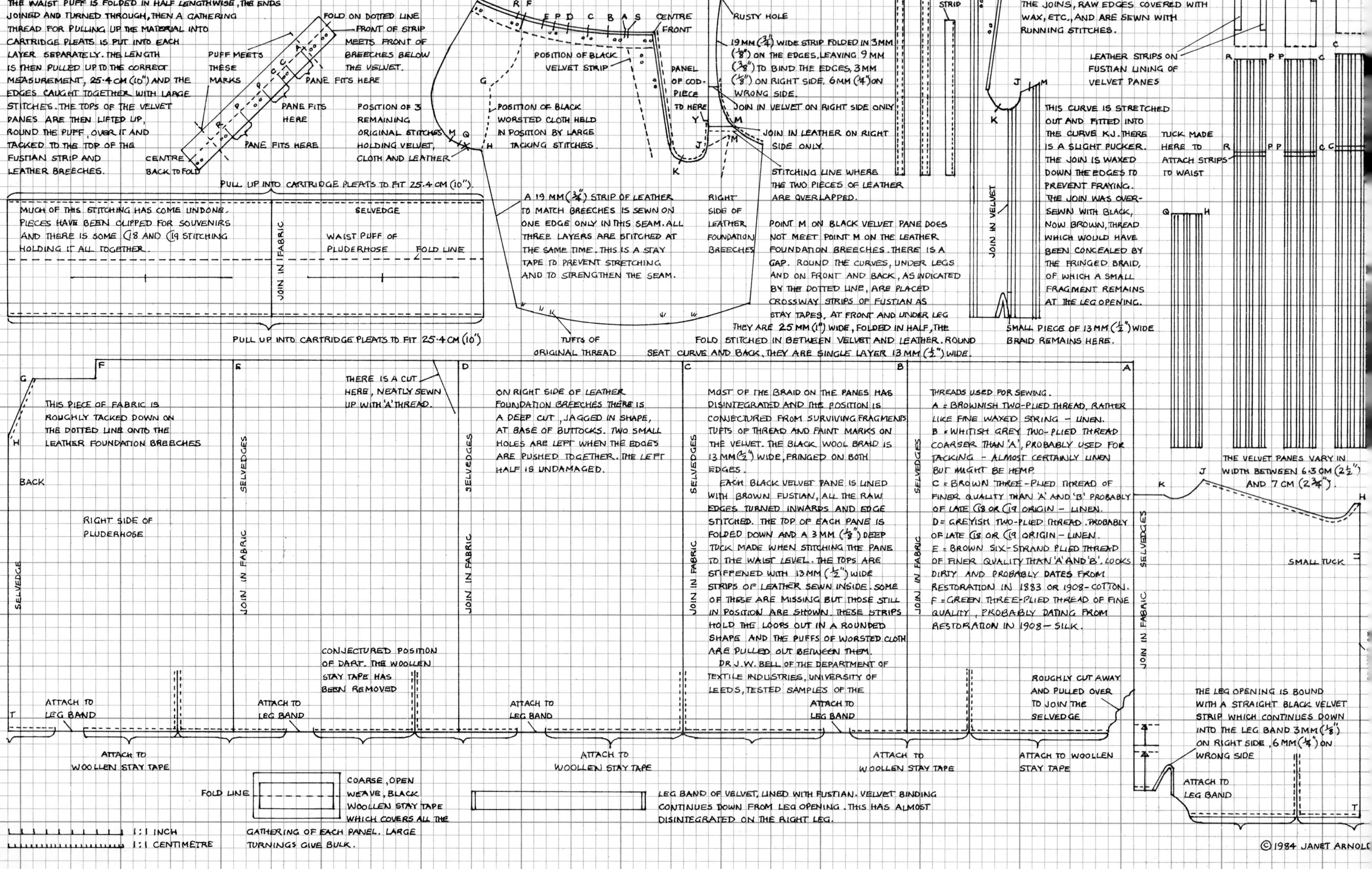

MUCH OF THIS STITCHING HAS COME UNDONE, PIECES HAVE BEEN CLIPPED FOR SOUVENIRS AND THERE IS SOME C18 AND C19 STITCHING HOLDING IT ALL TOGETHER.

FOLD ON DOTTED LINE
FRONT OF STRIP MEETS FRONT OF BREECHES BELOW THE VELVET.
PUFF MEETS THESE MARKS
PANE FITS HERE
PANE FITS HERE
POSITION OF 3 REMAINING ORIGINAL STITCHES M Q HOLDING VELVET, CLOTH AND LEATHER
PANE FITS HERE
CENTRE BACK TO FOLD

PULL UP INTO CARTRIDGE PLEATS TO FIT 25.4 CM (10")
SELVEDGE
WAIST PUFF OF PLUDERHOSE   FOLD LINE
JOIN IN FABRIC
PULL UP INTO CARTRIDGE PLEATS TO FIT 25.4 CM (10")

R F   E P D C B A S   CENTRE FRONT
POSITION OF BLACK VELVET STRIP
PANEL OF COD-PIECE TO HERE
POSITION OF BLACK WORSTED CLOTH HELD IN POSITION BY LARGE TACKING STITCHES.
G
RIGHT SIDE OF LEATHER FOUNDATION BREECHES
Y
M
M
J   M
K
A 19 MM (¾") STRIP OF LEATHER TO MATCH BREECHES IS SEWN ON ONE EDGE ONLY IN THIS SEAM. ALL THREE LAYERS ARE STITCHED AT THE SAME TIME. THIS IS A STAY TAPE TO PREVENT STRETCHING AND TO STRENGTHEN THE SEAM.
TUFTS OF ORIGINAL THREAD

ONE REMAINING POINT OF LEATHER MATCHING THE BREECHES LEFT IN THE RIGHT FRONT 9 MM (⅜") WIDE. NO METAL AGLETS LEFT.
RUSTY HOLE
19 MM (¾") WIDE STRIP FOLDED IN 3MM (⅛") ON THE EDGES, LEAVING 9 MM (⅜") TO BIND THE EDGES, 3 MM (⅛") ON RIGHT SIDE, 6MM (¼") ON WRONG SIDE.
JOIN IN VELVET ON RIGHT SIDE ONLY
JOIN IN LEATHER ON RIGHT SIDE ONLY.
STITCHING LINE WHERE THE TWO PIECES OF LEATHER ARE OVERLAPPED.
POINT M ON BLACK VELVET PANE DOES NOT MEET POINT M ON THE LEATHER FOUNDATION BREECHES. THERE IS A GAP. ROUND THE CURVES, UNDER LEGS AND ON FRONT AND BACK, AS INDICATED BY THE DOTTED LINE, ARE PLACED CROSSWAY STRIPS OF FUSTIAN AS STAY TAPES, AT FRONT AND UNDER LEG. THEY ARE 25 MM (1") WIDE, FOLDED IN HALF, THE FOLD STITCHED IN BETWEEN VELVET AND LEATHER. ROUND SEAT CURVE AND BACK, THEY ARE SINGLE LAYER 13 MM (½") WIDE.

CURVED SIDE BACK SEAM STRIP
CENTRE BACK STRIP
CENTRE BACK
LEG STRIP
J   M
K
JOIN IN VELVET
THIS CURVE IS STRETCHED OUT AND FITTED INTO THE CURVE K J. THERE IS A SLIGHT PUCKER. THE JOIN IS WAXED DOWN THE EDGES TO PREVENT FRAYING. THE JOIN WAS OVER-SEWN WITH BLACK, NOW BROWN, THREAD WHICH WOULD HAVE BEEN CONCEALED BY THE FRINGED BRAID, OF WHICH A SMALL FRAGMENT REMAINS AT THE LEG OPENING.
SMALL PIECE OF 13 MM (½") WIDE BRAID REMAINS HERE.

19 MM (¾") WIDE STRIPS OF LEATHER MATCHING THE BREECHES ARE SEWN OVER THE SEAMS INSIDE AT THE BACK, PROBABLY FOR COMFORT AS WELL AS TIDINESS. THEY CONCEAL ALL THE JOINS, RAW EDGES COVERED WITH WAX, ETC., AND ARE SEWN WITH RUNNING STITCHES.
LEATHER STRIPS ON FUSTIAN LINING OF VELVET PANES
R P P C
Q H
TUCK MADE HERE TO ATTACH STRIPS TO WAIST

F   F   E   D   C   B   A
THIS PIECE OF FABRIC IS ROUGHLY TACKED DOWN ON THE DOTTED LINE ONTO THE LEATHER FOUNDATION BREECHES
BACK
G
H
RIGHT SIDE OF PLUDERHOSE
SELVEDGE
JOIN IN FABRIC

THERE IS A CUT HERE, NEATLY SEWN UP WITH 'A' THREAD.
SELVEDGES

ON RIGHT SIDE OF LEATHER FOUNDATION BREECHES THERE IS A DEEP CUT, JAGGED IN SHAPE, AT BASE OF BUTTOCKS. TWO SMALL HOLES ARE LEFT WHEN THE EDGES ARE PUSHED TOGETHER. THE LEFT HALF IS UNDAMAGED.
SELVEDGES
JOIN IN FABRIC

MOST OF THE BRAID ON THE PANES HAS DISINTEGRATED AND THE POSITION IS CONJECTURED FROM SURVIVING FRAGMENTS, TUFTS OF THREAD AND FAINT MARKS ON THE VELVET. THE BLACK WOOL BRAID IS 13 MM (½") WIDE, FRINGED ON BOTH EDGES.
EACH BLACK VELVET PANE IS LINED WITH BROWN FUSTIAN, ALL THE RAW EDGES TURNED INWARDS AND EDGE STITCHED. THE TOP OF EACH PANE IS FOLDED DOWN AND A 3 MM (⅛") DEEP TUCK MADE WHEN STITCHING THE PANE TO THE WAIST LEVEL. THE TOPS ARE STIFFENED WITH 13 MM (½") WIDE STRIPS OF LEATHER SEWN INSIDE. SOME OF THESE ARE MISSING BUT THOSE STILL IN POSITION ARE SHOWN. THESE STRIPS HOLD THE LOOPS OUT IN A ROUNDED SHAPE AND THE PUFFS OF WORSTED CLOTH ARE PULLED OUT BETWEEN THEM.
DR J.W. BELL OF THE DEPARTMENT OF TEXTILE INDUSTRIES, UNIVERSITY OF LEEDS, TESTED SAMPLES OF THE
C
SELVEDGES
JOIN IN FABRIC

THREADS USED FOR SEWING.
A = BROWNISH TWO-PLIED THREAD, RATHER LIKE FINE WAXED STRING — LINEN.
B = WHITISH GREY TWO-PLIED THREAD COARSER THAN 'A', PROBABLY USED FOR TACKING — ALMOST CERTAINLY LINEN BUT MIGHT BE HEMP.
C = BROWN THREE-PLIED THREAD OF FINER QUALITY THAN 'A' AND 'B' PROBABLY OF LATE C18 OR C19 ORIGIN — LINEN.
D = GREYISH TWO-PLIED THREAD. PROBABLY OF LATE C18 OR C19 ORIGIN — LINEN.
E = BROWN SIX-STRAND PLIED THREAD OF FINER QUALITY THAN 'A' AND 'B'. LOOKS DIRTY AND PROBABLY DATES FROM RESTORATION IN 1883 OR 1908 — COTTON.
F = GREEN THREE-PLIED THREAD OF FINE QUALITY, PROBABLY DATING FROM RESTORATION IN 1908 — SILK.
B
SELVEDGES
JOIN IN FABRIC

K
J
THE VELVET PANES VARY IN WIDTH BETWEEN 6·3 CM (2½") AND 7 CM (2¾").
H
SMALL TUCK
A
SELVEDGES
JOIN IN FABRIC
THE LEG OPENING IS BOUND WITH A STRAIGHT BLACK VELVET STRIP WHICH CONTINUES DOWN INTO THE LEG BAND 3MM (⅛") ON RIGHT SIDE, 6 MM (¼") ON WRONG SIDE
ATTACH TO LEG BAND

CONJECTURED POSITION OF DART. THE WOOLLEN STAY TAPE HAS BEEN REMOVED

ATTACH TO LEG BAND
ATTACH TO LEG BAND
ATTACH TO LEG BAND
ATTACH TO LEG BAND
ATTACH TO LEG BAND
ROUGHLY CUT AWAY AND PULLED OVER TO JOIN THE SELVEDGE
ATTACH TO WOOLLEN STAY TAPE
ATTACH TO LEG BAND

ATTACH TO WOOLLEN STAY TAPE
ATTACH TO WOOLLEN STAY TAPE
ATTACH TO WOOLLEN STAY TAPE
ATTACH TO WOOLLEN STAY TAPE

1:1 INCH
1:1 CENTIMETRE
FOLD LINE
GATHERING OF EACH PANEL. LARGE TURNINGS GIVE BULK.
COARSE, OPEN WEAVE, BLACK WOOLLEN STAY TAPE WHICH COVERS ALL THE
LEG BAND OF VELVET, LINED WITH FUSTIAN. VELVET BINDING CONTINUES DOWN FROM LEG OPENING. THIS HAS ALMOST DISINTEGRATED ON THE RIGHT LEG.

© 1984 JANET ARNOLD

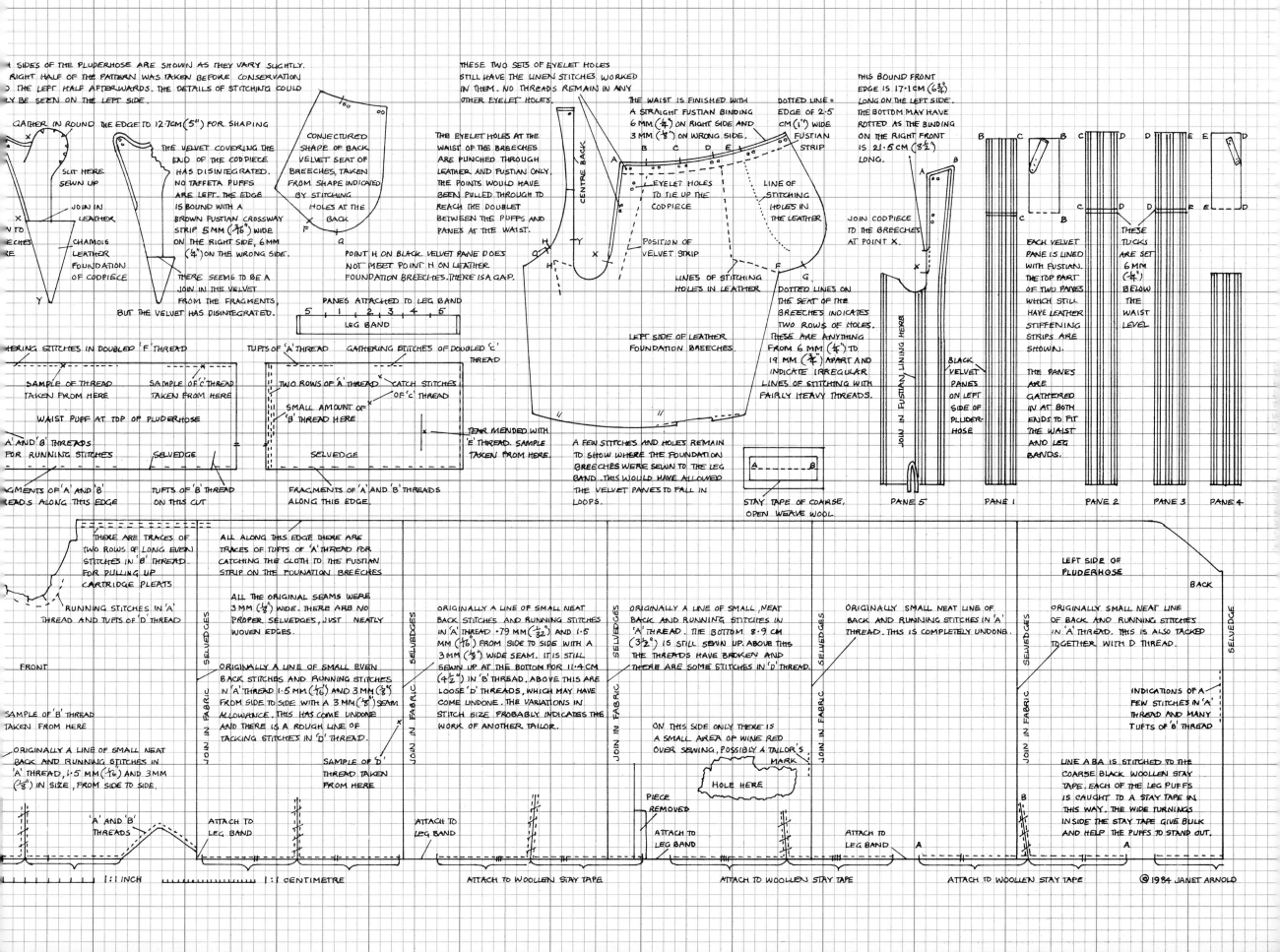

...SIDES OF THE PLUDERHOSE ARE SHOWN AS THEY VARY SLIGHTLY.
...RIGHT HALF OF THE PATTERN WAS TAKEN BEFORE CONSERVATION
... THE LEFT HALF AFTERWARDS. THE DETAILS OF STITCHING COULD
...LY BE SEEN ON THE LEFT SIDE.

THESE TWO SETS OF EYELET HOLES STILL HAVE THE LINEN STITCHES WORKED IN THEM. NO THREADS REMAIN IN ANY OTHER EYELET HOLES.

THE WAIST IS FINISHED WITH A STRAIGHT FUSTIAN BINDING 6 MM (¼") ON RIGHT SIDE AND 3 MM (⅛") ON WRONG SIDE.

DOTTED LINE = EDGE OF 2·5 CM (1") WIDE FUSTIAN STRIP

THIS BOUND FRONT EDGE IS 17·1 CM (6¾") LONG ON THE LEFT SIDE. THE BOTTOM MAY HAVE ROTTED AS THE BINDING ON THE RIGHT FRONT IS 21·5 CM (8½") LONG.

GATHER IN ROUND THE EDGE TO 12·7 CM (5") FOR SHAPING

THE VELVET COVERING THE END OF THE CODPIECE HAS DISINTEGRATED. NO TAFFETA PUFFS ARE LEFT. THE EDGE IS BOUND WITH A BROWN FUSTIAN CROSSWAY STRIP 5 MM (³⁄₁₆") WIDE ON THE RIGHT SIDE, 6 MM (¼") ON THE WRONG SIDE.

SLIT HERE SEWN UP

JOIN IN LEATHER

CHAMOIS LEATHER FOUNDATION OF CODPIECE

THERE SEEMS TO BE A JOIN IN THE VELVET FROM THE FRAGMENTS, BUT THE VELVET HAS DISINTEGRATED.

CONJECTURED SHAPE OF BACK VELVET SEAT OF BREECHES, TAKEN FROM SHAPE INDICATED BY STITCHING HOLES AT THE BACK

POINT H ON BLACK VELVET PANE DOES NOT MEET POINT H ON LEATHER FOUNDATION BREECHES. THERE IS A GAP.

THE EYELET HOLES AT THE WAIST OF THE BREECHES ARE PUNCHED THROUGH LEATHER AND FUSTIAN ONLY. THE POINTS WOULD HAVE BEEN PULLED THROUGH TO REACH THE DOUBLET BETWEEN THE PUFFS AND PANES AT THE WAIST.

CENTRE BACK

EYELET HOLES TO TIE UP THE CODPIECE

POSITION OF VELVET STRIP

LINE OF STITCHING HOLES IN THE LEATHER

LINES OF STITCHING HOLES IN LEATHER

DOTTED LINES ON THE SEAT OF THE BREECHES INDICATES TWO ROWS OF HOLES. THESE ARE ANYTHING FROM 6 MM (¼") TO 19 MM (¾") APART AND INDICATE IRREGULAR LINES OF STITCHING WITH FAIRLY HEAVY THREADS.

LEFT SIDE OF LEATHER FOUNDATION BREECHES

JOIN CODPIECE TO THE BREECHES AT POINT X.

EACH VELVET PANE IS LINED WITH FUSTIAN. THE TOP PART OF TWO PANES WHICH STILL HAVE LEATHER STIFFENING STRIPS ARE SHOWN.

THESE TUCKS ARE SET 6 MM (¼") BELOW THE WAIST LEVEL

THE PANES ARE GATHERED IN AT BOTH ENDS TO FIT THE WAIST AND LEG BANDS.

BLACK VELVET PANES ON LEFT SIDE OF PLUDERHOSE

JOIN IN FUSTIAN LINING HERE

PANES ATTACHED TO LEG BAND
5 1 2 3 4 5
LEG BAND

...THERING STITCHES IN DOUBLED 'E' THREAD

TUFTS OF 'A' THREAD

GATHERING STITCHES OF DOUBLED 'E' THREAD

SAMPLE OF THREAD TAKEN FROM HERE

SAMPLE OF 'C' THREAD TAKEN FROM HERE

TWO ROWS OF 'A' THREAD

CATCH STITCHES OF 'C' THREAD

WAIST PUFF AT TOP OF PLUDERHOSE

SMALL AMOUNT OF 'B' THREAD HERE

...'A' AND 'B' THREADS FOR RUNNING STITCHES

SELVEDGE

TEAR MENDED WITH 'E' THREAD. SAMPLE TAKEN FROM HERE.

SELVEDGE

...GMENTS OF 'A' AND 'B' ...READS ALONG THIS EDGE

TUFTS OF 'B' THREAD ON THIS CUT

FRAGMENTS OF 'A' AND 'B' THREADS ALONG THIS EDGE.

A FEW STITCHES AND HOLES REMAIN TO SHOW WHERE THE FOUNDATION BREECHES WERE SEWN TO THE LEG BAND. THIS WOULD HAVE ALLOWED THE VELVET PANES TO FALL IN LOOPS.

STAY TAPE OF COARSE, OPEN WEAVE WOOL

PANE 5   PANE 1   PANE 2   PANE 3   PANE 4

THERE ARE TRACES OF TWO ROWS OF LONG EVEN STITCHES IN 'B' THREAD FOR PULLING UP CARTRIDGE PLEATS

ALL ALONG THIS EDGE THERE ARE TRACES OF TUFTS OF 'A' THREAD FOR CATCHING THE CLOTH TO THE FUSTIAN STRIP ON THE FOUNDATION BREECHES

LEFT SIDE OF PLUDERHOSE

BACK

RUNNING STITCHES IN 'A' THREAD AND TUFTS OF 'D' THREAD

ALL THE ORIGINAL SEAMS WERE 3 MM (⅛") WIDE. THERE ARE NO PROPER SELVEDGES, JUST NEATLY WOVEN EDGES.

SELVEDGES

ORIGINALLY A LINE OF SMALL NEAT BACK STITCHES AND RUNNING STITCHES IN 'A' THREAD ·79 MM (¹⁄₃₂") AND 1·5 MM (¹⁄₁₆") FROM SIDE TO SIDE WITH A 3 MM (⅛") WIDE SEAM. IT IS STILL SEWN UP AT THE BOTTOM FOR 11·4 CM (4½") IN 'B' THREAD. ABOVE THIS ARE LOOSE 'D' THREADS, WHICH MAY HAVE COME UNDONE. THE VARIATIONS IN STITCH SIZE PROBABLY INDICATES THE WORK OF ANOTHER TAILOR.

SELVEDGES

ORIGINALLY A LINE OF SMALL, NEAT BACK AND RUNNING STITCHES IN 'A' THREAD. THE BOTTOM 8·9 CM (3½") IS STILL SEWN UP. ABOVE THIS THE THREADS HAVE BROKEN AND THERE ARE SOME STITCHES IN 'D' THREAD.

JOIN IN FABRIC

ORIGINALLY SMALL NEAT LINE OF BACK AND RUNNING STITCHES IN 'A' THREAD. THIS IS COMPLETELY UNDONE.

JOIN IN FABRIC

ORIGINALLY SMALL NEAT LINE OF BACK AND RUNNING STITCHES IN 'A' THREAD. THIS IS ALSO TACKED TOGETHER WITH 'D' THREAD.

SELVEDGE

FRONT

JOIN IN FABRIC

SELVEDGES

ORIGINALLY A LINE OF SMALL EVEN BACK STITCHES AND RUNNING STITCHES IN 'A' THREAD 1·5 MM (¹⁄₁₆") AND 3 MM (⅛") FROM SIDE TO SIDE WITH A 3 MM (⅛") SEAM ALLOWANCE. THIS HAS COME UNDONE AND THERE IS A ROUGH LINE OF TACKING STITCHES IN 'D' THREAD.

JOIN IN FABRIC

ON THIS SIDE ONLY THERE IS A SMALL AREA OF WINE RED OVER SEWING, POSSIBLY A TAILOR'S MARK

HOLE HERE

PIECE REMOVED

INDICATIONS OF A FEW STITCHES IN 'A' THREAD AND MANY TUFTS OF 'B' THREAD

LINE A BA IS STITCHED TO THE COARSE BLACK WOOLLEN STAY TAPE. EACH OF THE LEG PUFFS IS CAUGHT TO A STAY TAPE IN THIS WAY. THE WIDE TURNINGS INSIDE THE STAY TAPE GIVE BULK AND HELP THE PUFFS TO STAND OUT.

SAMPLE OF 'B' THREAD TAKEN FROM HERE

SAMPLE OF 'D' THREAD TAKEN FROM HERE

ORIGINALLY A LINE OF SMALL NEAT BACK AND RUNNING STITCHES IN 'A' THREAD, 1·5 MM (¹⁄₁₆") AND 3 MM (⅛") IN SIZE, FROM SIDE TO SIDE.

'A' AND 'B' THREADS

ATTACH TO LEG BAND

ATTACH TO LEG BAND

ATTACH TO LEG BAND

ATTACH TO LEG BAND

1:1 INCH   1:1 CENTIMETRE   ATTACH TO WOOLLEN STAY TAPE   ATTACH TO WOOLLEN STAY TAPE   ATTACH TO WOOLLEN STAY TAPE   © 1984 JANET ARNOLD

6C. Nils Sture's pluderhose are based on a foundation resembling chamois leather, probably deer skin. Panes of black velvet, lined with brown fustian and trimmed with black fringed wool braid are looped up, stitched to the waist, and then fall free over the gathered lengths of black cloth pulled out between the panes to form big puffs. Conservation work on the pluderhose commenced in the spring of 1976. I hardly liked to touch the crumbling fragments as the velvet had deteriorated to such an extent that the panes were disintegrating. The fustian linings were still intact, although very fragile in some places. The few tufts of thread and stitches visible from the outside were of nineteenth-century origin, like those on the narrow bands at the knee to which all the fullness was attached. These had been repaired with cotton sateen. I made drawings to clarify what could be seen on the right side and then began to draw the position of the original stitching holes in the leather foundation breeches on the left side, while Gunnel Berggrén, the conservator, started work on the

right half. We had discussed sixteenth-century stitching when I took patterns of the other two suits and after about half an hour she asked me if I would like to look at the crumbling area under the seat which had not previously been visible. There, concealed beneath the panes, were three stitches passing through velvet, cloth and leather foundation. These were undoubtedly of sixteenth-century origin and I later found another couple of sixteenth-century stitches holding a few scraps of velvet, from which all the pile was missing, to the other two layers on the back of the breeches at the right side. All this was proof that the black cloth had been part of the pluderhose when they were originally made.

6D. The front view of the pluderhose shows the velvet panes looped up and caught below the waist, with puffs of worsted cloth pulled out between them. The front was caught together and the cod-piece tied up with narrow leather points passing through pairs of eyelet holes. When the lengths of cloth from

the left leg were laid out on a large table all the tufts of linen stitches in the original seams, about 6 mm ($\frac{1}{4}$") away from the selvedges, were revealed (Fig. 101). Some stitches were still holding the seams together for short lengths but many had frayed with the springy quality of the cloth pulling them apart. They could be compared with other stitches known to be of sixteenth-century origin in the same garment in the velvet panes. Catch stitch was used here to hold the turnings down. The stitches put in round the waist in the eighteenth and nineteenth centuries to hold the breeches together had also broken.

6E. The back view of the pluderhose shows the plain area of velvet over the seat and pairs of eyelet holes round the waist through which points, or laces, were passed to be tied to the strip with eyelet holes inside the doublet waist. One point remains on the right front. All the cut edges of the velvet panes had been lightly daubed with wax to prevent fraying before they were stitched down. Evidence of

surviving garments shows that this technique was used in England in the seventeenth century. It appears to have started earlier as there are frequent deliveries of 'one pound of searing candle', which may have been used for this purpose, recorded from c1560 to the end of the century among the warrants for the Wardrobe of Robes, where the clothes worn by Queen Elizabeth I were made. R.M. Anderson also records the use of wax for this purpose in Spain in the early sixteenth century in her book *Hispanic Costume*. When a sample of this black wax, together with small samples of each type of thread and warp and weft of the cloth, were sent for testing to Dr J.W. Bell of the Department of Textile Industries, University of Leeds, he reported that, examined under the microscope, the wax had clusters of fine black silk fibres embedded in it. The colour was given by these fibres; the pile falls in a fine powder from the cut edge of some velvets as soon as the shears are lifted away. The areas where each type of thread was used are marked on the pattern.

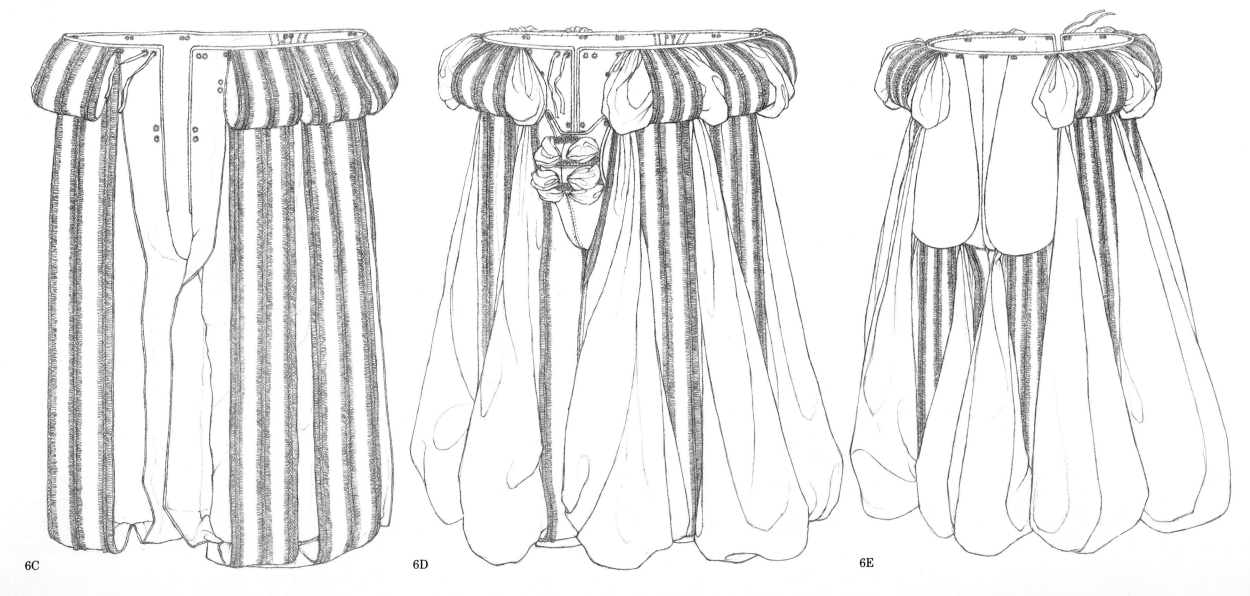

6C 6D 6E

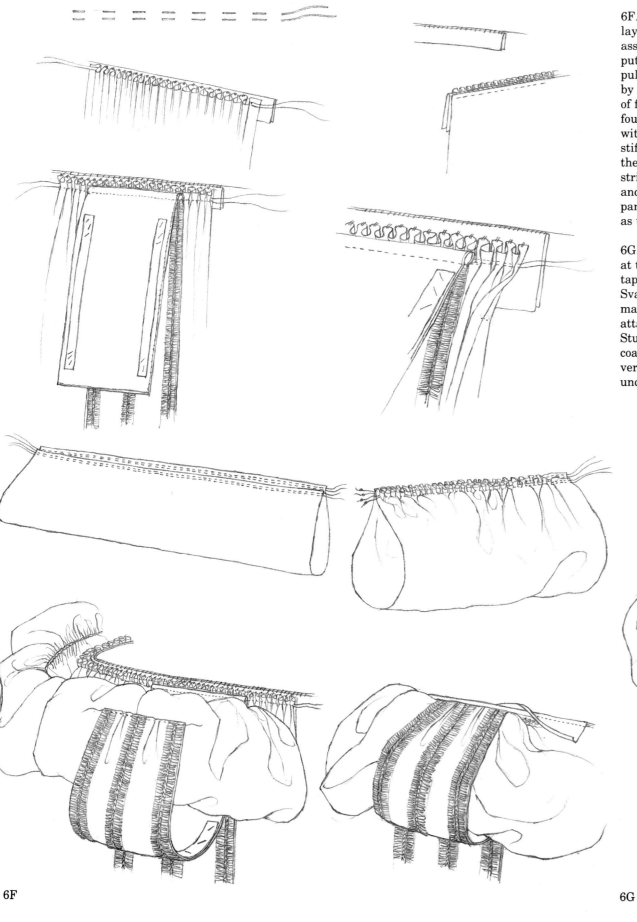

6F. A series of drawings showing how the various layers at the waist of Nils Sture's pluderhose were assembled. A row of parallel gathering threads is put through the edge of the worsted cloth and pulled up to form cartridge pleats. These are held by a stitch on the edge of each one to a folded strip of fustian which is over-stitched to the leather foundation at the waist. The velvet panes are lined with fustian and leather strips placed inside for stiffening. They are stitched to the waist just below the lines of gathering on the worsted cloth. The strip for the waist puff is gathered up separately and arranged inside the loops of the panes. Each pane is then stitched to the waist at the same time as the binding.

6G. The method of gathering the puffs of material at the bottom of the legs and attaching them to stay tapes (Fig. 102) proved to be identical to those in Svante Sture's suit (Fig. 92) although different material has been used. The silk puffs were attached to leather stay tapes, while those in Nils Sture's pluderhose were stitched to stays made of coarse wool. The cloth used for the pluderhose was very hard and springy in texture. The virtually uncrushable quality had made it impossible to press the seams flat and open in the normal way. Miss Ella McLeod identified the cloth as plain weave, ribbed worsted, the same fibre used for both warp and weft, with different spinning. The weft threads were thicker than the warp threads and not hard spun. Under microscopic examination by Dr Bell the cloth proved to be very dark brown, not black, and its appearance, both warp and weft, was consistent with that of English longwool-type fibres. It closely resembled a suit worn in c1655 by Karl X Gustavus of Sweden, which Miss Gudrun Ekstrand showed me at the Kungl. Livrustkammaren Stockholm (inv.no.3390), described as 'Dutch camlet' in an inventory of 1671. It was also similar in texture and weave to named samples of Norwich mohair camlets dated 1792, kept at the Stranger's Hall, Norwich, although heavier in weight. It would seem that camlet was the name for the material, not a term to describe fabric made from a particular fibre, as silk, camel's hair and worsted were variously employed in its manufacture in the sixteenth century. In *Baines Account of the Woollen Manufacture of England* (1875, reprinted 1970) camlet is described as a rough worsted material, especially valuable for resisting rain.

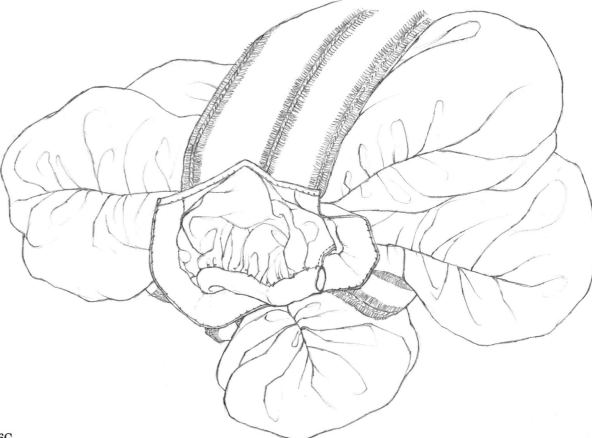

6F

6G

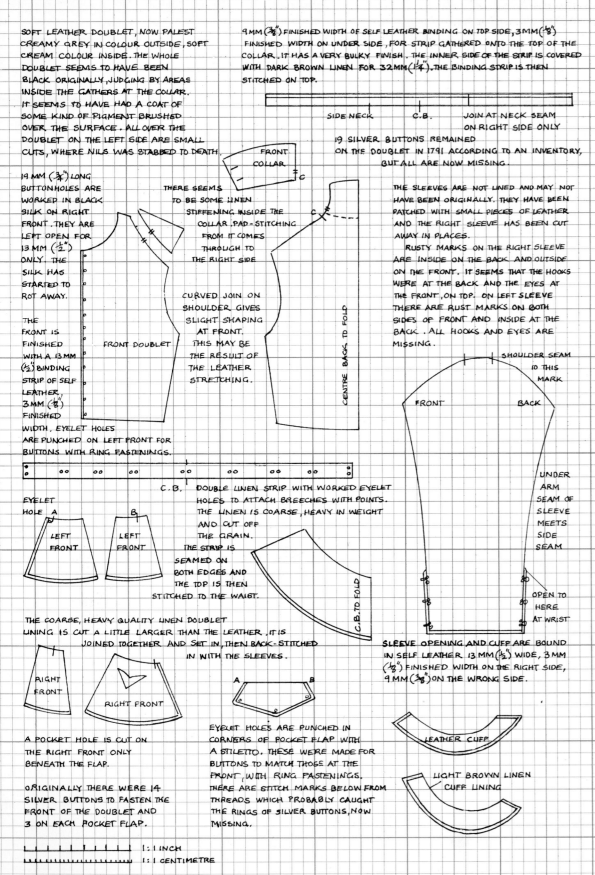

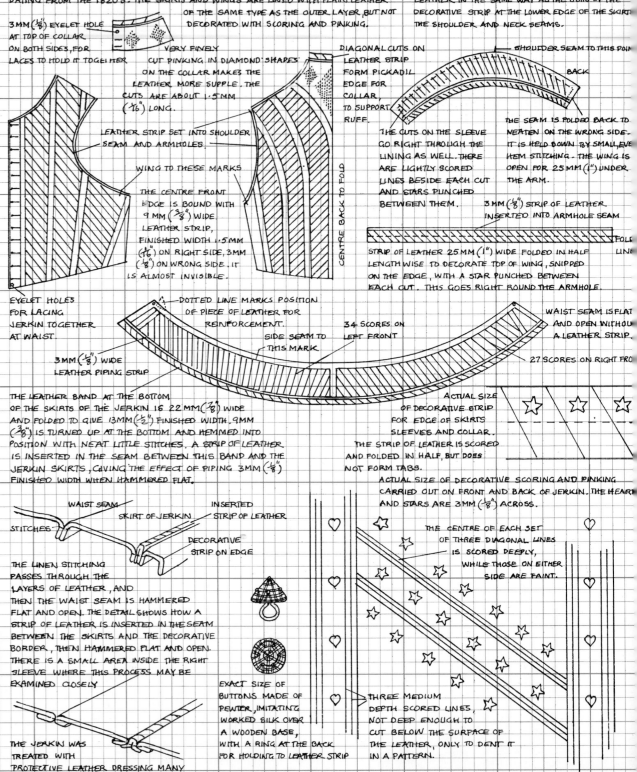

SOFT LEATHER DOUBLET, NOW PALEST CREAMY GREY IN COLOUR OUTSIDE, SOFT CREAM COLOUR INSIDE. THE WHOLE DOUBLET SEEMS TO HAVE BEEN BLACK ORIGINALLY, JUDGING BY AREAS INSIDE THE GATHERS AT THE COLLAR. IT SEEMS TO HAVE HAD A COAT OF SOME KIND OF PIGMENT BRUSHED OVER THE SURFACE. ALL OVER THE DOUBLET ON THE LEFT SIDE ARE SMALL CUTS, WHERE NILS WAS STABBED TO DEATH.

19 MM (¾") LONG BUTTONHOLES ARE WORKED IN BLACK SILK ON RIGHT FRONT. THEY ARE LEFT OPEN FOR 13 MM (½") ONLY. THE SILK HAS STARTED TO ROT AWAY.

THE FRONT IS FINISHED WITH A 13 MM (½") BINDING STRIP OF SELF LEATHER, 3 MM (⅛") FINISHED WIDTH. EYELET HOLES ARE PUNCHED ON LEFT FRONT FOR BUTTONS WITH RING FASTENINGS.

THERE SEEMS TO BE SOME LINEN STIFFENING INSIDE THE COLLAR, PAD-STITCHING FROM IT COMES THROUGH TO THE RIGHT SIDE

CURVED JOIN ON SHOULDER GIVES SLIGHT SHAPING AT FRONT. THIS MAY BE THE RESULT OF THE LEATHER STRETCHING.

FRONT COLLAR

FRONT DOUBLET

CENTRE BACK TO FOLD

9 MM (⅜") FINISHED WIDTH OF SELF LEATHER BINDING ON TOP SIDE, 3 MM (⅛") FINISHED WIDTH ON UNDER SIDE, FOR STRIP GATHERED ONTO THE TOP OF THE COLLAR. IT HAS A VERY BULKY FINISH. THE INNER SIDE OF THE STRIP IS COVERED WITH DARK BROWN LINEN FOR 32 MM (1¼"). THE BINDING STRIP IS THEN STITCHED ON TOP.

SIDE NECK — C.B. — JOIN AT NECK SEAM ON RIGHT SIDE ONLY

19 SILVER BUTTONS REMAINED ON THE DOUBLET IN 1791 ACCORDING TO AN INVENTORY, BUT ALL ARE NOW MISSING.

THE SLEEVES ARE NOT LINED AND MAY NOT HAVE BEEN ORIGINALLY. THEY HAVE BEEN PATCHED WITH SMALL PIECES OF LEATHER AND THE RIGHT SLEEVE HAS BEEN CUT AWAY IN PLACES.

RUSTY MARKS ON THE RIGHT SLEEVE ARE INSIDE ON THE BACK AND OUTSIDE ON THE FRONT. IT SEEMS THAT THE HOOKS WERE AT THE BACK AND THE EYES AT THE FRONT, ON TOP. ON LEFT SLEEVE THERE ARE RUST MARKS ON BOTH SIDES OF FRONT AND INSIDE AT THE BACK. ALL HOOKS AND EYES ARE MISSING.

SHOULDER SEAM TO THIS MARK

FRONT — BACK

UNDER ARM SEAM OF SLEEVE MEETS SIDE SEAM

OPEN TO HERE AT WRIST

C.B. DOUBLE LINEN STRIP WITH WORKED EYELET HOLES TO ATTACH BREECHES WITH POINTS. THE LINEN IS COARSE, HEAVY IN WEIGHT AND CUT OFF THE GRAIN. THE STRIP IS SEAMED ON BOTH EDGES AND THE TOP IS THEN STITCHED TO THE WAIST.

EYELET HOLE A — B

LEFT FRONT — LEFT FRONT

THE COARSE, HEAVY QUALITY LINEN DOUBLET LINING IS CUT A LITTLE LARGER THAN THE LEATHER. IT IS JOINED TOGETHER AND SET IN, THEN BACK-STITCHED IN WITH THE SLEEVES.

RIGHT FRONT

RIGHT FRONT

A POCKET HOLE IS CUT ON THE RIGHT FRONT ONLY BENEATH THE FLAP.

ORIGINALLY THERE WERE 14 SILVER BUTTONS TO FASTEN THE FRONT OF THE DOUBLET AND 3 ON EACH POCKET FLAP.

C.B. TO FOLD

SLEEVE OPENING AND CUFF ARE BOUND IN SELF LEATHER 13 MM (½") WIDE, 3 MM (⅛") FINISHED WIDTH ON THE RIGHT SIDE, 9 MM (⅜") ON THE WRONG SIDE.

A — B

EYELET HOLES ARE PUNCHED IN CORNERS OF POCKET FLAP WITH A STILETTO. THESE WERE MADE FOR BUTTONS TO MATCH THOSE AT THE FRONT, WITH RING FASTENINGS. THERE ARE STITCH MARKS BELOW FROM THREADS WHICH PROBABLY CAUGHT THE RINGS OF SILVER BUTTONS, NOW MISSING.

LEATHER CUFF

LIGHT BROWN LINEN CUFF LINING

DARK BROWN LEATHER JERKIN WITH DECORATIVE PINKING OF HEARTS AND STARS. THE COLLAR AND BODY OF THE JERKIN ARE UNLINED. TRACES OF SILK STITCHING ON THE FRONT SHOW THAT THERE MAY HAVE BEEN A SILK LINING AT ONE TIME, PROBABLY DATING FROM THE 1820s. THE SKIRTS AND WINGS ARE LINED WITH PLAIN LEATHER OF THE SAME TYPE AS THE OUTER LAYER, BUT NOT DECORATED WITH SCORING AND PINKING.

3 MM (⅛") EYELET HOLE AT TOP OF COLLAR ON BOTH SIDES, FOR LACES TO HOLD IT TOGETHER

VERY FINELY CUT PINKING IN DIAMOND SHAPES ON THE COLLAR MAKES THE LEATHER MORE SUPPLE. THE CUTS ARE ABOUT 1·5 MM (1/16") LONG.

LEATHER STRIP SET INTO SHOULDER SEAM AND ARMHOLES.

WING TO THESE MARKS

THE CENTRE FRONT EDGE IS BOUND WITH 9 MM (⅜") WIDE LEATHER STRIP, FINISHED WIDTH 1·5 MM (1/16") ON RIGHT SIDE, 3 MM (⅛") ON WRONG SIDE. IT IS ALMOST INVISIBLE.

EYELET HOLES FOR LACING JERKIN TOGETHER AT WAIST.

3 MM (⅛") WIDE LEATHER PIPING STRIP

THE LEATHER BAND AT THE BOTTOM OF THE SKIRTS OF THE JERKIN IS 22 MM (⅞") WIDE AND FOLDED TO GIVE 13 MM (½") FINISHED WIDTH. 9 MM (⅜") IS TURNED UP AT THE BOTTOM AND HEMMED INTO POSITION WITH NEAT LITTLE STITCHES. A STRIP OF LEATHER IS INSERTED IN THE SEAM BETWEEN THIS BAND AND THE JERKIN SKIRTS, GIVING THE EFFECT OF PIPING 3 MM (⅛") FINISHED WIDTH WHEN HAMMERED FLAT.

WAIST SEAM

SKIRT OF JERKIN

INSERTED STRIP OF LEATHER

STITCHES

DECORATIVE STRIP ON EDGE

THE LINEN STITCHING PASSES THROUGH THE LAYERS OF LEATHER, AND THEN THE WAIST SEAM IS HAMMERED FLAT AND OPEN. THE DETAIL SHOWS HOW A STRIP OF LEATHER IS INSERTED IN THE SEAM BETWEEN THE SKIRTS AND THE DECORATIVE BORDER, THEN HAMMERED FLAT AND OPEN. THERE IS A SMALL AREA INSIDE THE RIGHT SLEEVE WHERE THIS PROCESS MAY BE EXAMINED CLOSELY

EXACT SIZE OF BUTTONS MADE OF PEWTER, IMITATING WORKED SILK OVER A WOODEN BASE, WITH A RING AT THE BACK FOR HOLDING TO LEATHER STRIP

THE JERKIN WAS TREATED WITH PROTECTIVE LEATHER DRESSING MANY YEARS AGO. THIS HAS DARKENED THE LEATHER AND IT IS NOW DIFFICULT TO SEE EXACTLY HOW THE WORK WAS DONE.

DIAGONAL CUTS ON LEATHER STRIP FORM PICKADIL EDGE FOR COLLAR, TO SUPPORT RUFF.

THE CUTS ON THE SLEEVE GO RIGHT THROUGH THE LINING AS WELL. THERE ARE LIGHTLY SCORED LINES BESIDE EACH CUT AND STARS PUNCHED BETWEEN THEM.

3 MM (⅛") STRIP OF LEATHER INSERTED INTO ARMHOLE SEAM

STRIP OF LEATHER 25 MM (1") WIDE FOLDED IN HALF LENGTHWISE TO DECORATE TOP OF WING, SNIPPED ON THE EDGE, WITH A STAR PUNCHED BETWEEN EACH CUT. THIS GOES RIGHT ROUND THE ARMHOLE.

DOTTED LINE MARKS POSITION OF PIECE OF LEATHER FOR REINFORCEMENT.

SIDE SEAM TO THIS MARK

34 SCORES ON LEFT FRONT

WAIST SEAM IS FLAT AND OPEN WITHOUT A LEATHER STRIP.

27 SCORES ON RIGHT FRONT

DOTTED LINE INDICATES POSITION OF 13 MM (½") W THE ARMHOLE SEAM IS FINISHED WITH A STRIP OF LEATHER IN THE SAME WAY AS THE JOIN OF THE DECORATIVE STRIP AT THE LOWER EDGE OF THE SKIRT THE SHOULDER AND NECK SEAMS.

BACK

CENTRE BACK TO FOLD

THE SEAM IS FOLDED BACK TO NEATEN ON THE WRONG SIDE. IT IS HELD DOWN BY SMALL EVE HEM STITCHING. THE WING IS OPEN FOR 25 MM (1") UNDER THE ARM.

FOLD LINE

ACTUAL SIZE OF DECORATIVE STRIP FOR EDGE OF SKIRTS SLEEVES AND COLLAR.

THE STRIP OF LEATHER IS SCORED AND FOLDED IN HALF, BUT DOES NOT FORM TABS.

ACTUAL SIZE OF DECORATIVE SCORING AND PINKING CARRIED OUT ON FRONT AND BACK OF JERKIN. THE HEART AND STARS ARE 3 MM (⅛") ACROSS.

THE CENTRE OF EACH SET OF THREE DIAGONAL LINES IS SCORED DEEPLY, WHILE THOSE ON EITHER SIDE ARE FAINT.

THREE MEDIUM DEPTH SCORED LINES, NOT DEEP ENOUGH TO CUT BELOW THE SURFACE OF THE LEATHER, ONLY TO DENT IT IN A PATTERN.

7A. A youth's brown leather jerkin, decorated with rows of hearts and stars pinked between lines of scoring (Figs. 109–13). A photograph in the archive at the Museum of London shows a page wearing the jerkin, beside the figure of Queen Elizabeth I mounted on horseback, in a display at Lancaster House apparently dating from the 1930s. A label 22.2 × 9.5 cm (8¾ × 3¾″) stitched inside the jerkin has a written inscription:

'Tower 23rd October 1828. A date appears upon the interior of the Boots – 8th October 74 – It is therefore believed that the original dress may have been provided in the year 1774. A new dress for the figure of the Queen Elizabeth was furnished at the expense of the Board of Ordnance in the year 1827 And a new Dress for the Page in the year 1828. The Leather Jerkin is believed to be a dress of the time of Queen Elizabeth and was purchased at a sale of Antient Armour in the Year 1827 and was placed upon the Page on the 23rd October 1828.'

The earlier provenance of the jerkin is not known.

7B. Side view of wing, showing short slashes with rows of stars pinked between lines of scoring. The edge is bound with a folded strip of leather decorated in the same way. The wing is stitched to the armhole with a similar strip lying over the top of it.

7C. Inside the collar, showing the method used to attach decorative strip to top edge with a narrow strip of leather. The diamond shape of fine pinking makes the leather more supple. The large hole at the top, with one matching on the other front, would have had a ribbon or leather point tied through it, to pull the two sides together.

7A

7B

7C

c1560 Lord Astor, Hever Castle, Kent

8. A youth's red satin doublet, changing to light crimson under some lights, which probably came to Hever Castle about the beginning of the present century when the then William Waldorf Astor founded the collection of arms and armour. It may be an arming doublet (Fig. 117). A silver plate accompanying it is engraved in Spanish: 'Doublet worn in the siege of Goleta by Don Luis Hurtado de Mendoza, 3rd Count of Tendilla, 2nd Marquis of Mondejar, Captain General of the Cavalry of Charles V in 1535, with the signs of the two wounds he received on the side and left arm.'

There are, apparently, no authenticated arming doublets of this period surviving in museums for purposes of comparison but it seems likely that they too would have been lightly padded. Cotton wool padding is arranged loosely in wide panels between double rows of back-stitching. There are six worked eyelet holes over each sleevehead which may have been used for points to attach mail sleeves in the way seen in several paintings by Giovanni Battista Moroni and some unknown English painters. It should be noted, however, that these eyelet holes do not show signs of wear and strain, so may only have been used for decorative ribbon points. The doublet is similar in shape to several seen in Italian paintings of c1545–60 (Figs. 115–16).

NB: This doublet was purchased in 1983 by the Royal Scottish Museum, Edinburgh.

c1620 Los Angeles County Museum of Art

9. A jerkin in green silk woven with a design of stylized sprays of leaves and flowers of either Spanish or Italian origin, the gift of Mrs B. Houston Rehrig, purchased from Majorcas of London. Miss Natalie Rothstein describes the material as brocatelle, a lampas-woven fabric with silk warps that is characterized by a marked relief of the warp-faced weave, usually used for furnishings, dating from the 1620s. The early provenance of the jerkin is not known. In other garments of this period I have examined it is usual for the collar to be interlined with linen and lined with silk. Here the brocatelle is used for the lining, which indicates that the collar may have been recut from scraps at a later date, perhaps for the jerkin to be worn as fancy dress. The pieces of the body of the jerkin were individually mounted on to heavy linen and overhanded together. The original green silk lining has been replaced with a linen lining. Fragments of disintegrating brilliant grass-green silk lining remain inside the skirts: originally the jerkin was close to this colour but has now faded. The tabbed wings were probably stitched into the armholes originally and may have been moved for fancy dress, but it is not easy to distinguish stitch holes in this type of fabric so this can only be conjecture. The pattern shapes are similar to those of the doublets on page 85, both dating from c1615–20. This garment may have been made from pieces left over from some furnishings and not worn very much, as jerkins went out of fashion after about 1620. Jerkins were masculine garments occasionally copied by women; Queen Elizabeth I had a couple made in 1577, probably for riding. Paintings show that jerkins, sleeveless and worn over the doublet for extra warmth, could be made of leather, in material to match the doublet, or in fabric of totally different design and colour, providing a contrast. They were often decorated with pinking, slashing and braid. In paintings it is often difficult to detect the jerkin worn over a matching doublet when all the buttons are fastened, as the jerkin shoulder wings usually conceal those of the doublet. Even their wearers in the sixteenth century found difficulty in distinguishing the two garments. Valentine mistakes Thurio's jerkin for a doublet in *The Two Gentlemen of Verona* and turns his error into a punning joke. In the early 1600s portraits often show jerkins unfastened over the padded doublet (Fig. 122), apparently cut so that the fronts would not meet, although complete with buttons and worked buttonholes or loops. This jerkin appears to be an example of that style as it hangs better left open, the buttonholes show no signs of wear, and there are no buttons and buttonholes or loops on the collar.

8

9

.1560 PADDED DOUBLET LORD ASTOR, HEVER CASTLE, KENT.

DOUBLET IS MADE OF RED SATIN WHICH CHANGES TO CRIMSON IN SOME LIGHTS,
PALE STRAW WEFT AND RICH CRIMSON WARP THREADS. IT FASTENS AT THE CENTRE
IT WITH EIGHT BUTTONS AND WORKED BUTTONHOLES. THE TOP BUTTON IS MISSING.
E IS ONE PAIR OF WORKED EYELET HOLES AT THE CENTRE FRONT WAIST FOR A
T, OR LACE, TO PULL THE TWO SIDES TOGETHER.

A DOUBLED STRIP OF
SATIN 8MM (5/16"),
FINISHED WIDTH, CUT
PARALLEL TO THE
SELVEDGE, IS USED
FOR THE NECK
TRIMMING. IT IS
CLIPPED TO MAKE
APPROXIMATELY 25
LITTLE TABS. IT IS
DIFFICULT TO TELL
THE EXACT NUMBER
AS THE SATIN HAS
FRAYED AND MANY
OF THEM HAVE
DISINTEGRATED.

M (3/8") HOOK SEWN
EATH CENTRE FRONT
K EDGE, ON LEFT
AND EYE ON RIGHT
. FACING STRIP
ES IN WIDTH
19MM (3/4") TO
M (1") DOWN THE
RE FRONT. THE
ONHOLES ARE
KED IN RED SILK
UGH THIS AND THE
N LINING. THEY ARE
1 (3/4") LONG, WITH
ARE ENDS, AND AN
ING OF 13MM (1/2").
TOP OF EACH BUTTON
MM (3/8") IN DIAMETER
THE WORKED SHANK
MM (3/8") LONG. THE
ONS ARE 5MM (3/16")
C, MADE OF SATIN
TCHED OVER A
NDATION OF WHAT IS PROBABLY STIFF
DBOARD, THEN EMBROIDERED WITH
CHING RED SILK.

WADDING TO THE DOTTED LINE,
THICKER OVER THE SHOULDERS
AND AT THE ARMHOLES

FRONT SLEEVE
SEAM TO THIS
POINT

BACK SLEEVE
SEAM TO
THIS POINT

JOIN IN FABRIC

BACK

CENTRE BACK TO FOLD

THIS ROW OF STITCHING IS
1.5MM (1/16") AWAY FROM
THE CENTRE BACK.

THE WAIST IS STITCHED
1.5MM (1/16") AWAY FROM
THE EDGE ALL THE WAY
ROUND. AT THE FRONT OF
THE DOUBLET THERE ARE
TWO ROWS 1.5MM (1/16") AWAY
FROM THE EDGE, THEN 3MM
(1/8") APART.

EYELET HOLE
C.F.

THE WAIST STRIP WITH
WORKED EYELET HOLES FOR
POINTS, OR LACES, TO ATTACH
THE HOSE, IS MADE OF SATIN
LINED WITH WHITE LINEN,
INTERLINED WITH TWO LAYERS OF
STIFF LINEN. THIS IS VERY THICK AND
HEAVY, WITH A TEXTURE WHICH
RESEMBLES HESSIAN, AND IS THE
SAME TYPE AS THAT USED FOR
INTERLINING THE BACK AND
FRONT OF THE DOUBLET.

FRONT AND BACK OF THE DOUBLET
ARE MADE OF A LAYER OF
SATIN INTERLINED WITH
HEAVY, COARSE LINEN.
THE COTTON WADDING,
OR BOMBAST, IS PLACED
BETWEEN THESE TWO LAYERS. IT IS HELD IN POSITION BY
THE DOUBLE ROWS OF STITCHING SET 3MM (1/8") APART.
THE WADDING IS TAPERED OFF GRADUALLY TOWARDS
THE CENTRE FRONT AND THE WAIST AT THE FRONT, AND
THE DOTTED LINE AT THE BACK. THE FRONT AND TOP
OF THE SLEEVES ARE MORE HEAVILY WADDED THAN
ANYWHERE ELSE, BEING 9MM (3/8") THICK IN THESE
PLACES. THE WHITE LINEN LINING IS LOOSE AND THE
LINES OF RED SILK STITCHING DO NOT COME THROUGH IT.
THE WHITE LINEN THREADS HOLDING THE LINING TO THE
WAIST CAN BE SEEN CLEARLY. THE LINING REACHES TO
THE BOTTOM OF THE WAIST STRIP. THE EYELET HOLES ARE
WORKED THROUGH IT.

HOULDER
EAM TO THIS
OINT

FRONT

EYELET
ES ON THE
EVEHEAD
1.5MM (1/8")
DIAMETER
WORKED
ED SILK.

OPEN TO
HERE AT WRIST

TCHING ON
HIS SEAM IS
5MM (1/16")
ROM THE
DGE.

BUTTONHOLE IS THE SAME SIZE
THOSE AT THE FRONT OF THE DOUBLET
O WORKED WITH SQUARE ENDS. THE
TONS REMAIN ON BOTH SLEEVES
MATCH THOSE AT THE FRONT.

THE SLEEVE IS MADE OF A LAYER OF SATIN WITH A
LINING OF FAIRLY HEAVY WEAVE LINEN. THE COTTON
WADDING, OR BOMBAST, IS PLACED BETWEEN THESE TWO
LAYERS AND HELD IN POSITION BY THE ROWS OF STITCHING.
THE WRIST TABS ARE CUT IN ONE WITH THE SLEEVE. THE
LINEN LINING AND WADDING FINISHES JUST ABOVE THE BOTTOM
ROW OF STITCHING. FROM THIS LINE THE SATIN FACINGS ARE
PUT ON, 28MM (1 1/8") WIDE AT THE WRIST OPENING, CURVING UP
TO 4.4CM (1 3/4") AT THE FRONT SEAM. THE FOLDED EDGE OF THE
SLEEVE AT THE WRIST WAS CLIPPED TO FORM TABS AND HAS
NOW FRAYED. IT WAS NOT STIFFENED IN ANY WAY.

|---------| 1:1 INCH
|·········| 1:1 CENTIMETRE

9. c.1620 JERKIN LOS ANGELES COUNTY MUSEUM.

THE JERKIN IS MADE OF GREEN SILK WOVEN WITH A DESIGN OF STYLIZED SPRAYS OF LEAVES AND FLOWERS,
ENRICHED WITH GOLD METAL THREADS IN THE WEFT. EACH PIECE OF THE BODY OF THE JERKIN IS INDIVIDUALLY
MOUNTED ON TO HEAVY LINEN CANVAS, RESEMBLING HESSIAN. THE CANVAS IS NOT INCLUDED IN THE SEAMS.
THE RAW EDGES OF THE SILK ARE FOLDED BACK OVER THE CANVAS AND TACKED DOWN. THE PIECES ARE
THEN OVERHANDED TOGETHER. UNDER THE BUTTONHOLES, ON THE LEFT SIDE ONLY, IS A STRIP OF BRIGHT
GREEN SILK, NOT MATCHING THE FRAGMENTS OF LINING WHICH REMAIN ON THE TABBED SKIRTS.
THE BODY OF THE JERKIN IS LINED WITH LINEN WHICH HAS BEEN PUT IN AT A LATER DATE, PROBABLY TO REPLACE
A WORN GREEN SILK LINING.

DOTTED LINES MARK THE
POSITION OF THE WINGS

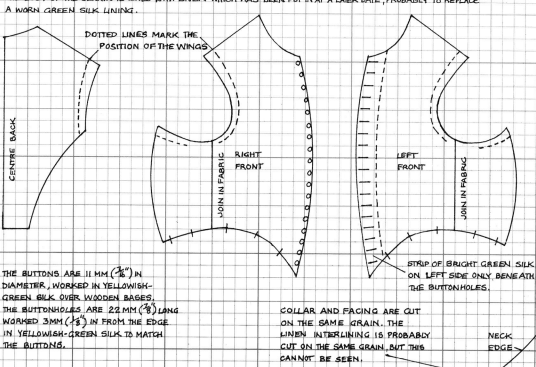

CENTRE BACK

JOIN IN FABRIC

RIGHT FRONT

LEFT FRONT

JOIN IN FABRIC

STRIP OF BRIGHT GREEN SILK
ON LEFT SIDE ONLY BENEATH
THE BUTTONHOLES.

THE BUTTONS ARE 11 MM (7/16") IN
DIAMETER, WORKED IN YELLOWISH-
GREEN SILK OVER WOODEN BASES.
THE BUTTONHOLES ARE 22 MM (7/8") LONG
WORKED 3MM (1/8") IN FROM THE EDGE
IN YELLOWISH-GREEN SILK TO MATCH
THE BUTTONS.

COLLAR AND FACING ARE CUT
ON THE SAME GRAIN. THE
LINEN INTERLINING IS PROBABLY
CUT ON THE SAME GRAIN, BUT THIS
CANNOT BE SEEN.

CENTRE
BACK

NECK
EDGE

FRONT

CENTRE
BACK

FRONT

THERE ARE FIVE TABS IN THE SKIRTS ON EACH SIDE OF THE JERKIN,
OVERLAPPING EACH OTHER TOWARDS THE BACK. EACH ONE IS
BACKED WITH LINEN CUT TO SHAPE. THE RAW EDGES OF THE
SILK ARE FOLDED ROUND THE EDGES AND TACKED DOWN.
A FEW SHREDS REMAIN OF THE GRASS GREEN SILK LINING.
THE TABS ARE TRIMMED WITH 6MM (1/4") WIDE GOLD METAL BRAID
AND OVERHANDED TO THE WAIST OF THE JERKIN.

SHOULDER SEAM
TO THIS MARK

FRONT

BACK SEAM TO
THIS MARK

EACH TAB OF THE WING IS BACKED WITH WHITE SATIN. THE
GREEN SILK IS DOUBLED ON THE FOLDED EDGE SO THAT NO
SATIN SHOWS. THE WINGS ARE TRIMMED WITH GOLD METAL
BRAID TO MATCH THE TABBED SKIRTS.

6MM (1/4") WIDE GOLD
METAL BRAID ROUND
EACH TAB OF THE WING.

THIS EDGE TO FOLD

© 1984 JANET ARNOLD

c1595–1610 Stibbert Museum, Florence

10.   A doublet in soft leather with a suede finish, originally cream and now discoloured unevenly to greyish white and buff. It is probably of Italian origin but the early provenance is not known. The whole doublet is interlined with linen and firmly padded (probably with cotton wool) on the chest, back, collar, wings and skirts. This padding, or bombast, is held in place between rows of stitching covered with plaited gold thread. The lower part of the doublet body is decorated with yellow silk and silver thread embroidery arranged between narrow raised panels, padded chevronwise. The front is stiffened beneath the embroidery with whalebones, bents or strips of wood, which may be felt but not seen. Lacing strips with worked eyelet holes are stitched on each side of the doublet waist, beneath the skirts, with a 17.7 cm (7″) gap between them at the back. Points, or laces, were tied through these holes to attach trunk-hose or breeches. Similar lacing strips are stitched inside the armhole for attaching a pair of sleeves: the points would have been hidden beneath the wings. The collar is cut without shaping at the back neck, continuing with the straight edge fitting the front. A similar method is used for cutting a roll collar today. A straight strip of silk, snipped in pickadil along the folded edge, is stitched inside the collar. The ruff would have been pinned to this to prevent it from becoming disarranged. The front fastens with lacing through eyelet holes worked between the rows of buttons on both sides. Ten buttons are missing at the bottom. This doublet should be compared with those on pages 82 and 83. The padding indicates that it was probably worn for fencing or some similar activity requiring protection over the chest. It may have been part of a page's livery, possibly worn with a leather hat similar to those in Figs. 241 and 244.

c1595–1605 Nederlands Kostuummuseum, The Hague

11A.   A youth's doublet in bright jade green and yellow cut and uncut velvet in a small regular pattern on a voided beige silk ground, giving an all-over effect of sage green. Parts of the cut velvet have a very long pile, giving the effect of slashed silk, heavily frayed at the edges. The style of the doublet is close to several seen in Italian paintings of the 1580s (Fig. 131) and this Italian velvet would seem to be an early example of many with similar small motifs depicted in portraits of the first two decades of the seventeenth century. The early provenance of the doublet is not known. The collar is cut in a similar way to that of the Stibbert Museum doublet but has a curved neck edge. A bias strip of brown silk, snipped along the folded edge, is stitched inside the collar for ruff or supportasse to be pinned to it in the same way as the Stibbert Museum doublet. The lower part of the doublet is stiffened with more whalebones than the Stibbert Museum doublet and may be compared with the woman's doublet on page 107. Both side back seams are open at the top with worked eyelet holes for lacing, which may be pulled tight to make a better fit in a similar way to Eleanora of Toledo's bodice on page 103. Eyelet holes are also worked round the upper part of the armholes, beneath the wings, for attaching the sleeves with points. The lacing strips with worked eyelet holes for attaching points to support the breeches are slightly shaped. They are stitched to the waistline on both fronts beneath the skirts with a gap between them at the back. The front fastens in the same way as the Stibbert Museum doublet, with lacing through eyelet holes worked between the buttons.

11B.   Detail of sleeve laced into armhole.

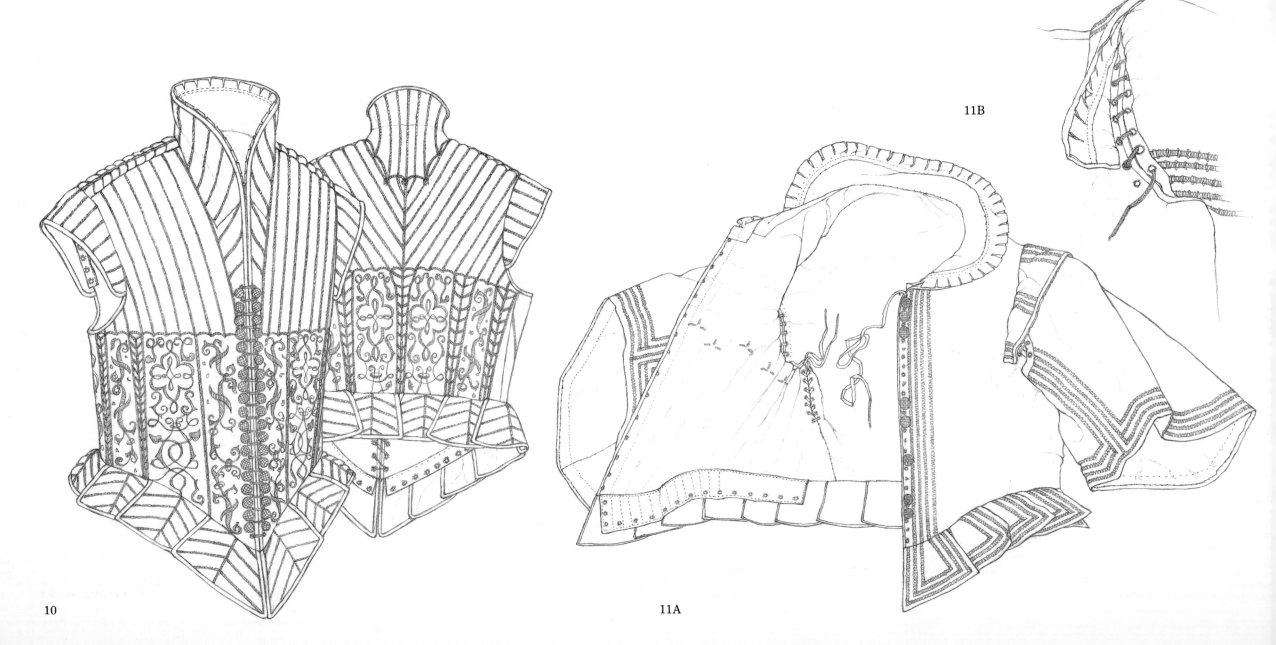

10

11A

11B

c.1595-1600 LEATHER DOUBLET   STIBBERT MUSEUM, FLORENCE

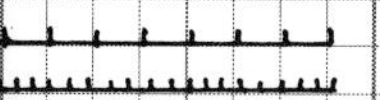

11. c.1595-1605 YOUTH'S DOUBLET   KOSTUUMMUSEUM, THE HAGUE. K1-X-1964.

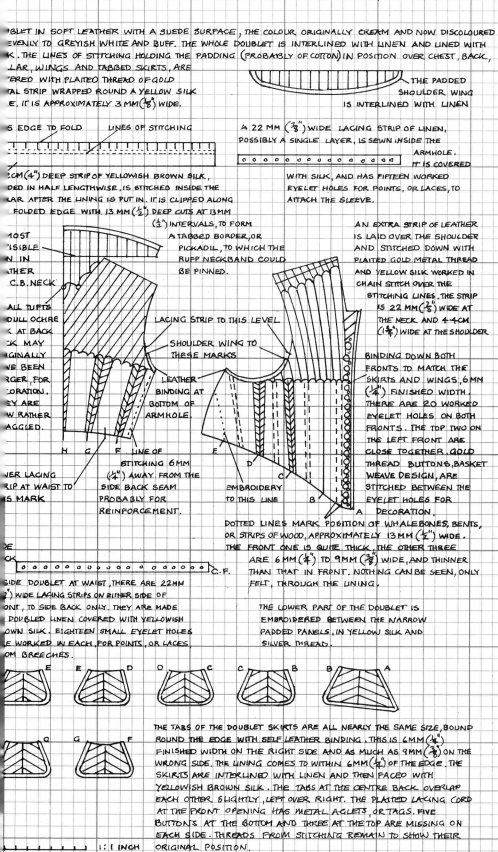

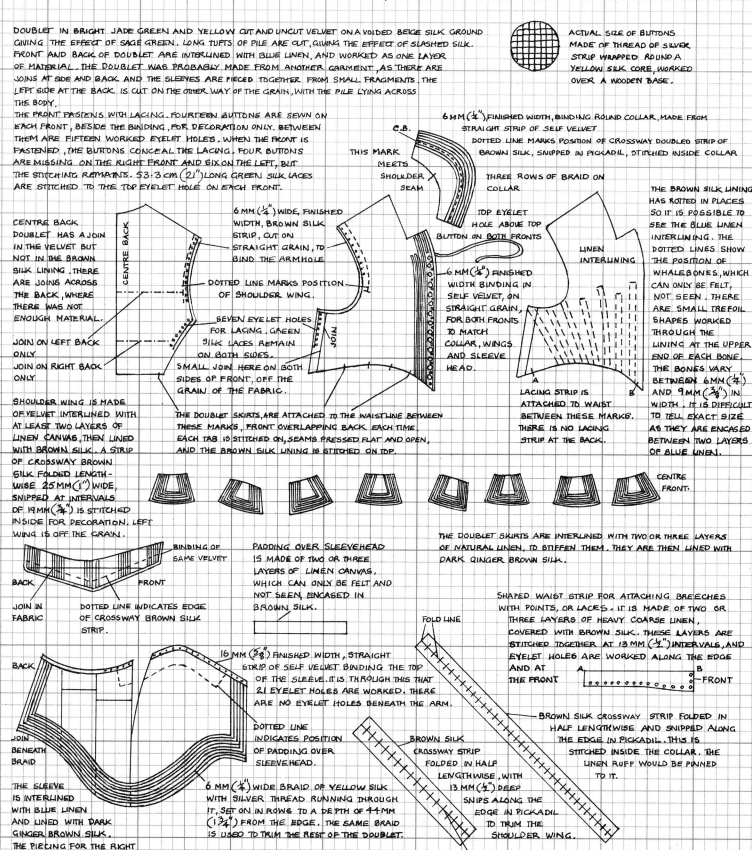

...BLET IN SOFT LEATHER WITH A SUEDE SURFACE, THE COLOUR ORIGINALLY CREAM AND NOW DISCOLOURED ...EVENLY TO GREYISH WHITE AND BUFF. THE WHOLE DOUBLET IS INTERLINED WITH LINEN AND LINED WITH ...K. THE LINES OF STITCHING HOLDING THE PADDING (PROBABLY OF COTTON) IN POSITION OVER CHEST, BACK, ...LAR, WINGS AND TABBED SKIRTS, ARE ...ERED WITH PLAITED THREAD OF GOLD ...AL STRIP WRAPPED ROUND A YELLOW SILK ...E. IT IS APPROXIMATELY 3 MM (⅛") WIDE.

THE PADDED SHOULDER WING IS INTERLINED WITH LINEN

...S EDGE TO FOLD   LINES OF STITCHING

A 22 MM (⅞") WIDE LACING STRIP OF LINEN, POSSIBLY A SINGLE LAYER, IS SEWN INSIDE THE ARMHOLE. IT IS COVERED WITH SILK, AND HAS FIFTEEN WORKED EYELET HOLES FOR POINTS, OR LACES, TO ATTACH THE SLEEVE.

...CM (4") DEEP STRIP OF YELLOWISH BROWN SILK, ...DED IN HALF LENGTHWISE, IS STITCHED INSIDE THE ...LAR AFTER THE LINING IS PUT IN. IT IS CLIPPED ALONG ...FOLDED EDGE WITH 13 MM (½") DEEP CUTS AT 13 MM (½") INTERVALS, TO FORM A TABBED BORDER, OR PICKADIL, TO WHICH THE RUFF NECKBAND COULD BE PINNED.

...10ST ...ISIBLE ...IN ...THER C.B. NECK

...ALL TUFTS ...DULL OCHRE ...K AT BACK ...MAY ...IGINALLY ...VE BEEN ...RGER, FOR ...ORATION ...EY ARE ...W. RATHER ...AGGLED.

AN EXTRA STRIP OF LEATHER IS LAID OVER THE SHOULDER AND STITCHED DOWN WITH PLAITED GOLD METAL THREAD AND YELLOW SILK WORKED IN CHAIN STITCH OVER THE STITCHING LINES. THE STRIP IS 22 MM (⅞") WIDE AT THE NECK AND 4.4 CM (1¾") WIDE AT THE SHOULDER.

SHOULDER WING TO THESE MARKS

LACING STRIP TO THIS LEVEL

LEATHER BINDING AT BOTTOM OF ARMHOLE

...ER LACING ...RIP AT WAIST TO ...IS MARK

LINE OF STITCHING 6 MM (¼") AWAY FROM THE SIDE BACK SEAM PROBABLY FOR REINFORCEMENT.

EMBROIDERY TO THIS LINE

BINDING DOWN BOTH FRONTS TO MATCH THE SKIRTS AND WINGS, 6 MM (¼") FINISHED WIDTH. THERE ARE 20 WORKED EYELET HOLES ON BOTH FRONTS. THE TOP TWO ON THE LEFT FRONT ARE CLOSE TOGETHER. GOLD THREAD BUTTONS, BASKET WEAVE DESIGN, ARE STITCHED BETWEEN THE EYELET HOLES FOR DECORATION.

DOTTED LINES MARK POSITION OF WHALEBONES, BENTS, OR STRIPS OF WOOD, APPROXIMATELY 13 MM (½") WIDE. THE FRONT ONE IS QUITE THICK, THE OTHER THREE ARE 6 MM (¼") TO 9 MM (⅜") WIDE, AND THINNER THAN THAT IN FRONT. NOTHING CAN BE SEEN, ONLY FELT, THROUGH THE LINING.

THE LOWER PART OF THE DOUBLET IS EMBROIDERED BETWEEN THE NARROW PADDED PANELS, IN YELLOW SILK AND SILVER THREAD.

C.F.

...DE ...CK

...SIDE DOUBLET AT WAIST, THERE ARE 22 MM ...") WIDE LACING STRIPS ON EITHER SIDE OF ...ONT, TO SIDE BACK ONLY, THEY ARE MADE ...DOUBLED LINEN COVERED WITH YELLOWISH ...OWN SILK. EIGHTEEN SMALL EYELET HOLES ...WORKED IN EACH, FOR POINTS, OR LACES, ...OM BREECHES.

THE TABS OF THE DOUBLET SKIRTS ARE ALL NEARLY THE SAME SIZE, BOUND ROUND THE EDGE WITH SELF LEATHER BINDING. THIS IS 6 MM (¼") FINISHED WIDTH ON THE RIGHT SIDE AND AS MUCH AS 9 MM (⅜") ON THE WRONG SIDE. THE SKIRTS ARE INTERLINED WITH LINEN AND THEN FACED WITH YELLOWISH BROWN SILK. THE TABS AT THE CENTRE BACK OVERLAP EACH OTHER SLIGHTLY, LEFT OVER RIGHT. THE PLAITED LACING CORD AT THE FRONT OPENING HAS METAL AGLETS, OR TAGS. FIVE BUTTONS AT THE BOTTOM AND THREE AT THE TOP ARE MISSING ON EACH SIDE. THREADS FROM STITCHING REMAIN TO SHOW THEIR ORIGINAL POSITION.

1: 1 INCH
1: 1 CM

DOUBLET IN BRIGHT JADE GREEN AND YELLOW CUT AND UNCUT VELVET ON A VOIDED BEIGE SILK GROUND GIVING THE EFFECT OF SAGE GREEN. LONG TUFTS OF PILE ARE CUT, GIVING THE EFFECT OF SLASHED SILK. FRONT AND BACK OF DOUBLET ARE INTERLINED WITH BLUE LINEN, AND WORKED AS ONE LAYER OF MATERIAL. THE DOUBLET WAS PROBABLY MADE FROM ANOTHER GARMENT, AS THERE ARE JOINS AT SIDE AND BACK AND THE SLEEVES ARE PIECED TOGETHER FROM SMALL FRAGMENTS. THE LEFT SIDE AT THE BACK IS CUT ON THE OTHER WAY OF THE GRAIN, WITH THE PILE LYING ACROSS THE BODY.

THE FRONT FASTENS WITH LACING. FOURTEEN BUTTONS ARE SEWN ON EACH FRONT, BESIDE THE BINDING, FOR DECORATION ONLY. BETWEEN THEM ARE FIFTEEN WORKED EYELET HOLES. WHEN THE FRONT IS FASTENED, THE BUTTONS CONCEAL THE LACING. FOUR BUTTONS ARE MISSING ON THE RIGHT FRONT AND SIX ON THE LEFT, BUT THE STITCHING REMAINS. 53.3 CM (21") LONG GREEN SILK LACES ARE STITCHED TO THE TOP EYELET HOLE ON EACH FRONT.

ACTUAL SIZE OF BUTTONS MADE OF THREAD OF SILVER STRIP WRAPPED ROUND A YELLOW SILK CORE, WORKED OVER A WOODEN BASE.

C.B.

THIS MARK MEETS SHOULDER SEAM

6 MM (¼") FINISHED WIDTH, BINDING ROUND COLLAR, MADE FROM STRAIGHT STRIP OF SELF VELVET. DOTTED LINE MARKS POSITION OF CROSSWAY DOUBLED STRIP OF BROWN SILK, SNIPPED IN PICKADIL, STITCHED INSIDE COLLAR

THREE ROWS OF BRAID ON COLLAR

TOP EYELET HOLE ABOVE TOP BUTTON ON BOTH FRONTS

LINEN INTERLINING

THE BROWN SILK LINING HAS ROTTED IN PLACES SO IT IS POSSIBLE TO SEE THE BLUE LINEN INTERLINING. THE DOTTED LINES SHOW THE POSITION OF WHALEBONES, WHICH CAN ONLY BE FELT, NOT SEEN. THERE ARE SMALL TREFOIL SHAPES WORKED THROUGH THE LINING AT THE UPPER END OF EACH BONE. THE BONES VARY BETWEEN 6 MM (¼") AND 9 MM (⅜") IN WIDTH. IT IS DIFFICULT TO TELL EXACT SIZE AS THEY ARE ENCASED BETWEEN TWO LAYERS OF BLUE LINEN.

CENTRE BACK DOUBLET HAS A JOIN IN THE VELVET BUT NOT IN THE BROWN SILK LINING. THERE ARE JOINS ACROSS THE BACK, WHERE THERE WAS NOT ENOUGH MATERIAL.

CENTRE BACK

6 MM (¼") WIDE, FINISHED WIDTH, BROWN SILK STRIP, CUT ON STRAIGHT GRAIN, TO BIND THE ARMHOLE

6 MM (¼") FINISHED WIDTH BINDING IN SELF VELVET, ON STRAIGHT GRAIN, FOR BOTH FRONTS TO MATCH COLLAR, WINGS AND SLEEVE HEAD.

JOIN ON LEFT BACK ONLY

JOIN ON RIGHT BACK ONLY

DOTTED LINE MARKS POSITION OF SHOULDER WING.

SEVEN EYELET HOLES FOR LACING. GREEN SILK LACES REMAIN ON BOTH SIDES. SMALL JOIN HERE ON BOTH SIDES OF FRONT, OFF THE GRAIN OF THE FABRIC.

JOIN

LACING STRIP IS ATTACHED TO WAIST BETWEEN THESE MARKS. THERE IS NO LACING STRIP AT THE BACK.

SHOULDER WING IS MADE OF VELVET INTERLINED WITH AT LEAST TWO LAYERS OF LINEN CANVAS, THEN LINED WITH BROWN SILK. A STRIP OF CROSSWAY BROWN SILK FOLDED LENGTHWISE 25 MM (1") WIDE, SNIPPED AT INTERVALS OF 19 MM (¾") IS STITCHED INSIDE FOR DECORATION. LEFT WING IS OFF THE GRAIN.

THE DOUBLET SKIRTS ARE ATTACHED TO THE WAISTLINE BETWEEN THESE MARKS, FRONT OVERLAPPING BACK EACH TIME. EACH TAB IS STITCHED ON, SEAMS PRESSED FLAT AND OPEN, AND THE BROWN SILK LINING IS STITCHED ON TOP.

THE DOUBLET SKIRTS ARE INTERLINED WITH TWO OR THREE LAYERS OF NATURAL LINEN, TO STIFFEN THEM. THEY ARE THEN LINED WITH DARK GINGER BROWN SILK.

SHAPED WAIST STRIP FOR ATTACHING BREECHES WITH POINTS, OR LACES. IT IS MADE OF TWO OR THREE LAYERS OF HEAVY COARSE LINEN, COVERED WITH BROWN SILK. THESE LAYERS ARE STITCHED TOGETHER AT 13 MM (½") INTERVALS, AND EYELET HOLES ARE WORKED ALONG THE EDGE AND AT THE FRONT

A   B   FRONT

BINDING OF SAME VELVET

BACK   FRONT

JOIN IN FABRIC

DOTTED LINE INDICATES EDGE OF CROSSWAY BROWN SILK STRIP.

PADDING OVER SLEEVEHEAD IS MADE OF TWO OR THREE LAYERS OF LINEN CANVAS, WHICH CAN ONLY BE FELT AND NOT SEEN, ENCASED IN BROWN SILK.

FOLD LINE

BROWN SILK CROSSWAY STRIP FOLDED IN HALF LENGTHWISE AND SNIPPED ALONG THE EDGE IN PICKADIL. THIS IS STITCHED INSIDE THE COLLAR. THE LINEN RUFF WOULD BE PINNED TO IT.

BACK

JOIN BENEATH BRAID

16 MM (⅝") FINISHED WIDTH, STRAIGHT STRIP OF SELF VELVET BINDING THE TOP OF THE SLEEVE. IT IS THROUGH THIS THAT 21 EYELET HOLES ARE WORKED. THERE ARE NO EYELET HOLES BENEATH THE ARM.

DOTTED LINE INDICATES POSITION OF PADDING OVER SLEEVEHEAD.

BROWN SILK CROSSWAY STRIP FOLDED IN HALF LENGTHWISE, WITH 13 MM (½") DEEP SNIPS ALONG THE EDGE IN PICKADIL TO TRIM THE SHOULDER WING.

THE SLEEVE IS INTERLINED WITH BLUE LINEN AND LINED WITH DARK GINGER BROWN SILK. THE PIECING FOR THE RIGHT SLEEVE IS SHOWN.

6 MM (¼") WIDE BRAID OF YELLOW SILK WITH SILVER THREAD RUNNING THROUGH IT, SET ON IN ROWS TO A DEPTH OF 4.4 CM (1¾") FROM THE EDGE. THE SAME BRAID IS USED TO TRIM THE REST OF THE DOUBLET.

FOLD LINE

© 1984 JANET ARNOLD

c1600–5 Grimsthorpe and Drummond Castle Trust Ltd, on loan to the Victoria and Albert Museum, London

12A. A suit consisting of doublet and trunk-hose, which is traditionally believed to have been worn by James I. However, Miss Avril Hart kindly gave me the following information which she pieced together from museum records. The suit was thought to have been acquired as a Coronation perquisite in 1603 by an ancestor of the Earl of Ancaster's family, the 13th Lord Willoughby de Eresby, who succeeded to the title in 1602. In 1937 J.L. Nevinson, in consultation with the 2nd Earl of Ancaster and A.R. Wagner, Portcullis Pursuivant of the College of Arms, concluded that the link with James I could only be traditional, as Lord Willoughby de Eresby would not have been eligible to receive Royal perquisites until he became Lord Great Chamberlain in the reign of Charles I. It is possible that Lord Willoughby himself wore it to the Coronation of James I, that the tradition began there and subsequently the suit became confused with later perquisites.

The suit is made from uncut velvet on a voided satin ground. The colour is now purple brown and was probably originally murrey or mulberry. The stylized design of sprays of leaves and curving stems has almost completely worn away on the front of the suit and what remains appears to be cut velvet, as the loops have powdered away. However, complete repeats of the uncut design may be seen on the canions and at the back of the trunk-hose (Fig. 143).

12B. The doublet is decorated with woven braid of purple-brown silk and metal thread (Fig. 142). It is all of the same design but in some areas, for example at the centre back and round the skirts, it is made with gold thread and yellow silk with some silver threads, while in other areas, for example round the neck and on the sleeves, it is made with gold thread and purple-brown silk. The difference between them is not noticeable at a cursory glance but the purple-brown braid seems to sparkle more: the silver in the yellow silk braid has tarnished and makes it look dull. The collar is very stiff. It is made of a layer of coarse natural-coloured linen, heavy in weight, with another layer of linen and one of heavy wool pad-stitched on top of it, cut away at the front for the buttonholes. Another layer of wool is pad-stitched over this again, reaching halfway up the collar. This is striped pale blue, red, yellow and dark brown in the weft with a green warp and quite heavily milled. The collar is then lined with purple-brown silk. An underpropper, or supportasse, would have been worn with this collar to hold up a linen band bordered with lace, or made entirely of lace. All forty-two buttons at the front are missing and also five at each wrist but they would have been similar to many seen on other doublets described in this book, with gold metal thread and purple-brown silk worked over wooden bases.

Although not very exaggerated, this seems to be the best surviving example of a peascod belly, which was popular in England from around 1575 to 1600. Stubbes described them in his *Anatomie of Abuses* in 1583 as

'beeing so harde-quilted, and stuffed, bombasted and sewed, as they can verie hardly eyther stoupe downe, or decline them selves to the grounde, soe styffe and sturdy they stand about them . . . certaine I am there was never any kinde of apparell ever invented, that could more disproportion the body of man than these Dublets with great bellies, hanging down beneath their pudenda, and stuffed with foure, five or six pound of bombast at the least.'

12A

12B

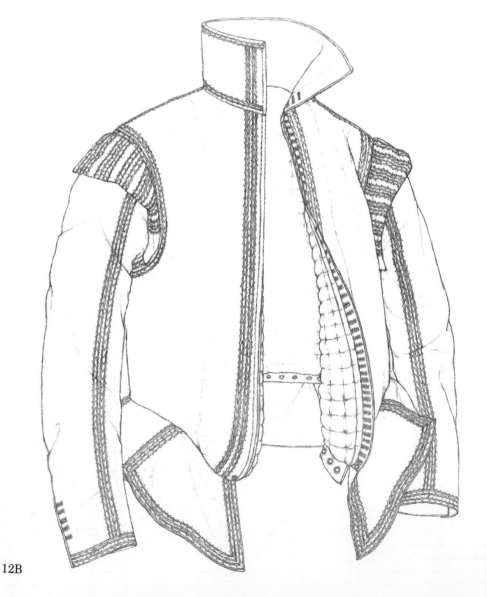

c.1600-5 DOUBLET AND TRUNK HOSE

GRIMSTHORPE AND DRUMMOND CASTLE TRUST LTD, ON LOAN TO THE VICTORIA AND ALBERT MUSEUM

DUBLET AND TRUNK HOSE IN PLE BROWN (PROBABLY GINALLY MULBERRY OURED) SILK, THE SATIN UND PATTERNED WITH NTRICATE IGN IN CUT VELVET

THREE PAIRS OF LINEN TAPE 9MM X 29.2CM (⅜ x 11½") WERE SEWN INSIDE FRONTS. ONLY ONE REMAINS. BOMBAST ON LEFT FRONT IS SET BACK 38MM (1½") TO ALLOW THE BUTTONHOLES TO FASTEN. ON RIGHT FRONT A BIAS CUT BINDING OF SELF FABRIC, TO WHICH THE 42 BUTTONS (ALL NOW MISSING) WERE SEWN, GOES OVER THE FRONT EDGE INCLUDING THE PADDING. IT IS 6MM (¼") WIDE ON R.S.

COLLAR IS 5MM (3/16") THICK AT LOWEST PART NEAR NECK.

FRONT COLLAR

THREE WORKED BUTTONHOLES AT BASE OF COLLAR

SLEEVE SEAM TO THIS POINT

WING TO THIS POINT

THERE IS A JOIN AT C.B. BENEATH THE R.BACK BRAID. THE YELLOW SELVEDGES ARE VISIBLE IN ONE PLACE, AS THE VELVET IS ROTTEN.

THE DOUBLET IS BACKED WITH A LAYER OF WHITE WOOLLEN CLOTH. INSIDE THIS IS A LINING OF WHITE FUSTIAN, PADDED WITH WHAT FEELS LIKE WOOL, BUT MAY BE COTTON WOOL.

THE DOUBLET IS TRIMMED WITH 8MM (5/16") BRAID WITH A3MM (⅛") GAP BETWEEN THE ROWS, MAKING A TOTAL WIDTH OF 20 MM (¾").

GUSSET SHAPE IN WHITE FUSTIAN FITS BETWEEN THE FACING AND EDGE OF LEFT FRONT, BY THE BUTTONHOLES. INSIDE BOTH FRONTS ARE FRAGMENTS OF PURPLE-BROWN SILK FACINGS 25MM (1") DEEP AT THE NECK, WIDENING TO 3.8CM (1½") ON THE LEFT FRONT AND 6.3CM (2½") ON THE RIGHT.

THE SLEEVES ARE INTERLINED WITH WHITE WOOL AND LINED WITH WHITE FUSTIAN. THERE ARE STRIPS OF PURPLE BROWN SILK BENEATH THE BUTTONHOLES AND WHERE THE BUTTONS WERE SEWN ON. ALL THE BUTTONS ARE NOW MISSING.

SHOULDER SEAM TO THIS MARK

LARGE AREAS OF THE DOUBLET AT TOP OF BACK AND SLEEVES HAVE ROTTED AWAY AND HAVE BEEN HEAVILY CONSERVED.

THE BUTTON HOLES ARE 20MM (¾") LONG WORKED WITH ROUND ENDS TOWARDS THE SEAM. THE OTHER ENDS ARE SQUARE.

C.B.

THE COLLAR IS MADE OF A LAYER OF COARSE, NATURAL COLOURED LINEN, HEAVY IN WEIGHT. PAD-STITCHED TO THIS IS ONE LAYER OF HEAVY WOOL ON TOP OF ANOTHER LAYER OF LINEN, CUT AWAY AT THE C.F. FOR THE BUTTONHOLES. ON TOP OF THIS, AT THE LOWER PART OF THE COLLAR, REACHING TO THE DOTTED LINE, IS PAD-STITCHED ANOTHER LAYER OF WOOL. OVER THIS IS A LAYER OF PURPLE BROWN SILK TAFFETA LINING, NOW ROTTEN. THE WOOL IS STRIPED PALE BLUE, RED YELLOW AND DARK BROWN IN THE WEFT AND GREEN IN THE WARP. IT IS QUITE HEAVILY MILLED.

SHOULDER SEAM TO THIS MARK

FRONT

SHOULDER WING IS FORMED OF LAYERS OF LINEN COVERED WITH PATTERNED VELVET AND TRIMMED WITH BRAID

THE CANIONS HAVE BEEN CONSERVED AND SOME PIECES OF LATER MATERIAL INSERTED. THIS SEEMS TO BE THE ORIGINAL SHAPE OF THE CANIONS. THEY ARE INTERLINED WITH WHITE WOOL AND BACKED WITH WHITE FUSTIAN.

JOIN IN FABRIC

CANION

JOIN ON RIGHT LEG ONLY

JOIN IN FABRIC

IT SEEMS AS IF THE LINING WAS MADE UP FIRST AND THE VELVET PUT OVER IT, AS THE SEAMS ARE SEWN FROM THE OUTSIDE. THIS JOIN WAS OPENED UNDER THE LEG AND A PIECE OF BLACK TWILLED COTTON INSERTED, PROBABLY DURING THE 19. THERE MAY ORIGINALLY HAVE BEEN AN OPENING HERE. THERE ARE NO TRACES OF HOOKS AND EYES LEFT.

CENTRE OF POCKET BAG

JOIN AND FOLD IN FABRIC

A 38 MM (1½") WIDE STRIP OF PURPLE BROWN SILK TAFFETA IS SEWN TO THE FUSTIAN BEHIND THE OPENING

JOIN AND FOLD IN FABRIC

OPEN ABOVE THIS MARK

APPROXIMATE SHAPE OF POCKET BAG MADE OF WHITE FUSTIAN, PATTERN TAKEN OF RIGHT SIDE ONLY. THE POCKET BAG HANGS BETWEEN THE FUSTIAN LINING AND WOOL AND VELVET LAYER

JOIN AND FOLD IN FABRIC

WORKED EYELET HOLES

THE FUSTIAN WAIST STRIP IS SET BACK NEARLY 25MM (1") FROM THE CENTRE FRONT TO ALLOW CLEARANCE FOR THE LACING HOLES AT THE FRONT

FRONT SKIRT TAB OVERLAPS TO THIS MARK

SECOND SKIRT TAB OVERLAPS TO THIS MARK

THIRD SKIRT TAB OVERLAPS TO THIS MARK

1

2

3

4

C.B.

THE OUTSIDE STRIP OF GOLD BRAID IS MISSING ON LEFT BACK, BUT STITCH HOLES REMAIN.

AT CENTRE BACK THE RIGHT SKIRT OVERLAPS THE LEFT.

FRONT

TO FOLD

C.B. TO FOLD

OPEN ABOVE THIS MARK

CENTRE BACK

THE WHITE FUSTIAN LINING OF THE BREECHES OR TRUNK HOSE IS MUCH SMALLER THAN THE VELVET AND PADDING. THE WAIST IS SLIGHTLY GATHERED TO EASE IT IN TO THE TOP OF THE WAISTBAND. IT IS HELD TO IT BY THE STRAIGHT STRIP OF BEIGE RIBBON BINDING. THE BOTTOM OF THE WAISTBAND REACHES TO THE DOTTED LINE.

GINALLY THE SKIRTS OR WAIST S, WERE INTERLINED WITH VY CANVAS, THEN LINED H PURPLE BROWN SILK FETA. THE SILK ST HAVE ROTTED THERE IS NOW A ER OF LINEN OVER CH ONE, PUT IN RING CONSERVATION RK.

FUSTIAN STRIP ROUND WAIST, INSIDE DOUBLET, INTERLINED WITH COARSE, HEAVY LINEN TO STIFFEN IT, FOR SUPPORTING THE BREECHES.

JOIN

A

X

A

VELVET WAISTBAND OF BREECHES, BACKED WITH WHITE LINEN. THE FUSTIAN BREECHES LINING REACHES TO TOP OF BAND. APPROX. 127 CM (50") WAIST.

SELVEDGE EDGE

THE BOTTOM OF THE LINING IS GATHERED UP TO FIT THE TOP OF THE CANION LINING

A LAYER OF WHITE WOOL, FAIRLY OPEN WEAVE, IS PLACED BELOW THE PATTERNED VELVET. THESE TWO LAYERS ARE WORKED TOGETHER TO MAKE THE BREECHES STAND OUT. BENEATH THIS IS A SMALLER LAYER OF COARSE LINEN OR HEMP, RATHER LIKE SACKING, AND THEN A LINING OF WHITE FUSTIAN

TOP OF THE ISTBAND IS UND WITH STRAIGHT GE SILK RIBBON DING, 5MM (3/16") ISHED WIDTH.

E SILK WAS IN A VERY AGILE CONDITION. ESE PATTERN SHAPES E APPROXIMATE AS EY WERE MEASURED EN THE SUIT WAS UNTED, RIGHT SIDE LY, TO AVOID HANDLING.

1:1 INCH

1:1 CM

CENTRE BACK

FLY FLAP ON THE RIGHT FRONT ONLY, IN PATTERNED VELVET BACKED WITH WHITE FUSTIAN

BEIGE SILK BINDING TO MATCH WAISTBAND

OPEN ABOVE X THIS POINT

TRUNK HOSE OR BREECHES

JOIN IN FABRIC

WORKED EYELET HOLES ON BOTH SIDES OF FRONT

x

x

x

x

JOIN IN FABRIC

JOIN IN FABRIC

Y

A

X= STITCHES MADE INSIDE BREECHES TO HOLD WOOL INTERLINING AND VELVET LAYERS TOGETHER IN LONG PLEATS. THERE MAY HAVE BEEN MORE STITCHES ORIGINALLY, BUT THESE ARE ALL THAT REMAIN ON THE RIGHT SIDE. THERE ARE FEWER ON THE LEFT.

B

THE LEG PLEATS IN TO FIT THE CANION 74 MM (29"). THE SEAM OF THE CANION MEETS POINT Y AT THE BACK.

THE WOVEN BRAID OF SILK AND METAL THREAD ON THE DOUBLET IS ALL OF THE SAME DESIGN, BUT SOME PARTS, E.G., CENTRE BACK AND ROUND THE SKIRTS, ARE OF GOLD THREAD AND YELLOW SILK. OTHER PARTS, E.G., ROUND NECK AND ON SLEEVES, ARE OF GOLD THREAD AND PURPLE BROWN SILK. THIS PURPLE BROWN SILK AND GOLD BRAID SEEMS TO SPARKLE MORE. THE SILVER THREAD IN THE OTHER BRAID HAS TARNISHED AND MAKES IT LOOK DULL.

THE POCKET SLIT IS BOUND WITH A STRAIGHT STRIP OF PATTERNED VELVET 6MM (¼") FINISHED WIDTH ON R.S. THERE ARE POCKETS ON BOTH SIDES.

JOIN IN FABRIC

JOIN IN FABRIC

© 1984 JANET ARNOLD

76 12C. The doublet is completely backed with a layer of white woollen cloth. Inside this is the lining of white fustian, padded with what feels like wool but may be cotton wool. Nothing can be seen. The fustian would have been cut a few inches longer than the doublet to allow for the amount taken up by the padding and quilting stitches. The padding, or bombast, thickens towards the front and a long fustian gusset is stitched between the outside of the padding and the edge of the left front by the buttonholes. It is 6 mm ($\frac{1}{4}$″) deep at the neck, widening to 22 mm ($\frac{7}{8}$″) below the waist. The bombast is held in position with long running stitches from the reverse side, only taking up small stitches on the fustian. These may be seen inside the doublet, giving a characteristic chequered appearance. Only one of three pairs of linen tapes sewn inside the centre front now remains. If this is a later addition, it seems to have replaced one which had broken off, as there are stitch marks which show the position of the others. It seems likely that the tapes were intended to hold the padding on both fronts butted together while the doublet was buttoned up. It would have been very difficult to fasten the doublet without them.

12D. The trunk-hose are interlined with white wool, fairly open in weave and quite springy. The velvet and wool are worked together as one layer. There is a smaller white fustian lining, made separately, inside the trunk-hose. Large fustian pocket bags hang between fustian lining and woollen interlining. These might have been stuffed with wadding or personal possessions to give extra fullness. John Bulwer, in his book *Anthropometamorphosis: Man Transform'd or The Artificial Changling* (1653) wrote that:

'. . . a Prisoner . . . who being to go before the Judge for a certaine cause he was accused of, it being at that time when the Law was in force against wearing Bayes

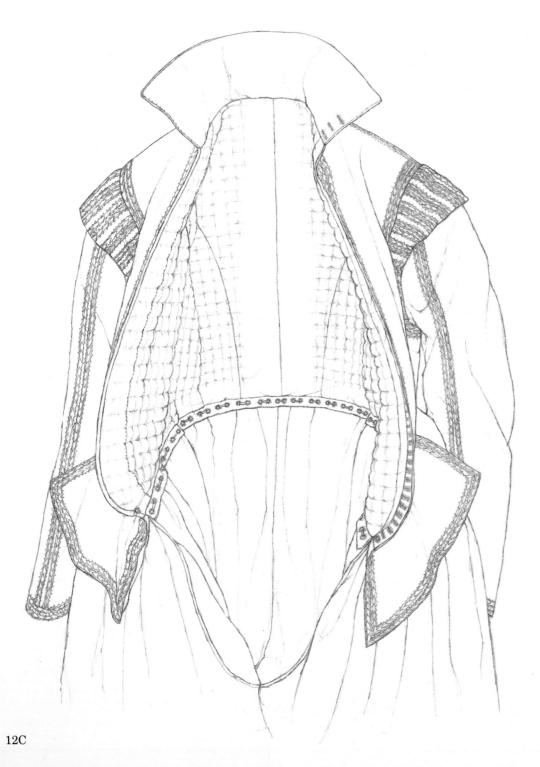

12C

12D

stuffed in their Breeches, and he then having stuffed his breeches very full, the Judges told him that he did weare his breeches contrary to the Law: who began to excuse himselfe of the offence, and endeavouring by little and little to discharge himselfe of that which he did weare within them, he drew out of his breeches a paire of Sheets, two Table Cloaths, ten Napkings, foure Shirts, a Brush, a Glasse, and a Combe, Night-caps, and other things of use saying (all the Hall being strewed with this furniture) your Highnesse may understand, that because I have no safer a store-house, these pockets do serve me for a roome to lay up my goods in, and though it be a straight prison, yet it is a store-house big enough for them, for I have many things more of value yet within it. And so his discharge was accepted and well laughed at, and they commanded him that he should not alter the furniture of his store-house, but that he should rid the Hall of his Stuffe, and keep them as it pleased him.'

12E.   The doublet skirts are lifted to show points threaded through eyelet holes at the waist. These are not worked in pairs: there are fifty holes in the waistband and sixty-two in the lacing strip inside the doublet waist. The waistband might apparently lie in front or behind the doublet lacing strip to suit the wearer. The doublet skirts would have concealed the ribbon ties. The cod-piece has been discarded and the front opening fastens with points through worked eyelet holes, backed with a large velvet flap. The opening is almost completely hidden by folds of material. The thigh-fitting extensions from the trunk-hose to the knee are canions. Separate stockings or nether stocks would be pulled up over the ends of the canions and often cross-gartered, or, if long and wide enough, the canions might be fastened over the stockings below the knee. Stockings were knitted by hand and also, after about 1600, on the stocking frame invented in 1589 by William Lee. Stubbes described them in his *Anatomie of Abuses* in 1583:
'Then have they nether-stocks to these gay hosen, not of cloth (though never so fine) for that is thought too base, but of Jarnsey worsted, silk, thred and such like, or else at the least of the finest yarn yt can be, so curiouslye knit with open seam down the leg, with quirks and clocks about the ancles, and sometimes (haply) interlaced with gold or silver threds, as is wonderful to behold. And to such insolency and outrage it is now growen, that every one (almost) though otherwise verie poor having scarce fortie shillings of wages by the yeer will be sure to have two or three paire of these silk nether-stocks, or else of the finest yarne that may be got.'

12F.   Velvet and interlining of white wool worked together as one layer makes the long darts above knee level very stiff. This helps to hold out the rounded shape of the trunk-hose. The effect may be seen in many examples of tomb sculpture of this date.

12E

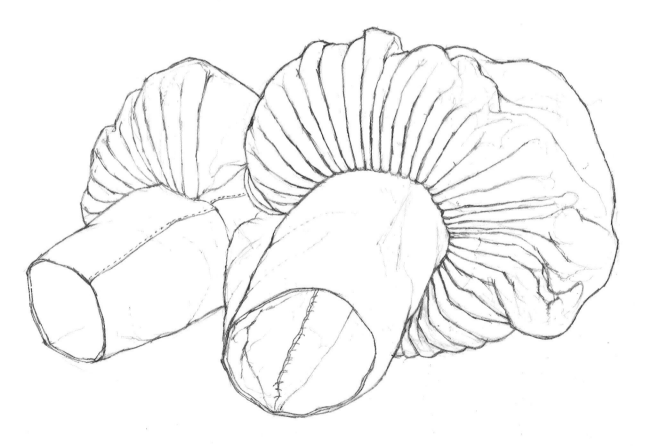

12F

13A.   A doublet in bright green satin, now slightly faded to yellowish green, with surface decoration of cutting and pinking, purchased in 1936, together with a suit of armour, from the Duke of Sachsen–Altenburg. It was said to be an arming doublet but the sleeves are not padded so this is not certain. It is similar in style to a red patterned velvet doublet, with matching breeches cut full at the waist and close below the knee, at the Niedersächsische Landesgalerie, Hanover. This suit was worn by

Herzog Moritz von Sachsen–Lauenburg, who died in 1612, and is illustrated in *Kostüme des 16. und 17. Jahrhunderts* by Eva Nienholdt. The green satin doublet is heavily padded and shows the continued use of the peascod belly by some men in Germany, even when the waist level had started to rise. The satin is decorated with an intricate pattern of parallel, interlocking pricked lines. Between them are rows of tiny pinks and in the centre of each pricked oval one large cut which reveals a layer of matching green lightweight silk beneath.

13B.   The front and sides of the doublet are padded with cotton wool laid on a foundation of white linen and stitched into position. The stitches are set in rows 13 mm (½″) apart from neck to waist and 16 mm (⅝″) apart round the body. The lightweight green silk and pinked green satin layers are mounted on top, worked together as one layer of material. The padded area on the left front is made separately from the buttonholes. The green silk layer is taken out to cover the padding, while the satin is backed with a strip of stiffened linen for the buttonholes. When buttons and buttonholes are fastened the two padded edges are butted together and lie flat beneath them.

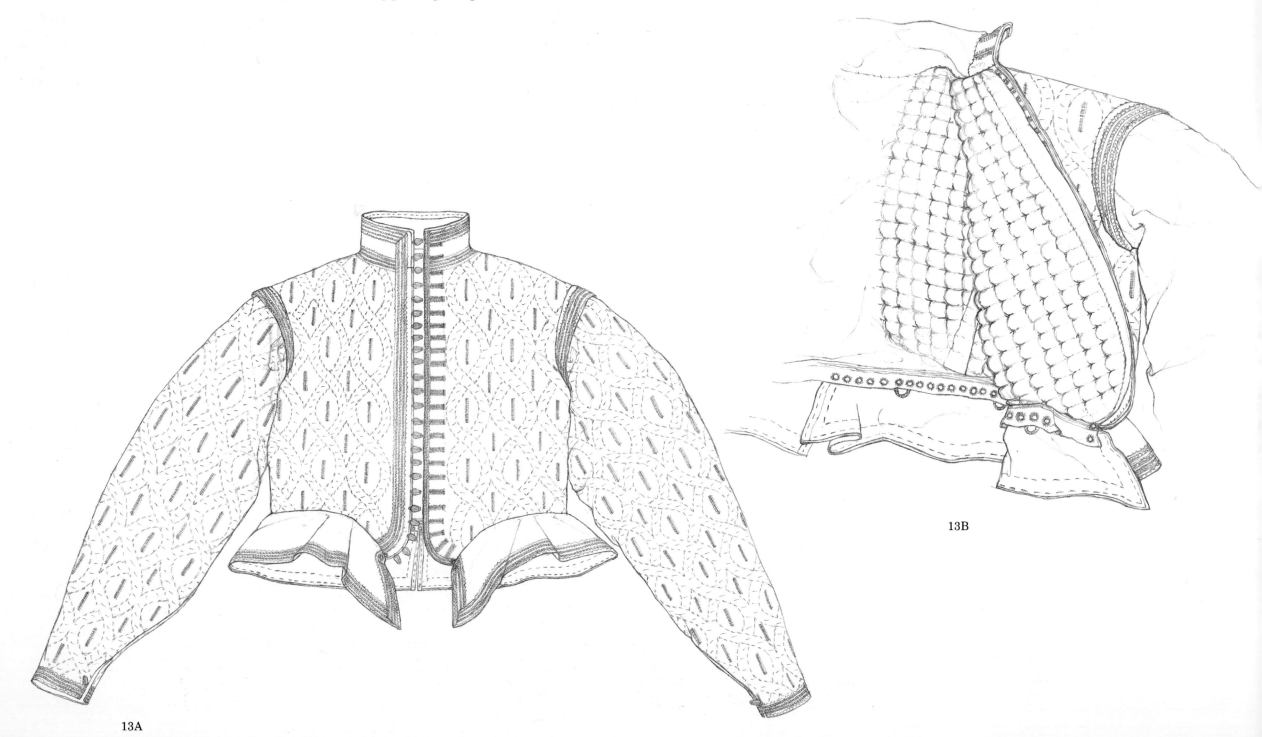

13A

13B

BLET IN BRIGHT GREEN SATIN, NOW SLIGHTLY YELLOWISH GREEN, BUT ORIGINALLY,
M THE UNFADED AREAS, WITH MORE BLUE IN IT. THE SILK FOR WEAVING WAS NOT
NLY DYED. THE COLOURS OF THE THREADS RANGE FROM YELLOWS THROUGH TO DEEP
ISH GREENS TO GIVE THIS RICH BRIGHT GREEN. THE DOUBLET IS CUT AND PINKED IN TWO
ES IN A DECORATIVE PATTERN. BENEATH THE CUTS MAY BE SEEN THE LINING OF MATCHING
EEN SILK. THIS IS OF A CHEAPER QUALITY
H NUMEROUS FLAWS. THIS TOO IS WOVEN WITH
DIFFERENT COLOURS OF GREEN AND YELLOW
NG THE FINAL COLOUR, BUT IT IS NOT A SHOT
FETA. THE WEIGHT IS SIMILAR TO JAP SILK.
HE FRONT AND SIDE OF THE DOUBLET ARE BOMBASTED
DDED WITH COTTON WOOL). THIS IS LAID ON A FOUNDATION
WHITE LINEN AND STITCHED INTO POSITION. THE LIGHTWEIGHT
EN SILK AND PINKED GREEN SATIN ARE MOUNTED ON
, WORKED TOGETHER AS ONE PIECE OF MATERIAL.

GREEN BRAID JUST OVER 13 MM (½") WIDE IS USED FOR TRIMMING

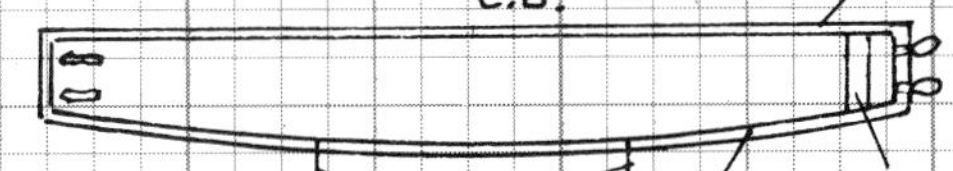

EDGE BOUND WITH SELF SATIN ON
STRAIGHT GRAIN, FINISHED WIDTH
3 MM (⅛").

C.B.

TO SHOULDER   BRAID

13 MM (½") BRAID
COVERS SEAM, HALF OVER
COLLAR, HALF OVER
DOUBLET NECKLINE

THE COLLAR IS INTERFACED WITH PALE BLUE STIFF
GLAZED LINEN, AND LINED WITH GREEN LIGHT-
WEIGHT SILK TO MATCH THE REST OF THE DOUBLET, AS
FAR AS THE BUTTONHOLES.

13 MM (½") BRAID OVER
SHOULDER SEAM.

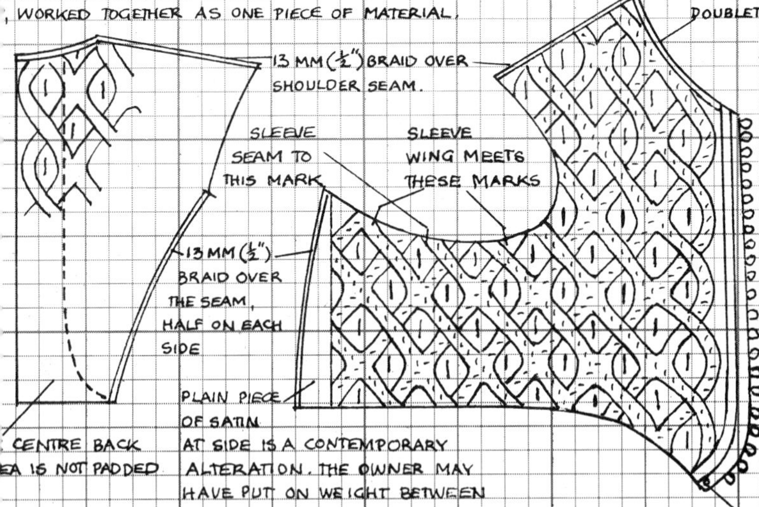

THE BUTTONS ARE 13 MM (½")
HIGH X 13MM (½") IN DIAMETER.
THEY ARE MADE OF WOOD
SLIGHTLY TAPERED TOWARDS
THE TOP. THE CENTRE OF
EACH IS HOLLOW AND THE
GREEN SILK CORDS ARE
PULLED THROUGH WITH A
TECHNIQUE STILL IN USE
FOR PASSEMENTERIE.
5MM (³⁄₁₆") LONG SHANKS
ARE WORKED IN LINEN
THREAD. THE BUTTONHOLES
ARE 22MM (⅞") LONG, WITH
SQUARE ENDS, WORKED VERY
NEATLY IN GREEN SILK.

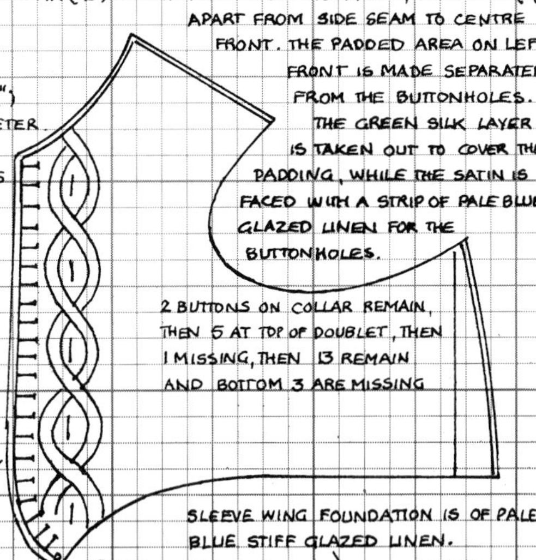

FOR THE BOMBAST, OR PADDING, THE STITCHES ARE SET
13 MM (½") APART FROM NECK TO WAIST, AND 16MM (⅝")
APART FROM SIDE SEAM TO CENTRE
FRONT. THE PADDED AREA ON LEFT
FRONT IS MADE SEPARATELY
FROM THE BUTTONHOLES.
THE GREEN SILK LAYER
IS TAKEN OUT TO COVER THE
PADDING, WHILE THE SATIN IS
FACED WITH A STRIP OF PALE BLUE
GLAZED LINEN FOR THE
BUTTONHOLES.

2 BUTTONS ON COLLAR REMAIN,
THEN 5 AT TOP OF DOUBLET, THEN
1 MISSING, THEN 13 REMAIN
AND BOTTOM 3 ARE MISSING

SLEEVE
SEAM TO
THIS MARK

SLEEVE
WING MEETS
THESE MARKS

13 MM (½") BRAID OVER
THE SEAM,
HALF ON EACH
SIDE

PLAIN PIECE
OF SATIN

SLEEVE WING FOUNDATION IS OF PALE
BLUE STIFF GLAZED LINEN.

BACK

CENTRE BACK
EA IS NOT PADDED
AT SIDE IS A CONTEMPORARY
ALTERATION. THE OWNER MAY
HAVE PUT ON WEIGHT BETWEEN
FITTINGS, OR THE TAILOR MAY
SIMPLY HAVE CUT IT TOO SMALL.

WORKED EYELET HOLES IN GREEN SILK MAY NOT HAVE
BEEN USED. THEY ARE VERY CLOSE TO THE WAIST
SEAM AND SHOW NO SIGNS OF WEAR.

BRAID

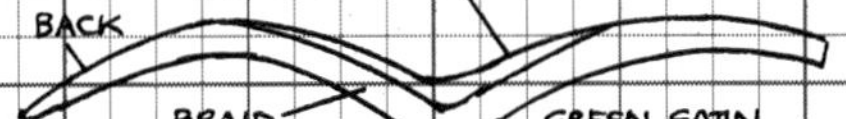

GREEN SATIN
IS MOUNTED ON TOP.
BRAID ON EDGE HELPS TO
STIFFEN IT FURTHER.

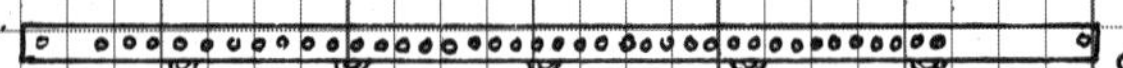

DOTTED LINE MARKS
POSITION OF WING

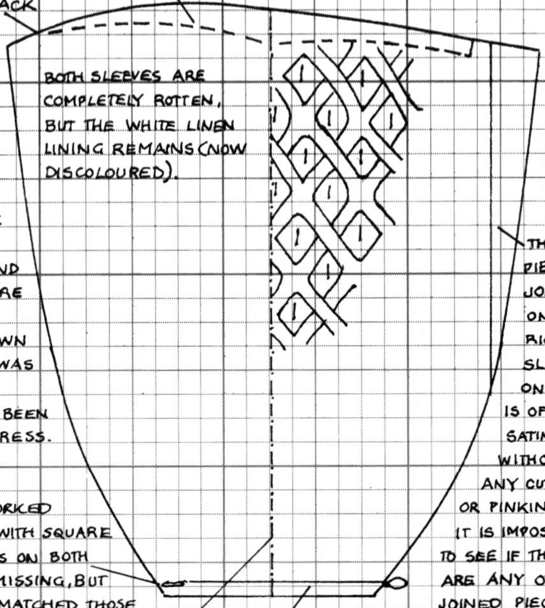

BACK

C.F.

LACING STRIP OF TWO LAYERS OF WHITE LINEN, SEAMED AT TOP AND
BOTTOM, STITCHED TO THE WAIST. 38 EYELET HOLES ON THE RIGHT FRONT
40 ON LEFT FRONT, ALL WORKED WITH LINEN THREAD. METAL HOOKS, NOW
RUSTY, ARE SEWN ON AS WELL. THE HOOKS ARE OF BLACK
METAL AND SEEM TO BE MADE OF SOME KIND OF COILED
WIRE. A STRIP OF GREEN STRIPED SELVEDGE CUT FROM THE
SATIN, 6MM (¼") FINISHED WIDTH, IS STITCHED OVER THE JOIN
AT THE WAIST.

WHEN THE PADDING IS ATTACHED TO RIGHT FRONT, THE GREEN SILK GOES ROUND TO THE
INSIDE FOR 9MM (⅜"). THE GREEN SATIN STOPS AT THE EDGE AND A STRAIGHT
STRIP OF GREEN SATIN, 3MM (⅛") FINISHED WIDTH, STARTING FROM THE TOP AND
EDGE OF THE COLLAR, IS STITCHED DOWN THE CENTRE FRONT. BESIDE THIS ARE
SEWN THE BUTTONS. SOME PADDING ON THE RIGHT BACK IS MISSING.
THE STITCHES ARE STILL THERE. A DEEP TUCK WAS TAKEN IN THE BACK, SEWN
WITH GREEN SILK AND WHITE LINEN THREAD, BADLY COBBLED. THIS WAS
PROBABLY PUT IN DURING THE LATE EIGHTEENTH CENTURY. THE
DOUBLET MAY HAVE BEEN
WORN FOR FANCY DRESS.

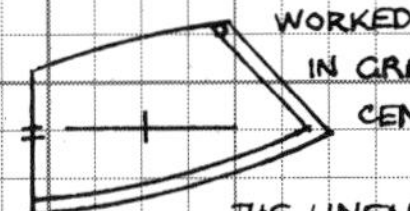

WORKED EYELET HOLE
IN GREEN SILK AT
CENTRE FRONT

THIS
JOIN

C.F.

THIS
PIECE IS
JOINED
ON THE
RIGHT
SLEEVE
ONLY. IT
IS OF PLAIN
SATIN,
WITHOUT
ANY CUTTING
OR PINKING.
IT IS IMPOSSIBLE
TO SEE IF THERE
ARE ANY OTHER
JOINED PIECES
AS THE SLEEVES
HAVE ALMOST
DISINTEGRATED.

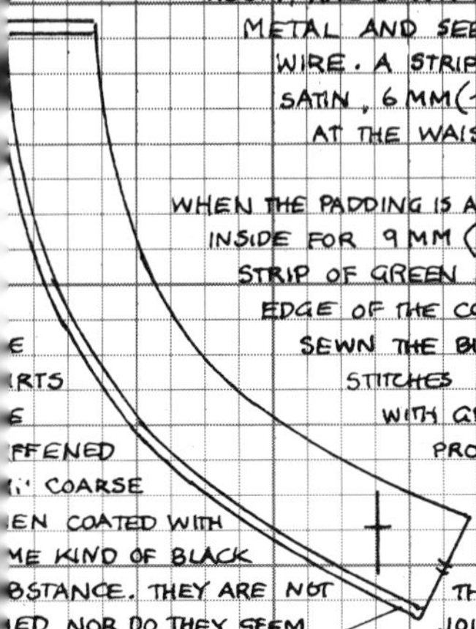

BOTH SLEEVES ARE
COMPLETELY ROTTEN,
BUT THE WHITE LINEN
LINING REMAINS (NOW
DISCOLOURED).

RTS
E
FFENED
N COARSE
EN COATED WITH
ME KIND OF BLACK
STANCE. THEY ARE NOT
ED, NOR DO THEY SEEM
HAVE BEEN.
AID ROUND
GE OF SKIRTS

IS SIMPLY
TO USE UP SMALL PIECES
OF MATERIAL, NOT FOR
CONSTRUCTION.

THE LINEN LINING IS CUT A
FRACTION LARGER THAN THE
SATIN TO ALLOW FOR THE COTTON
WOOL PADDING WHICH IS 19 MM
(¾") THICK. THERE ARE SMALL JOINS
IN THE LINING, AS IN THE SATIN, AT THE
SIDE FRONT.

25 MM (1") WORKED
BUTTONHOLE WITH SQUARE
END. BUTTONS ON BOTH
WRISTS ARE MISSING, BUT
WOULD HAVE MATCHED THOSE
ON FRONT.
JOIN IN GREEN
LIGHTWEIGHT SILK LAYER
WHICH IS VISIBLE AS SATIN IS ROTTEN

BRAID ON
END OF
SLEEVE FORMS
WRISTBAND

1:1 INCH   SIDE FRONT
1:1 CM

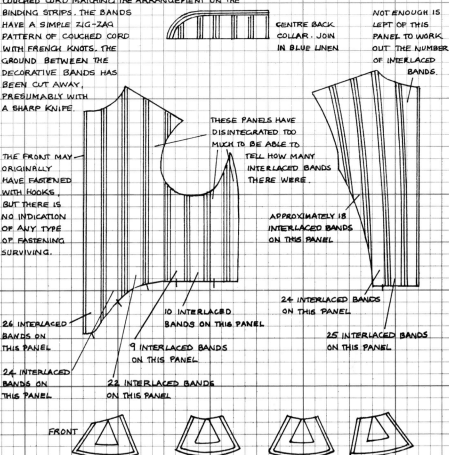

A JERKIN WHICH IS IN AN EXTREMELY FRAGILE CONDITION; SO MUCH HAS DISINTEGRATED THAT
IT IS DIFFICULT TO SEE HOW IT WAS MADE. THE PATTERN HAS BEEN TAKEN FROM THE
REMAINING FRAGMENTS, WITH AS LITTLE HANDLING AS POSSIBLE. ALL THE EDGES ARE
NOW BOUND WITH PALE BLUE SILK AND THE COLLAR IS JOINED TO THE NECKLINE TO FALL
AS A PETER PAN COLLAR. THIS RESTORATION WORK WAS PROBABLY CARRIED OUT EARLY
IN THE PRESENT CENTURY.
THE SURFACE IS CONSTRUCTED FROM NARROW VERTICAL PANELS OF BLACK SATIN EACH BOUND WITH
BIAS-CUT STRIPS OF BLACK SATIN, FINISHED WIDTH 6MM (¼"). THESE ARE DECORATED WITH THREE
ROWS OF COUCHED CORD, A NARROW ONE, 1MM (¹⁄₃₂) ON EITHER SIDE OF A THICKER ONE 1.5MM
(¹⁄₁₆") IN DIAMETER. THE PANELS ARE JOINED EDGE TO EDGE, THE STRIPS BUTTED TOGETHER. EACH
PANEL IS DECORATED WITH A PATTERN OF INTERLACED BANDS WHICH ARE DEFINED BY LINES OF
COUCHED CORD MATCHING THE ARRANGEMENT ON THE
BINDING STRIPS. THE BANDS
HAVE A SIMPLE ZIG-ZAG
PATTERN OF COUCHED CORD
WITH FRENCH KNOTS. THE
GROUND BETWEEN THE
DECORATIVE BANDS HAS
BEEN CUT AWAY,
PRESUMABLY WITH
A SHARP KNIFE.

CENTRE BACK
COLLAR. JOIN
IN BLUE LINEN

NOT ENOUGH IS
LEFT OF THIS
PANEL TO WORK
OUT THE NUMBER
OF INTERLACED
BANDS.

THESE PANELS HAVE
DISINTEGRATED TOO
MUCH TO BE ABLE TO
TELL HOW MANY
INTERLACED BANDS
THERE WERE.

APPROXIMATELY 18
INTERLACED BANDS
ON THIS PANEL

THE FRONT MAY
ORIGINALLY
HAVE FASTENED
WITH HOOKS,
BUT THERE IS
NO INDICATION
OF ANY TYPE
OF FASTENING
SURVIVING.

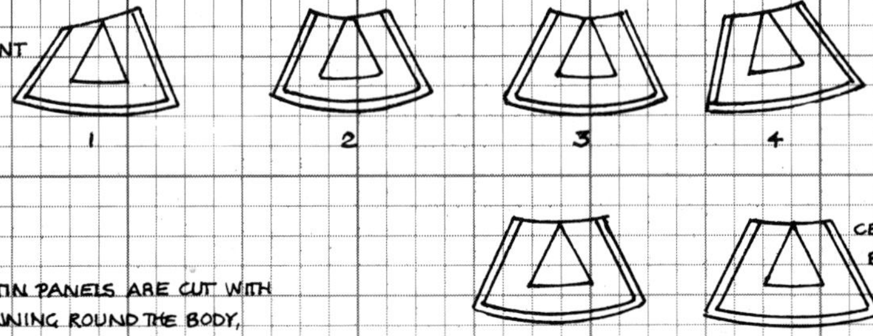

26 INTERLACED
BANDS ON
THIS PANEL

24 INTERLACED
BANDS ON
THIS PANEL

10 INTERLACED
BANDS ON THIS PANEL

9 INTERLACED BANDS
ON THIS PANEL

22 INTERLACED BANDS
ON THIS PANEL

24 INTERLACED BANDS
ON THIS PANEL

25 INTERLACED BANDS
ON THIS PANEL

FRONT

1   2   3   4

5   6

CENTRE
BACK

THE BLACK SATIN PANELS ARE CUT WITH
THE GRAIN RUNNING ROUND THE BODY,
SO THE CUT OUT AREAS ARE MOSTLY
ON THE BIAS GRAIN AND DO NOT FRAY TOO
BADLY. THE AREA TO BE CUT WAS PROBABLY
BRUSHED WITH GLUE SIZE ON THE BACK TO
PREVENT FRAYING. THIS LAYER OF CUT AND
EMBROIDERED SATIN IS THEN MOUNTED OVER
A LAYER OF BLACK SILK. MOST OF THIS HAS NOW
DISINTEGRATED AND ONLY A FEW FRAGMENTS REMAIN.
THE BLUE LINEN FOUNDATION BENEATH THESE LAYERS IS
PIECED TOGETHER AND HAS FADED BADLY IN SOME AREAS.

THE TABBED SKIRTS ARE
EMBROIDERED IN THE SAME
WAY AS THE BODY OF THE JERKIN
AND STITCHED TO THE WAIST
BETWEEN THE MARKS.

© 1984 JANET ARNOLD

c1590–1600 Hessisches Landesmuseum, Darmstadt

14.   A jerkin of embroidered black satin in a very fragile condition, which has undergone a considerable amount of restoration in the late nineteenth or early twentieth century. Its early provenance is not known. There is some difficulty in describing the original appearance of the jerkin but it has been included here as the decoration relates to clothes made of interlaced embroidered bands, worn by both men and women, depicted in Hilliard's miniatures (Figs. 153–4) and other portraits. It is not always easy to tell how the tailor achieved the effect of strapwork. In this one surviving example

the surface is constructed from narrow vertical panels of black satin, each bound with strips of black satin cut on the bias. These strips are decorated with three rows of couched cord. The panels are joined edge to edge, the strips butted together. Each panel is decorated with a pattern of interlaced bands which are defined by lines of couched cord. The bands have a simple zigzag pattern of couched cord with French knots. The ground between the bands has been cut away, presumably with a sharp knife, giving the effect of strapwork. Originally there was a layer of fine black silk beneath but most of this has rotted away.

c1610 Germanisches Nationalmuseum, Nürnberg

15.   A padded doublet, of unknown provenance, made of shot silk, described in the sixteenth century as 'changeable taffeta'. The rich blue warp and golden-yellow weft give the effect of rich russet with a blue bloom in unfaded areas, but the rest of the doublet now appears to be soft green with a blue or yellowish bloom, depending on the light. The silk is pinked in a trellis design which has cut the warp threads leaving the yellow wefts standing out, in some cases uncut. In the centre of each diamond shape are four diagonal cuts. The doublet is interlined with pale yellow linen and heavily

padded with cotton wool. This is placed inside a white linen lining and quilted into position with stitches set about 19 mm ($\frac{3}{4}$") apart from neck to waist and 22 mm ($\frac{7}{8}$") apart round the body. Almost all the cotton wool has been removed from the left front and the back but the stitch holes remain. The padding is made separately on the left front so that the buttons and buttonholes may be fastened: the edges of the padded lining are butted together and lie flat beneath the centre front.

14

15

c.1610 PADDED DOUBLET   GERMANISCHES NATIONALMUSEUM, NÜRNBERG. T1635

DOUBLET IS MADE OF SHOT (CHANGEABLE) SILK TAFFETA, WITH A RICH BLUE
[W]ARP AND GOLDEN YELLOW WEFT, WHICH GIVES THE EFFECT OF RICH RUSSET WITH
[B]LUE BLOOM IN SEVERAL AREAS UNDER THE SHOULDER WINGS. THE REST OF
[THE] DOUBLET NOW APPEARS AS A SOFT GREEN WITH A BLUE OR YELLOWISH BLOOM,
[DEP]ENDING ON THE LIGHT. THE SILK IS PINKED IN A TRELLIS
[DES]IGN WHICH HAS CUT THE WARP
[THR]EADS, LEAVING THE YELLOW WEFTS
[STA]NDING OUT. IN SOME CASES
[ARE] CUT. IN THE CENTRE OF
[EAC]H DIAMOND SHAPE ARE
[FOU]R DIAGONAL CUTS ACROSS
[WA]RP AND WEFT THREADS.
[THE] YELLOW THREADS HAVE
[COM]E TO THE SURFACE.

[THE] DOUBLET IS INTERLINED
[WIT]H PALE YELLOW LINEN. THE
[WHI]TE LINEN LINING IS CUT
[SLI]GHTLY LARGER THAN
[THE] DOUBLET PATTERN
[SHA]PES TO ALLOW FOR
[COT]TON WOOL WADDING.

[THE] BUTTONHOLES ARE
[WOR]KED WITH A 28MM (1⅛")
[WIDE] STRIP OF LINEN AND
[GRA]SS GREEN SILK OVER IT,
[RIG]HT TOGETHER WITH
[YEL]LOW SILK DOWN THE EDGE.
[THE] PADDED LINING IS
[COV]ERED OVER THE EDGE
[WIT]H GREEN SILK AND
[CAU]GHT DOWN AT THE END
[OF] THE BUTTONHOLES, SO THAT
[THE] BUTTONS MAY BE
[FAS]TENED.

[THE] 13MM (½") LONG BUTTON-
[HO]LES ARE WORKED IN THICK
[YEL]LOW SILK, SIMILAR TO
[MO]DERN BUTTONHOLE TWIST.
[TH]E BRAID ACTS AS
[THE] SQUARE ENDS
[TO] PREVENT
[STR]ETCHING.

[THE] TABS OF THE DOUBLET SKIRTS ARE INTERLINED WITH LINEN AND
[LIN]ED WITH BRIGHT GRASS GREEN SILK, HEMMED DOWN ROUND THE
[ED]GES WITH YELLOW SILK THREAD. THEY ARE STITCHED TO THE DOUBLET
[WA]IST, OVERLAPPING EACH OTHER SLIGHTLY FROM FRONT TO BACK.

[THE] EYELET HOLES FOR LACES AT THE
[BO]TTOM OF THE DOUBLET AT THE
[FR]ONT AND AT THE TOP OF THE FRONT
[WA]IST TAB ARE WORKED IN LINEN
[THR]EAD, OVER DOUBLE LINEN
[THR]EAD TO MAKE A FIRM EDGE.

CENTRE FRONT

CENTRE BACK COLLAR PROBABLY
TO FOLD, BUT COVERED BY BRAID
SO IT CANNOT BE SEEN.

ON LEFT SIDE, BRAID IS ON THE EDGE. ON RIGHT SIDE
IT IS SET BACK 9 MM (⅜") TO ALLOW FOR BUTTON STAND.

BRAID OVER THE
SHOULDER SEAM

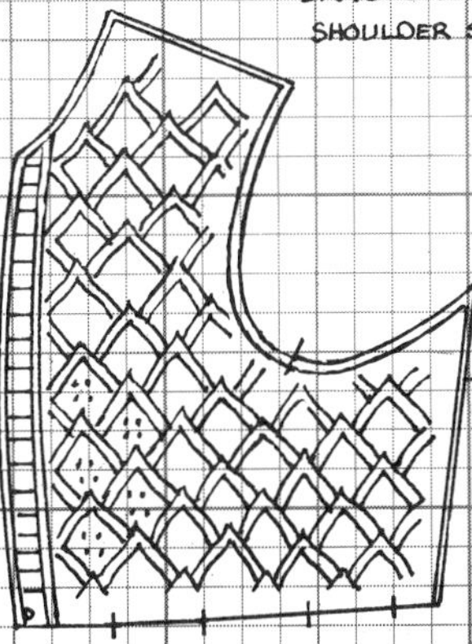

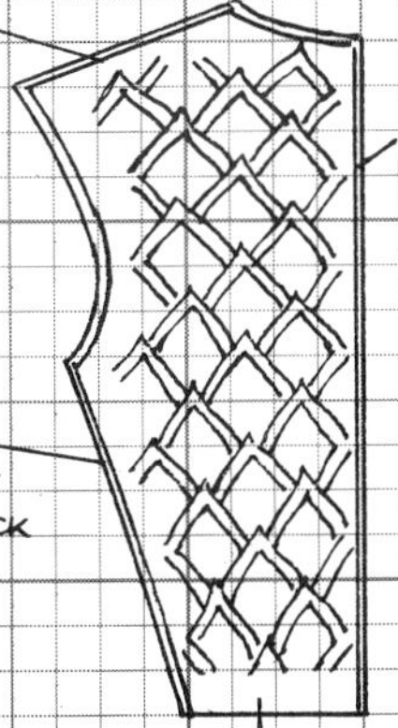

BRAID STITCHED
DOWN THE CENTRE
BACK, POSSIBLY
CONCEALING
A JOIN.

BRAID
OVER
THE
SIDE BACK
SEAM

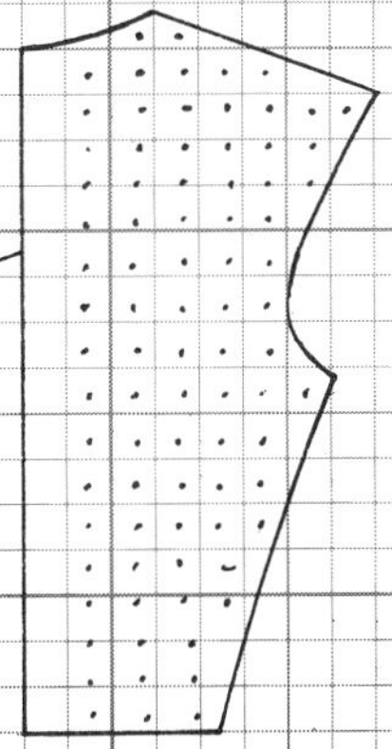

WAIST LEVEL
FRONT
SET BACK 6MM (¼")
FROM CENTRE FRONT
CENTRE BACK
TO FOLD
TO FOLD

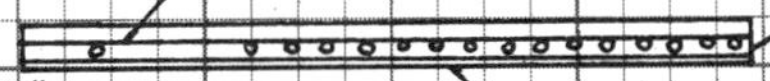

A LACING STRIP 22MM (⅞"), FINISHED WIDTH, TO ATTACH BREECHES WITH POINTS, OR
LACES, IS STITCHED TO WAISTLINE OF DOUBLET. IT IS MADE OF LINEN TO MATCH THE DOUBLET
LINING, INTERLINED WITH HEAVYWEIGHT LINEN. A 6 MM (¼") FINISHED WIDTH, STRIP OF LINEN
IS SEWN OVER THE JOIN. THE DOUBLET LINING IS HEMMED DOWN ON TOP OF THIS. THERE ARE
A FEW TUFTS OF COARSE LINEN THREAD (ALMOST LIKE STRING) ON THE BOTTOM EDGE OF THE STRIP, AND
HOLES WHERE THERE
WERE MORE.

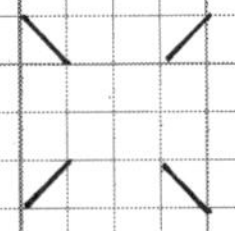

ACTUAL SIZE AND ARRANGEMENT
OF SETS OF FOUR DIAGONAL
CUTS IN THE TRELLIS DESIGN,
CARRIED OUT ON THE SHOT
SILK TAFFETA.

ACTUAL SIZE OF
BUTTON AND LINEN
SHANK.

ACTUAL SIZE OF TABLET WOVEN BRAID. THE
GOLDEN YELLOW AND PINKISH PURPLE SILK
THREADS HAVE NOW FADED TO SOFT YELLOWISH
BEIGE.

1:1 INCH
1:1 CENTIMETRE

THE COLLAR IS NOT VERY STIFF. IT SEEMS TO BE TWO LAYERS OF LINEN
PAD-STITCHED TOGETHER, BUT THERE MAY BE ANOTHER LAYER OF FINE
LINEN BETWEEN THEM. THE COLLAR IS COVERED ON THE OUTSIDE
WITH PINKED SHOT SILK AND INSIDE WITH PLAIN GREEN SILK. THIS
LINING HAS ROTTED AND A PIECE OF TURQUOISE SILK WAS STITCHED
IN TO CONSERVE IT DURING THE LATE NINETEENTH CENTURY. AT THE
SAME TIME A LOOP WAS PUT IN AT THE CENTRE BACK NECK.

THE COTTON WOOL WADDING WAS TESTED BY ERIKA WEILAND AND THE
TABLET WOVEN BRAID WAS EXAMINED BY ANNELIESE STREITER
IN THE TEXTILE CONSERVATION WORKSHOP.

CENTRE BACK TO FOLD

SHOULDER
WING TO
THESE
MARKS

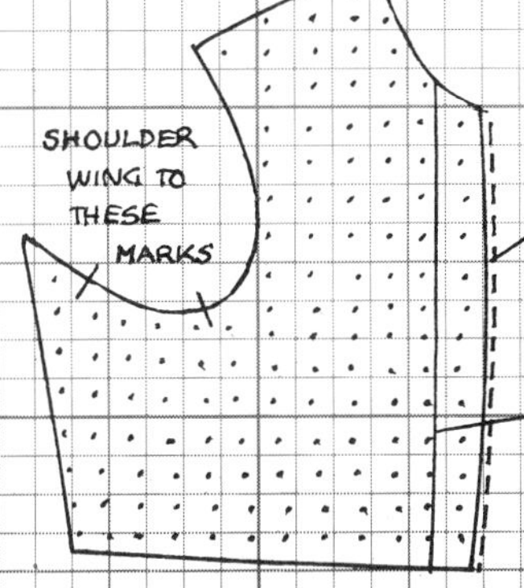

CENTRE FRONT OF
DOUBLET INDICATED
BY DOTTED LINE

FRONT EDGE OF
PADDED WHITE LINEN
LINING COVERED WITH
BIAS CUT GRASS GREEN SILK
TO THIS LINE.

A SMOOTH LAYER OF COTTON WOOL WADDING, OR BOMBAST,
IS PLACED INSIDE THE WHITE LINEN LINING AND QUILTED INTO
POSITION WITH STITCHES SET 19 MM (¾") AND 22 MM (⅞")
APART LENGTHWISE AND 22 MM (⅞") - 25MM (1") APART ACROSS
BACK AND CHEST. ALMOST ALL THE WADDING HAS BEEN REMOVED
FROM LEFT FRONT AND BACK, BUT STITCH
HOLES REMAIN.

SHOULDER SEAM
TO THIS MARK

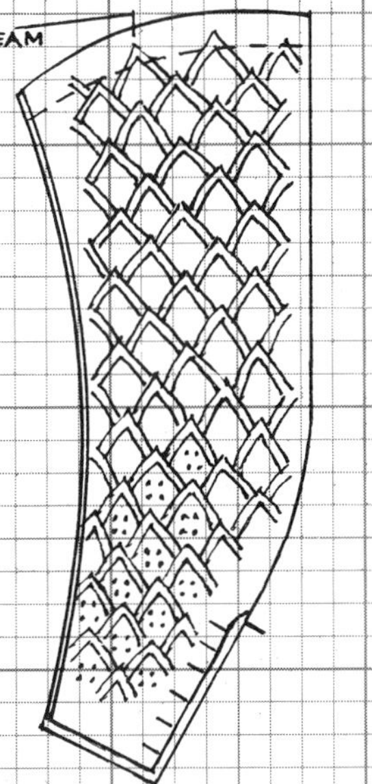

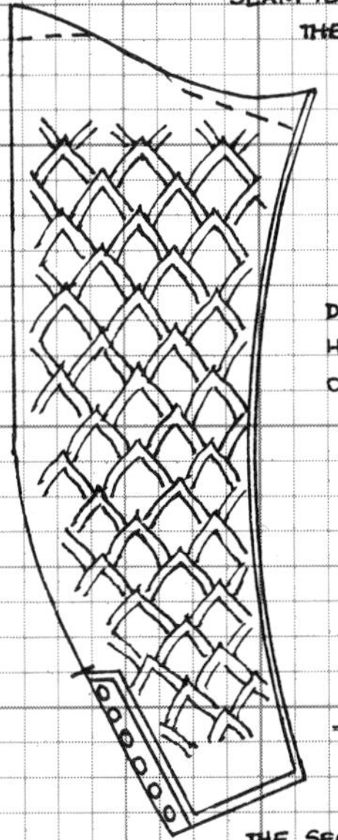

FRONT
SHOULDER SEAM MEETS THIS MARK 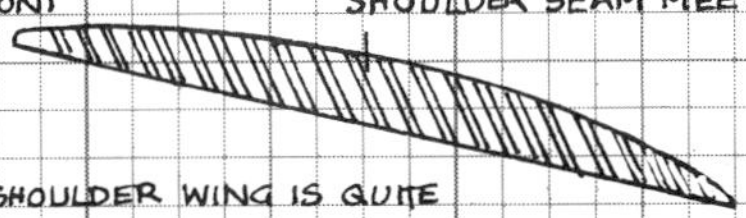
BACK

THE SHOULDER WING IS QUITE
STIFF. LINEN MATCHING THE DOUBLET
LINING MAY BE SEEN THROUGH THE SILK IN A FEW
PLACES. THERE IS PROBABLY A DOUBLE LAYER
WITH HEAVY WEIGHT LINEN BETWEEN. THE
WING IS COVERED WITH SHOT SILK AND BRAID
MOUNTED ON TOP. THIS IS FOLDED UNDER THE
EDGE FOR 6MM (¼") AND THEN FACED WITH A
PLAIN STRIP OF SHOT SILK TAFFETA.

THE BUTTONS ARE MADE WITH A WOODEN FOUNDATION 6MM (¼") DEEP
X 6MM (¼") IN DIAMETER. TWO YELLOW SILK THREADS, BORDERED WITH A
BLUE THREAD ON EACH SIDE, ARE WORKED OVER THE FOUNDATION IN
A BASKET WEAVE PATTERN. THIS SILK HAS NOW FADED TO BEIGE.
THE BUTTONS ARE SEWN ON WITH 5MM (³⁄₁₆") LINEN THREAD SHANKS.

SHOULDER SEAM
MEETS THIS POINT

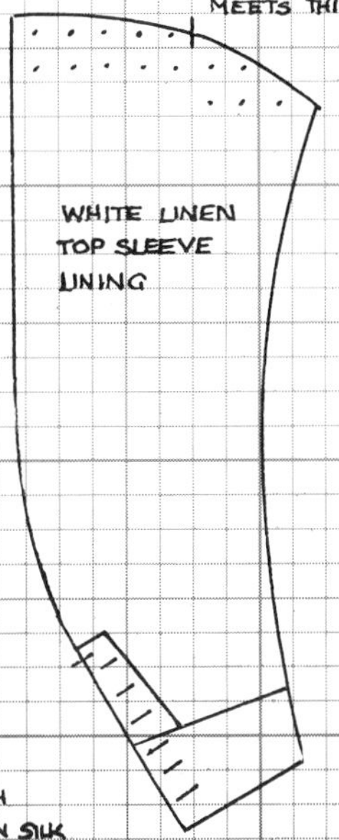

WHITE LINEN
TOP SLEEVE
LINING

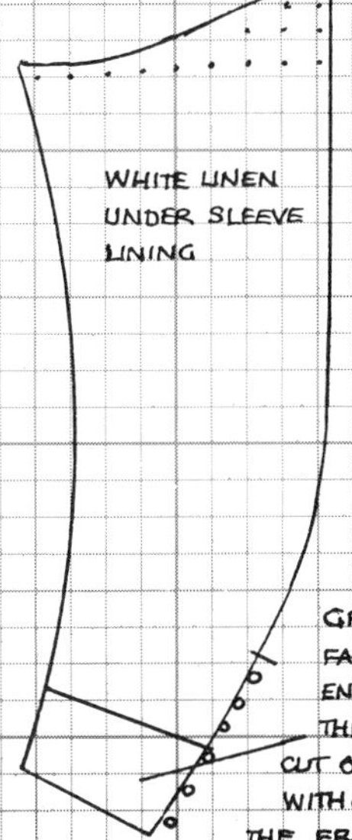

WHITE LINEN
UNDER SLEEVE
LINING

GRASS GREEN SILK
FACINGS AT THE
END OF THE SLEEVE.
THE BOTTOM PIECE IS
CUT ON THE CROSS,
WITHOUT A JOIN ON
THE FRONT SEAM.

THE SLEEVE IS INTERLINED WITH THE
SAME PALE YELLOW LINEN AS THE BODY
OF THE DOUBLET. IT IS LINED WITH WHITE
(NOW SLIGHTLY DISCOLOURED) LINEN. THE
TOP OF THE SLEEVE LINING IS LIGHTLY
PADDED WITH COTTON WOOL. THE INNER
SEAM IS JOINED UP AND THEN
THE LINING PUT INTO THE
SLEEVE AND THE
OUTER SEAM
HEMMED DOWN. ALL
THE RAW EDGES ARE
THUS CONCEALED.

DOTTED LINE OVER SLEEVE
HEAD INDICATES POSITION
OF SHOULDER WING

THE TOP TWO BUTTONS ARE
MISSING ON THE DOUBLET
FRONT.

THE SECOND BUTTON UP FROM
THE WRIST IS MISSING ON THE RIGHT SLEEVE, WHILE
THE SECOND BUTTON DOWN FROM THE TOP IS OF THE SAME DESIGN AS THE OTHERS BUT CARRIED
OUT IN BLUE SILK, PRESUMABLY A LATER REPLACEMENT. IT MAY HAVE BEEN A CLOSE MATCH
ORIGINALLY, BUT NOW LOOKS VERY DIFFERENT FROM THE OTHERS, WHICH HAVE FADED
MORE. ALL THE BUTTONS STILL
REMAIN ON THE LEFT SLEEVE.

© 1984 JANET ARNOLD

c1610 Germanisches Nationalmuseum, Nürnberg

16. A youth's doublet of cream-coloured leather with a suede finish, purchased in 1870 on the Munich art market, which is remarkably similar to one in the Royal Scottish Museum, Edinburgh. It proves to be a little larger and the padding is slightly less rigid, with buttonholes worked in apple-green silk, while those in the Edinburgh doublet are in a deeper shade of bluish green, but materials and sewing techniques are so much alike that both may have been made in the same tailor's workshop. Although not in such good condition as that in Edinburgh, the Nürnberg doublet is invaluable for study purposes as details of padding, interlining and stitching may be seen through holes in the lining. It had previously been thought by several costume and armour specialists that these padded leather doublets might be arming doublets but I felt that the padding was too stiff to allow armour to be worn on top and that it seemed to have been designed to protect the body from blows or cuts over the shoulders and upper arms which might be sustained when fighting with a quarterstaff or during fencing practice. Dr Leonie von Wilckens kindly traced a book in the Germanisches Nationalmuseum Library written in 1610 by Michael Hundt, a fencing master and citizen of Zeitz in Saxony: among the hundred woodcuts in *Ein new Künstliches Fechtbuch im Rappier* are several which show doublets with similar lines of stitching on chest and back. The sleeves are padded horizontally from shoulder to wrist (Fig. 165), thus giving even more protection than the vertical padding from shoulder to elbow. Both doublets are very well made from good-quality materials and would have fitted slim youths. It may be conjectured that they were made for pages at some German Court, early examples of protective clothing for fencing practice. Another example of a padded leather doublet, similar in design, may be seen on page 72.

c1610 Royal Scottish Museum, Edinburgh

17. This youth's doublet, almost identical to that in the Germanisches Museum, was bought in London at Christie's in 1977 after previously being advertised for sale in 1973. A third doublet matching these two very closely belonged to Cyril Andrade Esq in 1929. Both doublets here are made of creamy leather with a suede finish, heavily padded over the chest, back, at the tops of the sleeves and on the skirts, or waist tabs; the same methods of construction have been used. The body of each doublet is made of leather interlined with linen. Loosely spun cotton thread padding is packed tightly between these two layers, held in position by rows of stitching. It is likely that this cotton was spun for candlewicks. A loose linen lining, originally white, now discoloured, is stitched inside each doublet with a thin layer of cotton wool wadding caught inside it. The stitches holding the cotton wool in position are just visible on the right side of the linen. Not very much wadding is placed over the chest and back where the leather is heavily padded. This light quantity of wadding simply helps to keep the lower part of the doublet in shape. The sleeves are interlined with linen and padded in the same way as the doublet body, then lined with linen. The collar of each doublet is stiffened with an interlining of linen or hemp, which can just be seen through holes in the linen lining. This is pad-stitched through to the leather. Over this is placed the white linen lining used for the rest of the doublet. The pickadil, or tabbed border, is made from a doubled strip of leather, stitched to the top of the collar, snipped at intervals along the folded edge. Each doublet is decorated with narrow braid made from bright apple-green silk, now faded to yellow, and metal thread of gold strip wound round a yellow silk core. This is placed on top of all the lines of linen thread stitching holding the padding in position.

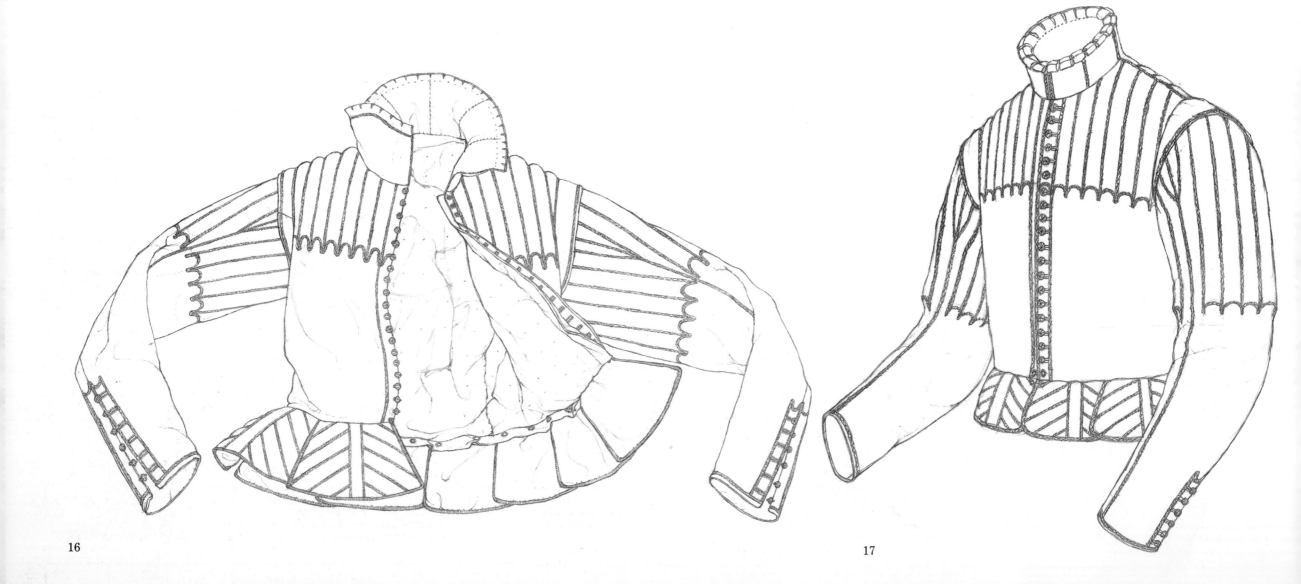

16

17

c.1610 PADDED LEATHER DOUBLET GERMANISCHES NATIONALMUSEUM, NÜRNBERG. T27.

17. c.1610 PADDED LEATHER DOUBLET ROYAL SCOTTISH MUSEUM, EDINBURGH. 1977.237.

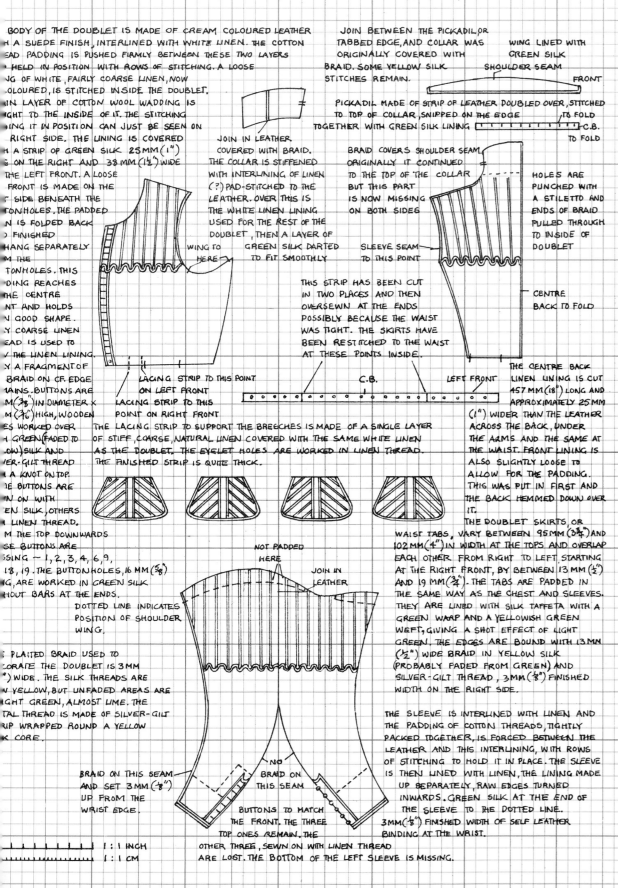

BODY OF THE DOUBLET IS MADE OF CREAM COLOURED LEATHER [WIT]H A SUEDE FINISH, INTERLINED WITH WHITE LINEN. THE COTTON [THR]EAD PADDING IS PUSHED FIRMLY BETWEEN THESE TWO LAYERS [AND] HELD IN POSITION WITH ROWS OF STITCHING. A LOOSE [LININ]G OF WHITE, FAIRLY COARSE LINEN, NOW [DISC]OLOURED, IS STITCHED INSIDE THE DOUBLET. [A TH]IN LAYER OF COTTON WOOL WADDING IS [CAU]GHT TO THE INSIDE OF IT. THE STITCHING [HOLD]ING IT IN POSITION CAN JUST BE SEEN ON [THE] RIGHT SIDE. THE LINING IS COVERED [WIT]H A STRIP OF GREEN SILK 25MM (1") [WIDE] ON THE RIGHT AND 38MM (1½") WIDE [ON] THE LEFT FRONT. A LOOSE [FLY] FRONT IS MADE ON THE [LEF]T SIDE BENEATH THE [BU]TTONHOLES. THE PADDED [LINE]N IS FOLDED BACK [AND] FINISHED [TO] HANG SEPARATELY [FRO]M THE [BUT]TONHOLES. THIS [PAD]DING REACHES [TO] THE CENTRE [FRON]T AND HOLDS [IN] GOOD SHAPE. [VER]Y COARSE LINEN [THRE]AD IS USED TO [SEW] THE LINEN LINING. [ONL]Y A FRAGMENT OF [THE] BRAID ON C.F. EDGE [REM]AINS. BUTTONS ARE [8 M]M(⅜") IN DIAMETER X [12 M]M(½") HIGH, WOODEN [BASES] WORKED OVER [WITH] GREEN (FADED TO [YELL]OW) SILK AND [SILV]ER-GILT THREAD. [THERE] IS A KNOT ON TOP. [THE]SE BUTTONS ARE [SEW]N ON WITH [GREE]N SILK, OTHERS [WITH] LINEN THREAD. [FRO]M THE TOP DOWNWARDS [THE]SE BUTTONS ARE [MIS]SING — 1, 2, 3, 4, 6, 9, [17,] 18, 19. THE BUTTONHOLES, 16MM (⅝") [LON]G, ARE WORKED IN GREEN SILK [WITHO]UT BARS AT THE ENDS. [THE]

JOIN BETWEEN THE PICKADIL OR TABBED EDGE, AND COLLAR WAS ORIGINALLY COVERED WITH BRAID. SOME YELLOW SILK STITCHES REMAIN.

WING LINED WITH GREEN SILK

SHOULDER SEAM

FRONT

PICKADIL MADE OF STRIP OF LEATHER DOUBLED OVER, STITCHED TO TOP OF COLLAR, SNIPPED ON THE EDGE TOGETHER WITH GREEN SILK LINING

TO FOLD C.B. TO FOLD

JOIN IN LEATHER COVERED WITH BRAID. THE COLLAR IS STIFFENED WITH INTERLINING OF LINEN (?) PAD-STITCHED TO THE LEATHER. OVER THIS IS THE WHITE LINEN LINING USED FOR THE REST OF THE DOUBLET, THEN A LAYER OF GREEN SILK DARTED TO FIT SMOOTHLY

WING TO HERE

SLEEVE SEAM TO THIS POINT

BRAID COVERS SHOULDER SEAM, ORIGINALLY IT CONTINUED TO THE TOP OF THE COLLAR BUT THIS PART IS NOW MISSING ON BOTH SIDES

HOLES ARE PUNCHED WITH A STILETTO AND ENDS OF BRAID PULLED THROUGH TO INSIDE OF DOUBLET

CENTRE BACK TO FOLD

THIS STRIP HAS BEEN CUT IN TWO PLACES AND THEN OVERSEWN AT THE ENDS POSSIBLY BECAUSE THE WAIST WAS TIGHT. THE SKIRTS HAVE BEEN RESTITCHED TO THE WAIST AT THESE POINTS INSIDE.

LACING STRIP TO THIS POINT ON LEFT FRONT

LACING STRIP TO THIS POINT ON RIGHT FRONT

C.B.

LEFT FRONT

THE CENTRE BACK LINEN LINING IS CUT 457MM (18") LONG AND APPROXIMATELY 25MM (1") WIDER THAN THE LEATHER ACROSS THE BACK, UNDER THE ARMS AND THE SAME AT THE WAIST. FRONT LINING IS ALSO SLIGHTLY WIDER TO ALLOW FOR THE PADDING. THIS WAS PUT IN FIRST AND THE BACK HEMMED DOWN OVER IT.

THE LACING STRIP TO SUPPORT THE BREECHES IS MADE OF A SINGLE LAYER OF STIFF, COARSE, NATURAL LINEN COVERED WITH THE SAME WHITE LINEN AS THE DOUBLET. THE EYELET HOLES ARE WORKED IN LINEN THREAD. THE FINISHED STRIP IS QUITE THICK.

NOT PADDED HERE

JOIN IN LEATHER

DOTTED LINE INDICATES POSITION OF SHOULDER WING.

[THE] PLAITED BRAID USED TO [DEC]ORATE THE DOUBLET IS 3MM [(⅛")] WIDE. THE SILK THREADS ARE [NOW] YELLOW, BUT UNFADED AREAS ARE [BRI]GHT GREEN, ALMOST LIME. THE [MET]AL THREAD IS MADE OF SILVER-GILT [STR]IP WRAPPED ROUND A YELLOW [SIL]K CORE.

BRAID ON THIS SEAM AND SET 3MM (⅛") UP FROM THE WRIST EDGE.

NO BRAID ON THIS SEAM

JOIN IN LEATHER

BUTTONS TO MATCH THE FRONT. THE THREE TOP ONES REMAIN. THE OTHER THREE, SEWN ON WITH LINEN THREAD ARE LOST. THE BOTTOM OF THE LEFT SLEEVE IS MISSING.

THE DOUBLET SKIRTS, OR WAIST TABS, VARY BETWEEN 95MM (3¾") AND 102MM (4") IN WIDTH AT THE TOPS AND OVERLAP EACH OTHER FROM RIGHT TO LEFT STARTING AT THE RIGHT FRONT, BY BETWEEN 13MM (½") AND 19MM (¾"). THE TABS ARE PADDED IN THE SAME WAY AS THE CHEST AND SLEEVES. THEY ARE LINED WITH SILK TAFFETA WITH A GREEN WARP AND A YELLOWISH GREEN WEFT, GIVING A SHOT EFFECT OF LIGHT GREEN. THE EDGES ARE BOUND WITH 13MM (½") WIDE BRAID IN YELLOW SILK (PROBABLY FADED FROM GREEN) AND SILVER-GILT THREAD, 3MM (⅛") FINISHED WIDTH ON THE RIGHT SIDE.

THE SLEEVE IS INTERLINED WITH LINEN AND THE PADDING OF COTTON THREADS, TIGHTLY PACKED TOGETHER, IS FORCED BETWEEN THE LEATHER AND THIS INTERLINING, WITH ROWS OF STITCHING TO HOLD IT IN PLACE. THE SLEEVE IS THEN LINED WITH LINEN, THE LINING MADE UP SEPARATELY, RAW EDGES TURNED INWARDS. GREEN SILK AT THE END OF THE SLEEVE TO THE DOTTED LINE. 3MM (⅛") FINISHED WIDTH OF SELF LEATHER BINDING AT THE WRIST.

1 : 1 INCH
1 : 1 CM

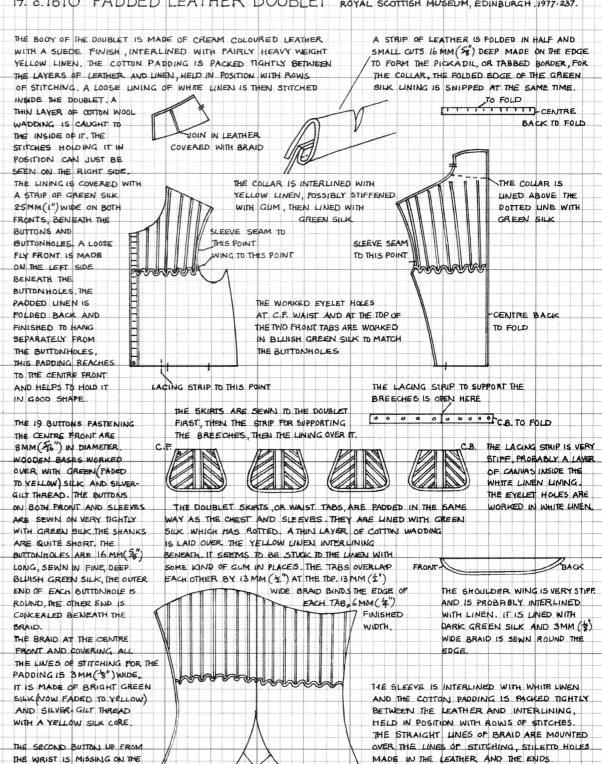

THE BODY OF THE DOUBLET IS MADE OF CREAM COLOURED LEATHER WITH A SUEDE FINISH, INTERLINED WITH FAIRLY HEAVY WEIGHT YELLOW LINEN. THE COTTON PADDING IS PACKED TIGHTLY BETWEEN THE LAYERS OF LEATHER AND LINEN, HELD IN POSITION WITH ROWS OF STITCHING. A LOOSE LINING OF WHITE LINEN IS THEN STITCHED INSIDE THE DOUBLET. A THIN LAYER OF COTTON WOOL WADDING IS CAUGHT TO THE INSIDE OF IT. THE STITCHES HOLDING IT IN POSITION CAN JUST BE SEEN ON THE RIGHT SIDE. THE LINING IS COVERED WITH A STRIP OF GREEN SILK 25MM (1") WIDE ON BOTH FRONTS, BENEATH THE BUTTONS AND BUTTONHOLES. A LOOSE FLY FRONT IS MADE ON THE LEFT SIDE BENEATH THE BUTTONHOLES. THE PADDED LINEN IS FOLDED BACK AND FINISHED TO HANG SEPARATELY FROM THE BUTTONHOLES. THIS PADDING REACHES TO THE CENTRE FRONT AND HELPS TO HOLD IT IN GOOD SHAPE.

THE 19 BUTTONS FASTENING THE CENTRE FRONT ARE 8MM (5/16") IN DIAMETER. WOODEN BASES WORKED OVER WITH GREEN (FADED TO YELLOW) SILK AND SILVER-GILT THREAD. THE BUTTONS ON BOTH FRONT AND SLEEVES ARE SEWN ON VERY TIGHTLY WITH GREEN SILK. THE SHANKS ARE QUITE SHORT. THE BUTTONHOLES ARE 16MM (⅝") LONG, SEWN IN FINE, DEEP BLUISH GREEN SILK. THE OUTER END OF EACH BUTTONHOLE IS ROUND, THE OTHER END IS CONCEALED BENEATH THE BRAID.

THE BRAID AT THE CENTRE FRONT AND COVERING ALL THE LINES OF STITCHING FOR THE PADDING IS 3MM (⅛") WIDE. IT IS MADE OF BRIGHT GREEN SILK (NOW FADED TO YELLOW) AND SILVER-GILT THREAD WITH A YELLOW SILK CORE.

THE SECOND BUTTON UP FROM THE WRIST IS MISSING ON THE LEFT SLEEVE AND THE FOURTH BUTTON UP FROM THE WRIST ON THE RIGHT SLEEVE. ON THE LEFT SLEEVE THE TOP BUTTON IS MADE WITH A DIFFERENT SHADE OF GREEN SILK.

JOIN IN LEATHER COVERED WITH BRAID

THE COLLAR IS INTERLINED WITH YELLOW LINEN, POSSIBLY STIFFENED WITH GUM, THEN LINED WITH GREEN SILK

SLEEVE SEAM TO THIS POINT

WING TO THIS POINT

THE WORKED EYELET HOLES AT C.F. WAIST AND AT THE TOP OF THE TWO FRONT TABS ARE WORKED IN BLUISH GREEN SILK TO MATCH THE BUTTONHOLES

LACING STRIP TO THIS POINT

THE SKIRTS ARE SEWN TO THE DOUBLET FIRST, THEN THE STRIP FOR SUPPORTING THE BREECHES, THEN THE LINING OVER IT.

C.F.

THE DOUBLET SKIRTS, OR WAIST TABS, ARE PADDED IN THE SAME WAY AS THE CHEST AND SLEEVES. THEY ARE LINED WITH GREEN SILK WHICH HAS ROTTED. A THIN LAYER OF COTTON WADDING IS LAID OVER THE YELLOW LINEN INTERLINING BENEATH. IT SEEMS TO BE STUCK TO THE LINEN WITH SOME KIND OF GUM IN PLACES. THE TABS OVERLAP EACH OTHER BY 13MM (½") AT THE TOP. 13MM (½") WIDE BRAID BINDS THE EDGE OF EACH TAB, 6MM (¼") FINISHED WIDTH.

NO BRAID ON THIS SEAM

OPEN TO THIS POINT

BUTTONHOLES ON LEFT SLEEVE ARE WORKED IN SILK MATCHING THOSE ON THE FRONT. ON RIGHT SLEEVE THE SILK IS NOW YELLOWISH GREEN.

A STRIP OF LEATHER IS FOLDED IN HALF AND SMALL CUTS 16MM (⅝") DEEP MADE ON THE EDGE TO FORM THE PICKADIL, OR TABBED BORDER, FOR THE COLLAR. THE FOLDED EDGE OF THE GREEN SILK LINING IS SNIPPED AT THE SAME TIME.

TO FOLD
CENTRE BACK TO FOLD

THE COLLAR IS LINED ABOVE THE DOTTED LINE WITH GREEN SILK

SLEEVE SEAM TO THIS POINT

CENTRE BACK TO FOLD

THE LACING STRIP TO SUPPORT THE BREECHES IS OPEN HERE

C.B. TO FOLD

C.B.

THE LACING STRIP IS VERY STIFF, PROBABLY A LAYER OF CANVAS INSIDE THE WHITE LINEN LINING. THE EYELET HOLES ARE WORKED IN WHITE LINEN.

FRONT

BACK

THE SHOULDER WING IS VERY STIFF AND IS PROBABLY INTERLINED WITH LINEN. IT IS LINED WITH DARK GREEN SILK AND 3MM (⅛") WIDE BRAID IS SEWN ROUND THE EDGE.

FINISHED WIDTH.

THE SLEEVE IS INTERLINED WITH WHITE LINEN AND THE COTTON PADDING IS PACKED TIGHTLY BETWEEN THE LEATHER AND INTERLINING, HELD IN POSITION WITH ROWS OF STITCHES. THE STRAIGHT LINES OF BRAID ARE MOUNTED OVER THE LINES OF STITCHING. STILETTO HOLES MADE IN THE LEATHER AND THE ENDS PUSHED THROUGH TO THE WRONG SIDE. THE LONG STRIP OF BRAID AT THE BOTTOM IS PUT ON LAST, ARRANGED IN A SERIES OF CURVES. THE SLEEVE IS LINED WITH WHITE LINEN, COVERED FOR A SHORT DISTANCE AT THE WRISTS WITH GREEN SILK.

© 1984 JANET ARNOLD

c1615–20 Hessisches Landesmuseum, Darmstadt

18. A doublet in deep reddish-plum-coloured satin decorated with narrow stone-coloured silk braid and rows of pinking. Its early provenance is not known. The slightly pointed front, the area of wool pad-stitched over the shoulders, the waist level and two-piece sleeve may be compared with Sir Richard (?) Cotton's suit, which can be precisely dated to 1618 by his portrait (Fig. 190). The doublet is interlined with black linen, now faded to dark brown. A layer of black corded silk was originally placed over this, beneath the satin, but most of this has now disintegrated, except on the skirts where it remains in good condition. This would have shown through the pinking holes. The pinking may have been done after the layers were tacked together as some of the black linen and black silk are cut as

well. A layer of black wool is pad-stitched to the linen over the shoulders to prevent wrinkles around the armholes. It is layered to prevent any ridges showing through the satin. The doublet is lined with natural linen, the side seams set back from those in the satin, presumably to avoid bulk. A stiffened linen strip with worked eyelet holes for points to attach the breeches is stitched inside the waist. The belly-piece is made of four layers of black linen and one of thick, lovat-green felted woollen cloth, all pad-stitched together, tapering out gradually so that no ridges can be seen. A strip of braid, folded in half to make a loop, is stitched on the belly-piece on both fronts, to be tied across, holding both sides together before buttoning the doublet.

c1615–20 Lord Middleton Collection, Museum of Costume and Textiles, Nottingham

19A. A doublet in ivory silk with thin silver strip in the weft and a woven pattern of stylized floral motifs in heavier metal thread of gold strip wrapped round a silk core and pink, blue, greeny-brown and turquoise silk. The doublet has apparently been in Baron Middleton's family since the seventeenth century. It is similar to many doublets in portraits dating from c1615–20 (Figs. 179 and 200). The doublet is completely interlined with heavy linen canvas, with a narrow strip of linen pad-stitched down both fronts for extra stiffness beneath buttons and buttonholes. Over the shoulders, under the arms and across the back is a layer of brown woollen cloth, slightly felted, which is pad-stitched to the linen interlining. The doublet is lined with pink silk. This drawing shows the conjectured appearance of the doublet in its original condition.

19B. Although some early doublets were made without sleeve wings, this doublet appears to have had them removed at some time and the left sleeve reset with the seam lower than the right at the back. All the buttons have been removed and tufts of yellow silk indicate the original position of lines of gold braid. On the right side of the collar are four long tufts of thread, the remains of button shanks. On the left side are four punched holes, about 19 mm ($\frac{3}{4}$″) in from the edge, for loop buttonholes, now missing. These would have been made of plaited cord or narrow braid pushed through the holes and stitched firmly at the back. Eyelet holes for points to attach the breeches are worked in the tabs forming the skirts of the doublet, instead of a waist strip. The ribbon points would have been tied in decorative bows. This drawing shows the present appearance of the doublet.

18   19A   19B

c.1615-20 DOUBLET HESSISCHES LANDESMUSEUM, DARMSTADT

...BLET IN DEEP REDDISH PLUM SATIN DECORATED WITH NARROW STONE COLOURED SILK
...AID AND ROWS OF PINKING. IT IS INTERLINED WITH BLACK LINEN, NOW FADED TO DARK
...WN. A LAYER OF BLACK CORDED SILK WAS ORIGINALLY PLACED OVER THIS, BENEATH THE
...IN, BUT MOST OF THIS HAS NOW DISINTEGRATED, EXCEPT ON THE SKIRTS, WHERE IT REMAINS
...OOD CONDITION. THIS WOULD HAVE SHOWN THROUGH THE PINKED HOLES WHICH HAVE
...YED TO SHOW THE STONE-COLOURED
...ET THREADS AGAINST THE RICH
...M WARP. THE PINKING MAY HAVE
...N CARRIED OUT AFTER THE
...BLET WAS MADE UP, AS SOME
...THE BLACK LINEN AND BLACK
...K IS CUT AS WELL. THE PINKS
...Y BETWEEN 6MM (¼") AND 13 MM (½")
...RANGED ON THE BIAS GRAIN.

...WORKED
...TONHOLES, BUT
...THE BUTTONS
...E MISSING
...THE
...NT
...D ON
...RIGHT
...EYE. 3
...MAIN ON
...T SLEEVE

TWO 16MM (⅝") LOOPS MADE
FROM PIECES OF CORD 3.2 CM
(1¼") LONG FOLDED IN HALF
ON THE LEFT SIDE.

BRAID COVERS SHOULDER
SEAM
DOUBLE ROWS
OF BRAID 3MM (⅛")
WIDE WITH 3MM
(⅛") OR 1.5MM (¹⁄₁₆")
GAP BETWEEN
THEM.

FRONT
AND
SLEEVE
SEAM
MEET
THIS MARK

CENTRE BACK
TO FOLD

CENTRE BACK TO FOLD

THE COLLAR IS MADE OF ONE OR
TWO VERY THICK LAYERS OF
COARSE LINEN, PAD-STITCHED
TOGETHER. OVER THIS ARE
LAYERS OF BLACK LINEN,
BLACK SILK AND PLUM
SATIN. THE COLLAR IS LINED
WITH STONE AND BLACK SHOT
SILK TAFFETA. THE FINAL THICKNESS
OF THE COLLAR
IS NEARLY
6MM (¼").

THE SIDE BACK SEAM OF THE NATURAL LINEN
LINING OF THE DOUBLET BODY IS SET ABOUT
13 MM (½") BACK FROM THE SEAM IN THE SATIN,
PRESUMABLY TO AVOID BULK. THE SEAMS
ALMOST MEET AT THE TOP.

BLACK WOOL IS PAD-STITCHED
TO THE LINEN OVER THE SHOULDER
TO THE DOTTED LINE AT BOTH
FRONT AND BACK. IT IS LAYERED
AND TAPERED OUT SO THAT
THERE ARE NO RIDGES TO BE
SEEN.

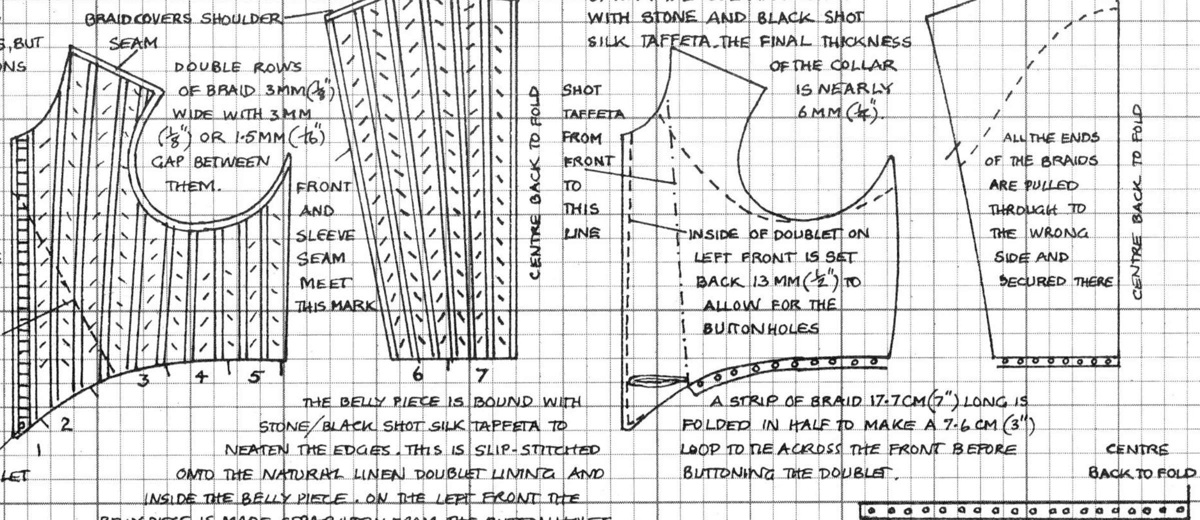

ALL THE ENDS
OF THE BRAIDS
ARE PULLED
THROUGH TO
THE WRONG
SIDE AND
SECURED THERE

CENTRE BACK TO FOLD

SHOT
TAFFETA
FROM
FRONT
TO
THIS
LINE

INSIDE OF DOUBLET ON
LEFT FRONT IS SET
BACK 13 MM (½") TO
ALLOW FOR THE
BUTTONHOLES

THE BELLY PIECE IS BOUND WITH
STONE/BLACK SHOT SILK TAFFETA TO
NEATEN THE EDGES. THIS IS SLIP-STITCHED
ONTO THE NATURAL LINEN DOUBLET LINING AND
INSIDE THE BELLY PIECE. ON THE LEFT FRONT THE
...KED EYELET   BELLY PIECE IS MADE SEPARATELY FROM THE BUTTON HOLES
...LES   SO THAT THE DOUBLET MAY BE FASTENED.

A STRIP OF BRAID 17.7CM (7") LONG IS
FOLDED IN HALF TO MAKE A 7.6 CM (3")
LOOP TO TIE ACROSS THE FRONT BEFORE
BUTTONING THE DOUBLET.

CENTRE
BACK TO FOLD

...TED LINE
...RKS
...TION OF
...LY-PIECE

1   2   3   4   5   6   7

1   2   3   4   5   6   7

...E SKIRTS ARE CUT FROM ODD SCRAPS OF MATERIAL
...IS DOES NOT SHOW VERY MUCH AS THE SATIN
...S A DULL SURFACE. IT IS HEAVY IN WEIGHT
...D OF GOOD QUALITY. EACH SKIRT TAB IS
...TERLINED WITH STIFF BLACK SILK AND SHOT
...TH SHOT SILK TAFFETA, STONE-COLOURED
...RP AND BLACK WEFT. THERE
...APPARENTLY NO LINEN
...TERLINING.

A 5.1 CM (2") WIDE STRIP OF LINEN,
FOLDED IN HALF LENGTHWISE
ROUND A STRIP OF STIFFENED LINEN,
IS STITCHED TO THE WAIST OF THE
DOUBLET, SHOWING FOR 16 MM
(⅝") BENEATH THE LINING. 38
EYELET HOLES ARE WORKED IN
IT FOR POINTS TO SUPPORT THE
BREECHES. THE TURNINGS FROM
THE SKIRTS AND THIS STRIP MAKE
THE WAIST VERY BULKY.

THE SHOULDER WING FEELS AS IF
IT IS INTERLINED WITH JUST THE BLACK
LINEN AND BLACK SILK. IT IS LINED
UNDERNEATH WITH
BLACK AND STONE
SHOT SILK
TAFFETA

SHOULDER SEAM
TO THIS MARK.

FRONT   THE WING IS CUT WITH
BACK   THE GRAIN RUNNING ACROSS.

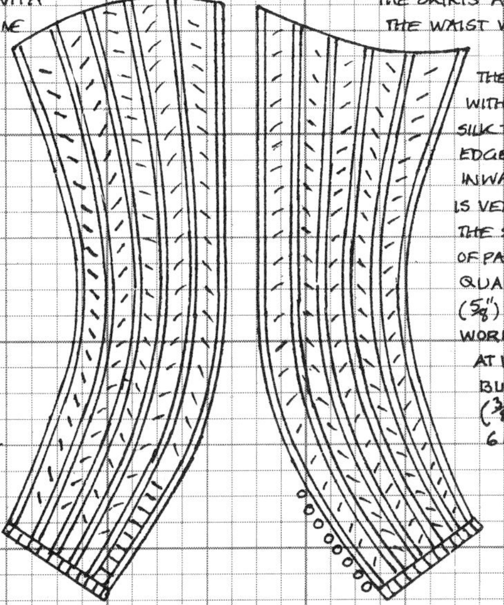

THE SLEEVE IS LINED
WITH BLACK/STONE SHOT
SILK TAFFETA. ALL THE RAW
EDGES ARE TURNED
INWARDS, SO THAT IT
IS VERY NEAT ALTHOUGH
THE STITCHING IS NOT
OF PARTICULARLY FINE
QUALITY. EIGHT 16MM
(⅝") BUTTONHOLES ARE
WORKED IN STONE SILK
AT WRIST OPENING. THE
BUTTONS ARE 9MM
(⅜") IN DIAMETER AND
6MM (¼") HIGH, MADE OF
STONE SILK WORKED
OVER A WOOLLEN
FOUNDATION. ONLY
THREE BUTTONS
REMAIN ON THE
LEFT SLEEVE.

THE BELLY-PIECE IS MADE OF SEVERAL
LAYERS PAD-STITCHED TOGETHER AND
TAPERING OUT GRADUALLY SO THAT
NO RIDGES CAN BE SEEN. IT IS OVER SEWN
TIGHTLY TOGETHER AT THE BOTTOM

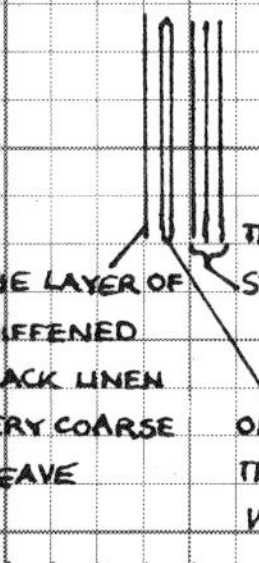

...E LAYER OF   THREE LAYERS OF
...FFENED   STIFFENED BLACK LINEN,
...CK LINEN   VERY COARSE WEAVE.
...RY COARSE
...EAVE   ONE LAYER OF 6MM (¼")
                   THICK FELTED LOVAT GREEN
                   WOOLLEN CLOTH.

DIAGRAM SHOWING 16MM (⅝")
DEEP PLEATED STRIP IN BLACK
AND STONE SHOT
SILK TAFFETA
AT WRIST.

1 : 1 INCH
1 : 1 CM

19. c.1615-20 DOUBLET LORD MIDDLETON COLLECTION, MUSEUM OF COSTUME AND TEXTILES, NOTTINGHAM

DOUBLET IN IVORY SILK WITH THIN SILVER STRIP IN THE
WEFT AND A WOVEN PATTERN OF STYLIZED FLORAL
MOTIFS IN HEAVIER METAL THREAD, OF GOLD STRIP
WRAPPED ROUND A SILK CORE, WITH PINK AND BLUE
SILK. THE DOUBLET BODY IS INTERLINED WITH
HEAVY LINEN CANVAS MATCHING THAT FOR
THE SKIRTS. A 5.1 CM (2") WIDE STRIP OF LINEN
CANVAS IS PAD-STITCHED ON TO THIS INTERLINING
AT THE FRONT ON BOTH SIDES, TO DOTTED LINE
-------------. THE PAD-STITCHING IS CARRIED OUT
WITH LINEN THREAD, SIMILAR TO FINE STRING.

FRONT EDGE OF DOUBLET IS BOUND WITH
6MM (¼") FINISHED WIDTH BIAS-CUT
IVORY SILK

FRONT SEAM OF
SLEEVE TO
THIS MARK

SMALL
PINK
SILK
COVERED
CANVAS
TAB, WITH
WORKED
EYELET
HOLE TO
TIE ACROSS
FRONT
BEFORE
BUTTONING
DOUBLET

LINES OF TUFTS OF
YELLOW SILK INDICATE
STITCHING LINES OF
GOLD BRAID WHICH
HAVE BEEN REMOVED

A   TWO WORKED
     EYELET HOLES

A   B   C

THE COLLAR IS BACKED WITH LINEN CANVAS. A PIECE OF STIFF CARD-
BOARD, WITH THE TEXTURE OF BLOTTING PAPER, IS PLACED ON TOP OF IT.
OVER THIS IS A LAYER OF COARSE, LOOSELY WOVEN WHITE WOOLLEN
CLOTH, PAD-STITCHED THROUGH THE CARDBOARD TO THE LINEN
CANVAS. THE IVORY SILK IS CAUGHT DOWN OVER IT. THE COLLAR IS
LINED WITH PINK SHOT SILK TAFFETA.

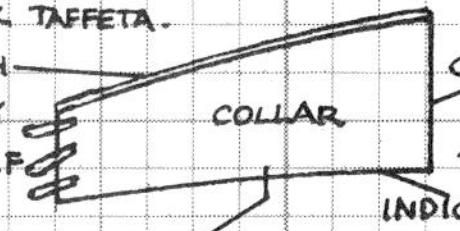

A 6MM (¼") FINISHED WIDTH
STRAIGHT BINDING OF IVORY
SILK IS SEWN OVER
TOP EDGE OF COLLAR.
3 HOLES ARE PUNCHED
19MM (¾") FROM C.F.
EDGE FOR LOOPS,
NOW MISSING.

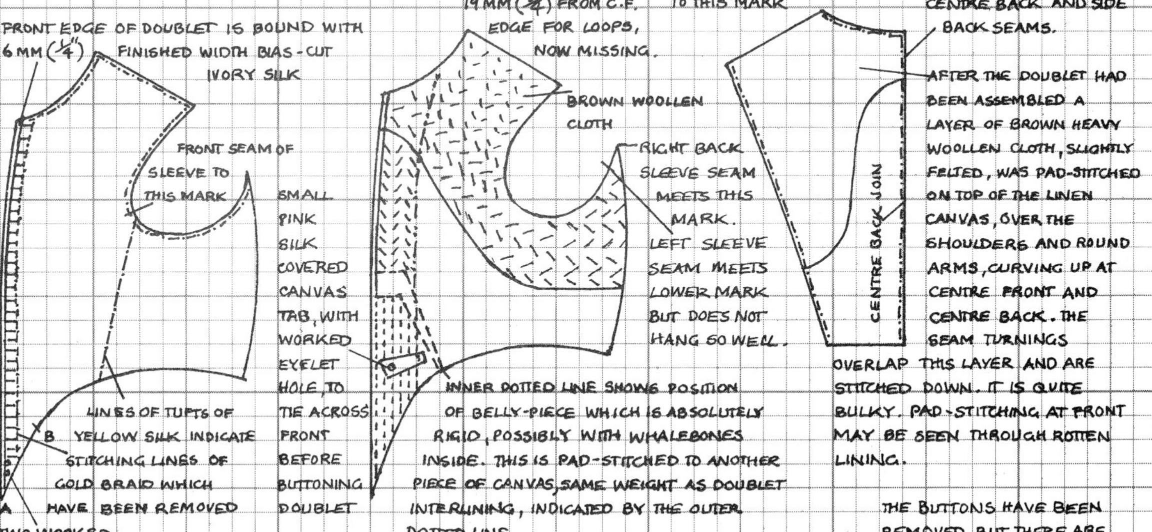

CENTRE BACK JOIN
COLLAR
C.F.

SHOULDER SEAM
TO THIS MARK

TUFTS OF YELLOW SILK
INDICATE POSITION OF LINE OF
GOLD BRAID ON NECK SEAM,
CENTRE BACK AND SIDE
BACK SEAMS.

BROWN WOOLLEN
CLOTH

RIGHT BACK
SLEEVE SEAM
MEETS THIS
MARK.
LEFT SLEEVE
SEAM MEETS
LOWER MARK
BUT DOES NOT
HANG SO WELL.

CENTRE BACK JOIN

INNER DOTTED LINE SHOWS POSITION
OF BELLY-PIECE WHICH IS ABSOLUTELY
RIGID, POSSIBLY WITH WHALEBONES
INSIDE. THIS IS PAD-STITCHED TO ANOTHER
PIECE OF CANVAS, SAME WEIGHT AS DOUBLET
INTERLINING, INDICATED BY THE OUTER
DOTTED LINE.

AFTER THE DOUBLET HAD
BEEN ASSEMBLED A
LAYER OF BROWN HEAVY
WOOLLEN CLOTH, SLIGHTLY
FELTED, WAS PAD-STITCHED
ON TOP OF THE LINEN
CANVAS, OVER THE
SHOULDERS AND ROUND
ARMS, CURVING UP AT
CENTRE FRONT AND
CENTRE BACK. THE
SEAM TURNINGS
OVERLAP THIS LAYER AND ARE
STITCHED DOWN. IT IS QUITE
BULKY. PAD-STITCHING AT FRONT
MAY BE SEEN THROUGH ROTTEN
LINING.

THE BUTTONS HAVE BEEN
REMOVED BUT THERE ARE
TRACES OF YELLOW SILK
WHERE THEY WERE SEWN
ON BESIDE A STRIP OF
GOLD BRAID, ON RIGHT
FRONT. ON LEFT FRONT
31 BUTTONHOLES, JUST
OVER 16 MM (⅝") WIDE
ARE WORKED IN
YELLOW SILK

C   D   E   SIDE BACK SEAM

A   B   C   D   E

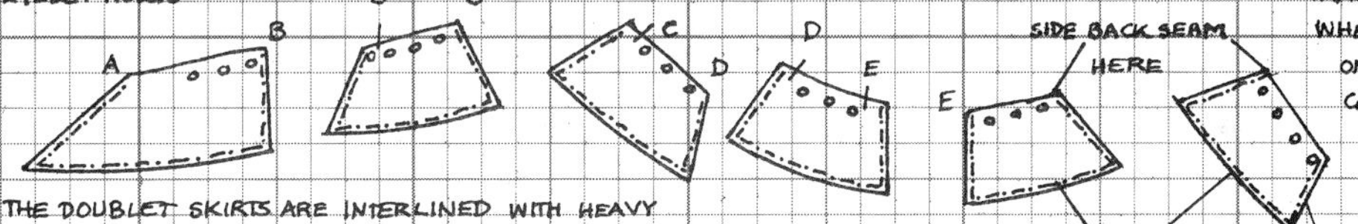

TUFTS OF YELLOW SILK STITCHING
ROUND EDGES OF TABS INDICATE
ORIGINAL POSITION OF GOLD BRAID

C.B.

THE DOUBLET SKIRTS ARE INTERLINED WITH HEAVY
NATURAL LINEN CANVAS. THE IVORY SILK IS
MOUNTED ON TOP AND THE TURNINGS CAUGHT DOWN
OVER THE EDGE. ROSE PINK SHOT SILK TAFFETA (PINK WARP,
WHITE WEFT) LINING CUT TO THE SAME SHAPE AND HEMMED
DOWN OVER THE IVORY SILK TURNINGS, CONCEALING ALL
THE RAW EDGES. EYELET HOLES ARE WORKED IN YELLOW
SILK THROUGH ALL THE LAYERS. THE TABS OVERLAP EACH
OTHER FROM FRONT TO BACK. THEY MEET AT THE CENTRE BACK
AT THE TOP, AND MAY OVERLAP EITHER WAY BELOW.

ON THE SHOULDER SEAMS, THE ROTTEN LINING REVEALS
THAT THE IVORY SILK WAS PROBABLY SEWN TOGETHER
FIRST, THEN THE LINEN LAYER PUT IN AND CAUGHT
DOWN ROUND THE NECK, ARMHOLES, CENTRE
FRONT AND OTHER EDGES.
THE SLIGHTLY FELTED BROWN
WOOLLEN CLOTH WAS
PAD-STITCHED IN
AND THE
SHOULDER SEAMS
SEWN DOWN
OVER THE TOP.

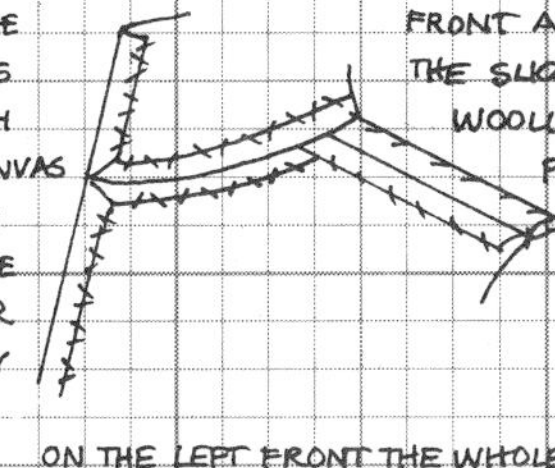

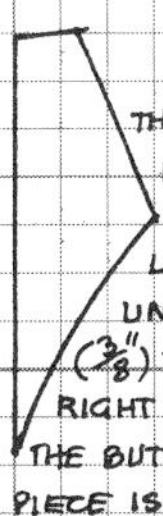

THIS PART OF THE
BELLY PIECE IS
BUILT UP WITH
LAYERS OF CANVAS
UNTIL IT IS 9MM
(⅜") THICK. ON THE
RIGHT FRONT, UNDER
THE BUTTONS, THE BELLY
PIECE IS BUILT INTO
THE DOUBLET, BEING
CUT AWAY A
FRACTION AT THE
BOTTOM TO ALLOW
FOR TWO WORKED
EYELET HOLES.

ON THE LEFT FRONT THE WHOLE OF THE LONG CANVAS
STRIP, BELLY PIECE AND 9MM (⅜") WIDE WHALEBONE
ARE ATTACHED TO THE PINK SHOT SILK LINING. THEY
ARE SEPARATE FROM THE DOUBLET, BEING
ATTACHED AT NECK AND WAIST ONLY. THIS
MAKES THE FRONT SUFFICIENTLY PLIABLE TO
FASTEN THE BUTTONHOLES.

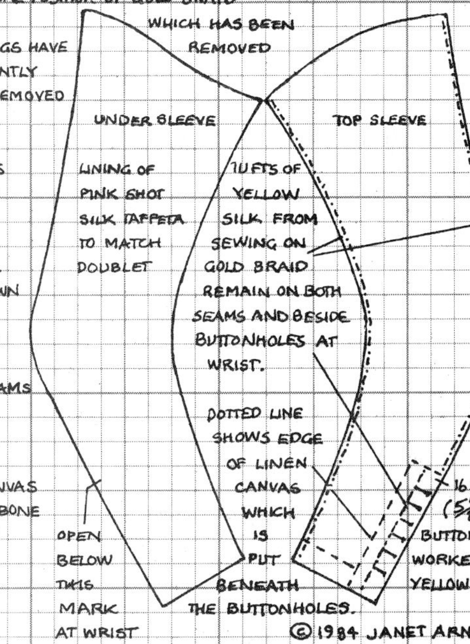

THE WINGS HAVE
APPARENTLY
BEEN REMOVED

WHICH HAS BEEN
REMOVED

UNDER SLEEVE   TOP SLEEVE

LINING OF
PINK SHOT
SILK TAFFETA
TO MATCH
DOUBLET

TUFTS OF
YELLOW
SILK FROM
SEWING ON
GOLD BRAID
REMAIN ON BOTH
SEAMS AND BESIDE
BUTTONHOLES AT
WRIST.

DOTTED LINE
SHOWS EDGE
OF LINEN
CANVAS
WHICH
IS
PUT
BENEATH
THE BUTTONHOLES

OPEN
BELOW
THIS
MARK
AT WRIST

16MM
(⅝")
BUTTONHOLES
WORKED IN
YELLOW SILK

© 1984 JANET ARNOLD.

c1615–25 Bayerisches Nationalmuseum, Munich

20. A doublet in warm orange-tan satin, now faded in places, decorated with rows of pinking. Its early provenance is not known. The doublet is interlined with coarse linen, matching in colour but now faded to natural in many areas, which would have shown through the pinked holes. The body of the doublet, collar and sleeve ends are also lined with white linen. In some places this is also covered with saffron-yellow silk. The pinking is carried out in well-defined areas, avoiding the seams on the body of the doublet and away from the ends of the sleeves. The plain area on the shoulders would have been hidden under the linen falling band, that round the waist by a belt (Fig. 187) and that at the bottom of the sleeves by lace-trimmed linen cuffs (Fig. 190). This doublet is softer to handle than other doublets studied here: it does not have extra linen stiffening at the front beneath the buttons and

buttonholes, nor felted woollen cloth pad-stitched over the shoulders, nor a stiffened belly-piece. This may be a doublet for summer wear or one which foreshadows the softer lines seen in the 1640s and 1650s when the waist level rose again. The back collar is cut in one with the body of the doublet, a technique seen in earlier examples in this book. The collar is interlined with heavy linen and lined with saffron-yellow silk. The bottom of the centre back seam of the doublet is also lined with saffron-yellow silk and appears to have been open originally but later stitched down. The skirts are cut in two pieces, with an opening at the back, interlined with very heavy linen canvas and then lined with orange-tan linen. Eyelet holes are worked in the skirts for points to support the breeches. These would probably have been made of satin and tied in decorative bows.

c1615–20 Germanisches Nationalmuseum, Nürnberg

21. A pair of soft greenish-brown weft striped cut and uncut velvet breeches made for a very large man. The early provenance is not known. These are the type described by Stubbes in his *Anatomie of Abuses* (1583) as:

'Venetian-hosen, they reach beneath the knee to the gartering place of the Leg, where they are tyed finely with silk points or some such like, and laied on also with rewes of lace, or gardes . . . yet notwithstanding all this is not sufficient, except they be made of silk, velvet, saten, damask and other such precious things beside.'

This pair of breeches closely resembles those worn by Prince Maurits of Nassau in his portrait dating from about 1616 (Fig. 187). Dr Mary de Jong kindly

showed me a series of engravings of the Princes of Nassau, after Van de Venne, made in 1616–17 and this portrait is among them. The breeches are now in a very fragile condition, much of the velvet in a state of disintegration with age, and the drawing shows them as they would have appeared originally. The breeches were worn slightly above the natural waist level and there are large hooks sewn to the waistband for eyes attached to a reinforced strip inside the doublet waist. This is an early example of the use of hooks to support breeches. By the 1630s hooks and eyes had replaced points and eyelet holes, probably because they were much easier and quicker to fasten. Ribbon points increased in size and continued into the 1630s as decorative features at the waist of the doublet.

20

21

c.1615-25 DOUBLET   BAYERISCHES NATIONALMUSEUM, MUNICH. T4094

21. c.1615-20 BREECHES OR VENETIANS   GERMANISCHES NATIONALMUSEUM, NÜRNBERG.

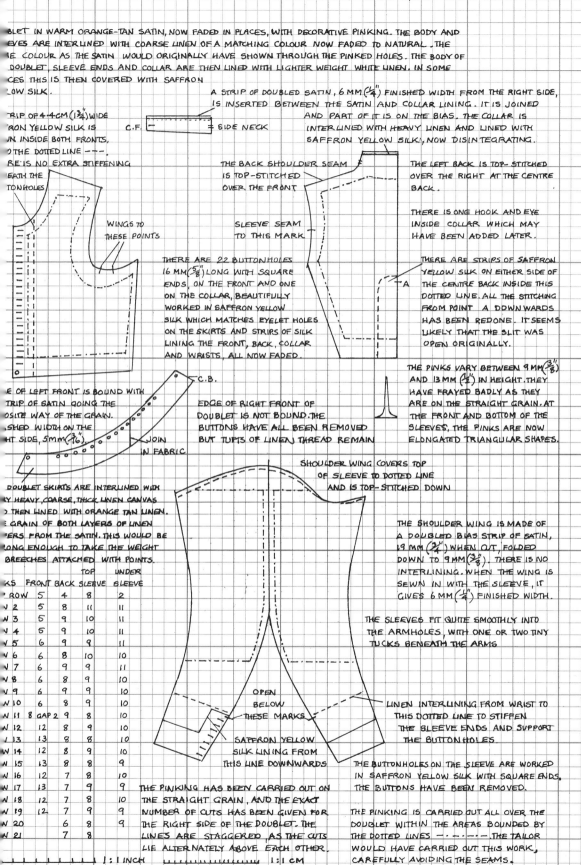

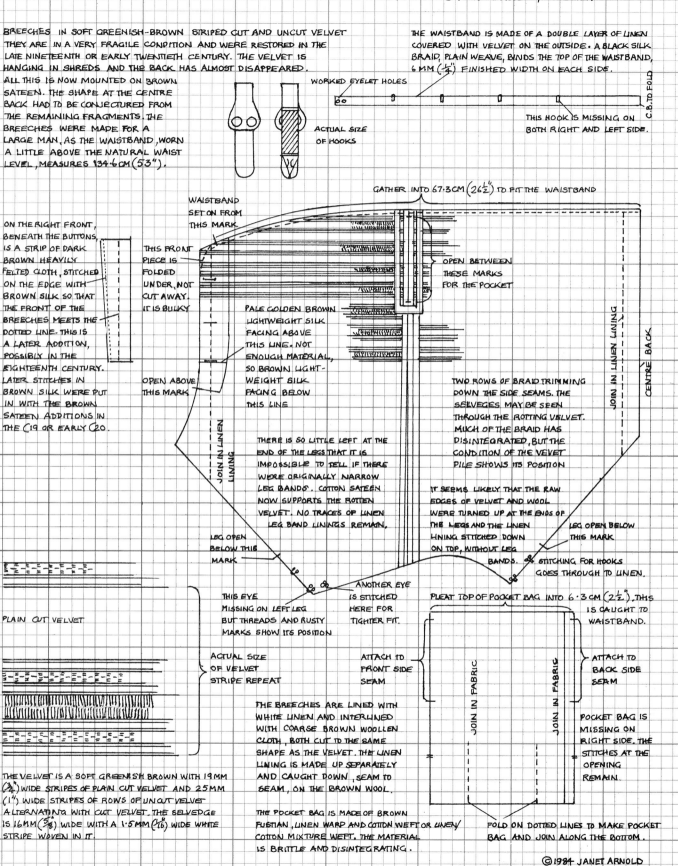

...BLET IN WARM ORANGE-TAN SATIN, NOW FADED IN PLACES, WITH DECORATIVE PINKING. THE BODY AND
...EVES ARE INTERLINED WITH COARSE LINEN OF A MATCHING COLOUR NOW FADED TO NATURAL. THE
...E COLOUR AS THE SATIN WOULD ORIGINALLY HAVE SHOWN THROUGH THE PINKED HOLES. THE BODY OF
...DOUBLET, SLEEVE ENDS AND COLLAR ARE THEN LINED WITH LIGHTER WEIGHT WHITE LINEN. IN SOME
...CES THIS IS THEN COVERED WITH SAFFRON
...LOW SILK.

A STRIP OF DOUBLED SATIN, 6 MM (¼") FINISHED WIDTH FROM THE RIGHT SIDE,
IS INSERTED BETWEEN THE SATIN AND COLLAR LINING. IT IS JOINED
AND PART OF IT IS ON THE BIAS. THE COLLAR IS
INTERLINED WITH HEAVY LINEN AND LINED WITH
SAFFRON YELLOW SILK, NOW DISINTEGRATING.

...RIP OF 4·4CM (1¾") WIDE
...RON YELLOW SILK IS
...N INSIDE BOTH FRONTS,
...O THE DOTTED LINE — — —
...RE IS NO EXTRA STIFFENING
...EATH
...TON HOLES

C.F.   SIDE NECK

THE BACK SHOULDER SEAM
IS TOP-STITCHED
OVER THE FRONT

THE LEFT BACK IS TOP-STITCHED
OVER THE RIGHT AT THE CENTRE
BACK.

WINGS TO
THESE POINTS

SLEEVE SEAM
TO THIS MARK

THERE IS ONE HOOK AND EYE
INSIDE COLLAR WHICH MAY
HAVE BEEN ADDED LATER.

THERE ARE 22 BUTTONHOLES
16 MM (⅝") LONG WITH SQUARE
ENDS, ON THE FRONT AND ONE
ON THE COLLAR, BEAUTIFULLY
WORKED IN SAFFRON YELLOW
SILK WHICH MATCHES EYELET HOLES
ON THE SKIRTS AND STRIPS OF SILK
LINING THE FRONT, BACK, COLLAR
AND WRISTS, ALL NOW FADED.

THERE ARE STRIPS OF SAFFRON
YELLOW SILK ON EITHER SIDE OF
THE CENTRE BACK INSIDE THIS
DOTTED LINE. ALL THE STITCHING
FROM POINT A DOWNWARDS
HAS BEEN REDONE. IT SEEMS
LIKELY THAT THE SLIT WAS
OPEN ORIGINALLY.

A

THE PINKS VARY BETWEEN 9 MM (⅜")
AND 13 MM (½") IN HEIGHT. THEY
HAVE FRAYED BADLY AS THEY
ARE ON THE STRAIGHT GRAIN. AT
THE FRONT AND BOTTOM OF THE
SLEEVES, THE PINKS ARE NOW
ELONGATED TRIANGULAR SHAPES.

...E OF LEFT FRONT IS BOUND WITH
...TRIP OF SATIN GOING THE
...OSITE WAY OF THE GRAIN.
...SHED WIDTH ON THE
...HT SIDE, 5MM (3/16")

C.B.

EDGE OF RIGHT FRONT OF
DOUBLET IS NOT BOUND. THE
BUTTONS HAVE ALL BEEN REMOVED
BUT TUFTS OF LINEN THREAD REMAIN

JOIN
IN FABRIC

...DOUBLET SKIRTS ARE INTERLINED WITH
...RY HEAVY, COARSE, THICK LINEN CANVAS
...THEN LINED WITH ORANGE TAN LINEN.
...E GRAIN OF BOTH LAYERS OF LINEN
...ERS FROM THE SATIN. THIS WOULD BE
...RONG ENOUGH TO TAKE THE WEIGHT
...BREECHES ATTACHED WITH POINTS.

SHOULDER WING COVERS TOP
OF SLEEVE TO DOTTED LINE
AND IS TOP-STITCHED DOWN

THE SHOULDER WING IS MADE OF
A DOUBLED BIAS STRIP OF SATIN,
19 MM (¾") WHEN CUT, FOLDED
DOWN TO 9MM (⅜"). THERE IS NO
INTERLINING. WHEN THE WING IS
SEWN IN WITH THE SLEEVE, IT
GIVES 6 MM (¼") FINISHED WIDTH.

	TOP	UNDER		
KS	FRONT	BACK	SLEEVE	SLEEVE
ROW 1	5	4	8	2½
2				
3	5	9	10	11
4	5	9	10	11
5				
6	6	8	9	10
7	6	9	10	11
8				
9	6	9		10
10	6	8		10
11	8 GAP 2	9	8	10
12	12	8		10
13	13			10
14	12	8		10
15	13	8		9
16	12	7		10
17	13	7		9
18	12	7		10
19	12	7	9	9
20		6	8	9
21	7	8		

THE SLEEVES FIT QUITE SMOOTHLY INTO
THE ARMHOLES, WITH ONE OR TWO TINY
TUCKS BENEATH THE ARMS

OPEN
BELOW
THESE MARKS

LINEN INTERLINING FROM WRIST TO
THIS DOTTED LINE TO STIFFEN
THE SLEEVE ENDS AND SUPPORT
THE BUTTONHOLES

SAFFRON YELLOW
SILK LINING FROM
THIS LINE DOWNWARDS

THE BUTTONHOLES ON THE SLEEVE ARE WORKED
IN SAFFRON YELLOW SILK WITH SQUARE ENDS.
THE BUTTONS HAVE BEEN REMOVED.

THE PINKING HAS BEEN CARRIED OUT ON
THE STRAIGHT GRAIN, AND THE EXACT
NUMBER OF CUTS HAS BEEN GIVEN FOR
THE RIGHT SIDE OF THE DOUBLET. THE
LINES ARE STAGGERED AS THE CUTS
LIE ALTERNATELY ABOVE EACH OTHER.

THE PINKING IS CARRIED OUT ALL OVER THE
DOUBLET WITHIN THE AREAS BOUNDED BY
THE DOTTED LINES — · — · — · THE TAILOR
WOULD HAVE CARRIED OUT THIS WORK,
CAREFULLY AVOIDING THE SEAMS.

1:1 INCH   1:1 CM   © 1984 JANET ARNOLD

BREECHES IN SOFT GREENISH-BROWN STRIPED CUT AND UNCUT VELVET.
THEY ARE IN A VERY FRAGILE CONDITION AND WERE RESTORED IN THE
LATE NINETEENTH OR EARLY TWENTIETH CENTURY. THE VELVET IS
HANGING IN SHREDS AND THE BACK HAS ALMOST DISAPPEARED.
ALL THIS IS NOW MOUNTED ON BROWN
SATEEN. THE SHAPE AT THE CENTRE
BACK HAD TO BE CONJECTURED FROM
THE REMAINING FRAGMENTS. THE
BREECHES WERE MADE FOR A
LARGE MAN, AS THE WAISTBAND, WORN
A LITTLE ABOVE THE NATURAL WAIST
LEVEL, MEASURES 134·6CM (53").

THE WAISTBAND IS MADE OF A DOUBLE LAYER OF LINEN
COVERED WITH VELVET ON THE OUTSIDE. A BLACK SILK
BRAID, PLAIN WEAVE, BINDS THE TOP OF THE WAISTBAND,
6 MM (¼") FINISHED WIDTH ON EACH SIDE.

WORKED EYELET HOLES

ACTUAL SIZE
OF HOOKS

THIS HOOK IS MISSING ON
BOTH RIGHT AND LEFT SIDE.

C.B. TO FOLD

GATHER INTO 67·3CM (26½") TO FIT THE WAISTBAND

WAISTBAND
SET ON FROM
THIS MARK

ON THE RIGHT FRONT,
BENEATH THE BUTTONS
IS A STRIP OF DARK
BROWN HEAVILY
FELTED CLOTH, STITCHED
ON THE EDGE WITH
BROWN SILK SO THAT
THE FRONT OF THE
BREECHES MEETS THE
DOTTED LINE. THIS IS
A LATER ADDITION,
POSSIBLY IN THE
EIGHTEENTH CENTURY.
LATER STITCHES IN
BROWN SILK WERE PUT
IN WITH THE BROWN
SATEEN ADDITIONS IN
THE C19 OR EARLY C20.

THIS FRONT
PIECE IS
FOLDED
UNDER, NOT
CUT AWAY.
IT IS BULKY

PALE GOLDEN BROWN
LIGHTWEIGHT SILK
FACING ABOVE
THIS LINE. NOT
ENOUGH MATERIAL,
SO BROWN LIGHT-
WEIGHT SILK
FACING BELOW
THIS LINE

OPEN BETWEEN
THESE MARKS
FOR THE POCKET

OPEN ABOVE
THIS MARK

JOIN IN LINEN LINING

CENTRE BACK

TWO ROWS OF BRAID TRIMMING
DOWN THE SIDE SEAMS. THE
SELVEDGES MAY BE SEEN
THROUGH THE ROTTING VELVET.
MUCH OF THE BRAID HAS
DISINTEGRATED, BUT THE
CONDITION OF THE VELVET
PILE SHOWS ITS POSITION

THERE IS SO LITTLE LEFT AT THE
END OF THE LEGS THAT IT IS
IMPOSSIBLE TO TELL IF THERE
WERE ORIGINALLY NARROW
LEG BANDS. COTTON SATEEN
NOW SUPPORTS THE ROTTEN
VELVET. NO TRACES OF LINEN
LEG BAND LININGS REMAIN.

IT SEEMS LIKELY THAT THE RAW
EDGES OF VELVET AND WOOL
WERE TURNED UP AT THE ENDS OF
THE LEGS AND THE LINEN
LINING STITCHED DOWN
ON TOP, WITHOUT LEG
BANDS. STITCHING FOR HOOKS
GOES THROUGH TO LINEN.

LEG OPEN BELOW
THIS MARK

JOIN IN LINEN LINING

LEG OPEN
BELOW THIS
MARK

THIS EYE
MISSING ON LEFT LEG
BUT THREADS AND RUSTY
MARKS SHOW ITS POSITION

ANOTHER EYE
IS STITCHED
HERE FOR
TIGHTER FIT.

PLEAT TOP OF POCKET BAG INTO 6·3CM (2½"). THIS
IS CAUGHT TO
WAISTBAND.

PLAIN CUT VELVET

ACTUAL SIZE
OF VELVET
STRIPE REPEAT

ATTACH TO
FRONT SIDE
SEAM

ATTACH TO
BACK SIDE
SEAM

JOIN IN FABRIC

JOIN IN FABRIC

THE BREECHES ARE LINED WITH
WHITE LINEN AND INTERLINED
WITH COARSE BROWN WOOLLEN
CLOTH, BOTH CUT TO THE SAME
SHAPE AS THE VELVET. THE LINEN
LINING IS MADE UP SEPARATELY
AND CAUGHT DOWN, SEAM TO
SEAM, ON THE BROWN WOOL.

THE POCKET BAG IS MADE OF BROWN
FUSTIAN, LINEN WARP AND COTTON WEFT OR LINEN/
COTTON MIXTURE WEFT. THE MATERIAL
IS BRITTLE AND DISINTEGRATING.

THE VELVET IS A SOFT GREENISH BROWN WITH 19MM
(¾") WIDE STRIPES OF PLAIN CUT VELVET AND 25MM
(1") WIDE STRIPES OF ROWS OF UNCUT VELVET
ALTERNATING WITH CUT VELVET. THE SELVEDGE
IS 16MM (⅝") WIDE WITH A 1·5MM (1/16") WIDE WHITE
STRIPE WOVEN IN IT.

POCKET BAG IS
MISSING ON
RIGHT SIDE. THE
STITCHES AT THE
OPENING
REMAIN.

FOLD ON DOTTED LINES TO MAKE POCKET
BAG AND JOIN ALONG THE BOTTOM.

88

22A. A suit consisting of doublet and trunk-hose in creamy stone satin, backed with blue silk, slashed and pinked to reveal a white silk underlining. Over fifteen hours were spent taking the pattern and this close study resulted in almost instant recognition of the suit in a photograph of a portrait said to be of Sir Richard Cotton by Daniel Mytens (Fig. 190), sold at Sotheby's on 19 July 1961 formerly the property of the late Mr E. Peter Jones. Museum accession records stated that the suit was one of the Cotton family heirlooms, formerly at Etwall Hall in Derbyshire, and the gift of Lady Spickernell in 1938. The County Borough of Derby Central Library possesses 'An account and schedule of papers, deeds etc., at Etwall Hall in the County of Derby relating to the Cotton Estates' taken in August 1820, which includes material for the early seventeenth century, but there is no trace of the papers either there, or in the Record Offices of Derbyshire, Shropshire or Staffordshire. The papers may have included bills from tailor and portrait painter. There seemed to be no trace of any 'Sir Richard' but Dr John Newman kindly sent a few extracts from the will of Sir Rowland Cotton, who

left some beautiful clothes of the same quality as this suit. His effigy is shown in Figs. 198–9, wearing full trunk-hose. There may have been some confusion with names and perhaps the portrait shows Sir Rowland rather than Sir Richard Cotton, wearing his suit, although he appears to be younger than forty-one, Sir Rowland's age in 1618.

22B. On first sight the doublet appeared to be made of pinkish-cream satin with a faint stripe but this was caused by lines of couching holding the disintegrating material together over a backing of very pale pink rayon to reinforce it. There were also small areas of cream paint, presumably to cover discolorations. Fortunately the suit had undergone relatively little unpicking to enable conservation work to be carried out and had been restitched with the utmost care in exactly the same places. The belly-piece is made of four layers of stiff linen canvas pad-stitched together and two tabs with eyelet holes were laced across the front to pull the two sides together before any attempt was made to fasten the buttons.

22C. The full gathered trunk-hose were made of a layer of satin and blue silk worked as one layer, slashed and pinked, then laid over a layer of fine white silk which has almost disintegrated. Beneath this is a layer of white wool, open weave and springy in texture, cut to the same shape, which provides the padding. All these layers are gathered in cartridge pleats at top and legs to fit waistband and canions. A smaller white fustian lining, which reaches the top of the waistband, is stitched inside. This helps to hold the fullness in position, standing out over the canions. The fly front fastens with buttons and worked buttonholes.

22A

22B

22C

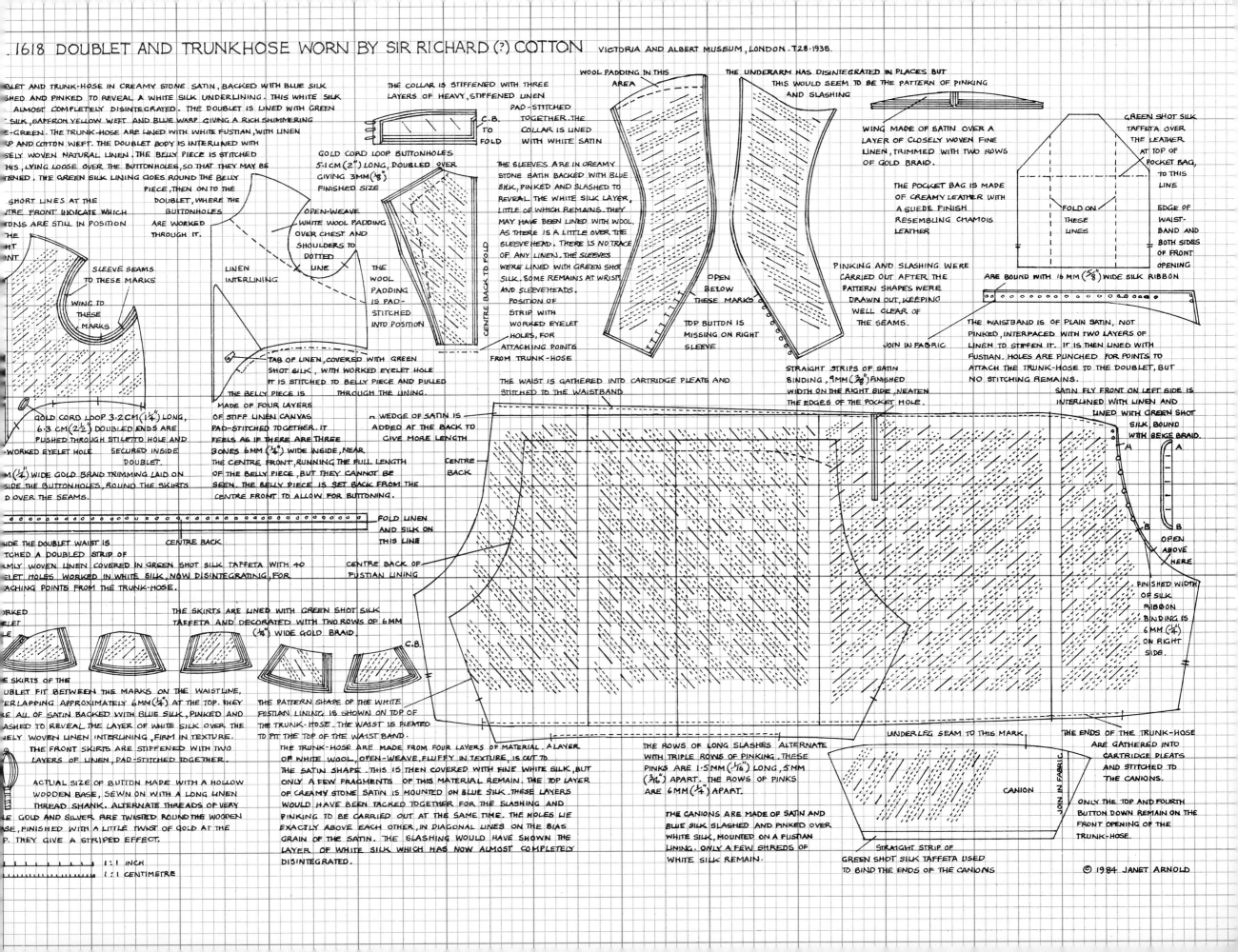

1618 DOUBLET AND TRUNKHOSE WORN BY SIR RICHARD (?) COTTON

VICTORIA AND ALBERT MUSEUM, LONDON. T28-1938.

DOUBLET AND TRUNK-HOSE IN CREAMY STONE SATIN, BACKED WITH BLUE SILK [SLA]SHED AND PINKED TO REVEAL A WHITE SILK UNDERLINING. THIS WHITE SILK [IS] ALMOST COMPLETELY DISINTEGRATED. THE DOUBLET IS LINED WITH GREEN [SI]LK, SAFFRON YELLOW WEFT AND BLUE WARP GIVING A RICH SHIMMERING [BLU]E-GREEN. THE TRUNK-HOSE ARE LINED WITH WHITE FUSTIAN, WITH LINEN [WAR]P AND COTTON WEFT. THE DOUBLET BODY IS INTERLINED WITH [CLO]SELY WOVEN NATURAL LINEN. THE BELLY PIECE IS STITCHED [OVER] THIS, LYING LOOSE OVER THE BUTTONHOLES, SO THAT THEY MAY BE [FAS]TENED. THE GREEN SILK LINING GOES ROUND THE BELLY PIECE, THEN ON TO THE DOUBLET, WHERE THE BUTTONHOLES ARE WORKED THROUGH IT.

[THE] SHORT LINES AT THE [CEN]TRE FRONT INDICATE WHICH [BUT]TONS ARE STILL IN POSITION

SLEEVE SEAMS TO THESE MARKS

WING TO THESE MARKS

LINEN INTERLINING

GOLD CORD LOOP BUTTONHOLES 5.1 CM (2") LONG, DOUBLED OVER GIVING 3MM (⅛") FINISHED SIZE

OPEN-WEAVE WHITE WOOL PADDING OVER CHEST AND SHOULDERS TO DOTTED LINE

THE WOOL PADDING IS PAD-STITCHED INTO POSITION

TAB OF LINEN, COVERED WITH GREEN SHOT SILK, WITH WORKED EYELET HOLE IT IS STITCHED TO BELLY PIECE AND PULLED THROUGH THE LINING.

GOLD CORD LOOP 3.2 CM (1¼") LONG, 6.3 CM (2½") DOUBLED ENDS ARE PUSHED THROUGH STILETTO HOLE AND [WORKED] EYELET HOLE SECURED INSIDE DOUBLET.

[6]M (¼") WIDE GOLD BRAID TRIMMING LAID ON [EITHER] SIDE THE BUTTONHOLES, ROUND THE SKIRTS [AND] OVER THE SEAMS.

THE BELLY PIECE IS MADE OF FOUR LAYERS OF STIFF LINEN CANVAS PAD-STITCHED TOGETHER. IT FEELS AS IF THERE ARE THREE BONES 6MM (¼") WIDE INSIDE, NEAR THE CENTRE FRONT, RUNNING THE FULL LENGTH OF THE BELLY PIECE, BUT THEY CANNOT BE SEEN. THE BELLY PIECE IS SET BACK FROM THE CENTRE FRONT TO ALLOW FOR BUTTONING.

A WEDGE OF SATIN IS ADDED AT THE BACK TO GIVE MORE LENGTH

CENTRE BACK TO FOLD

THE COLLAR IS STIFFENED WITH THREE LAYERS OF HEAVY, STIFFENED LINEN

PAD-STITCHED TOGETHER. THE COLLAR IS LINED WITH WHITE SATIN

C.B. TO FOLD

THE SLEEVES ARE IN CREAMY STONE SATIN BACKED WITH BLUE SILK, PINKED AND SLASHED TO REVEAL THE WHITE SILK LAYER, LITTLE OF WHICH REMAINS. THEY MAY HAVE BEEN LINED WITH WOOL, AS THERE IS A LITTLE OVER THE SLEEVE HEAD. THERE IS NO TRACE OF ANY LINEN. THE SLEEVES WERE LINED WITH GREEN SHOT SILK. SOME REMAINS AT WRIST AND SLEEVEHEADS. POSITION OF STRIP WITH WORKED EYELET HOLES, FOR ATTACHING POINTS FROM TRUNK-HOSE

THE WAIST IS GATHERED INTO CARTRIDGE PLEATS AND STITCHED TO THE WAISTBAND

CENTRE BACK TO FOLD

CENTRE BACK

FOLD LINEN AND SILK ON THIS LINE

CENTRE BACK

CENTRE BACK OF FUSTIAN LINING

WOOL PADDING IN THIS AREA

OPEN BELOW THESE MARKS

TOP BUTTON IS MISSING ON RIGHT SLEEVE

THE UNDERARM HAS DISINTEGRATED IN PLACES BUT THIS WOULD SEEM TO BE THE PATTERN OF PINKING AND SLASHING

PINKING AND SLASHING WERE CARRIED OUT AFTER THE PATTERN SHAPES WERE DRAWN OUT, KEEPING WELL CLEAR OF THE SEAMS.

JOIN IN FABRIC

STRAIGHT STRIPS OF SATIN BINDING, 9MM (⅜") FINISHED WIDTH ON THE RIGHT SIDE, NEATEN THE EDGES OF THE POCKET HOLE.

WING MADE OF SATIN OVER A LAYER OF CLOSELY WOVEN FINE LINEN, TRIMMED WITH TWO ROWS OF GOLD BRAID.

THE POCKET BAG IS MADE OF CREAMY LEATHER WITH A SUEDE FINISH RESEMBLING CHAMOIS LEATHER

GREEN SHOT SILK TAFFETA OVER THE LEATHER AT TOP OF POCKET BAG, TO THIS LINE

FOLD ON THESE LINES

EDGE OF WAIST-BAND AND BOTH SIDES OF FRONT OPENING

[THEY] ARE BOUND WITH 16 MM (⅝") WIDE SILK RIBBON

THE WAISTBAND IS OF PLAIN SATIN, NOT PINKED, INTERFACED WITH TWO LAYERS OF LINEN TO STIFFEN IT. IT IS THEN LINED WITH FUSTIAN. HOLES ARE PUNCHED FOR POINTS TO ATTACH THE TRUNK-HOSE TO THE DOUBLET, BUT NO STITCHING REMAINS.

SATIN FLY FRONT ON LEFT SIDE IS INTERLINED WITH LINEN AND LINED WITH GREEN SHOT SILK BOUND WITH BEIGE BRAID.

A / A

B / B

OPEN ABOVE HERE

FINISHED WIDTH OF SILK RIBBON BINDING IS 6MM (¼") ON RIGHT SIDE.

[INSIDE] THE DOUBLET WAIST IS [STI]TCHED A DOUBLED STRIP OF [FIR]MLY WOVEN LINEN COVERED IN GREEN SHOT SILK TAFFETA WITH 40 [EYE]LET HOLES WORKED IN WHITE SILK, NOW DISINTEGRATING, FOR [ATT]ACHING POINTS FROM THE TRUNK-HOSE.

[W]ORKED [EYE]LET [HOLE]

THE SKIRTS ARE LINED WITH GREEN SHOT SILK TAFFETA AND DECORATED WITH TWO ROWS OF 6MM (¼") WIDE GOLD BRAID.

C.B.

[TH]E SKIRTS OF THE [DO]UBLET FIT BETWEEN THE MARKS ON THE WAISTLINE, [THEY] ARE ALL OF SATIN BACKED WITH BLUE SILK, PINKED AND [SL]ASHED TO REVEAL THE LAYER OF WHITE SILK OVER THE [FI]NELY WOVEN LINEN INTERLINING, FIRM IN TEXTURE. THE FRONT SKIRTS ARE STIFFENED WITH TWO LAYERS OF LINEN, PAD-STITCHED TOGETHER.

ACTUAL SIZE OF BUTTON MADE WITH A HOLLOW WOODEN BASE, SEWN ON WITH A LONG LINEN THREAD SHANK. ALTERNATE THREADS OF VERY [PA]LE GOLD AND SILVER ARE TWISTED ROUND THE WOODEN [BA]SE, FINISHED WITH A LITTLE TWIST OF GOLD AT THE [TO]P. THEY GIVE A STRIPED EFFECT.

1:1 INCH
1:1 CENTIMETRE

THE PATTERN SHAPE OF THE WHITE FUSTIAN LINING IS SHOWN ON TOP OF THE TRUNK-HOSE. THE WAIST IS PLEATED TO FIT THE TOP OF THE WAIST BAND.

THE TRUNK-HOSE ARE MADE FROM FOUR LAYERS OF MATERIAL. A LAYER OF WHITE WOOL, OPEN-WEAVE, FLUFFY IN TEXTURE, IS CUT TO THE SATIN SHAPE. THIS IS THEN COVERED WITH FINE WHITE SILK, BUT ONLY A FEW FRAGMENTS OF THIS MATERIAL REMAIN. THE TOP LAYER OF CREAMY STONE SATIN IS MOUNTED ON BLUE SILK. THESE LAYERS WOULD HAVE BEEN TACKED TOGETHER FOR THE SLASHING AND PINKING TO BE CARRIED OUT AT THE SAME TIME. THE HOLES LIE EXACTLY ABOVE EACH OTHER, IN DIAGONAL LINES ON THE BIAS GRAIN OF THE SATIN. THE SLASHING WOULD HAVE SHOWN THE LAYER OF WHITE SILK WHICH HAS NOW ALMOST COMPLETELY DISINTEGRATED.

THE ROWS OF LONG SLASHES ALTERNATE WITH TRIPLE ROWS OF PINKING. THESE PINKS ARE 1.5MM (1/16") LONG, 5MM (3/16") APART. THE ROWS OF PINKS ARE 6MM (¼") APART.

THE CANIONS ARE MADE OF SATIN AND BLUE SILK SLASHED AND PINKED OVER WHITE SILK, MOUNTED ON A FUSTIAN LINING. ONLY A FEW SHREDS OF WHITE SILK REMAIN.

STRAIGHT STRIP OF GREEN SHOT SILK TAFFETA USED TO BIND THE ENDS OF THE CANIONS

UNDERLEG SEAM TO THIS MARK

CANION

JOIN IN FABRIC

THE ENDS OF THE TRUNK-HOSE ARE GATHERED INTO CARTRIDGE PLEATS AND STITCHED TO THE CANIONS.

ONLY THE TOP AND FOURTH BUTTON DOWN REMAIN ON THE FRONT OPENING OF THE TRUNK-HOSE.

© 1984 JANET ARNOLD

23A.   A suit consisting of doublet and trunk hose. The early provenance is not known. The satin ground, of a colour between light crimson and geranium, has an applied layer of soft, creamy leather with a suede finish, cut in a trellis design with carnations, or gillyflowers, in the spaces. The design is similar to that of the doublet in Richard Sackville, 3rd Earl of Dorset's portrait (Fig. 200). Presumably the pattern shapes of the suit were drawn out on the leather, then the trellis shapes lightly scored on each one and the design of carnations traced out. The pieces of leather would then have been placed on top of the satin, stretched taut in an embroidery frame, giving generous turnings to allow for the amount which would be taken up with the stitching, or quilting as Alcega described it in 1589. Every shape was then outlined with small, even back stitches in pale pink silk, now faded. Large areas were then skilfully cut away to reveal the satin below.

23B.   The doublet has a supportasse, or underpropper, attached to the collar. It is made of several layers of linen pad-stitched together, probably stiffened with whalebones as there are no rust marks from an iron or steel framework. Small scraps of ivory silk are pieced together, disregarding the grain of the material, to cover the linen. Additional pieces of ivory silk are also stitched inside the doublet collar. This is all covered with a strip of ivory silk which hides the raw edges and acts as a collar lining. A standing band of linen bordered with lace, or entirely of lace, stiffly starched, would have been worn with this doublet. The front is stiffened with a belly-piece made of layers of coarse linen with rows of stitching in linen thread holding strips of whalebone between them. The left side of the belly-piece is made slightly smaller than the right. It is set back under the buttonholes so that when the buttons are fastened the edges of the belly-piece butt together in the centre front and lie flat to give a smooth line. Eyelet holes are worked in the tabs forming the skirts of the doublet. Some are to take the long points supporting the breeches, others for short decorative points, some of which are still in position. From 1560 to about 1610 points were hidden beneath the doublet skirts, fastened through eyelet holes worked in a band at the waist. This fashion for having the points tied through the doublet skirts and seen in the first decade of the seventeenth century became more widespread in the second decade. Extra points were tied on for decoration and gradually heavy metal hooks and eyes replaced the functional points during the 1620s. The decorative points remained round the waist of the doublet until the 1630s.

23A

23B

.c.1615-20 DOUBLET AND TRUNK HOSE   MUSEO PARMIGIANINO, REGGIO EMILIA

3LET AND TRUNK-HOSE IN LIGHT CRIMSON SATIN AND SOFT CREAMY LEATHER A SUEDE FINISH RESEMBLING HEAVY CHAMOIS LEATHER. THE MOTIFS ARE ANGED IN 10.7 CM (4¼") X 12.7 CM (5") IDENTICAL REPEATS. THE LEATHER LD PROBABLY HAVE BEEN MARKED OUT IN TRELLIS SHAPES FIRST, THEN PATTERN OF CARNATIONS DRAWN OUT. THE LEATHER IS OUTLINED WITH SMALL, N BACK-STITCHES IN PALE PINK SILK THREAD, NOW FADED. THE BRAID USED FOR ORATION IS MADE OF A SOFT SHADE OF YELLOW SILK, 6 MM (¼") WIDE, FOLDED N BOTH EDGES TO GIVE 3 MM (⅛") FINISHED WIDTH. THIS GIVES A RAISED EFFECT. E IS A 13 MM (½") LOOP BUTTONHOLE OF THIS BRAID AT THE BASE OF THE COLLAR. DOUBLET BODY IS INTERLINED WITH COARSE LINEN, ALMOST LIKE HESSIAN OUCH, BUT NOT SO COARSELY WOVEN. THE SAME MATERIAL IS O FOR THE BELLY PIECE. THE DOUBLET IS THEN LINED WITH RAL LINEN. SAFFRON YELLOW SILK IS USED TO FACE THE BLET FOR 3.2 MM (1¼") ON THE RIGHT FRONT AND BENEATH BUTTON HOLES HE LEFT FRONT, TO COVER THE YPIECE. 27 ONHOLES ARE KED IN CREAMY- OWISH SILK M (½") APART. Y ARE 16 MM) LONG, ROUND S AT CENTRE T, SQUARE THE OTHER END.

EXTRA LAYER OF LINEN IN THIS AREA

EXTRA LAYER OF LINEN IN THIS AREA

SLEEVE SEAM TO THIS MARK

WING TO THESE MARKS

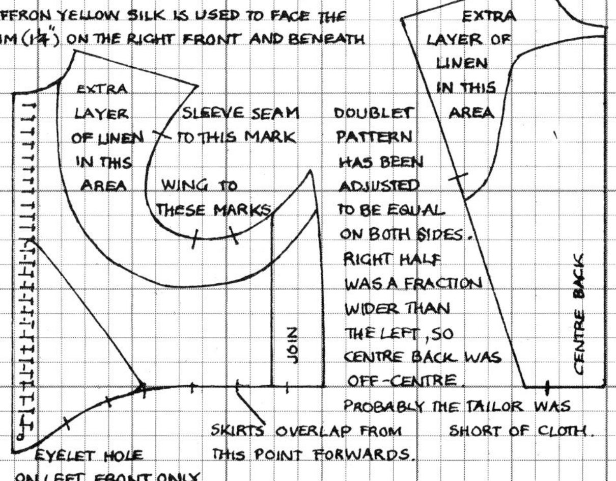

DOUBLET PATTERN HAS BEEN ADJUSTED TO BE EQUAL ON BOTH SIDES. RIGHT HALF WAS A FRACTION WIDER THAN THE LEFT, SO CENTRE BACK WAS OFF-CENTRE

CENTRE BACK

JOIN

EYELET HOLE ON LEFT FRONT ONLY

SKIRTS OVERLAP FROM THIS POINT FORWARDS.

SHORT OF CLOTH. PROBABLY THE TAILOR WAS

THE SHOULDER WING IS MADE OF TWO LAYERS OF LINEN COVERED WITH LIGHT CRIMSON SATIN, DECORATED WITH 44 PINKED STRIPS OF LEATHER. THE STRIPS ARE ALTERNATELY 3 MM (⅛") WIDE PLAIN AND 6 MM (¼") WIDE WITH PINKED EDGES, SET ABOUT 1.5 MM (1/16") APART

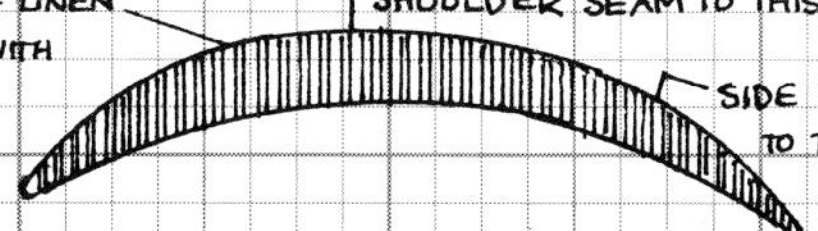

THE SLEEVE IS LINED WITH LINEN. OVER THIS IS LAID SAFFRON YELLOW SILK, AS FAR AS THE DOTTED LINE, AT THE WRIST AND THE SIDES OF THE OPENING, 6.9 MM (2¾") DEEP AT THE WRIST AND 25 MM (1") AT THE SIDES. THE BUTTONS MATCH THOSE FASTENING THE DOUBLET FRONT. TOP BUTTON IS MISSING ON LEFT SLEEVE

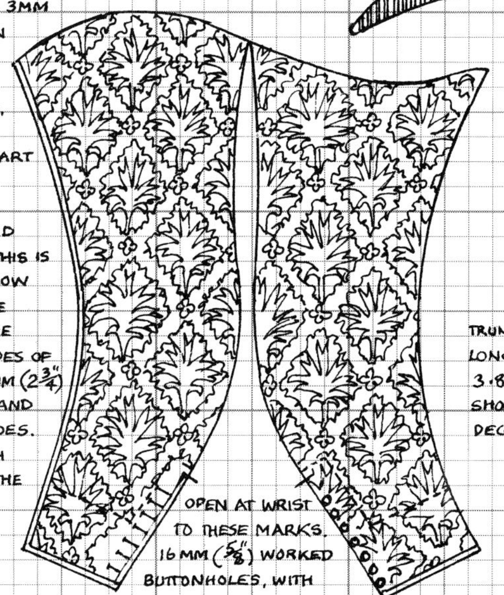

OPEN AT WRIST TO THESE MARKS. 16 MM (⅝") WORKED BUTTONHOLES, WITH SQUARE AND ROUNDED ENDS

SHOULDER SEAM TO THIS MARK

SIDE BACK SEAM TO THIS MARK

THE POINTS AT THE DOUBLET WAIST ARE MADE OF THE SAME SATIN AS THE DOUBLET. THEY ARE 25 MM (1") WIDE AND 38.1 CM (15") LONG, CUT ON THE STRAIGHT GRAIN AND TURNED UNDER ON THE EDGES, HELD DOWN WITH RUNNING STITCHES. THE HEMS ARE 1.5 MM (1/16") WIDE AND ARE FRAYING SLIGHTLY, AS IT IS ONLY A SINGLE TURNING. THE ENDS ARE CAUGHT INTO AGLETS, OR TAGS, OF SOME METAL WHICH HAS RUSTED. THESE ARE 4.7 CM (1⅞") LONG. SOME OF THE ORIGINAL VIVID LIGHT CRIMSON REMAINS, BUT MOST OF THE RIBBONS HAVE FADED TO A DIRTY WINE COLOUR. THE POINTS IN THE WAISTBAND OF THE TRUNK-HOSE ARE 40.6 CM (16") LONG WITH METAL AGLETS 3.8 CM (1½") LONG. THE SHORTER POINTS ARE FOR DECORATION ONLY.

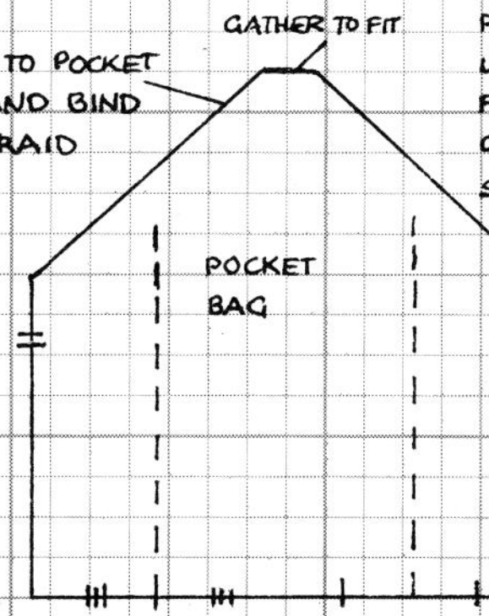

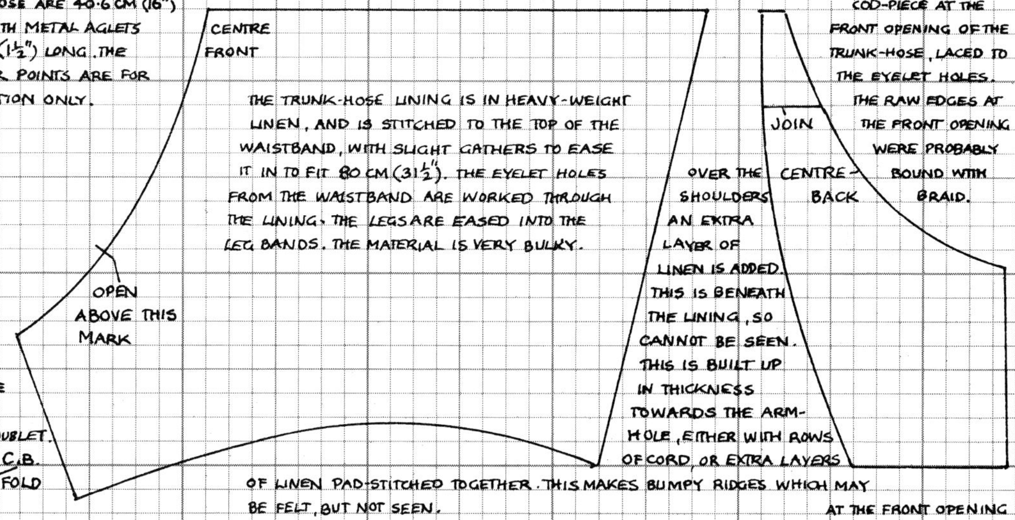

CENTRE FRONT

OPEN ABOVE THIS MARK

C.B. FOLD

WAISTBAND OF DOUBLE LAYER OF HEAVY LINEN COVERED WITH LEATHER 3 MM (⅛") THICK, CUT ON A SLIGHT CURVE, MEASURING 80 CM (31½") AT THE TOP, 91.4 CM (36") AT THE BOTTOM. IT IS 3.8 CM (1½") DEEP, PIECED IN SEVERAL PLACES. THERE ARE 9 PAIRS OF EYELET HOLES TO FASTEN POINTS TO DOUBLET.

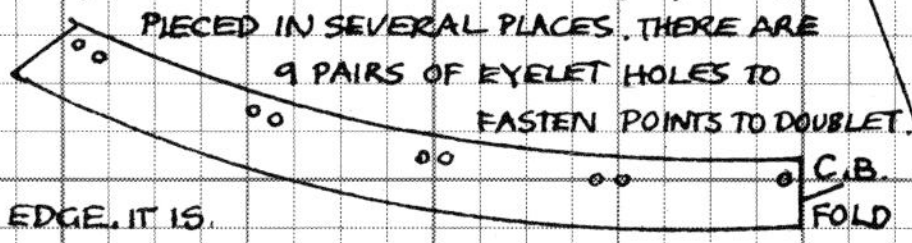

ATTACH TO POCKET HOLE AND BIND WITH BRAID

GATHER TO FIT

POCKET BAG

POCKET BAG IN CREAM LEATHER WITH A SUEDE FINISH SIMILAR TO CHAMOIS LEATHER. THE SHAPE IS APPROXIMATE AS THE LEATHER WAS TOO STIFF TO PULL OUT AND MEASURE PRECISELY.

JOIN

OVER THE SHOULDERS

CENTRE BACK

THERE MAY ORIGINALLY HAVE BEEN A COD-PIECE AT THE FRONT OPENING OF THE TRUNK-HOSE, LACED TO THE EYELET HOLES. THE RAW EDGES AT THE FRONT OPENING WERE PROBABLY BOUND WITH BRAID.

AN EXTRA LAYER OF LINEN IS ADDED THIS IS BENEATH THE LINING, SO CANNOT BE SEEN. THIS IS BUILT UP IN THICKNESS TOWARDS THE ARM-HOLE, EITHER WITH ROWS OF CORD, OR EXTRA LAYERS

THE TRUNK-HOSE LINING IS IN HEAVY-WEIGHT LINEN, AND IS STITCHED TO THE TOP OF THE WAISTBAND, WITH SLIGHT GATHERS TO EASE IT IN TO FIT 80 CM (31½"). THE EYELET HOLES FROM THE WAISTBAND ARE WORKED THROUGH THE LINING. THE LEGS ARE EASED INTO THE LEG BANDS. THE MATERIAL IS VERY BULKY.

BELLYPIECE IS MADE OF LAYERS OF LINEN TCHED TOGETHER IN ROWS WITH STRIPS OF WHALEBONE BETWEEN THEM, GRADING IN THICKNESS FROM 9 MM (⅜") AT CENTRE FRONT WAIST TO 1.5 MM (1/16") AT TOP AND SIDES. IT FEELS AS IF THERE ARE ELEVEN STRIPS OF WHALEBONE. THE BELLY- PIECE IS MADE SEPARATELY FROM THE DOUBLET AND SET BACK 13 MM (½") M THE EDGE BENEATH THE BUTTON- ES ON THE LEFT FRONT. IT IS CAUGHT THE LINEN LINING AND SAFFRON LOW SILK TO KEEP IT IN POSITION. E SHAPE GIVEN IS FOR THE RIGHT NT. THE LEFT SIDE IS SMALLER E DOTTED LINE BENEATH BUTTON- ES).

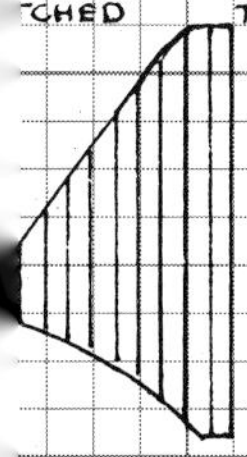

THE SUPPORTASSE IS ATTACHED TO THE COLLAR. IT IS MADE OF SEVERAL LAYERS OF LINEN PAD-STITCHED TOGETHER, PROBABLY STIFFENED WITH WHALEBONES, AS THERE ARE NO RUST MARKS FROM IRON OR STEEL. THE SUPPORTASSE RUCKLES SLIGHTLY AROUND THE EDGE. IT IS MADE OF SMALL SCRAPS OF IVORY SILK ON DIFFERENT GRAINS PIECED TOGETHER, SO IT IS DIFFICULT TO TAKE AN ACCURATE PATTERN. THERE ARE ADDITIONAL PIECES OF IVORY SILK WHICH ARE STITCHED INSIDE THE DOUBLET COLLAR. THIS IS ALL COVERED WITH A STRIP OF IVORY SILK WHICH CONCEALS THE RAW EDGES AND ACTS AS A COLLAR LINING.

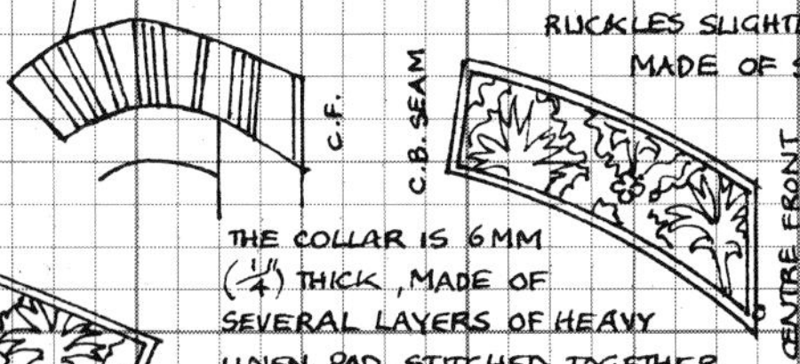

C.F.

C.B. SEAM

CENTRE FRONT

THE COLLAR IS 6 MM (¼") THICK, MADE OF SEVERAL LAYERS OF HEAVY LINEN PAD-STITCHED TOGETHER COVERED WITH LIGHT CRIMSON SATIN AND APPLIED LEATHER AND LINED WITH IVORY SATIN.

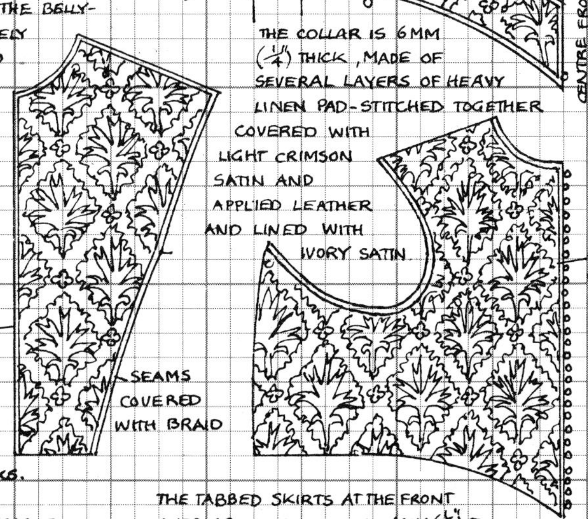

AN ADDITIONAL STRIP OF BRAID IS PLACED ON C.F. ON LEFT SIDE, AS WELL AS THAT BINDING THE EDGE.

FRONT OPEN TO THIS MARK

PIECE OF PLAIN LEATHER SIMILAR TO HEAVY CHAMOIS

IN THIS AREA, TO THE LINE, THE PATTERN IS STITCHED ON THE LEATHER, BUT NOT CUT OUT

THE TRUNK-HOSE WAIST IS GATHERED INTO CARTRIDGE PLEATS, TO FIT WAISTBAND, 80 CM (36") FOR WHOLE WAIST MEASUREMENT.

OF LINEN PAD-STITCHED TOGETHER. THIS MAKES BUMPY RIDGES WHICH MAY BE FELT, BUT NOT SEEN.

INSIDE THE TOP OF THE TRUNK-HOSE, ATTACHED TO THE BOTTOM OF THE WAISTBAND, IS STITCHED A PIECE OF COARSE WOOL WITH HORSEHAIR ATTACHED TO IT (FOR PADDING) TO THIS DOTTED LINE.

OPEN HERE FOR POCKET AND BOUND WITH BRAID.

AT THE FRONT OPENING OF THE TRUNKHOSE THERE IS A SMALL HOOK ON LEFT SIDE AT THE TOP. ANOTHER SMALL HOOK ON RIGHT SIDE AND AN EYE ON LEFT SIDE AT THE BOTTOM, ALL APPARENTLY ORIGINAL. THERE ARE ALSO EYELET HOLES.

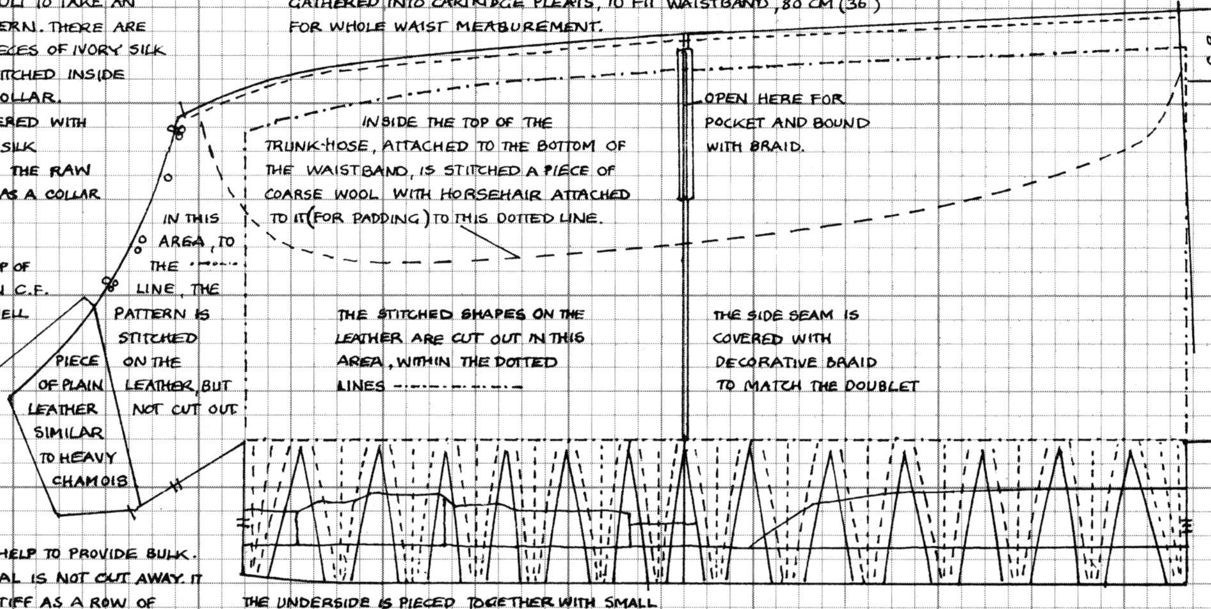

C.B.

CENTRE BACK DOUBLET IS TO A FOLD AND OUTLINED WITH 6 MM (¼") WIDE BRAID FOLDED DOWN TO 3 MM (⅛"). THE EFFECT IS OF BUTTONHOLE STITCHING.

BUTTONS ARE 6 MM (¼") HIGH X 6 MM (¼") DIAMETER, SEWN ON WITH 3 MM (⅛") SHANKS. Y ARE WORKED IN SILK, POSSIBLY PINK GINALLY, NOW FADED TO A YELLOWISH COLOUR.

SEAMS COVERED WITH BRAID

THE TABBED SKIRTS AT THE FRONT OVERLAP EACH OTHER BY 6 MM (¼") TO 9 MM (⅜") WHERE THEY ARE STITCHED ON.

C.F.

THE DARTS HELP TO PROVIDE BULK. THE MATERIAL IS NOT CUT AWAY. IT FEELS AS STIFF AS A ROW OF WHALEBONES.

THE STITCHED SHAPES ON THE LEATHER ARE CUT OUT IN THIS AREA, WITHIN THE DOTTED LINES ------

THE SIDE SEAM IS COVERED WITH DECORATIVE BRAID TO MATCH THE DOUBLET

PLAIN LEATHER SIMILAR TO CHAMOIS LEATHER

THE UNDERSIDE IS PIECED TOGETHER WITH SMALL PIECES OF LEATHER. THESE DO NOT SHOW. THE PIECING VARIES SLIGHTLY ON EACH SIDE.

LEG BAND OF LEATHER OVER A LINEN BASE, WITH 34 WORKED EYELET HOLES FOR LACING POINTS. IT IS VERY STIFF.

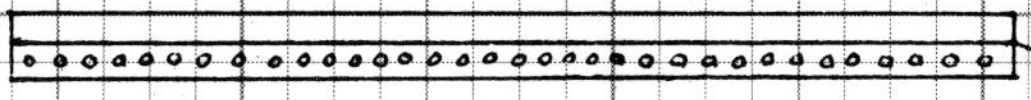

1:1 INCH

1:1 CENTIMETRE

THE DOUBLET SKIRTS ARE INTERLINED WITH LINEN, LINED WITH SAFFRON YELLOW SILK AND BOUND WITH BRAID 6 MM (¼") FINISHED WIDTH ON THE RIGHT SIDE. EACH TAB HAS A CARNATION LEATHER MOTIF.

FOLD LINE

© 1984 JANET ARNOLD

92

23C. The trunk-hose are similar to many seen in English miniatures and paintings in the second decade of the seventeenth century (Figs. 179 and 201). They are lined with heavyweight linen and beneath this, caught to the bottom of the waistband, is a layer of coarse wool with horsehair attached to it (Fig. 207) to support the mass of gathering and give a rounded shape. The front fastens with hooks and eyes, which appear to be contemporary, but there are also worked eyelet holes for points or laces. There may originally have been a small cod-piece attached to the front opening, laced to the eyelet holes, perhaps removed shortly after the suit was made because it was unfashionable. The raw edges at the front opening were probably bound with braid but this has worn away. The eyelet holes at the waist are worked through the lining and some of the points remain, made of straight strips of the same satin as the suit, with metal aglets. Both these long functional points and the short decorative ones on the doublet are cut on the straight grain. The edges are held down with running stitches, fraying slightly as it is only a single turning. The side seams are covered with decorative silk braid, of a soft shade of yellow matching that trimming the doublet. Both side seams are open at the top for large pocket bags made of cream leather with a suede finish, similar to chamois leather.

23D. The leather is left uncut under the legs of the trunk-hose, although the pattern is worked. This, together with all the back-stitching and the long darts, helps to hold the rounded shape. The darts are so rigid that they feel like a row of whalebones. Other methods of stiffening trunk-hose included stuffing them with bran, according to one story told by John Bulwer in his book *Anthropo-metamorphosis: Man Transform'd or The Artificial Changling* (1653):

'At the time when the fashion came up of wearing Trunk-hose, some young men used so to stuffe them with rags, and other like things, that you might find some that used such inventions to extend them in compasse with as great eagernesse, as the women did take pleasure to weare great and stately Verdingales. . . . The Author of the Spanish Gallant tells us a story of what happened to one that thought he excelled so much in this fashion, that he stuffed a Follado of Velvet, that he did weare, with branne, and being set in seemely manner amongst some Ladies, to whom he desired to shew his bravery and neatnesse, as he was talking merrily of something that pleased him, he was so excedingly taken with delight that possessed him, that he could not take notice of a small rent which was made, with a naile of the chaire he sat upon, in one of his two pockets of branne (who though the harme was but in his hose, yet he found it after in his heart), for, as he was moving and stroaking himselfe (with much gallantry) the bran began to drop out by little and little, without his perceiving it, but the Ladies that sat over against him and saw it (it being by his motion like meale that commeth from the Mill as it grindeth) laughed much at it, and looked one upon another, and the Gallant supposing that his good behaviour, mirth and sporting, was pleasing to them, laughed with the Ladies for company; and it so much pleased him, that the more he strove to delight the company the more the Mill did grind forth the branne; the laughter by little and little encreased, and he appeared as confident as a man that had shed much bloud by a wound, untill he espied the heape of branne, which came out of his hose, and then he began to recall himselfe, and dissembling his shame, he took his leave and departed.'

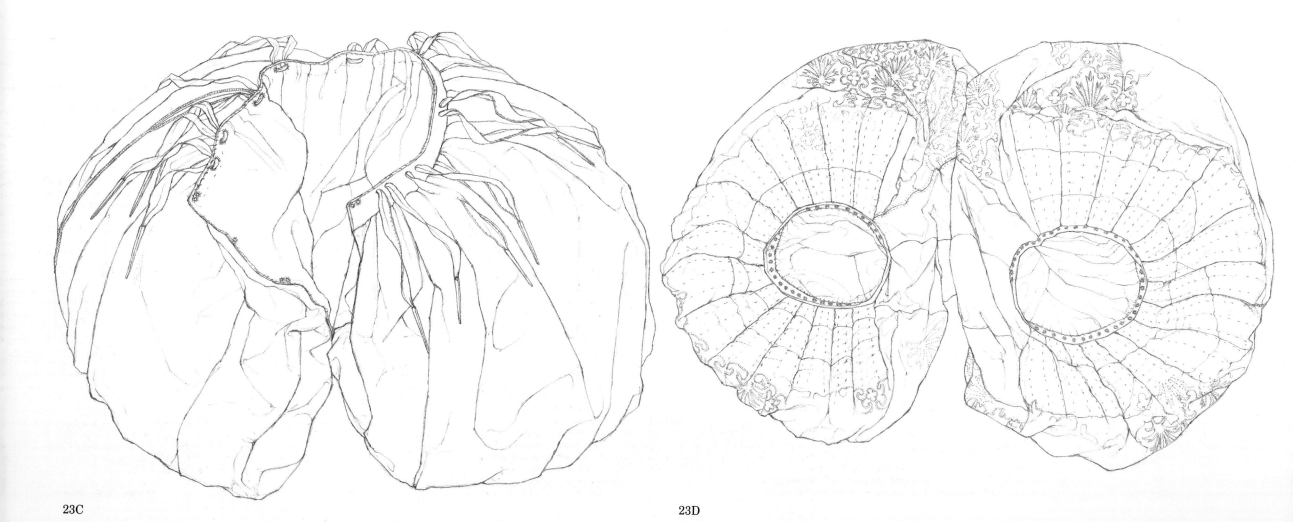

23C

23D

+1567 FELT BONNET WITH WOOL PILE

ALA CATHEDRAL

-CROWNED BONNET, OR CAP, MADE OF FELT WITH A TUFTED PILE OF BLACK RYA
L WITH A SILKY FINISH. THE TECHNIQUE OF LOOPED CUT STITCHES CREATES THE
ECT OF A DEEP, THICK, VELVETY PILE. THIS IS A SIMPLER METHOD THAN THAT USED
THE HIGH-CROWNED HAT FROM NÜRNBERG (25) BECAUSE THE FELT WOULD
E GRIPPED THE WOOL SECURELY, WHEREAS SILK WOULD HAVE BEEN LIABLE
SLIP AND REQUIRED BACK STITCHING.

PINK SILK BRIM LINING, 6.9 CM (2¾") WIDE, WITH 6 MM
(¼") SEAM ALLOWANCE ON THE INNER EDGE. MUCH
OF THE SEAM ALLOWANCE HAS DISINTEGRATED
BUT SOME OF THE STITCH HOLES REMAIN ON THE
DOTTED LINE. ON THE OUTER EDGE A 9 MM
(⅜") TURNING IS ALLOWED.

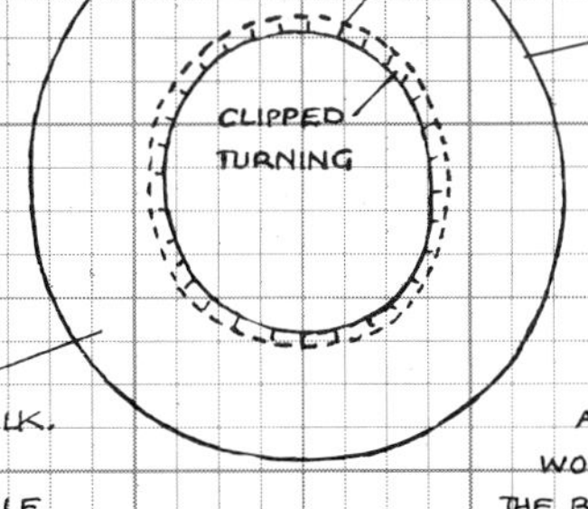

CLIPPED
TURNING

TRACES OF BLACK SILK TAFFETA
REMAIN IN THE STITCHING
ROUND THE OUTER EDGE, AND
A FEW TUFTS OF STITCHING IN
DARK BROWN OR BLACK
SILK. ORIGINALLY THERE MAY
HAVE BEEN A BLACK SILK BRIM
LINING WHICH WAS REPLACED
WITH PINK SILK WHEN WORN OUT.
A FEW FRAGMENTS OF FELT WITH
WOOLLEN PILE REMAIN STITCHED TO
THE BRIM LINING.

RE ARE NO
S IN THE SILK.
S CUT IN A
PLETE CIRCLE.

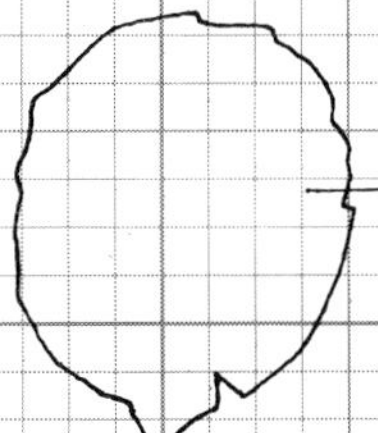

FRAGMENT OF PLAIN FELT, PROBABLY
CIRCULAR ORIGINALLY, WHICH WOULD HAVE
SUPPORTED THE CROWN OF THE HAT AND
PREVENTED IT FROM SAGGING WITH THE
WEIGHT OF THE PILE. IT WAS PROBABLY
SHAPED TO COME TO THE INNER EDGE OF THE
CROWN. NO TRACE OF A CURVED AREA REMAINS
NOR ANY PIECES BENEATH THE FELT WITH THE
PILE LEFT ON THE SILK BRIM LINING.

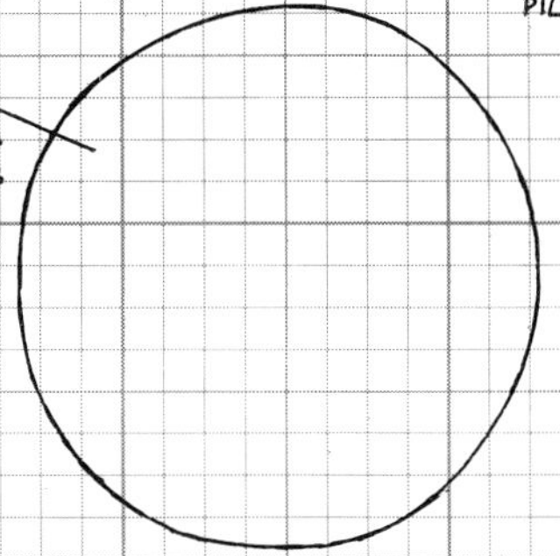

JECTURED
APE OF FLAT
OWN. ONLY A
FRAGMENTS
MAIN.

DIAGRAM TO SHOW
CONJECTURED METHOD OF
WORKING THE PILE ON THE
SURFACE OF THE FELT.

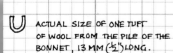

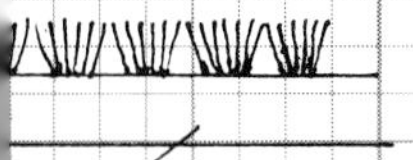

TUAL SIZE OF WOOL
E AND FELT TOGETHER,
M (⁵⁄₁₆") DEEP.

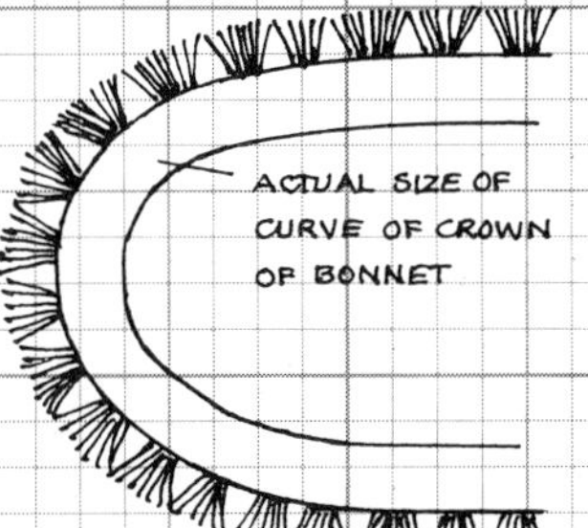

ACTUAL SIZE OF
CURVE OF CROWN
OF BONNET

U ACTUAL SIZE OF ONE TUFT
OF WOOL FROM THE PILE OF THE
BONNET, 13 MM (½") LONG.

|‖‖‖‖‖| 1 : 1 INCH   ‖‖‖‖‖‖‖‖‖‖‖‖‖‖   1 : 1 CENTIMETRE

25. c.1565-1600 FELT HAT WITH SILK PILE

GERMANISCHES NATIONALMUSEUM, NÜRNBERG. T32.

HIGH CROWNED HAT MADE OF THICK FELT, SIMILAR TO CARPET FELT, WITH A TUFTED PILE OF
WHAT APPEARS TO BE SIX-STRAND SPUN SILK. THE FELT IS 5 MM (³⁄₁₆") THICK AND WITH THE
PILE IT VARIES BETWEEN 6 MM (¼") AND 8 MM (⁵⁄₁₆") THICK. THE CROWN IS INTERLINED
WITH A LAYER OF COARSE LINEN, CLOSELY WOVEN, ORIGINALLY NATURAL COLOUR, NOW
DISCOLOURED. SOME CAN BE SEEN THROUGH THE ROTTEN BLACK SILK LINING.
THE FELT FOUNDATION WAS MOULDED FIRST, PROBABLY WITH STEAM OVER A WOODEN
BLOCK. IT IS ALL IN ONE PIECE INCLUDING THE BRIM, AND STIFFENED INSIDE WITH SOME
KIND OF GLUE. THE BRIM IS NOT INTERLINED WITH LINEN. THE EFFECT OF A PLUSH PILE IS
GIVEN BY APPARENTLY WORKING SMALL NEAT EVEN BACK STITCHES, LEAVING A LOOP
EVERY ALTERNATE STITCH OVER THE WHOLE HAT.

CIRCUMFERENCE
OF HAT AT TOP
IS 58.4 CM (23"),
AT BASE IT IS
58.4 CM (23").
INSIDE
MEASUREMENT
IS 55.8 CM (22").
HEIGHT OF HAT TO THE
PLACE WHERE IT
ROUNDS OVER THE TOP
IS 19 CM (7½"). IT IS
APPROXIMATELY 13 MM (½")
HIGHER IN THE CENTRE,
MAKING A TOTAL HEIGHT
OF 20.3 CM (8").

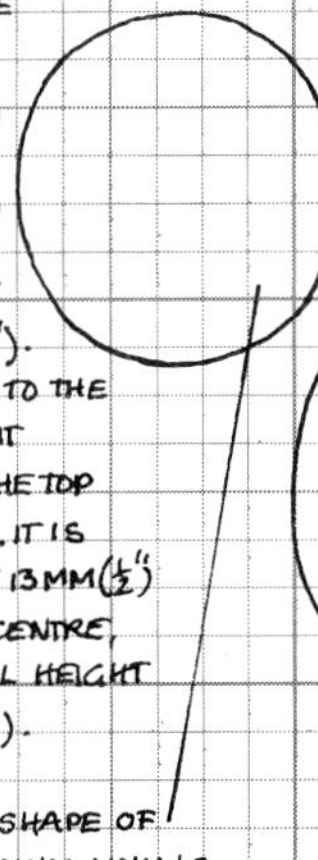

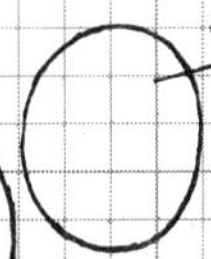

SHAPE OF TOP OF CROWN WHERE THE
STITCHES ARE IN APPROXIMATELY FORTY
STRAIGHT ROWS GIVING A TWILLED EFFECT

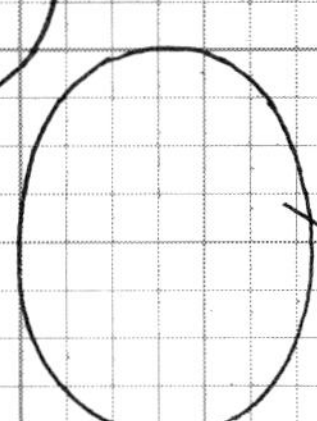

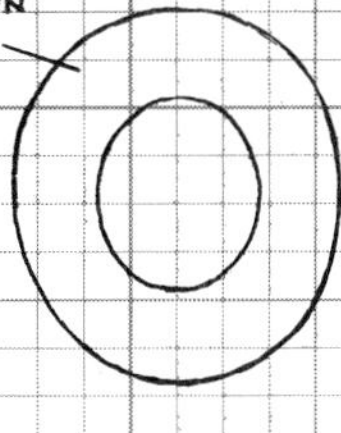

SHAPE OF CROWN
FROM CENTRE TO
SIDES, WHERE
STITCHES ARE
ARRANGED
IN CIRCLES

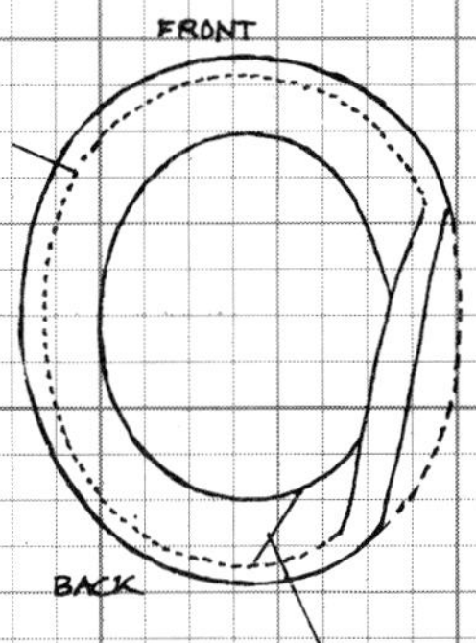

SHAPE OF INSIDE
BASE OF CROWN

CONJECTURED SHAPE OF
BLACK SILK CROWN LINING.

THE ROWS OF STITCHING GIVING THE
LONG PILE ARE STAGGERED SO THAT
THE EFFECT IS OF A TWILL WEAVE. AFTER
THE LOOPS WERE CUT THE PILE WOULD HAVE
BEEN SHORN TO GIVE THE EFFECT OF BLACK
VELVET OR PLUSH. MOST OF THE PILE HAS
NOW DISINTEGRATED, BUT IT IS BLACK THICK
AND SILKY WHERE IT REMAINS. IT IS
5 MM (³⁄₁₆") HIGH APPROXIMATELY.

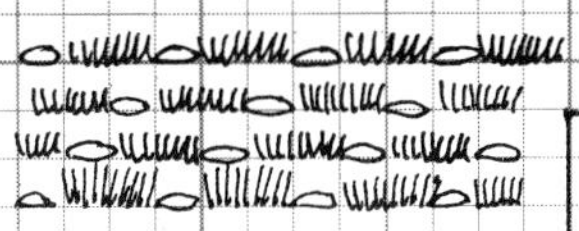

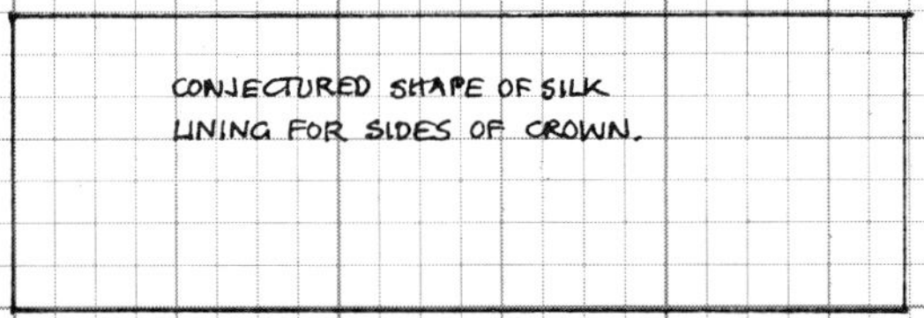

THE STITCHES SEEM TO
BE WORKED IN ROWS UP
AND DOWN THE HAT.
ENLARGED DIAGRAM
SHOWS PROPORTIONS OF
STITCHES AND LOOPS.

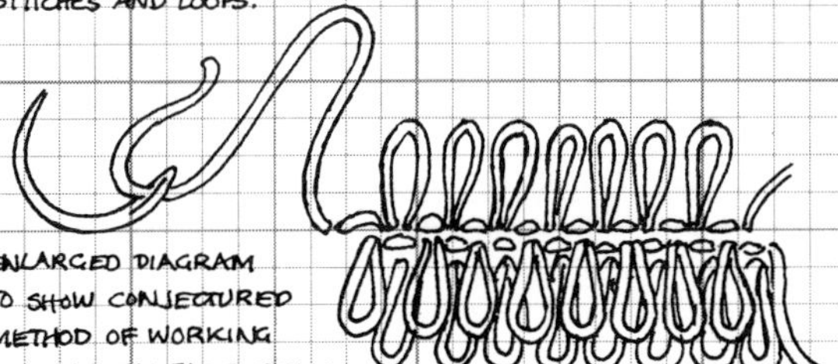

ENLARGED DIAGRAM
TO SHOW CONJECTURED
METHOD OF WORKING
THE PILE ON THE SURFACE
OF THE FELT, PRESUMABLY
WITH A CURVED NEEDLE.

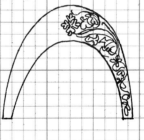

FRONT

ON THE LEFT
SIDE THE BRIM
IS CURLED UP.
BLACK AND
WHITE
OSTRICH
FEATHERS
WITH A
RUCHED
STRIP OF
BLACK SILK
RIBBON HAVE
REPLACED THE
ORIGINALS.

BRIM OF HAT
LINED TO THE
DOTTED LINE

BACK

JOIN IN BLACK
SILK LINING

CONJECTURED SHAPE OF SILK
LINING FOR SIDES OF CROWN.

THE LINING OF THE CROWN HAS ROTTED AWAY SO THE PATTERN
SHAPE CANNOT BE TAKEN ACCURATELY. ALL THE REMAINING
FRAGMENTS SHOW THAT IT WAS PIECED TOGETHER FROM
SMALL REMNANTS OF SILK. BRIM AND CROWN LINING WERE
JOINED TOGETHER BEFORE BEING PUT INTO THE HAT.

EXAMINATION UNDER THE
MICROSCOPE SHOWS THAT
THE SPUN SILK DOES NOT
HAVE MUCH TWIST. 2 MM
(¹⁄₁₆") FOR EACH BACK STITCH
AND 3 MM (⅛") FOR PILE,
SO THE STITCHES ARE VERY
CLOSE TOGETHER.
THE PILE IS VERY TIGHT
AND HAS A LUSTROUS SHEEN.

26. c.1600 VELVET AND FELT MORION HAT

GERMANISCHES NATIONALMUSEUM, NÜRNBERG. T34.

THE MORION HAT IS MOULDED FROM THICK FELT RESEMBLING MODERN FELT UNDERLAY FOR
CARPETS. THE CREST IS PINCHED TOGETHER AND STITCHED THROUGH AT THE BASE, OVER THE
TOP OF THE HAT, WITH WHITE LINEN THREAD. INSIDE THE FELT IS BRUSHED OVER WITH SIZE, A
STIFFENING AGENT MADE FROM PROTEIN GLUE: THERE ARE SOME TRACES OF IT VISIBLE
ON THE SURFACE OF THE FELT, WHICH WERE TESTED BY ERIKA WEILAND AND ANNELIESE
STREITER IN THE TEXTILE CONSERVATION WORKSHOP.
THE BRIM IS COVERED WITH LINEN WHICH IS TAKEN ROUND THE EDGE OF THE FELT FOR 6 MM (¼").
THE FELT IS 3 MM (⅛") THICK. THE LINEN IS SEWN DOWN WITH LARGE STITCHES IN LINEN
THREAD. THE CREST IS COVERED WITH LINEN AND OVER THIS EMBROIDERED BLACK VELVET. THE
LINEN WAS USED AS THE BACKING FOR THIS EMBROIDERY. MOST OF THE VELVET PILE HAS
DISINTEGRATED. THE TOP SEAM IS STITCHED THEN THE MATERIAL TURNED THROUGH AND EASED
OVER THE FELT. IT IS THEN STITCHED TO THE FELT AT THE BASE OF THE CREST. THE SIDES OF
THE HAT ARE COVERED WITH BLACK VELVET EMBROIDERED WITH GOLD THREAD, HEMMED TO THE
BOTTOM OF THE CREST. THE BRIM IS COVERED WITH EMBROIDERED VELVET BACKED WITH LINEN,
WHICH IS HEMMED TO THE BOTTOM OF THE HAT. THERE IS NO TRACE OF A LINING.

ALL THE BLACK VELVET PILE HAS DISINTEGRATED, LEAVING
ONLY TINY FRAGMENTS ROUND THE SEAM AT THE JOIN OF
THE CROWN AND CREST. THE SILK GROUND HAS DISCOLOURED
TO BROWN.

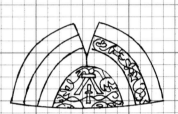

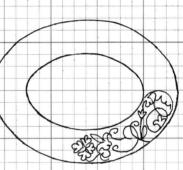

THE EMBROIDERY IS CARRIED OUT IN
COUCHED GOLD METAL THREAD WITH A BROWN
SILK CORE, WITH SILVER BULLION FOR THE
TREFOIL AND SOME OF THE OTHER LEAF
SHAPES. SOME ARE RAISED WITH A PADDING
OF LINEN THREADS. IN THE CENTRE OF THE
TREFOIL LEAF ON TOP OF THE CREST IS A
LOOPED STRIP OF PARCHMENT COVERED
WITH GOLD THREAD, 1.5 MM (¹⁄₁₆") WIDE. THE
INITIALS A I ARE IN GOLD THREAD OVER A
PADDING OF LINEN THREADS. SOME OF THE
SILVER BULLION EMBROIDERY SEEMS TO
HAVE BEEN CLEANED.

THESE THREADS ARE USED
FOR THE EMBROIDERY.
1. TREFOIL LEAVES = SILVER BULLION
OUTLINED IN GOLD THREAD WITH BROWN
SILK CORE.
2. LEAVES = GOLD THREAD WITH BROWN
SILK CORE.
3. HEAVY STEMS = SILVER THREAD WITH BROWN
SILK CORD, TWO STRANDS TWISTED TOGETHER,
OUTLINED WITH GOLD THREAD WITH BROWN
SILK CORE.
4. SEPARATE PIECES OF BULLION ARE PUT
OVER THE STEMS, OR POSSIBLY TINY
PIECES OF COILED WIRE WITH A SILK
THREAD THROUGH EACH TO HOLD
THEM DOWN.

QUARTER-SCALE DIAGRAM OF
EMBROIDERY ON SIDE OF HAT

© 1984 JANET ARNOLD

27. c.1575-1600 SILK HAT GERMANISCHES NATIONALMUSEUM NÜRNBERG. T1220.

HAT IN BROWN CORDED SILK LINED WITH LIGHTWEIGHT BROWN SILK. BOTH LAYERS ARE CUT TO THE SAME SHAPE. THE PIECES ARE DAUBED WITH WAX ALONG THE CUT EDGES TO PREVENT FRAYING. THE BRIM IS MADE OF TWO LAYERS OF CORDED SILK, WITHOUT ANY STIFFENING. THE CROWN IS PLEATED UP, LINING AND CORDED SILK WORKED AS ONE LAYER, AND STITCHED TO THE EDGE OF THE TOP SIDE OF THE BRIM. THE UNDERSIDE OF THE BRIM IS HEMMED DOWN OVER THE LINING WITH BROWN SILK THREAD. THE HATBAND CONCEALS THE JOIN OF BRIM AND CROWN AND ALL THE STITCHES, BUT IT IS JUST POSSIBLE TO SEE TRACES OF WAX ON THE RAW EDGES OF THE BRIM. A FRAGMENT OF WAX WAS TESTED BY MISS ERIKA WEILAND IN THE TEXTILE CONSERVATION WORKSHOP.

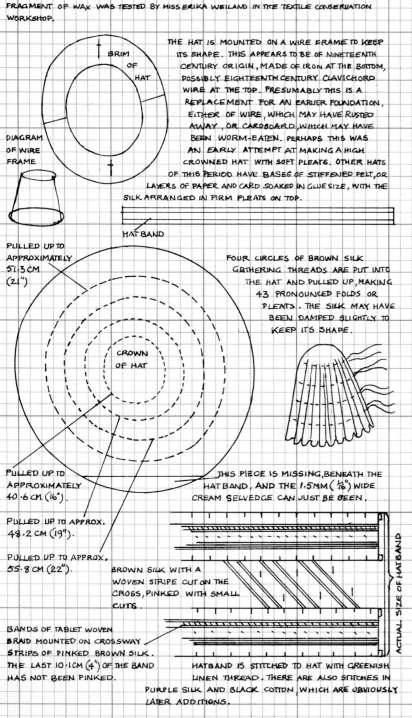

DIAGRAM OF WIRE FRAME

BRIM OF HAT

THE HAT IS MOUNTED ON A WIRE FRAME TO KEEP ITS SHAPE. THIS APPEARS TO BE OF NINETEENTH CENTURY ORIGIN, MADE OF IRON AT THE BOTTOM, POSSIBLY EIGHTEENTH CENTURY CLAVICHORD WIRE AT THE TOP. PRESUMABLY THIS IS A REPLACEMENT FOR AN EARLIER FOUNDATION, EITHER OF WIRE, WHICH MAY HAVE RUSTED AWAY, OR CARDBOARD WHICH MAY HAVE BEEN WORM-EATEN. PERHAPS THIS WAS AN EARLY ATTEMPT AT MAKING A HIGH CROWNED HAT WITH SOFT PLEATS. OTHER HATS OF THIS PERIOD HAVE BASES OF STIFFENED FELT, OR LAYERS OF PAPER AND CARD SOAKED IN GLUE SIZE, WITH THE SILK ARRANGED IN FIRM PLEATS ON TOP.

HAT BAND

PULLED UP TO APPROXIMATELY 51.3 CM (21")

CROWN OF HAT

FOUR CIRCLES OF BROWN SILK GATHERING THREADS ARE PUT INTO THE HAT AND PULLED UP, MAKING 43 PRONOUNCED FOLDS OR PLEATS. THE SILK MAY HAVE BEEN DAMPED SLIGHTLY TO KEEP ITS SHAPE.

PULLED UP TO APPROXIMATELY 40.6 CM (16").

PULLED UP TO APPROX. 48.2 CM (19").

PULLED UP TO APPROX. 55.8 CM (22").

THIS PIECE IS MISSING, BENEATH THE HATBAND, AND THE 1.5MM (1/16") WIDE CREAM SELVEDGE CAN JUST BE SEEN.

BROWN SILK WITH A WOVEN STRIPE CUT ON THE CROSS, PINKED WITH SMALL CUTS.

BANDS OF TABLET WOVEN BRAID MOUNTED ON CROSSWAY STRIPS OF PINKED BROWN SILK. THE LAST 10.1 CM (4") OF THE BAND HAS NOT BEEN PINKED.

ACTUAL SIZE OF HATBAND

HATBAND IS STITCHED TO HAT WITH GREENISH LINEN THREAD. THERE ARE ALSO STITCHES IN PURPLE SILK AND BLACK COTTON, WHICH ARE OBVIOUSLY LATER ADDITIONS.

1:1 INCH   1:1 CENTIMETRE

28. c.1600-10 HIGH CROWNED VELVET HAT GERMANISCHES NATIONALMUSEUM, NÜRNBERG, T33.

HAT IN RICH PINK VELVET, NOW FADED TO PALE BEIGE/PINK IN PLACES. IT IS LINED WITH BRILLIANT PINK SILK. THE FOUNDATION IS MADE OF HAIRY FELT. THIS WAS MOULDED TO SHAPE FIRST OF ALL, PROBABLY WITH STEAM OVER A WOODEN BLOCK. THERE MAY BE A LINEN COVERING OVER THIS, DARTED AND CLIPPED TO SHAPE. THIS BASE SEEMS TO HAVE BEEN PAINTED, OR DIPPED IN GLUE SIZE, OR SOME OTHER STIFFENING AGENT. THE VELVET IS INTERLINED WITH A LAYER OF PAPER FROM THE OUTER EDGE OF THE CIRCLE TO THE DOTTED LINE — · — · — · — · —. THREE ROWS OF GATHERING STITCHES PULL THE VELVET INTO SHAPE, TWO OF THEM THROUGH PAPER AND VELVET. 36 PLEATS ARE THEN STROKED INTO IT. IT LOOKS AS IF THREADS HAD BEEN TIED ROUND THE HAT 31MM (1¼") DOWN FROM THE TOP, AS THE VELVET IS CRUSHED IN PLACES, PRESUMABLY WHILE STEAMING THE PLEATS INTO POSITION. THE TOP OF THE HAT CROWN IS QUITE SMOOTH AND FLAT.

VELVET COVERING FOR HAT CROWN

THE LINES OF GATHERING — — PULL UP TO 48.2 CM (19") AT THE TOP, 59.7 CM (23½") ROUND THE CENTRE AND 62.2 CM (24½") ROUND THE BASE OF THE CROWN, WHERE IT IS JOINED TO THE BRIM.

THE SIDE OF THE HAT CROWN IS MADE OF FELT. THIS MAY BE MOULDED TOGETHER WITH BRIM AND TOP OF CROWN, OR CUT AND STITCHED, THE EDGES BUTTED TOGETHER TO GIVE A FLAT SURFACE. THERE MAY BE A LAYER OF LINEN ON TOP OF THE FELT, FOR EXTRA STIFFNESS. THE BRILLIANT PINK SILK LINING IS DARTED TO FIT. THE FELT IS CUT WITHOUT ANY TURNINGS.

THERE ARE MARKS OF CRUSHING ON THE VELVET BRIM, WHERE THERE WAS SOME KIND OF CORD TRIMMING

SIDE OF HAT CROWN

THE BRIM OF THE HAT IS MADE OF 3MM (⅛") THICK FELT. THIS MAY HAVE BEEN MOULDED FROM THE SAME PIECE AS THE CROWN, OR STITCHED ON SEPARATELY. NOTHING CAN BE SEEN.

TOP OF HAT CROWN

TOP OF HAT CROWN HAS AN INTERLINING OF PAPER BENEATH THE PINK SILK LINING.

CLIPPED TURNING

BRIM OF HAT

THE FELT BRIM IS COVERED WITH LINEN ON THE UNDERSIDE. THIS HAS A 25MM (1") WIDE INNER TURNING, CLIPPED AND STUCK DOWN INSIDE CROWN, AND TO FELT BRIM. THE BRIM MAY BE COVERED WITH LINEN ON THE UPPER SIDE AS WELL. VELVET IS THEN PUT ON TOP, PULLED ROUND THE EDGE, CLIPPED AND STUCK DOWN. PINK SILK CROWN LINING AND BRIM LINING ARE STITCHED TOGETHER AND THEN SEWN INSIDE THE HAT.

PINK SILK LINING FOR SIDE OF CROWN

29. c.1600-10 LEATHER HAT GERMANISCHES NATIONALMUSEUM, NÜRNBERG. T1593.

HAT IN EMBROIDERED CREAM LEATHER, WITH SUEDE FINISH, NOW DISCOLOURED TO VERY PALE GREY. IT IS MADE OF EIGHT SHAPED PIECES OF FELT (TO BOTTOM DOTTED LINE — — —). THE FELT IS BUTTED TOGETHER TO MAKE A SMOOTH SURFACE AND JOINED. ONE LAYER OF LINEN, CUT TO THE SAME SHAPE, IS PUT ON TOP OF THE FELT AND ANOTHER BELOW. THESE ARE CUT TO THE ZIG-ZAG LINE. ROWS OF STITCHING MAY BE SEEN THROUGH THE SILK LINING INSIDE THE HAT. THE FELT BRIM IS STITCHED TO THE CROWN AND THIS FOUNDATION IS THEN BRUSHED OR SOAKED WITH GLUE SIZE OF SOME KIND TO MAKE IT STIFF. THE ZIG-ZAG EDGES OF LINEN ARE STROKED DOWN OVER THE FELT

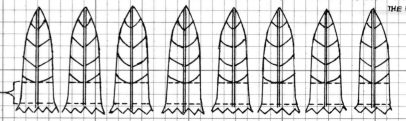

POSITION OF HAT-BAND.

THE EDGE OF THE BRIM IS BOUND WITH A STRIP OF LEATHER FROM THE RIGHT SIDE, HOLDING FELT AND LEATHER TOGETHER. IT IS ROLLED OVER THE EDGE AND STITCHED ON THE DOTTED LINE. THE ZIG-ZAG EDGE IS STUCK TO THE FELT UNDERSIDE.

BRIM

THE BRIM IS MADE FROM FELT COVERED WITH LEATHER, SHAPE CUT TO OUTER LINE, IVORY SILK LINING CUT TO INNER LINE.

SHELL SHAPE ON BACK OF HAT MAY HAVE HELD A FEATHER. IT IS MADE OVER A PARCHMENT SHAPE PADDED WITH HAIR AND SOME COTTON THREADS AT THE TOP.

THE BRIM MEASURES 83.1 CM (32¾") ROUND THE OUTER EDGE

IVORY SILK TAFFETA LINING FOR SIDE OF CROWN, WITH ONE JOIN. THE LINING SEEMS TO BE GLUED TO THE LINEN LAYER.

SILK HAT TOP LINING

LINES OF EMBROIDERY MATCHING THOSE ON THE SEAMS OF THE CROWN.

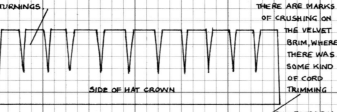

LINE OF 3-PLY CORD, 1 SILVER THREAD AND 2 SILK.

DETAIL OF EMBROIDERY OVER SEAMS OF CROWN

⊕ BUTTON ON TOP OF HAT 22 MM (⅞") IN DIAMETER, WORKED IN SILVER THREAD WITH A SILK CORE, THEN CAUGHT DOWN WITH SILK THREAD.

THE HATBAND MEASURES 63.5 CM (25") WHERE BRIM MEETS CROWN AND 55.8 CM (22") AT TOP OF HATBAND. THE LEATHER IS EASED IN TO FIT THE SHAPE, OVER FIRM PADDING.

BADGE AT FRONT OF HAT-BAND IS MADE OF LEATHER MATCHING THE HAT. THE CENTRE IS COVERED WITH IVORY SILK EMBROIDERED WITH 4 FLEURS-DE-LYS IN SILVER METAL THREAD. FAINT TRACES REMAIN OF A SILVER METAL THREAD DESIGN IN THE S...

INSIDE THE HAT IS A BAND OF IVORY SATIN, VERY GREASY AND WORN. THERE ARE TWO JOINS AND THE MATERIAL IS OFF THE GRAIN. THERE IS A GATHERING THREAD RUNNING THROUGH THE EDGE.

THE JOINS IN THE FELT FOUNDATION COME UNDER LINES OF EMBROIDERY. ROWS OF LARGE DIAGONAL STITCHES ARE VISIBLE BENEATH THE SILK LINING

THE EMBROIDERED LEATHER PANELS ARE BUTTED TOGETHER FOR SMOOTH JOINS ALL OF WHICH ARE COVERED WITH COUCHED SILVER THREAD, WITH A SILK CORE, THEN WORKED WITH CHAIN STITCH IN IVORY SILK, NOW DISCOLOURED, DOWN THE CENTRE. FINISHED WIDTH OF THIS DECORATION IS 3MM (⅛").

THE LAYERS OF FELT AND LEATHER ARE STAGGERED WHEN PUT TOGETHER SO THAT THE SEAMS DO NOT LIE ON TOP OF EACH OTHER.

POSITION OF...

[CRIM]SON VELVET CLOAK CUT IN A FULL CIRCLE, LINED THROUGHOUT WITH NATURAL LINEN. THE VELVET
55·8 CM (22") WIDE, WITH 22MM (⅞) WIDE ACID GREEN SELVEDGES, WOVEN WITH TWO FINE WHITE
[AN]D BEIGE STRIPES. THE VELVET HAS A CREAM SILK GROUND WHICH IS SLIGHTLY FLAWED IN ONE OR
[TW]O PLACES, WITH FINE STRIPES IN THE WARP. THE VELVET PILE STANDS ALMOST UPRIGHT AND THERE
[IS] HARDLY ANY CHANGE OF COLOUR WHEN THE GARMENT IS MOVED. THE LINEN LINING IS JOINED
[AT] THE CENTRE BACK ONLY. THE FABRIC IS WIDE ENOUGH TO DO WITHOUT OTHER JOINS. THERE IS
[A] JOIN ACROSS THE COLLAR TO PIECE THE VELVET. ALTHOUGH THE GRAIN DOES NOT MATCH, THE JOIN
[IS] HARDLY VISIBLE. THE COLLAR LINING IS IN NATURAL LINEN, CUT ON THE BIAS.

[EM]BROIDERY IS CARRIED OUT IN COUCHED GOLD
[ME]TAL CORD FOR THE LINEAR DESIGN, WITH
[THE] CENTRES OF THE MOTIFS IN FINER
[SILV]ER METAL CORD.

[BOT]H FRONTS AND THE HEMLINE
[ARE] BORDERED WITH A
[THI]CK BRAID OF CRIMSON
[SIL]K AND GOLD
[TH]READ WITH A
[YEL]LOW SILK CORE.
[G]IVES THE
[APP]EARANCE
[OF] AN
[UN]CUT
[FRI]NGE

THE COLLAR IS INTERFACED WITH PINK LINEN CUT ON THE SAME
GRAIN, THROUGH WHICH THE EMBROIDERY IS WORKED.

CENTRE
BACK   COLLAR
TO FOLD

ORIGINAL
HOOKS
AND EYES STILL
IN POSITION

THREE LOOPS OF COARSE LINEN THREAD
RESEMBLING STRING ARE SEWN INSIDE
THE COLLAR. ALL THREE LOOPS
MEASURE 4·4 CM (1¾) ON THE
DOUBLE, BUT MORE OF THE FRONT
LOOPS ARE SEWN DOWN. THESE
ARE PROBABLY FOR CORDS
TO SUPPORT THE COLLAR
FROM THE SHOULDERS

JOIN IN FABRIC

CENTRE BACK JOIN IN FABRIC

JOIN IN FABRIC

DIRECTION OF
VELVET PILE

DIRECTION OF
VELVET PILE

JOIN IN FABRIC

JOIN IN FABRIC

1 : 1 INCH
1 : 1 CENTIMETRE

CENTRE
BACK TO FOLD

COLLAR LINING OF NATURAL LINEN

SHORT CLOAK IN RED SATIN WITH AN APPLIED DESIGN OF ACID YELLOW SATIN
GIVING THE EFFECT OF GOLD. THIS IS OUTLINED WITH CORD OF BLUE LINEN
THREAD COVERED WITH ACID-YELLOW SILK. THIS IS TWISTED TIGHTLY ROUND
AND COUCHED DOWN WITH YELLOW SILK. THE ADDITIONAL DECORATION IS GIVEN
BY FRENCH KNOTS IN PINK AND BLUE SILK. THE LINING IS OF NATURAL LINEN,
VERY LIGHT BROWN IN COLOUR. SOME COTTON MATERIAL, A NINETEENTH CENTURY
ADDITION, IS STITCHED TO THE NECK TO REINFORCE ROTTING SATIN. THE EMBROIDERY
DESIGN INCLUDES POMEGRANATES, LEOPARDS, A BIRD, ACORNS, ROSES AND
FANTASTIC FLOWERS
ENCLOSED IN A BORDER   THE RED SATIN IS 56·4 CM (22¼")
WITH TREFOIL SHAPES   WIDE, WITH 9MM (⅜") WIDE
CUT IN AN INTERLOCKING   GREEN SELVEDGES.
PATTERN FROM ONE STRIP
OF YELLOW SATIN. THE
TWO STRIPS OF SATIN ARE
SEPARATED AND COUCHED
DOWN AS A CONTINUOUS
BORDER DESIGN.

THE EMBROIDERY DESIGN
APPEARS TO DATE FROM
THE SIXTEENTH CENTURY,
BUT THE EXECUTION IS
RATHER COARSE. THE
TECHNIQUE IS SIMILAR
TO THAT OF A DATED
EXAMPLE OF 1630 AT
THE NORDISKA MUSEET,
STOCKHOLM.

THE RAW EDGES OF THE
COLLAR ARE TURNED IN
AND THEN THE TOP OF THE
COLLAR IS HEMMED ONTO
THE UNDERSIDE, WHICH IS
CUT IN ONE WITH THE
CLOAK. THERE IS NO
STIFFENING.
THIS COLLAR IS NOW A
CRYSTALLIZED FASHION,
BEING ONLY A LITTLE FLAP
AT THE CENTRE BACK.
THE CLOAK IS SAID TO HAVE
BEEN WORN BY A FOOL,
OR PERHAPS A DWARF,
AT THE ANSBACH COURT,
PROBABLY IN THE EARLY
YEARS OF THE SEVENTEENTH
CENTURY.

THERE ARE
SEVERAL SMALL
JOINS IN THE
SATIN, AT THE BACK.

ACTUAL SIZE OF ACID YELLOW SATIN APPLIED DESIGN

© 1984 JANET ARNOLD

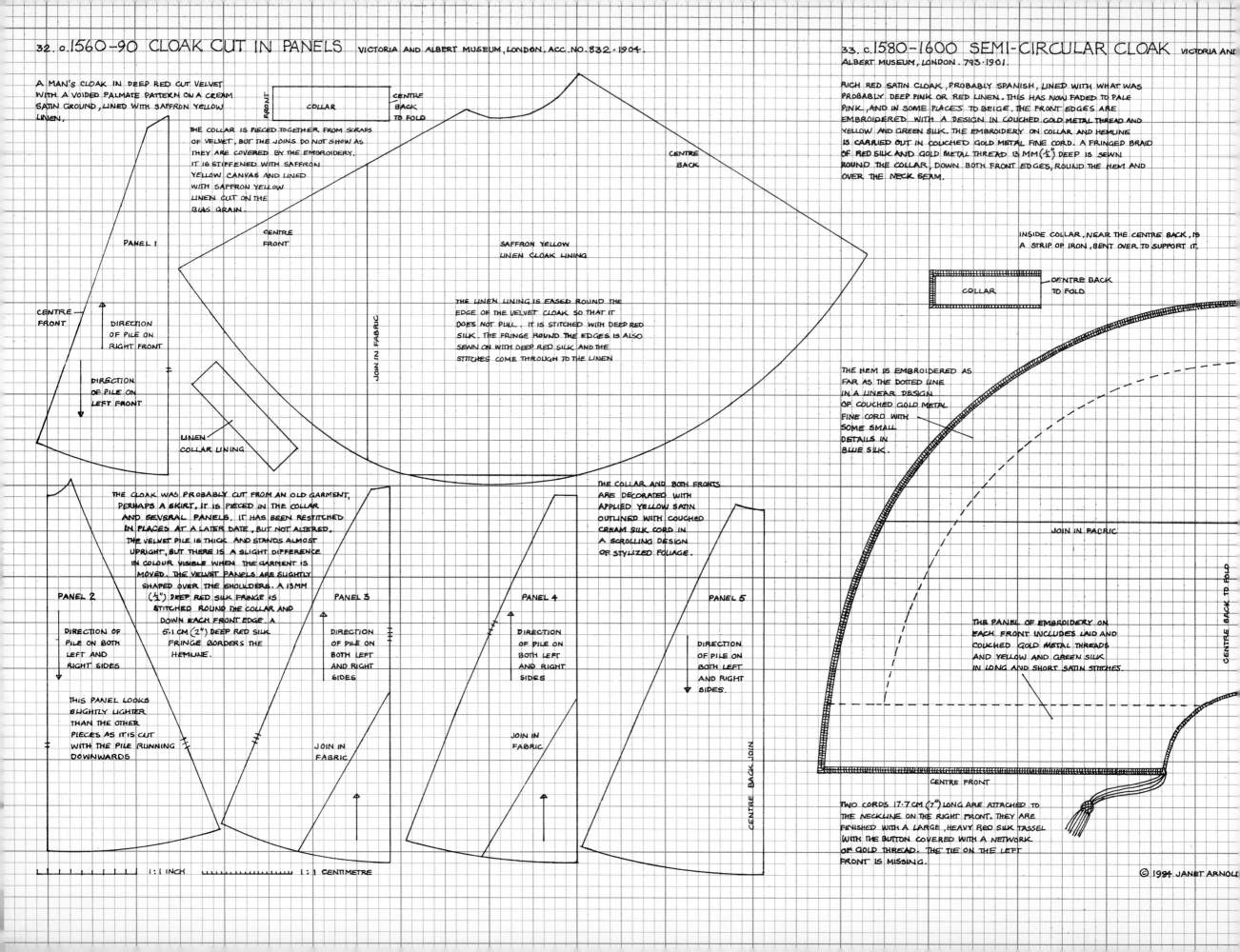

32. c.1560-90 CLOAK CUT IN PANELS VICTORIA AND ALBERT MUSEUM, LONDON. ACC. NO. 832-1904.

A MAN'S CLOAK IN DEEP RED CUT VELVET
WITH A VOIDED PALMATE PATTERN ON A CREAM
SATIN GROUND, LINED WITH SAFFRON YELLOW
LINEN.

FRONT

COLLAR

CENTRE
BACK
TO FOLD

THE COLLAR IS PIECED TOGETHER FROM SCRAPS
OF VELVET, BUT THE JOINS DO NOT SHOW AS
THEY ARE COVERED BY THE EMBROIDERY.
IT IS STIFFENED WITH SAFFRON
YELLOW CANVAS AND LINED
WITH SAFFRON YELLOW
LINEN CUT ON THE
BIAS GRAIN.

PANEL 1

CENTRE
FRONT

CENTRE
BACK

CENTRE
FRONT

DIRECTION
OF PILE ON
RIGHT FRONT

DIRECTION
OF PILE ON
LEFT FRONT

SAFFRON YELLOW
LINEN CLOAK LINING

JOIN IN FABRIC

THE LINEN LINING IS EASED ROUND THE
EDGE OF THE VELVET CLOAK SO THAT IT
DOES NOT PULL. IT IS STITCHED WITH DEEP RED
SILK. THE FRINGE ROUND THE EDGES IS ALSO
SEWN ON WITH DEEP RED SILK AND THE
STITCHES COME THROUGH TO THE LINEN

LINEN
COLLAR LINING

THE CLOAK WAS PROBABLY CUT FROM AN OLD GARMENT,
PERHAPS A SKIRT. IT IS PIECED IN THE COLLAR
AND SEVERAL PANELS. IT HAS BEEN RESTITCHED
IN PLACES AT A LATER DATE, BUT NOT ALTERED.
THE VELVET PILE IS THICK AND STANDS ALMOST
UPRIGHT, BUT THERE IS A SLIGHT DIFFERENCE
IN COLOUR VISIBLE WHEN THE GARMENT IS
MOVED. THE VELVET PANELS ARE SLIGHTLY
SHAPED OVER THE SHOULDERS. A 13MM
(½") DEEP RED SILK FRINGE IS
STITCHED ROUND THE COLLAR AND
DOWN EACH FRONT EDGE. A
5.1 CM (2") DEEP RED SILK
FRINGE BORDERS THE
HEMLINE.

PANEL 2

PANEL 3

PANEL 4

PANEL 5

DIRECTION OF
PILE ON BOTH
LEFT AND
RIGHT SIDES

DIRECTION
OF PILE ON
BOTH LEFT
AND RIGHT
SIDES

DIRECTION
OF PILE ON
BOTH LEFT
AND RIGHT
SIDES

DIRECTION
OF PILE ON
BOTH LEFT
AND RIGHT
SIDES.

THIS PANEL LOOKS
SLIGHTLY LIGHTER
THAN THE OTHER
PIECES AS IT IS CUT
WITH THE PILE RUNNING
DOWNWARDS

JOIN IN
FABRIC

JOIN IN
FABRIC

CENTRE BACK JOIN

1:1 INCH   1:1 CENTIMETRE

33. c.1580-1600 SEMI-CIRCULAR CLOAK VICTORIA AND
ALBERT MUSEUM, LONDON. 793-1901.

RICH RED SATIN CLOAK, PROBABLY SPANISH, LINED WITH WHAT WAS
PROBABLY DEEP PINK OR RED LINEN. THIS HAS NOW FADED TO PALE
PINK, AND IN SOME PLACES TO BEIGE. THE FRONT EDGES ARE
EMBROIDERED WITH A DESIGN IN COUCHED GOLD METAL THREAD AND
YELLOW AND GREEN SILK. THE EMBROIDERY ON COLLAR AND HEMLINE
IS CARRIED OUT IN COUCHED GOLD METAL FINE CORD. A FRINGED BRAID
OF RED SILK AND GOLD METAL THREAD 13 MM (½") DEEP IS SEWN
ROUND THE COLLAR, DOWN BOTH FRONT EDGES, ROUND THE HEM AND
OVER THE NECK SEAM.

INSIDE COLLAR, NEAR THE CENTRE BACK, IS
A STRIP OF IRON, BENT OVER TO SUPPORT IT.

COLLAR

CENTRE BACK
TO FOLD

THE HEM IS EMBROIDERED AS
FAR AS THE DOTTED LINE
IN A LINEAR DESIGN
OF COUCHED GOLD METAL
FINE CORD WITH
SOME SMALL
DETAILS IN
BLUE SILK.

THE COLLAR AND BOTH FRONTS
ARE DECORATED WITH
APPLIED YELLOW SATIN
OUTLINED WITH COUCHED
CREAM SILK CORD IN
A SCROLLING DESIGN
OF STYLIZED FOLIAGE.

JOIN IN FABRIC

CENTRE BACK TO FOLD

THE PANEL OF EMBROIDERY ON
EACH FRONT INCLUDES LAID AND
COUCHED GOLD METAL THREADS
AND YELLOW AND GREEN SILK
IN LONG AND SHORT SATIN STITCHES.

CENTRE FRONT

TWO CORDS 17.7 CM (7") LONG ARE ATTACHED TO
THE NECKLINE ON THE RIGHT FRONT. THEY ARE
FINISHED WITH A LARGE, HEAVY RED SILK TASSEL
WITH THE BUTTON COVERED WITH A NETWORK
OF GOLD THREAD. THE TIE ON THE LEFT
FRONT IS MISSING.

© 1984 JANET ARNOLD

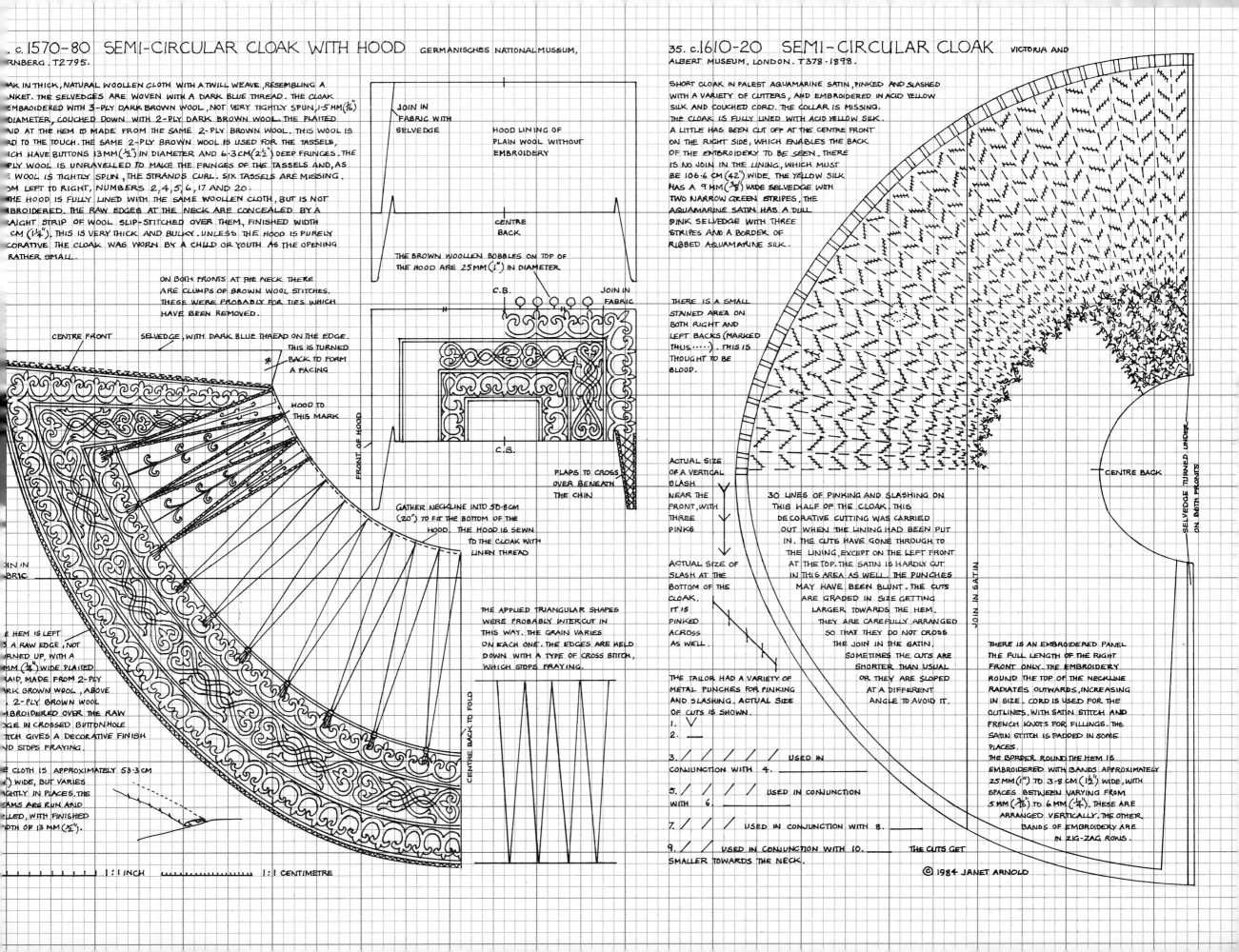

. c.1570-80 SEMI-CIRCULAR CLOAK WITH HOOD GERMANISCHES NATIONALMUSEUM,
RNBERG. T2795.

...AK IN THICK, NATURAL WOOLLEN CLOTH WITH A TWILL WEAVE, RESEMBLING A
...NKET. THE SELVEDGES ARE WOVEN WITH A DARK BLUE THREAD. THE CLOAK
...EMBROIDERED WITH 3-PLY DARK BROWN WOOL, NOT VERY TIGHTLY SPUN, 1·5 MM (1/16")
...DIAMETER, COUCHED DOWN WITH 2-PLY DARK BROWN WOOL. THE PLAITED
...AID AT THE HEM IS MADE FROM THE SAME 2-PLY BROWN WOOL. THIS WOOL IS
...RD TO THE TOUCH. THE SAME 2-PLY BROWN WOOL IS USED FOR THE TASSELS,
...ICH HAVE BUTTONS 13 MM (1/2") IN DIAMETER AND 6·3 CM (2 1/2") DEEP FRINGES. THE
...PLY WOOL IS UNRAVELLED TO MAKE THE FRINGES OF THE TASSELS AND, AS
...E WOOL IS TIGHTLY SPUN, THE STRANDS CURL. SIX TASSELS ARE MISSING.
...OM LEFT TO RIGHT, NUMBERS 2,4,5,6,17 AND 20.
...THE HOOD IS FULLY LINED WITH THE SAME WOOLLEN CLOTH, BUT IS NOT
...BROIDERED. THE RAW EDGES AT THE NECK ARE CONCEALED BY A
...RAIGHT STRIP OF WOOL SLIP-STITCHED OVER THEM, FINISHED WIDTH
... CM (1 1/4"). THIS IS VERY THICK AND BULKY. UNLESS THE HOOD IS PURELY
...CORATIVE THE CLOAK WAS WORN BY A CHILD OR YOUTH AS THE OPENING
...RATHER SMALL.

ON BOTH FRONTS AT THE NECK THERE
ARE CLUMPS OF BROWN WOOL STITCHES.
THESE WERE PROBABLY FOR TIES WHICH
HAVE BEEN REMOVED.

CENTRE FRONT
SELVEDGE, WITH DARK BLUE THREAD ON THE EDGE.
THIS IS TURNED
BACK TO FORM
A FACING

HOOD TO
THIS MARK

FRONT OF HOOD

JOIN IN
FABRIC WITH
SELVEDGE

HOOD LINING OF
PLAIN WOOL WITHOUT
EMBROIDERY

CENTRE
BACK

THE BROWN WOOLLEN BOBBLES ON TOP OF
THE HOOD ARE 25 MM (1") IN DIAMETER

C.B.   JOIN IN
              FABRIC

C.B.

FLAPS TO CROSS
OVER BENEATH
THE CHIN

GATHER NECKLINE INTO 50·8 CM
(20") TO FIT THE BOTTOM OF THE
HOOD. THE HOOD IS SEWN
TO THE CLOAK WITH
LINEN THREAD

THE APPLIED TRIANGULAR SHAPES
WERE PROBABLY INTERCUT IN
THIS WAY. THE GRAIN VARIES
ON EACH ONE. THE EDGES ARE HELD
DOWN WITH A TYPE OF CROSS STITCH,
WHICH STOPS FRAYING.

CENTRE BACK TO FOLD

...IN IN
...BRIC

...E HEM IS LEFT
... A RAW EDGE, NOT
...RNED UP, WITH A
...MM (1/4") WIDE PLAITED
...AID, MADE FROM 2-PLY
...RK BROWN WOOL, ABOVE
... 2-PLY BROWN WOOL
...MBROIDERED OVER THE RAW
...GE IN CROSSED BUTTONHOLE
...TCH GIVES A DECORATIVE FINISH
...ND STOPS FRAYING.

...E CLOTH IS APPROXIMATELY 53·3 CM
...") WIDE, BUT VARIES
...GHTLY IN PLACES. THE
...AMS ARE RUN AND
...LLED, WITH FINISHED
...DTH OF 13 MM (1/2").

1:1 INCH   1:1 CENTIMETRE

35. c.1610-20 SEMI-CIRCULAR CLOAK VICTORIA AND
ALBERT MUSEUM, LONDON. T378·1898.

SHORT CLOAK IN PALEST AQUAMARINE SATIN, PINKED AND SLASHED
WITH A VARIETY OF CUTTERS, AND EMBROIDERED IN ACID YELLOW
SILK AND COUCHED CORD. THE COLLAR IS MISSING.
THE CLOAK IS FULLY LINED WITH ACID YELLOW SILK.
A LITTLE HAS BEEN CUT OFF AT THE CENTRE FRONT
ON THE RIGHT SIDE, WHICH ENABLES THE BACK
OF THE EMBROIDERY TO BE SEEN. THERE
IS NO JOIN IN THE LINING, WHICH MUST
BE 106·6 CM (42") WIDE. THE YELLOW SILK
HAS A 9 MM (3/8") WIDE SELVEDGE WITH
TWO NARROW GREEN STRIPES. THE
AQUAMARINE SATIN HAS A DULL
PINK SELVEDGE WITH THREE
STRIPES AND A BORDER OF
RIBBED AQUAMARINE SILK.

THERE IS A SMALL
STAINED AREA ON
BOTH RIGHT AND
LEFT BACKS (MARKED
THUS ......). THIS IS
THOUGHT TO BE
BLOOD.

ACTUAL SIZE
OF A VERTICAL
SLASH
NEAR THE
FRONT, WITH
THREE
PINKS

ACTUAL SIZE OF
SLASH AT THE
BOTTOM OF THE
CLOAK.
IT IS
PINKED
ACROSS
AS WELL.

THE TAILOR HAD A VARIETY OF
METAL PUNCHES FOR PINKING
AND SLASHING. ACTUAL SIZE
OF CUTS IS SHOWN.
1. V
2. —
3. / / / / / USED IN
CONJUNCTION WITH 4. —
5. / / / USED IN CONJUNCTION
WITH 6. —
7. / / / USED IN CONJUNCTION WITH 8. —
9. / / USED IN CONJUNCTION WITH 10. — THE CUTS GET
SMALLER TOWARDS THE NECK.

30 LINES OF PINKING AND SLASHING ON
THIS HALF OF THE CLOAK. THIS
DECORATIVE CUTTING WAS CARRIED
OUT WHEN THE LINING HAD BEEN PUT
IN. THE CUTS HAVE GONE THROUGH TO
THE LINING, EXCEPT ON THE LEFT FRONT
AT THE TOP. THE SATIN IS HARDLY CUT
IN THIS AREA AS WELL. THE PUNCHES
MAY HAVE BEEN BLUNT. THE CUTS
ARE GRADED IN SIZE GETTING
LARGER TOWARDS THE HEM.
THEY ARE CAREFULLY ARRANGED
SO THAT THEY DO NOT CROSS
THE JOIN IN THE SATIN.
SOMETIMES THE CUTS ARE
SHORTER THAN USUAL
OR THEY ARE SLOPED
AT A DIFFERENT
ANGLE TO AVOID IT.

CENTRE BACK

SELVEDGE TURNED UNDER

SELVEDGE TURNED UNDER ON BOTH FRONTS

JOIN IN SATIN

THERE IS AN EMBROIDERED PANEL
THE FULL LENGTH OF THE RIGHT
FRONT ONLY. THE EMBROIDERY
ROUND THE TOP OF THE NECKLINE
RADIATES OUTWARDS, INCREASING
IN SIZE. CORD IS USED FOR THE
OUTLINES, WITH SATIN STITCH AND
FRENCH KNOTS FOR FILLINGS. THE
SATIN STITCH IS PADDED IN SOME
PLACES.
THE BORDER ROUND THE HEM IS
EMBROIDERED WITH BANDS APPROXIMATELY
25 MM (1") TO 3·8 CM (1 1/2") WIDE, WITH
SPACES BETWEEN VARYING FROM
5 MM (3/16") TO 6 MM (1/4"). THESE ARE
ARRANGED VERTICALLY. THE OTHER
BANDS OF EMBROIDERY ARE
IN ZIG-ZAG ROWS.

© 1984 JANET ARNOLD

c1600–10   The National Trust, Hardwick Hall, Derbyshire

36A.   A loose gown in rich deep wine satin, bordered and lined throughout with matching velvet. The collar is interlined with pink heavy linen canvas, pad-stitched to the satin. Both layers are sewn to the neck of the gown and the velvet undercollar is cut large enough to overlap on the right side, forming a decorative border round the edge of the collar. Separate bands of bias-cut velvet, edged with narrow strips of bias-cut satin, are stitched down both fronts, round the hem, on the vents at centre back and side seams and round the pockets.

The style and size of the gown make it seem likely to have been worn by a man. However, it has been associated by tradition with the Countess of Shrewsbury, 'Bess of Hardwick'. She married four times and outlived her last husband George, 6th Earl of Shrewsbury, who died in 1590. She died in 1608 aged eighty-eight. As J.L. Nevinson points out, it would not have been unsuitable wear for an elderly lady with the dominant personality and masculine character of Bess of Hardwick.

36B.   Each tab of the shoulder wing is made individually, stiffened with linen canvas and bordered with bias-cut satin strips.

36C.   The loops which fasten the front of the gown are made from a continuous length of wine cord. Holes are punched through satin and narrow satin strip bordering the decorative velvet band to allow loops of cord to protrude. They are stitched firmly into position between the satin outer layer and velvet lining. All the buttons are missing.

c1605–15   Sir Ralph Verney, Claydon House (The National Trust), near Aylesbury

37.   A rich purple silk damask loose gown with hanging sleeves, lined with deep grey silk shag, now faded. By tradition this was worn, together with matching nightcap and slippers, by Sir Francis Verney who died in 1615 at Messina. J.L. Nevinson suggests that he may have left it behind him on his last visit to Claydon in 1608. The back is gathered up and stitched to the front shoulders and the collar, the raw edges being covered by a narrow green silk ribbon which also acts as a stay tape. Two more green silk ribbons are stitched to the armholes across the back at shoulder-blade level, acting as stay tapes to hold the pleats in position. The hanging sleeves are fastened with buttons of silver and gold metal thread and purple silk worked over wooden bases with plaited loops of matching threads. They can be left unfastened for the arm in the doublet sleeve to pass through at elbow level. Alternatively part of the sleeve can hang free if a hook and eye are undone under the wing (Fig. 270). The arm then passes through this aperture as shown in the drawing. Sleeves, armholes, front edges, hem and pockets are all trimmed with gold braid.

36A

36B

36C

37

.c.1600-10 LOOSE GOWN   THE NATIONAL TRUST, HARDWICK HALL, DERBYSHIRE.

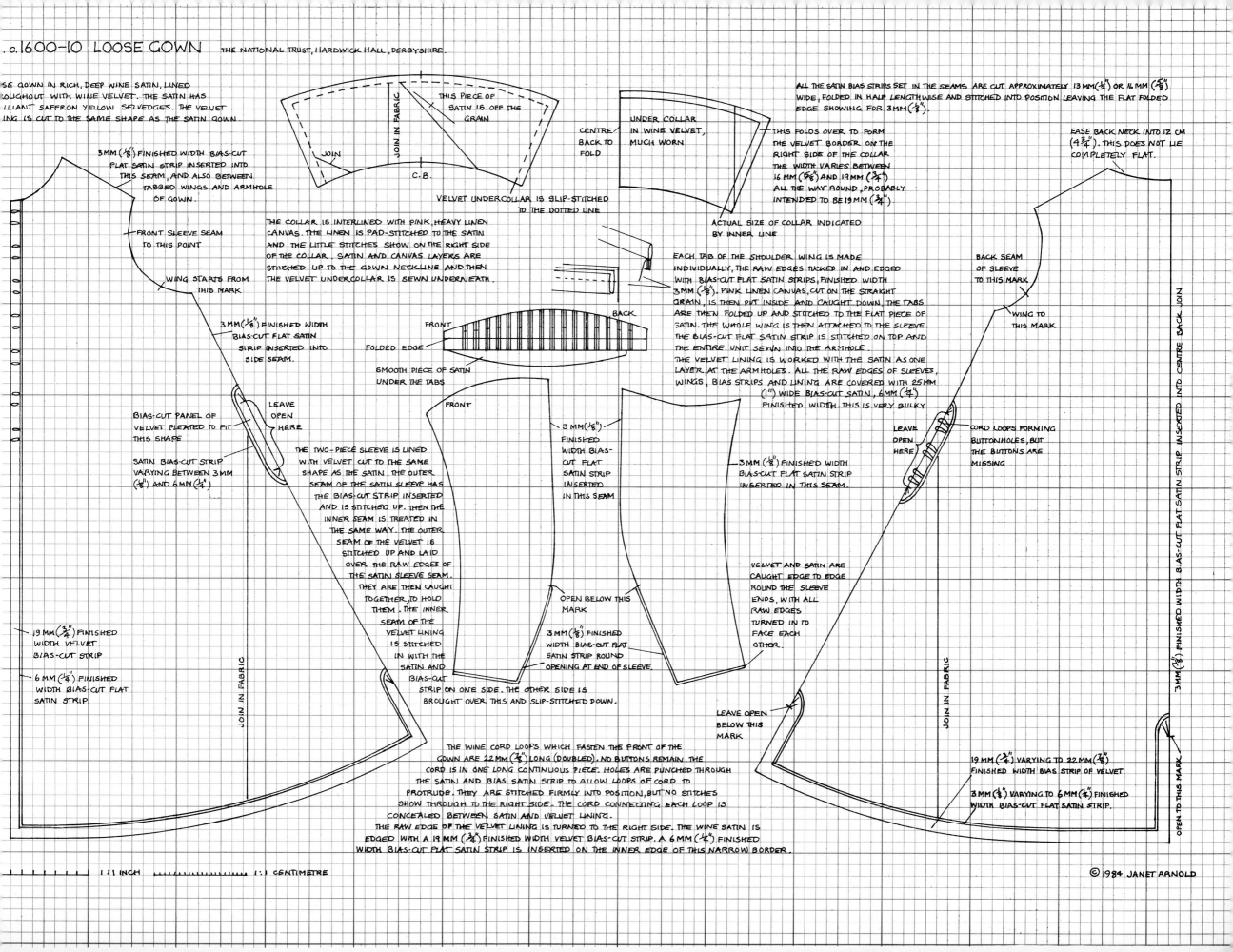

SE GOWN IN RICH, DEEP WINE SATIN, LINED ROUGHOUT WITH WINE VELVET. THE SATIN HAS LLIANT SAFFRON YELLOW SELVEDGES. THE VELVET ING IS CUT TO THE SAME SHAPE AS THE SATIN GOWN.

ALL THE SATIN BIAS STRIPS SET IN THE SEAMS ARE CUT APPROXIMATELY 13 MM (½") OR 16 MM (⅝") WIDE, FOLDED IN HALF LENGTHWISE AND STITCHED INTO POSITION LEAVING THE FLAT FOLDED EDGE SHOWING FOR 3 MM (⅛").

3 MM (⅛") FINISHED WIDTH BIAS-CUT FLAT SATIN STRIP INSERTED INTO THIS SEAM, AND ALSO BETWEEN TABBED WINGS AND ARMHOLE OF GOWN.

THIS PIECE OF SATIN IS OFF THE GRAIN

JOIN IN FABRIC

JOIN

CENTRE BACK TO FOLD

C.B.

UNDER COLLAR IN WINE VELVET, MUCH WORN

THIS FOLDS OVER TO FORM THE VELVET BORDER ON THE RIGHT SIDE OF THE COLLAR THE WIDTH VARIES BETWEEN 16 MM (⅝") AND 19 MM (¾") ALL THE WAY ROUND, PROBABLY INTENDED TO BE 19 MM (¾").

EASE BACK NECK INTO 12 CM (4¾"). THIS DOES NOT LIE COMPLETELY FLAT.

VELVET UNDERCOLLAR IS SLIP-STITCHED TO THE DOTTED LINE

ACTUAL SIZE OF COLLAR INDICATED BY INNER LINE

FRONT SLEEVE SEAM TO THIS POINT

THE COLLAR IS INTERLINED WITH PINK, HEAVY LINEN CANVAS. THE LINEN IS PAD-STITCHED TO THE SATIN AND THE LITTLE STITCHES SHOW ON THE RIGHT SIDE OF THE COLLAR, SATIN AND CANVAS LAYERS ARE STITCHED UP TO THE GOWN NECKLINE AND THEN THE VELVET UNDERCOLLAR IS SEWN UNDERNEATH.

BACK SEAM OF SLEEVE TO THIS MARK

WING STARTS FROM THIS MARK

EACH TAB OF THE SHOULDER WING IS MADE INDIVIDUALLY, THE RAW EDGES TUCKED IN AND EDGED WITH BIAS-CUT FLAT SATIN STRIPS, FINISHED WIDTH 3 MM (⅛"). PINK LINEN CANVAS, CUT ON THE STRAIGHT GRAIN, IS THEN PUT INSIDE AND CAUGHT DOWN. THE TABS ARE THEN FOLDED UP AND STITCHED TO THE FLAT PIECE OF SATIN. THE WHOLE WING IS THEN ATTACHED TO THE SLEEVE. THE BIAS-CUT FLAT SATIN STRIP IS STITCHED ON TOP AND THE ENTIRE UNIT SEWN INTO THE ARMHOLE. THE VELVET LINING IS WORKED WITH THE SATIN AS ONE LAYER AT THE ARMHOLES. ALL THE RAW EDGES OF SLEEVES, WINGS, BIAS STRIPS AND LINING ARE COVERED WITH 25 MM (1") WIDE BIAS-CUT SATIN, 6 MM (¼") FINISHED WIDTH. THIS IS VERY BULKY

WING TO THIS MARK

FRONT

BACK

3 MM (⅛") FINISHED WIDTH BIAS-CUT FLAT SATIN STRIP INSERTED INTO SIDE SEAM.

FOLDED EDGE

SMOOTH PIECE OF SATIN UNDER THE TABS

FRONT

BIAS-CUT PANEL OF VELVET PLEATED TO FIT THIS SHAPE

LEAVE OPEN HERE

SATIN BIAS-CUT STRIP VARYING BETWEEN 3 MM (⅛") AND 6 MM (¼")

THE TWO-PIECE SLEEVE IS LINED WITH VELVET CUT TO THE SAME SHAPE AS THE SATIN. THE OUTER SEAM OF THE SATIN SLEEVE HAS THE BIAS-CUT STRIP INSERTED AND IS STITCHED UP. THEN THE INNER SEAM IS TREATED IN THE SAME WAY. THE OUTER SEAM OF THE VELVET IS STITCHED UP AND LAID OVER THE RAW EDGES OF THE SATIN SLEEVE SEAM. THEY ARE THEN CAUGHT TOGETHER, TO HOLD THEM. THE INNER SEAM OF THE VELVET LINING IS STITCHED IN WITH THE SATIN AND BIAS-CUT STRIP ON ONE SIDE. THE OTHER SIDE IS BROUGHT OVER THIS AND SLIP-STITCHED DOWN.

3 MM (⅛") FINISHED WIDTH BIAS-CUT FLAT SATIN STRIP INSERTED IN THIS SEAM

3 MM (⅛") FINISHED WIDTH BIAS-CUT FLAT SATIN STRIP INSERTED IN THIS SEAM.

LEAVE OPEN HERE

CORD LOOPS FORMING BUTTONHOLES, BUT THE BUTTONS ARE MISSING

VELVET AND SATIN ARE CAUGHT EDGE TO EDGE ROUND THE SLEEVE ENDS, WITH ALL RAW EDGES TURNED INTO FACE EACH OTHER.

19 MM (¾") FINISHED WIDTH VELVET BIAS-CUT STRIP

6 MM (¼") FINISHED WIDTH BIAS-CUT FLAT SATIN STRIP.

OPEN BELOW THIS MARK

3 MM (⅛") FINISHED WIDTH BIAS-CUT FLAT SATIN STRIP ROUND OPENING AT END OF SLEEVE.

LEAVE OPEN BELOW THIS MARK

3 MM (⅛") FINISHED WIDTH BIAS-CUT FLAT SATIN STRIP INSERTED INTO CENTRE BACK JOIN

JOIN IN FABRIC

JOIN IN FABRIC

THE WINE CORD LOOPS WHICH FASTEN THE FRONT OF THE GOWN ARE 22 MM (⅞") LONG (DOUBLED). NO BUTTONS REMAIN. THE CORD IS IN ONE LONG CONTINUOUS PIECE. HOLES ARE PUNCHED THROUGH THE SATIN AND BIAS SATIN STRIP TO ALLOW LOOPS OF CORD TO PROTRUDE. THEY ARE STITCHED FIRMLY INTO POSITION, BUT NO STITCHES SHOW THROUGH TO THE RIGHT SIDE. THE CORD CONNECTING EACH LOOP IS CONCEALED BETWEEN SATIN AND VELVET LINING. THE RAW EDGE OF THE VELVET LINING IS TURNED TO THE RIGHT SIDE. THE WINE SATIN IS EDGED WITH A 19 MM (¾") FINISHED WIDTH VELVET BIAS-CUT STRIP. A 6 MM (¼") FINISHED WIDTH BIAS-CUT FLAT SATIN STRIP IS INSERTED ON THE INNER EDGE OF THIS NARROW BORDER.

19 MM (¾") VARYING TO 22 MM (⅞") FINISHED WIDTH BIAS STRIP OF VELVET

3 MM (⅛") VARYING TO 6 MM (¼") FINISHED WIDTH BIAS-CUT FLAT SATIN STRIP.

OPEN TO THIS MARK

1 : 1 INCH   1 : 1 CENTIMETRE

© 1984 JANET ARNOLD

37. c.1605-15 LOOSE GOWN WITH SHAG LINING BY TRADITION WORN BY SIR FRANCIS VERNEY

SIR RALPH VERNEY, CLAYDON HOUSE (NATIONAL TRUST) NEAR AYLESBURY

LOOSE GOWN IN RICH PURPLE SILK DAMASK, WITH MATCHING NIGHTCAP AND SLIPPERS BY TRADITION WORN BY SIR FRANCIS VERNEY, WHO DIED IN 1615 IN MESSINA. THE GOWN IS LINED WITH DEEP GREY SILK SHAG, NOW FADED, WHICH RESEMBLES FUR.

THE PURPLE SILK DAMASK GOWN AND GREY SILK SHAG LINING ARE MADE UP SEPARATELY. THE RAW EDGES ARE TURNED IN TOWARDS EACH OTHER AND THE GOWN IS STITCHED NEATLY ALL ROUND. THE BACK IS GATHERED INTO SMALL CARTRIDGE PLEATS TO FIT THE SHOULDER AND COLLAR AND STITCHED INTO POSITION. THIS SEAM IS COVERED BY A STRIP OF GREEN RIBBON.

GATHERED INTO 13·9CM (5½") IN SMALL CARTRIDGE PLEATS TO FIT FRONT SHOULDER

GATHERED INTO 7·6CM (3") TO FIT COLLAR

WING ATTACHED TO THIS LINE

THIS PART STICKS OUT FOR SLEEVE ATTACHMENT

OPEN PART OF HANGING SLEEVE TO THIS POINT

WINGS END HERE

SEAM OF HANGING SLEEVE TO THIS POINT

TOP COLLAR IN GREY SILK SHAG

CENTRE BACK TO FOLD

UNDER COLLAR IN PURPLE SILK DAMASK

CENTRE BACK TO FOLD

THIS PART STICKS OUT BENEATH THE WING FOR SLEEVE ATTACHMENT

WING IS ATTACHED TO THIS LINE

TWO GREEN SILK STAY RIBBONS, 13MM (½") X 43·1 CM (17"), ARE STITCHED INTO THE ARMHOLES, AND HOLD THE PLEATS IN POSITION ACROSS THE BACK.

WORKED BARS HOLDING TABS OF WING TOGETHER.

FRONT

SHOULDER SEAM TO THIS MARK

BACK

THIS EDGE TO FOLD

LINES OF BRAID

EACH TAB OF THE SHOULDER WING IS MADE OF STIFF BLACK BUCKRAM AND THE PURPLE DAMASK IS MOUNTED ON TOP, THE RAW EDGES CAUGHT DOWN BENEATH. THE DAMASK IS NOT ALL ON THE STRAIGHT GRAIN, AS THE TABS ARE CUT FROM ODD SCRAPS. THE TABS ARE THEN FOLDED IN HALF AND STITCHED TOGETHER FROM SHOULDERHEAD TO THE LITTLE MARKS. BRAID IS SEWN ON, CURVING BACK FROM BENEATH THE TABS, NOT CUTTING THE ENDS OFF. THE WING IS THEN STITCHED INTO THE ARMHOLE.

THE PURPLE SILK DAMASK SLEEVE AND GREY SILK SHAG LINING ARE MADE UP SEPARATELY. THE RAW EDGES ARE TURNED IN TOWARDS EACH OTHER AND THE SLEEVE IS STITCHED NEATLY ALL THE WAY ROUND. THE SLEEVE IS THEN HALF-STITCHED INTO THE ARMHOLE BENEATH THE WINGS, WHICH CONCEAL THE LINE OF SHAG STICKING OUT BENEATH THE DAMASK.

SIX BUTTONS ARE SEWN ON THE SEAM FOR DECORATIVE PURPOSES ONLY

THIS PART OF THE SLEEVE IS LEFT HANGING FREE. WHEN THE HOOK IS UNDONE, THE ARM PASSES THROUGH THIS OPENING. IF THE HOOK AND EYE ARE FASTENED, THE ARM EMERGES THROUGH AN APERTURE MADE BY LEAVING BUTTONS AND LOOPS UNFASTENED AT ELBOW LEVEL ON THE FRONT OF THE SLEEVE.

HOOK   EYE

THE UPPER PART AND BACK OF SLEEVE ARE STITCHED INTO THE GOWN.

THE ACORN TYPE BUTTONS ARE 13MM (½") DEEP AND 13MM (½") IN DIAMETER. THEY ARE MADE OF SILVER, GOLD AND PURPLE SILK THREADS WORKED OVER WOODEN BASES.

DECORATIVE BANDS OF GOLD METAL BRAID 9MM (⅜") WIDE SET DIAGONALLY IN PAIRS ON THE HANGING SLEEVES

. TWO BANDS OF GOLD METAL BRAID 9MM (⅜") WIDE SET 3MM (⅛") APART AND 3MM (⅛") AWAY FROM THE EDGE ON THE FRONT, AT THE HEM ROUND THE ARMHOLES AND ON SIDE SEAMS.

CENTRE FRONT

JOIN IN FABRIC

THREE BUTTONS ARE SEWN ON THE SEAM FOR DECORATIVE PURPOSES ONLY

BOTTOM OF SLEEVE OPEN BELOW THIS LEVEL

THERE ARE 46 BUTTONS AND LOOPS DOWN THE FRONT OPENING OF THE HANGING SLEEVE. THE LOOPS ARE MADE OF PLAITED SILVER, GOLD AND PURPLE SILK THREADS. THEY ARE 16MM (⅝") WIDE AND EXTEND FOR ABOUT 5MM (³⁄₁₆") OVER THE EDGE OF THE SLEEVE

ACTUAL SIZE OF BUTTONHOLE LOOPS

JOIN IN FABRIC

TWO BANDS OF GOLD METAL BRAID 9MM (⅜") WIDE SET 3MM (⅛") APART AND 3MM (⅛") AWAY FROM THE HEM.

CENTRE BACK JOIN

THREE BUTTONS AT THE TOP ARE FOR DECORATION. BELOW THIS LEVEL THE BUTTONS ARE FASTENED WITH CORD LOOPS.

OPEN BELOW THIS MARK

1:1 INCH   1:1 CENTIMETRE

© 1984 JANET ARNOLD

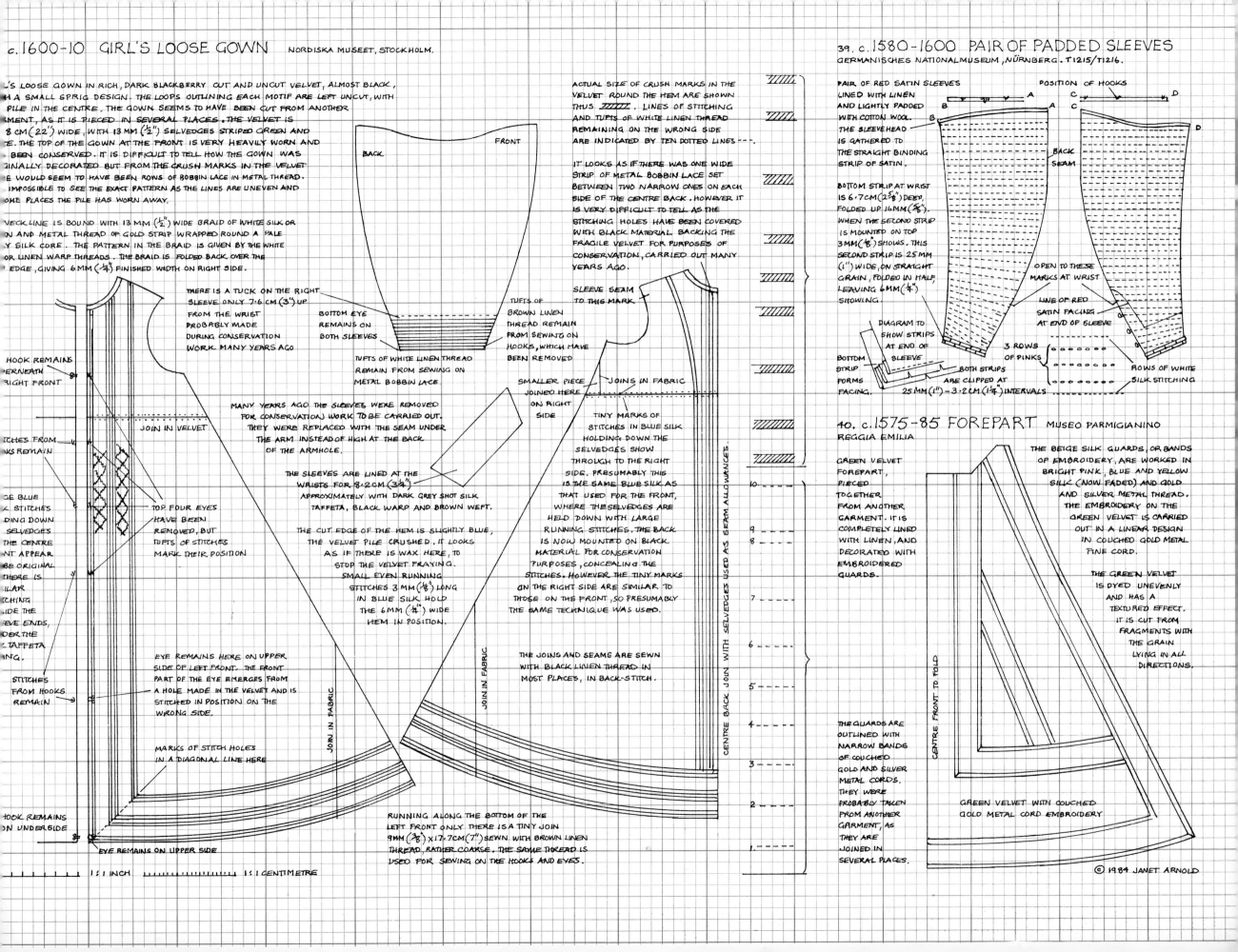

c.1600-10 GIRL'S LOOSE GOWN   NORDISKA MUSEET, STOCKHOLM.

...'S LOOSE GOWN IN RICH, DARK BLACKBERRY CUT AND UNCUT VELVET, ALMOST BLACK, ...H A SMALL SPRIG DESIGN. THE LOOPS OUTLINING EACH MOTIF ARE LEFT UNCUT, WITH ...PILE IN THE CENTRE, THE GOWN SEEMS TO HAVE BEEN CUT FROM ANOTHER ...RMENT, AS IT IS PIECED IN SEVERAL PLACES. THE VELVET IS ...8 CM (22") WIDE, WITH 13 MM (½") SELVEDGES STRIPED GREEN AND ...E. THE TOP OF THE GOWN AT THE FRONT IS VERY HEAVILY WORN AND ...BEEN CONSERVED. IT IS DIFFICULT TO TELL HOW THE GOWN WAS ...INALLY DECORATED BUT FROM THE CRUSH MARKS IN THE VELVET ...E WOULD SEEM TO HAVE BEEN ROWS OF BOBBIN LACE IN METAL THREAD. ...IMPOSSIBLE TO SEE THE EXACT PATTERN AS THE LINES ARE UNEVEN AND ...OME PLACES THE PILE HAS WORN AWAY.

...NECKLINE IS BOUND WITH 13 MM (½") WIDE BRAID OF WHITE SILK OR ...N AND METAL THREAD OF GOLD STRIP WRAPPED ROUND A PALE ...Y SILK CORE. THE PATTERN IN THE BRAID IS GIVEN BY THE WHITE ...OR LINEN WARP THREADS. THE BRAID IS FOLDED BACK OVER THE ...EDGE, GIVING 6 MM (¼") FINISHED WIDTH ON RIGHT SIDE.

HOOK REMAINS ...ERNEATH ...RIGHT FRONT

...TCHES FROM ...KS REMAIN

...E BLUE ...K STITCHES ...DING DOWN ...SELVEDGES ...THE CENTRE ...NT APPEAR ...BE ORIGINAL ...THERE IS ...ILAR ...CHING ...IDE THE ...VE ENDS, ...ER THE ...TAFFETA ...ING.

...STITCHES ...FROM HOOKS ...REMAIN

HOOK REMAINS ...ON UNDERSIDE

...EYE REMAINS ON UPPER SIDE

JOIN IN VELVET

TOP FOUR EYES HAVE BEEN REMOVED, BUT TUFTS OF STITCHES MARK THEIR POSITION

THERE IS A TUCK ON THE RIGHT SLEEVE ONLY 7.6 CM (3") UP FROM THE WRIST PROBABLY MADE DURING CONSERVATION WORK MANY YEARS AGO

MANY YEARS AGO THE SLEEVES WERE REMOVED FOR CONSERVATION WORK TO BE CARRIED OUT. THEY WERE REPLACED WITH THE SEAM UNDER THE ARM INSTEAD OF HIGH AT THE BACK OF THE ARMHOLE.

THE SLEEVES ARE LINED AT THE WRISTS FOR 8.2 CM (3¼") APPROXIMATELY WITH DARK GREY SHOT SILK TAFFETA, BLACK WARP AND BROWN WEFT.

THE CUT EDGE OF THE HEM IS SLIGHTLY BLUE, THE VELVET PILE CRUSHED. IT LOOKS AS IF THERE IS WAX HERE, TO STOP THE VELVET FRAYING. SMALL EVEN RUNNING STITCHES 3 MM (⅛") LONG IN BLUE SILK HOLD THE 6 MM (¼") WIDE HEM IN POSITION.

EYE REMAINS HERE ON UPPER SIDE OF LEFT FRONT. THE FRONT PART OF THE EYE EMERGES FROM A HOLE MADE IN THE VELVET AND IS STITCHED IN POSITION ON THE WRONG SIDE.

MARKS OF STITCH HOLES IN A DIAGONAL LINE HERE

BACK   FRONT

BOTTOM EYE REMAINS ON BOTH SLEEVES

TUFTS OF WHITE LINEN THREAD REMAIN FROM SEWING ON METAL BOBBIN LACE.

JOIN IN FABRIC

SMALLER PIECE JOINED HERE ON RIGHT SIDE

TUFTS OF BROWN LINEN THREAD REMAIN FROM SEWING ON HOOKS, WHICH HAVE BEEN REMOVED

SLEEVE SEAM TO THIS MARK

JOINS IN FABRIC

TINY MARKS OF STITCHES IN BLUE SILK HOLDING DOWN THE SELVEDGES SHOW THROUGH TO THE RIGHT SIDE. PRESUMABLY THIS IS THE SAME BLUE SILK AS THAT USED FOR THE FRONT, WHERE THE SELVEDGES ARE HELD DOWN WITH LARGE RUNNING STITCHES. THE BACK IS NOW MOUNTED ON BLACK MATERIAL FOR CONSERVATION PURPOSES, CONCEALING THE STITCHES. HOWEVER THE TINY MARKS ON THE RIGHT SIDE ARE SIMILAR TO THOSE ON THE FRONT, SO PRESUMABLY THE SAME TECHNIQUE WAS USED.

THE JOINS AND SEAMS ARE SEWN WITH BLACK LINEN THREAD IN MOST PLACES, IN BACK-STITCH.

RUNNING ALONG THE BOTTOM OF THE LEFT FRONT ONLY THERE IS A TINY JOIN 9 MM (⅜") X 17.7 CM (7") SEWN WITH BROWN LINEN THREAD, RATHER COARSE. THE SAME THREAD IS USED FOR SEWING ON THE HOOKS AND EYES.

ACTUAL SIZE OF CRUSH MARKS IN THE VELVET ROUND THE HEM ARE SHOWN THUS ⨏⨏⨏⨏. LINES OF STITCHING AND TUFTS OF WHITE LINEN THREAD REMAINING ON THE WRONG SIDE ARE INDICATED BY TEN DOTTED LINES ---.

IT LOOKS AS IF THERE WAS ONE WIDE STRIP OF METAL BOBBIN LACE SET BETWEEN TWO NARROW ONES ON EACH SIDE OF THE CENTRE BACK. HOWEVER IT IS VERY DIFFICULT TO TELL AS THE STITCHING HOLES HAVE BEEN COVERED WITH BLACK MATERIAL BACKING THE FRAGILE VELVET FOR PURPOSES OF CONSERVATION, CARRIED OUT MANY YEARS AGO.

JOIN IN FABRIC

CENTRE BACK JOIN WITH SELVEDGES USED AS SEAM ALLOWANCES.

10
9
8
7
6
5
4
3
2
1

╠══════╣ 1:1 INCH   ╠══════╣ 1:1 CENTIMETRE

39. c.1580-1600 PAIR OF PADDED SLEEVES
GERMANISCHES NATIONALMUSEUM, NÜRNBERG. T1215/T1216.

PAIR OF RED SATIN SLEEVES LINED WITH LINEN AND LIGHTLY PADDED WITH COTTON WOOL. THE SLEEVEHEAD IS GATHERED TO THE STRAIGHT BINDING STRIP OF SATIN.

BOTTOM STRIP AT WRIST IS 6.7 CM (2⅝") DEEP, FOLDED UP 16 MM (⅝"). WHEN THE SECOND STRIP IS MOUNTED ON TOP 3 MM (⅛") SHOWS. THIS SECOND STRIP IS 25 MM (1") WIDE, ON STRAIGHT GRAIN, FOLDED IN HALF, LEAVING 6 MM (¼") SHOWING.

POSITION OF HOOKS

A   C   D
B   A   C

BACK SEAM

OPEN TO THESE MARKS AT WRIST

LINE OF RED SATIN FACING AT END OF SLEEVE

DIAGRAM TO SHOW STRIPS AT END OF SLEEVE

BOTTOM STRIP FORMS FACING

BOTH STRIPS ARE CLIPPED AT 25 MM (1") – 3.2 CM (1¼") INTERVALS

3 ROWS OF PINKS

ROWS OF WHITE SILK STITCHING

40. c.1575-85 FOREPART MUSEO PARMIGIANINO
REGGIA EMILIA

GREEN VELVET FOREPART, PIECED TOGETHER FROM ANOTHER GARMENT. IT IS COMPLETELY LINED WITH LINEN, AND DECORATED WITH EMBROIDERED GUARDS.

THE BEIGE SILK GUARDS, OR BANDS OF EMBROIDERY, ARE WORKED IN BRIGHT PINK, BLUE AND YELLOW SILK (NOW FADED) AND GOLD AND SILVER METAL THREAD. THE EMBROIDERY ON THE GREEN VELVET IS CARRIED OUT IN A LINEAR DESIGN IN COUCHED GOLD METAL FINE CORD.

THE GREEN VELVET IS DYED UNEVENLY AND HAS A TEXTURED EFFECT. IT IS CUT FROM FRAGMENTS WITH THE GRAIN LYING IN ALL DIRECTIONS.

THE GUARDS ARE OUTLINED WITH NARROW BANDS OF COUCHED GOLD AND SILVER METAL CORDS. THEY WERE PROBABLY TAKEN FROM ANOTHER GARMENT, AS THEY ARE JOINED IN SEVERAL PLACES.

CENTRE FRONT TO FOLD

GREEN VELVET WITH COUCHED GOLD METAL CORD EMBROIDERY

© 1984 JANET ARNOLD

c1600–10 Nordiska Museet, Stockholm

38. Young girl's loose gown with long sleeves in rich, dark blackberry colour (almost black) cut and uncut velvet, which came to the museum in 1905. Its early provenance is not known. None of the metal bobbin lace remains but crush marks, with some tufts of thread and stitch holes, are left in the velvet. The gown may have been pieced together from another garment as there are several joins in the fabric. The front fastens with hooks and eyes. Most are now missing but tufts of thread remain to show their position. The rings of the eyes are pushed through the velvet and sewn to the wrong side of the gown. During conservation work in the early years of the century the sleeves were removed for mounting and replaced with the seam under the arm, as is usual in the twentieth century, instead of high at the back on the outside of the arm. The drawing shows the gown as it might have looked originally. The design for the bobbin lace has been taken from the impression in the velvet and surviving examples in the Victoria and Albert Museum.

+1562 Palazzo Pitti, Florence

41A. A satin gown and velvet bodice or 'bodies' worn by Eleanora of Toledo, wife of Cosimo I de'Medici, who died of malaria in 1562, aged forty. She was buried in these clothes in the Sagrestia Vecchia of San Lorenzo in Florence. In 1791 all the Medici coffins, except those in the marble tombs, were removed to the vaults of the Capella di Principe of San Lorenzo. An article, initialled G.S.P., 'Esumazione e Ricognizione delle Ceneri dei Principe Medici fatta nell'anno 1857', printed in *Archivo Storico Italiano* in 1888, explains that when the coffins were opened in 1857 there was no memorial found to record this corpse which had not been embalmed. Medical inspection showed that the bones were not those of someone younger than thirty, nor those of an old woman, and were assumed to be those of Eleanora. The corpse was dressed in a 'raso bianco' (white satin) floor-length gown, richly embroidered with 'gallone' (braid) on the bodice, down the skirt and round the hem. Under this gown was another of 'velluto color chermisi' (crimson velvet) with crimson silk stockings and black leather shoes, badly decayed. The net round her braided hair was similar to that in the Bronzino portrait in the Uffizi Gallery. The coffin had been violated and any jewels removed.

Only fragments now remain: the white satin has discoloured to pale golden yellow and the crimson velvet to a brownish red. Almost all the right side of the satin skirt has rotted away and there is no trace of a skirt for the crimson velvet bodice, nor of the hair net and the leather shoes, but the stockings and garters have survived (Figs. 292–4).

41B. The velvet bodice fastens at the front with hooks and eyes, probably eighteen pairs, although many have corroded and disappeared. It would have been lined with linen, from the evidence of the armholes and neckline, which are closely oversewn with matching silk. This stitching is slightly loose and would appear to have held two layers of material together originally. It is not certain if this was a 'pair of bodies' or corset with bents to stiffen it set in the linen lining (Fig. 330) or a 'petticoat bodies' to support a petticoat, or under-skirt, of matching velvet. There are stitch holes at the waist but no trace of any velvet skirt, although the description of 1857 would seem to indicate that there was one originally, Further evidence is needed.

41C. The velvet bodice is shaped in the same way as the satin with two seams at the back. Fragments of the lining, or possibly a binding strip, remain inside the waist.

38

41A

41B

41C

41D. The body had probably been turned over in the tomb by robbers looking for jewels not long after burial, as the back of the bodice, complete with lacing on both side back seams, has survived almost intact (Fig. 286). All the satin at the front had virtually disintegrated with the decomposing corpse. Many hours were spent straightening the embroidered velvet guards which gave the shape and the drawing shows how it would have looked originally. The embroidery was carried out in couched gold metal thread and cord on a brown velvet ground, probably black originally but now discoloured. This velvet has been cut away to reveal the satin beneath, giving a raised effect. The guards may have been used first on a black velvet gown. No sleeves appear to have survived, nor is there any evidence of stitching or eyelet holes for lacing on the shoulders. It may be conjectured that sleeves were attached by small cord loops and jewelled buttons, like those in Fig. 287.

41E. The back of the bodice shows the original lacing through eyelet holes, which enabled the wearer to achieve a close fit. The holes appear to be worked unevenly but this is usual practice and, when laced up, the waistline lies level. Around the waist of the gown are small stitch holes where the skirt was attached. The bodice would have been lined with linen, from the evidence of stitch holes round the neck, but none remains.

41D

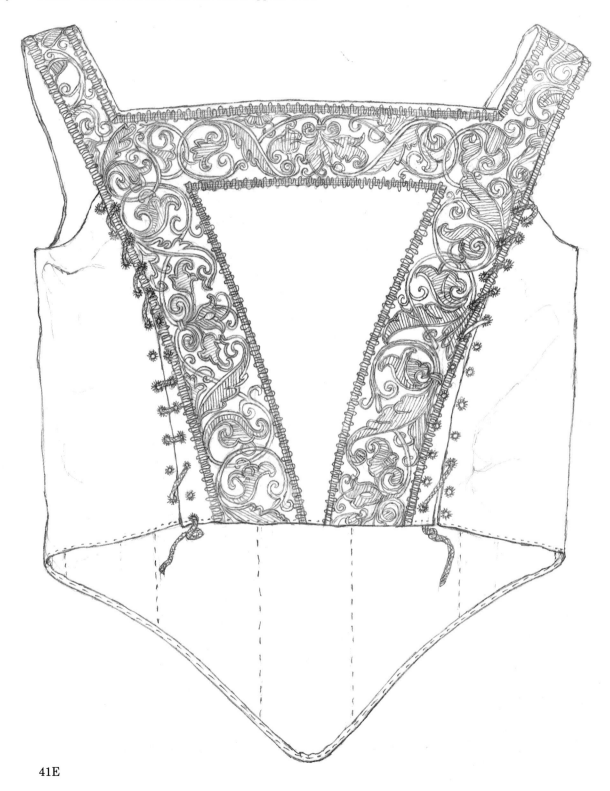

41E

SATIN GOWN, NOW GOLDEN YELLOW RANGING TO PALE CHARTREUSE, BUT DESCRIBED AS WHITE WHEN THE TOMB WAS OPENED IN 1857, DECORATED WITH VELVET GUARDS EMBROIDERED WITH GOLD METAL THREAD. TESTS BY PAOLO BENSI IN 1986 SHOW THAT THE SATIN WAS ORIGINALLY PALE CHARTREUSE IN COLOUR. UNDER THE SATIN BODICE IS A RICH RUST-RED VELVET BODICE, POSSIBLY CRIMSON ORIGINALLY.

THE DISCOVERY OF MORE FRAGMENTS OF SATIN IN 1986 ALLOWED THE PATTERN SHAPES TO BE REVISED, ALTHOUGH THEY STILL COULD NOT BE MEASURED WITH COMPLETE ACCURACY AS SO MUCH OF THE FRONT BODICE HAD DISINTEGRATED, AND THE SKIRT FRAGMENTS STRETCHED AND SHRANK BY ABOUT 25MM (1") DURING THE TIME WHEN THEY WERE LAID OUT FOR CONSERVATION WORK. THE PATTERN OF THE SATIN BODICE WAS PIECED TOGETHER FROM THE MEASUREMENTS OF THE BACK, THE EMBROIDERED GUARDS, AND WHAT REMAINED OF THE SATIN AT THE FRONT. THE SATIN BODICE WAS ORIGINALLY LINED WITH CLOSELY WOVEN FINE LINEN AND TINY FRAGMENTS REMAIN BY THE THIRD AND SIXTH EYELET HOLES FROM THE TOP ON THE LEFT SIDE OF THE BACK. FRAGMENTS OF LINEN OF A MORE OPEN WEAVE REMAINING BENEATH THE STITCHING FROM THE GUARDS SHOW THAT BOTH FRONT AND BACK WERE INTERLINED FOR EXTRA SUPPORT. THE SEAM ALLOWANCES WERE TURNED IN OVER THE INTERLINING TO MAKE NEAT EDGES AND THE EMBROIDERED GUARDS MOUNTED ON THE SATIN. HOLES FROM STITCHING REMAIN 3 MM (⅛") AWAY FROM THE FOLDED EDGE OF THE TURNING AT BODICE WAIST. THE BODICE MAY HAVE BEEN TOP-STITCHED TO THE SATIN FROM THE RIGHT SIDE AND THE LINING HEMMED DOWN TO CONCEAL THE RAW EDGES INSIDE, BUT THERE IS INSUFFICIENT EVIDENCE TO BE CERTAIN.

THE RICH RUST-RED VELVET BODICE FASTENS AT THE CENTRE FRONT WITH HOOKS AND EYES WHICH HAVE CORRODED, BUT THERE SEEM TO HAVE BEEN 18 PAIRS. TWO OR THREE HOOKS WERE FIRMLY EMBEDDED IN THE VELVET AS IF THE FRONTS HAD BEEN WRAPPED OVER EACH OTHER FOR THE BURIAL. THE SATIN BODICE LACES UP ON BOTH SIDE BACK SEAMS, WITH OPENINGS IN THE SKIRT SEAMS BELOW CONCEALED BENEATH THE PLEATS. THE EYELET HOLES AT THE TOP OF THE BODICE OPENINGS ARE WORKED THROUGH THE RICHLY EMBROIDERED GUARDS AND METAL BRAID. ALMOST ALL THE STITCHING HAS DISINTEGRATED BUT THE STILETTO HOLES REMAIN.

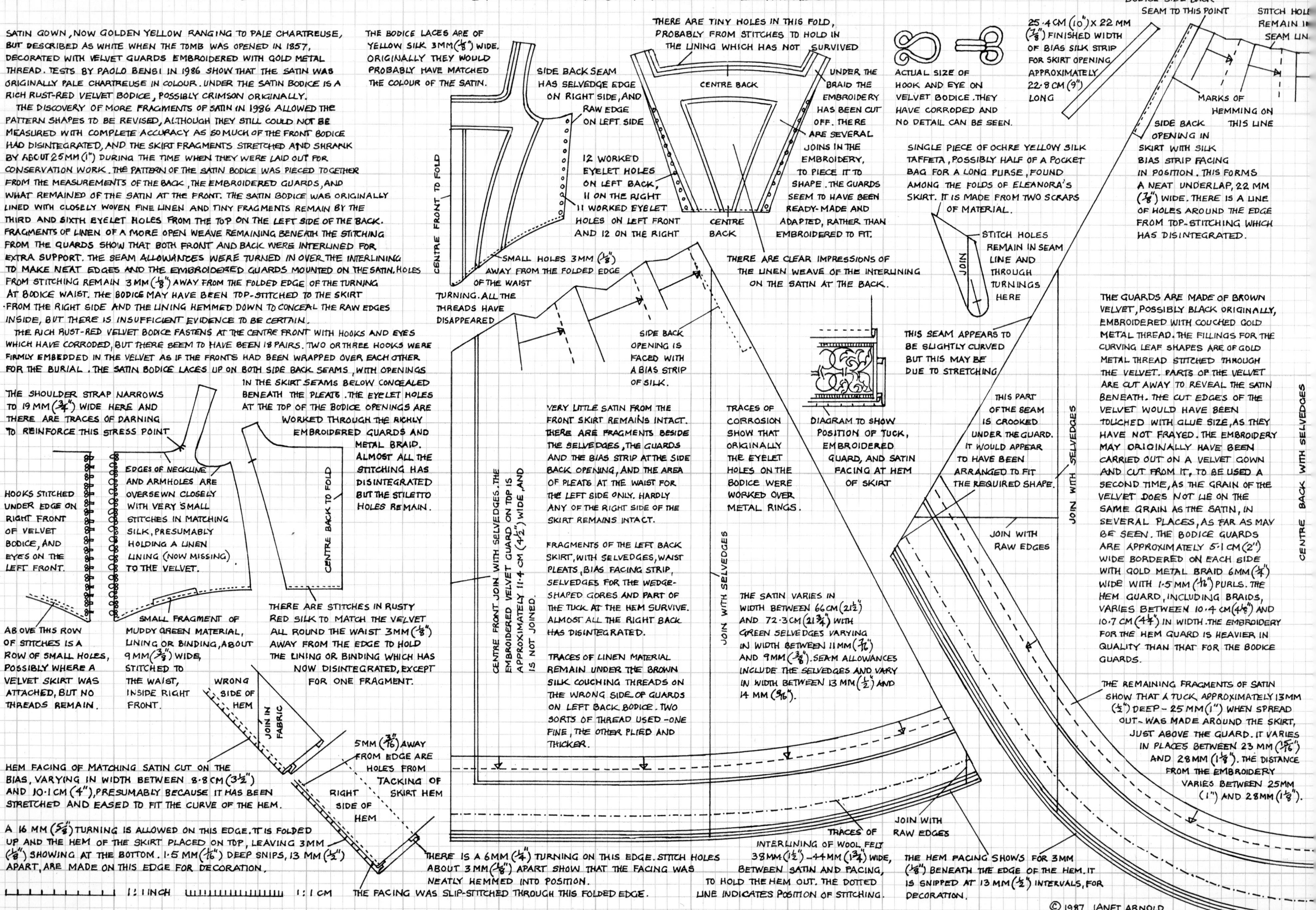

THE SHOULDER STRAP NARROWS TO 19 MM (¾") WIDE HERE AND THERE ARE TRACES OF DARNING TO REINFORCE THIS STRESS POINT

HOOKS STITCHED UNDER EDGE ON RIGHT FRONT OF VELVET BODICE, AND EYES ON THE LEFT FRONT.

EDGES OF NECKLINE AND ARMHOLES ARE OVERSEWN CLOSELY WITH VERY SMALL STITCHES IN MATCHING SILK, PRESUMABLY HOLDING A LINEN LINING (NOW MISSING) TO THE VELVET.

ABOVE THIS ROW OF STITCHES IS A ROW OF SMALL HOLES, POSSIBLY WHERE A VELVET SKIRT WAS ATTACHED, BUT NO THREADS REMAIN.

SMALL FRAGMENT OF MUDDY GREEN MATERIAL, LINING OR BINDING, ABOUT 9MM (⅜") WIDE, STITCHED TO THE WAIST, INSIDE RIGHT FRONT.

WRONG SIDE OF HEM

THERE ARE STITCHES IN RUSTY RED SILK TO MATCH THE VELVET ALL ROUND THE WAIST 3MM (⅛") AWAY FROM THE EDGE TO HOLD THE LINING OR BINDING WHICH HAS NOW DISINTEGRATED, EXCEPT FOR ONE FRAGMENT.

JOIN IN FABRIC

HEM FACING OF MATCHING SATIN CUT ON THE BIAS, VARYING IN WIDTH BETWEEN 8.8 CM (3½") AND 10.1 CM (4"), PRESUMABLY BECAUSE IT HAS BEEN STRETCHED AND EASED TO FIT THE CURVE OF THE HEM.

5MM (³⁄₁₆") AWAY FROM EDGE ARE HOLES FROM TACKING OF SKIRT HEM

RIGHT SIDE OF HEM

A 16 MM (⅝") TURNING IS ALLOWED ON THIS EDGE. IT IS FOLDED UP AND THE HEM OF THE SKIRT PLACED ON TOP, LEAVING 3MM (⅛") SHOWING AT THE BOTTOM. 1.5 MM (¹⁄₁₆") DEEP SNIPS, 13 MM (½") APART, ARE MADE ON THIS EDGE FOR DECORATION.

THE BODICE LACES ARE OF YELLOW SILK 3MM (⅛") WIDE. ORIGINALLY THEY WOULD PROBABLY HAVE MATCHED THE COLOUR OF THE SATIN.

SIDE BACK SEAM HAS SELVEDGE EDGE ON RIGHT SIDE, AND RAW EDGE ON LEFT SIDE

12 WORKED EYELET HOLES ON LEFT BACK, 11 ON THE RIGHT
11 WORKED EYELET HOLES ON LEFT FRONT AND 12 ON THE RIGHT

CENTRE FRONT TO FOLD

SMALL HOLES 3MM (⅛") AWAY FROM THE FOLDED EDGE OF THE WAIST

TURNING. ALL THE THREADS HAVE DISAPPEARED

CENTRE BACK TO FOLD

SIDE BACK OPENING IS FACED WITH A BIAS STRIP OF SILK.

VERY LITTLE SATIN FROM THE FRONT SKIRT REMAINS INTACT. THERE ARE FRAGMENTS BESIDE THE SELVEDGES, THE GUARDS AND THE BIAS STRIP AT THE SIDE BACK OF PLEATS AT THE WAIST FOR THE LEFT SIDE ONLY. HARDLY ANY OF THE RIGHT SIDE OF THE SKIRT REMAINS INTACT.

FRAGMENTS OF THE LEFT BACK SKIRT, WITH SELVEDGES, WAIST PLEATS, BIAS FACING STRIP, SELVEDGES FOR THE WEDGE-SHAPED GORES AND PART OF THE TUCK AT THE HEM SURVIVE. ALMOST ALL THE RIGHT BACK HAS DISINTEGRATED.

TRACES OF LINEN MATERIAL REMAIN UNDER THE BROWN SILK COUCHING THREADS ON THE WRONG SIDE OF GUARDS ON LEFT BACK BODICE. TWO SORTS OF THREAD USED – ONE FINE, THE OTHER PLIED AND THICKER.

CENTRE FRONT JOIN WITH SELVEDGES. THE EMBROIDERED VELVET GUARD ON TOP IS APPROXIMATELY 11.4 CM (4½") WIDE AND IS NOT JOINED.

THE BODICE LACES ARE OF YELLOW SILK

SIDE BACK SEAM HAS SELVEDGE EDGE ON RIGHT SIDE, AND RAW EDGE ON LEFT SIDE

THERE ARE TINY HOLES IN THIS FOLD, PROBABLY FROM STITCHES TO HOLD IN THE LINING WHICH HAS NOT SURVIVED

CENTRE BACK

UNDER THE BRAID THE EMBROIDERY HAS BEEN CUT OFF. THERE ARE SEVERAL JOINS IN THE EMBROIDERY, TO PIECE IT TO SHAPE. THE GUARDS SEEM TO HAVE BEEN READY-MADE AND ADAPTED, RATHER THAN EMBROIDERED TO FIT.

CENTRE BACK

THERE ARE CLEAR IMPRESSIONS OF THE LINEN WEAVE OF THE INTERLINING ON THE SATIN AT THE BACK.

SIDE BACK OPENING IS FACED WITH A BIAS STRIP OF SILK.

TRACES OF CORROSION SHOW THAT ORIGINALLY THE EYELET HOLES ON THE BODICE WERE WORKED OVER METAL RINGS.

DIAGRAM TO SHOW POSITION OF TUCK, EMBROIDERED GUARD, AND SATIN FACING AT HEM OF SKIRT

THE SATIN VARIES IN WIDTH BETWEEN 66 CM (21½") AND 72.3 CM (21¾") WITH GREEN SELVEDGES VARYING IN WIDTH BETWEEN 11MM (⁷⁄₁₆") AND 9MM (⅜"). SEAM ALLOWANCES INCLUDE THE SELVEDGES AND VARY IN WIDTH BETWEEN 13 MM (½") AND 14 MM (⁹⁄₁₆").

JOIN WITH SELVEDGES

THERE IS A 6MM (¼") TURNING ON THIS EDGE. STITCH HOLES ABOUT 3MM (⅛") APART SHOW THAT THE FACING WAS NEATLY HEMMED INTO POSITION.

TRACES OF INTERLINING OF WOOL FELT 38MM (1½") – 44MM (1¾") WIDE, BETWEEN SATIN AND PACING, TO HOLD THE HEM OUT. THE DOTTED LINE INDICATES POSITION OF STITCHING.

JOIN WITH RAW EDGES

THE FACING WAS SLIP-STITCHED THROUGH THIS FOLDED EDGE.

ACTUAL SIZE OF HOOK AND EYE ON VELVET BODICE. THEY HAVE CORRODED AND NO DETAIL CAN BE SEEN.

SINGLE PIECE OF OCHRE YELLOW SILK TAFFETA, POSSIBLY HALF OF A POCKET BAG FOR A LONG PURSE, FOUND AMONG THE FOLDS OF ELEANORA'S SKIRT. IT IS MADE FROM TWO SCRAPS OF MATERIAL.

STITCH HOLES REMAIN IN SEAM LINE AND THROUGH TURNINGS HERE

JOIN

THIS SEAM APPEARS TO BE SLIGHTLY CURVED BUT THIS MAY BE DUE TO STRETCHING

THIS PART OF THE SEAM IS CROOKED UNDER THE GUARD. IT WOULD APPEAR TO HAVE BEEN ARRANGED TO FIT THE REQUIRED SHAPE.

JOIN WITH RAW EDGES

25.4 CM (10") X 22 MM (⅞") FINISHED WIDTH OF BIAS SILK STRIP FOR SKIRT OPENING APPROXIMATELY 22.8 CM (9") LONG

STITCH HOLE REMAIN IN SEAM LIN

MARKS OF HEMMING ON SIDE BACK. THIS LINE OPENING IN SKIRT WITH SILK BIAS STRIP FACING IN POSITION. THIS FORMS A NEAT UNDERLAP, 22 MM (⅞") WIDE. THERE IS A LINE OF HOLES AROUND THE EDGE FROM TOP-STITCHING WHICH HAS DISINTEGRATED.

THE GUARDS ARE MADE OF BROWN VELVET, POSSIBLY BLACK ORIGINALLY, EMBROIDERED WITH COUCHED GOLD METAL THREAD. THE FILLINGS FOR THE CURVING LEAF SHAPES ARE OF GOLD METAL THREAD STITCHED THROUGH THE VELVET. PARTS OF THE VELVET ARE CUT AWAY TO REVEAL THE SATIN BENEATH. THE CUT EDGES OF THE VELVET WOULD HAVE BEEN TOUCHED WITH GLUE SIZE, AS THEY HAVE NOT FRAYED. THE EMBROIDERY MAY ORIGINALLY HAVE BEEN CARRIED OUT ON A VELVET GOWN AND CUT FROM IT, TO BE USED A SECOND TIME, AS THE GRAIN OF THE VELVET DOES NOT LIE ON THE SAME GRAIN AS THE SATIN, IN SEVERAL PLACES, AS FAR AS MAY BE SEEN. THE BODICE GUARDS ARE APPROXIMATELY 5.1 CM (2") WIDE BORDERED ON EACH SIDE WITH GOLD METAL BRAID 6MM (¼") WIDE WITH 1.5 MM (¹⁄₁₆") PURLS. THE HEM GUARD, INCLUDING BRAIDS, VARIES BETWEEN 10.4 CM (4⅛") AND 10.7 CM (4¼") IN WIDTH. THE EMBROIDERY FOR THE HEM GUARD IS HEAVIER IN QUALITY THAN THAT FOR THE BODICE GUARDS.

CENTRE BACK WITH SELVEDGES

THE REMAINING FRAGMENTS OF SATIN SHOW THAT A TUCK, APPROXIMATELY 13MM (½") DEEP – 25MM (1") WHEN SPREAD OUT – WAS MADE AROUND THE SKIRT, JUST ABOVE THE GUARD. IT VARIES IN PLACES BETWEEN 23 MM (¹⁵⁄₁₆") AND 28MM (1⅛"). THE DISTANCE FROM THE EMBROIDERY VARIES BETWEEN 25MM (1") AND 28MM (1⅛").

THE HEM FACING SHOWS FOR 3MM (⅛") BENEATH THE EDGE OF THE HEM. IT IS SNIPPED AT 13MM (½") INTERVALS, FOR DECORATION.

JOIN WITH SELVEDGES

JOIN WITH SELVEDGES

1: 1 INCH   1 : 1 CM

© 1987 JANET ARNOLD

42A. A velvet gown with hanging sleeves in which Gräfin Katharina zur Lippe was buried in the crypt of Augustiner-Nonnenkirche zu Blomberg. She died in 1600 aged six. The deep sandy golden-brown cut velvet in a geometric design on a voided soft old-gold silk ground may have discoloured from dark brown on ivory. The under-sleeves are in dark sage-green velvet, now faded to brownish sage green, embroidered with couched gold and silver twisted cord (Fig. 301). These were probably cut from another garment as the design does not fit the shape. Only fragments of the hanging sleeves remain. The gown is decorated with guards of gold and silver metal bobbin lace and fastens at the front with hooks and eyes. These are hidden beneath ribbon bows with tiny tassels, which have replaced what were probably ribbon points with decorative aglets, which have disintegrated.

42B. The tabbed wings are shaped and were probably intended to stand as shoulder rolls originally but no padding remains. There is an opening on the right shoulder as well as at the front.

42A

42B

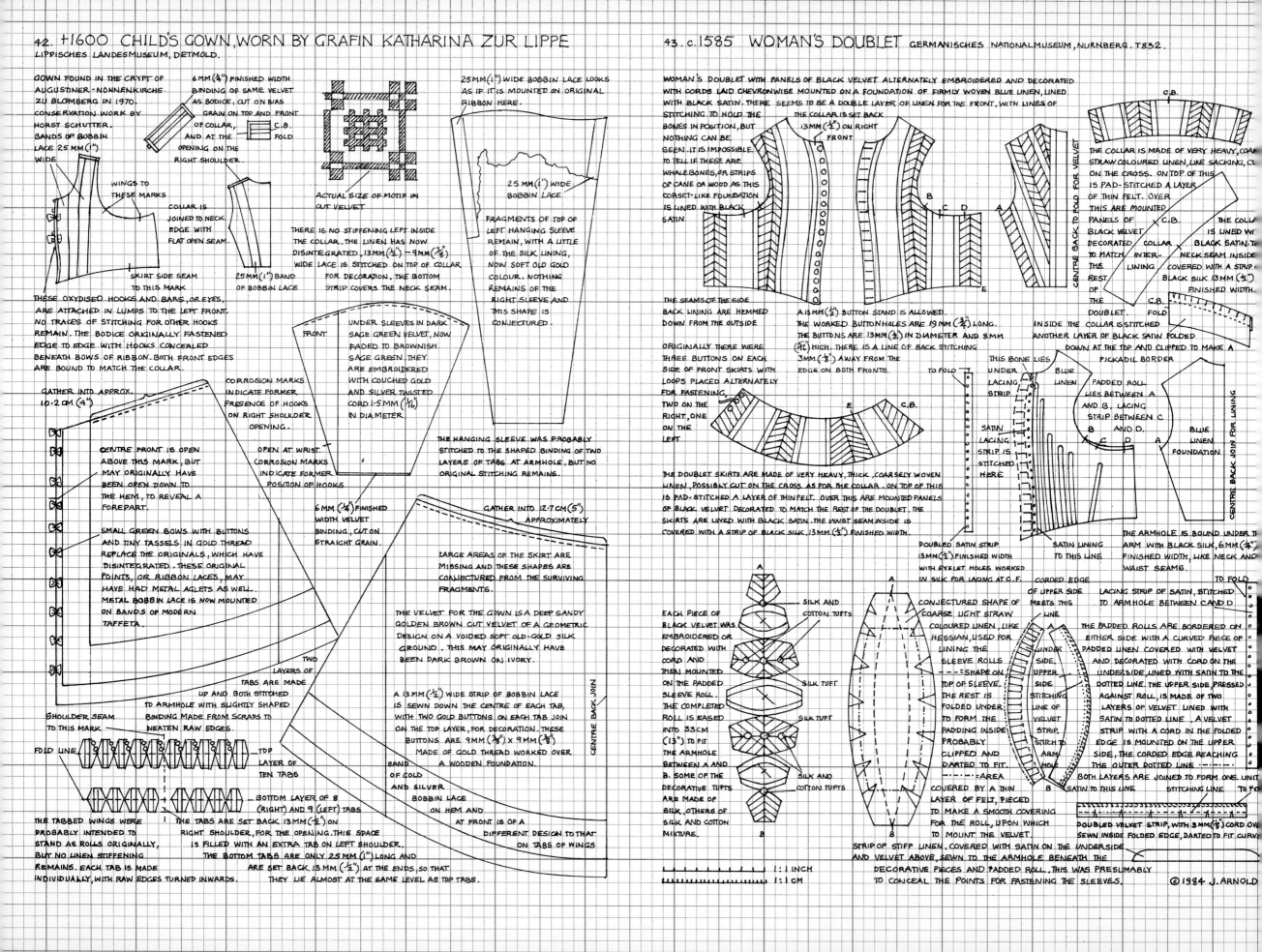

42. +1600 CHILD'S GOWN, WORN BY GRÄFIN KATHARINA ZUR LIPPE. LIPPISCHES LANDESMUSEUM, DETMOLD.

43. c.1585 WOMAN'S DOUBLET. GERMANISCHES NATIONALMUSEUM, NÜRNBERG. T832.

© 1984 J. ARNOLD

c1585 Germanisches Nationalmuseum, Nürnberg

43A. An embroidered black velvet doublet with high, standing collar, rigid body and stiffened skirts which was purchased in 1893 from Mr Böhler, an art dealer in Munich, and was said to have come from the collection of a painter in Paris. Nothing is known of its early history. The doublet has a decidedly masculine appearance and has previously been described as that of a young man. The absence of a linen strip with worked eyelet holes at the waist, to which breeches or trunk-hose would have been attached by points, the slightly curved shape of the centre front, the lacing strips beneath the buttons and buttonholes and the shoulder rolls

suggested that this garment might have been worn by a girl or a slim young woman. In England Phillip Stubbes complained in his *Anatomie of Abuses*, published in 1583, that 'The women also there have dublettes and jerkins as men have here, buttoned up the breast, and made with winges, weltes and pinions on the shoulder pointes, as mannes apparell is, for all the worlde, and though this be a kinde of attire appropriate onely to man, yet they blush not to weare it.'

The arrangement of whalebones or bents inside this doublet were positioned to control the shape of the bust in a similar way to those in a surviving 'pair of bodies' or corset (page 112) and the theory was

finally confirmed by a small German gouache painting dated 1586 of a young woman playing the virginals, wearing a doublet remarkably similar in design (Figs. 302–3). It seems likely from the evidence of this picture that the doublet is German and may well have been made in about 1585. The doublet fastens with buttons and sixteen worked buttonholes with cord loops on collar and skirts, which lie edge to edge as they are too thick to overlap. There are two loops on the collar, one on each side, and three on the skirts, two on the right and one on the left. The buttons are made of knotted cotton, worked over tightly packed rag or wooden foundations, covered with black velvet and

a cover of knotted black silk thread is worked over the top.

43B. Much of the embroidery and velvet has disintegrated but enough is left to show that the doublet was of high-quality workmanship and made for a fashionable person of rank and wealth. The surface of the doublet is made of strips of black velvet cut on the straight grain, embroidered with a chevron arrangement of silk cord. These are placed beside strips cut on the bias, embroidered with a flowing design of stylized fleurs-de-lys and leaves. There are slight variations of width in these strips to suit the pattern shapes of the doublet.

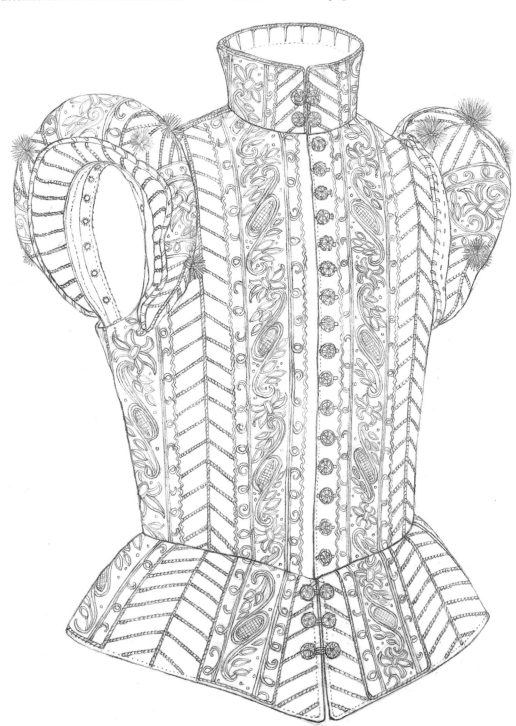

43A

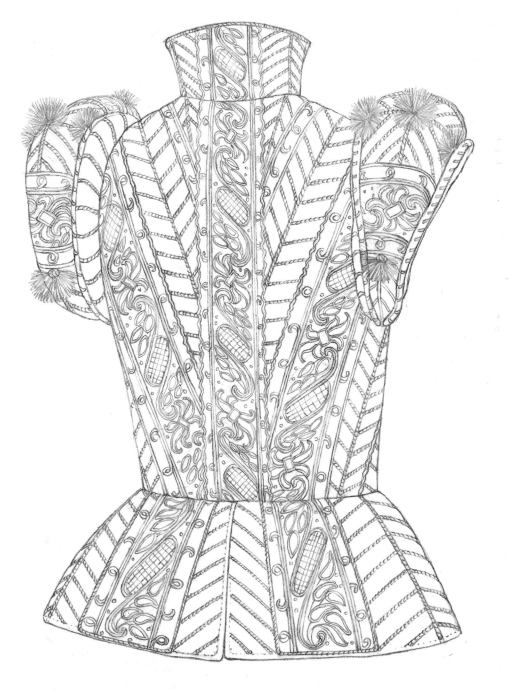

43B

43C. The narrower strips of velvet, cut on the straight grain, are padded between the chevrons made by the cords with a mixture of hemp and tiny threads of orange wool, probably unravelled from an old garment. The cords forming the chevrons are slightly under 1.5 mm ($\frac{1}{16}''$) in diameter. Some are Z and others S twist but both types are made with a cotton core. The heavier black silk cords outlining the edges of the panels, nearly 3 mm ($\frac{1}{8}''$) in diameter, are also made with cotton cores. Both leaf and flower shapes on the wider velvet strips are worked in black silk over a padding of spun linen or hemp threads. The central shapes between the fleurs-de-lys are covered with fine, twill weave black silk, caught down with a chequered design of black silk threads giving the effect of a net (Fig. 306). The strips of velvet are bordered with heavy black silk cords (silk S and cotton core Z twist). This cord is twisted tightly until it curls and is still held in position in many places by a thin three-strand cotton thread (Z twist), probably black originally, now brown. No traces of a silk covering for this thin cotton thread remain. Experiments carried out by Miss Anneliese Streiter in the Textile Conservation Workshop showed that the cotton core for the thick cord would have been twisted more tightly than the silk covering it. The thin cotton thread held taut in the resultant curves kept the twist open. Miss Erika Weiland tested fibres from various parts of the doublet with the Neocarmine W test and examined them under the microscope.

The padded shoulder rolls are made of a pale straw-coloured linen or hemp, similar in texture to hessian, folded in and pleated to shape. Pieces of felt, joined together with butted edges, are stitched on top. Shaped pieces of embroidered velvet are mounted over this smooth surface. Decorative tufts, formed like tassels, two of black silk and six of cotton and silk mixture, are stitched to each roll for decoration. Shaped pieces of black velvet, padded and decorated with cord, are placed on either side of each shoulder roll. A satin lacing strip with twenty worked eyelet holes is stitched inside the armhole for sleeves to be attached with points. A strip of linen, covered with satin on one side and velvet on the other, is sewn to the armhole, satin side outwards, facing the arm, presumably to hide the points when the sleeve was laced in. Good examples of fashionable sleeve rolls in France may be seen in the Valois tapestries designed for Catherine de'Medici in c1575–80 and in England worn by Queen Elizabeth I in several portraits in the 1570s and 1580s. A drawing by Hilliard of c1588 (Fig. 283) shows embroidered linen sleeves beneath prominent sleeve rolls, similar to those of the young lady playing the virginals (Figs. 302–3).

43D. The foundation of the doublet is a layer of firmly woven blue linen, lined with black satin. There is a double layer of linen for the front of the doublet to stiffen it. Lines of stitching hold six whalebones (or possibly bents) in position on either side but they can only be felt, not seen, through the black satin lining. On either side of the centre front, beneath the buttonholes, are lacing strips made of folded pieces of satin with nineteen eyelet holes worked in each one. The waist seam is neatened with a strip of satin.

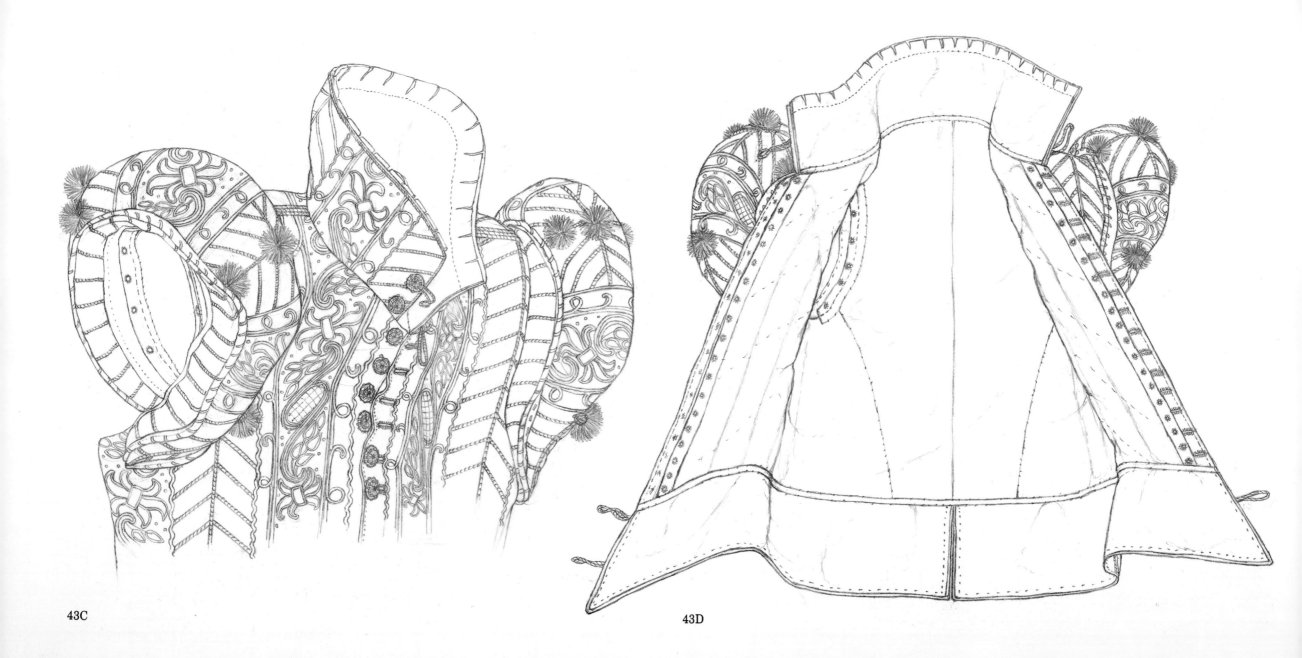

43C

43D

c1570–80 Germanisches Nationalmuseum, Nürnberg

44A. A kirtle in ivory silk with detachable sleeves worn under the black velvet gown on pages 109–11. The early provenance is unknown but it was probably acquired by the museum in the 1870s. The kirtle is made of coarse linen covered with ivory silk. The latter is in a very fragile state. The centre front of the skirt is interlined with pink linen to below knee level and a narrower strip is placed all the way round the hem to stiffen it. The bottom of the kirtle is covered with ivory silk, with silver metal strip in the weft (Fig. 315). The front panel is covered with soft ivory silk with very fine silver threads in the weft, embroidered with black silk and bluish-grey metal spangles (Fig. 313). Two bands of black and white bobbin net are stitched above the hem of the kirtle (Fig. 311). Details of the wider one may be seen in Figs. 314, 316–17, showing the applied motifs of black silk outlined with black silk braid enriched with metal strip. The kirtle laces up at the centre back and there are worked eyelet holes round the armhole for attaching the sleeves with points or laces.

44B. Each kirtle sleeve is made of palest pink linen, lined with ivory silk taffeta. The lower half is covered with ivory embroidered silk to match the front panel. The top is covered first with ivory silk taffeta and then with a layer of ivory embroidered silk. Eyelet holes are worked round the sleevehead for attaching the sleeve to the kirtle with points.

c1570–80 Germanisches Nationalmuseum, Nürnberg

45A. The black velvet loose gown, which was worn over the ivory silk kirtle, is similar to that worn by Anna Sophia, Herzogin zu Mecklenburg, in her portrait dated 1574 (Fig. 310). The side view shows the gored panel added because the velvet was not wide enough. The pile of the velvet has almost disappeared.

44A

44B

45A

A KIRTLE WITH DETACHABLE SLEEVES IN IVORY SILK, WITH SILK PANELS EMBROIDERED IN BLACK SILK AND SEQUINS. THE PATTERN OF THE RIGHT SIDE IS GIVEN. THE LEFT SIDE IS FRAGILE AT THE FRONT, BUT IN GOOD CONDITION AT THE BACK. THE RIGHT SIDE IS FRAGILE AT THE FRONT AND VERY FRAGILE AT THE BACK, BUT THE SILK HAS A COMPLETE ARMHOLE BINDING STRIP. THE LEFT SIDE IS SLIGHTLY PUCKERED ON THE SIDE SEAM AT THE BACK. MUCH OF THE BLACK SILK EMBROIDERY HAS FADED AND DISCOLOURED TO BROWN.

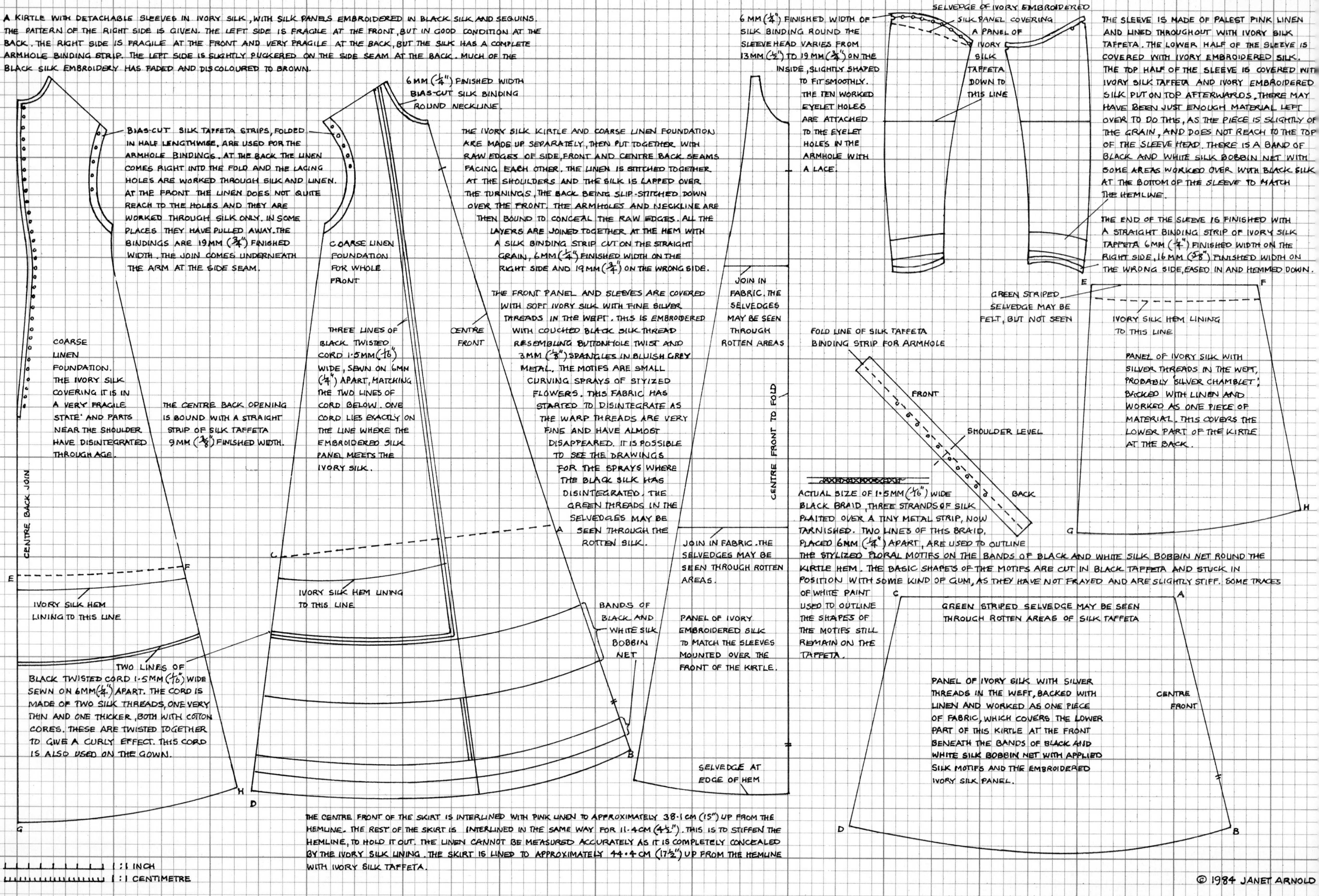

6MM (¼") FINISHED WIDTH BIAS-CUT SILK BINDING ROUND NECKLINE

BIAS-CUT SILK TAFFETA STRIPS, FOLDED IN HALF LENGTHWISE, ARE USED FOR THE ARMHOLE BINDINGS. AT THE BACK THE LINEN COMES RIGHT INTO THE FOLD AND THE LACING HOLES ARE WORKED THROUGH SILK AND LINEN. AT THE FRONT THE LINEN DOES NOT QUITE REACH TO THE HOLES AND THEY ARE WORKED THROUGH SILK ONLY. IN SOME PLACES THEY HAVE PULLED AWAY. THE BINDINGS ARE 19MM (¾") FINISHED WIDTH. THE JOIN COMES UNDERNEATH THE ARM AT THE SIDE SEAM.

COARSE LINEN FOUNDATION FOR WHOLE FRONT

COARSE LINEN FOUNDATION. THE IVORY SILK COVERING IT IS IN A VERY FRAGILE STATE AND PARTS NEAR THE SHOULDER HAVE DISINTEGRATED THROUGH AGE.

THE CENTRE BACK OPENING IS BOUND WITH A STRAIGHT STRIP OF SILK TAFFETA 9MM (⅜") FINISHED WIDTH.

CENTRE BACK JOIN

THE IVORY SILK KIRTLE AND COARSE LINEN FOUNDATION ARE MADE UP SEPARATELY, THEN PUT TOGETHER WITH RAW EDGES OF SIDE, FRONT AND CENTRE BACK SEAMS FACING EACH OTHER. THE LINEN IS STITCHED TOGETHER AT THE SHOULDERS AND THE SILK IS LAPPED OVER THE TURNINGS, THE BACK BEING SLIP-STITCHED DOWN OVER THE FRONT. THE ARMHOLES AND NECKLINE ARE THEN BOUND TO CONCEAL THE RAW EDGES. ALL THE LAYERS ARE JOINED TOGETHER AT THE HEM WITH A SILK BINDING STRIP CUT ON THE STRAIGHT GRAIN, 6MM (¼") FINISHED WIDTH ON THE RIGHT SIDE AND 19MM (¾") ON THE WRONG SIDE.

THE FRONT PANEL AND SLEEVES ARE COVERED WITH SOFT IVORY SILK WITH FINE SILVER THREADS IN THE WEFT. THIS IS EMBROIDERED WITH COUCHED BLACK SILK THREAD RESEMBLING BUTTONHOLE TWIST AND 3MM (⅛") SPANGLES IN BLUISH GREY METAL. THE MOTIFS ARE SMALL CURVING SPRAYS OF STYLIZED FLOWERS. THIS FABRIC HAS STARTED TO DISINTEGRATE AS THE WARP THREADS ARE VERY FINE AND HAVE ALMOST DISAPPEARED. IT IS POSSIBLE TO SEE THE DRAWINGS FOR THE SPRAYS WHERE THE BLACK SILK HAS DISINTEGRATED, THE GREEN THREADS IN THE SELVEDGES MAY BE SEEN THROUGH THE ROTTEN SILK.

THREE LINES OF BLACK TWISTED CORD 1·5MM (1/16") WIDE, SEWN ON 6MM (¼") APART, MATCHING THE TWO LINES OF CORD BELOW. ONE CORD LIES EXACTLY ON THE LINE WHERE THE EMBROIDERED SILK PANEL MEETS THE IVORY SILK.

CENTRE FRONT

CENTRE FRONT TO FOLD

JOIN IN FABRIC. THE SELVEDGES MAY BE SEEN THROUGH ROTTEN AREAS.

JOIN IN FABRIC, THE SELVEDGES MAY BE SEEN THROUGH ROTTEN AREAS

6MM (¼") FINISHED WIDTH OF SILK BINDING ROUND THE SLEEVE HEAD VARIES FROM 13MM (½") TO 19MM (¾") ON THE INSIDE, SLIGHTLY SHAPED TO FIT SMOOTHLY. THE TEN WORKED EYELET HOLES ARE ATTACHED TO THE EYELET HOLES IN THE ARMHOLE WITH A LACE.

SELVEDGE OF IVORY EMBROIDERED SILK PANEL COVERING A PANEL OF IVORY SILK TAFFETA DOWN TO THIS LINE

THE SLEEVE IS MADE OF PALEST PINK LINEN AND LINED THROUGHOUT WITH IVORY SILK TAFFETA. THE LOWER HALF OF THE SLEEVE IS COVERED WITH IVORY EMBROIDERED SILK. THE TOP HALF OF THE SLEEVE IS COVERED WITH IVORY SILK TAFFETA AND IVORY EMBROIDERED SILK PUT ON TOP AFTERWARDS. THERE MAY HAVE BEEN JUST ENOUGH MATERIAL LEFT OVER TO DO THIS, AS THE PIECE IS SLIGHTLY OF THE GRAIN, AND DOES NOT REACH TO THE TOP OF THE SLEEVE HEAD. THERE IS A BAND OF BLACK AND WHITE SILK BOBBIN NET WITH SOME AREAS WORKED OVER WITH BLACK SILK AT THE BOTTOM OF THE SLEEVE TO MATCH THE HEMLINE.

THE END OF THE SLEEVE IS FINISHED WITH A STRAIGHT BINDING STRIP OF IVORY SILK TAFFETA 6MM (¼") FINISHED WIDTH ON THE RIGHT SIDE, 16MM (⅝") FINISHED WIDTH ON THE WRONG SIDE, EASED IN AND HEMMED DOWN.

GREEN STRIPED SELVEDGE MAY BE FELT, BUT NOT SEEN

FOLD LINE OF SILK TAFFETA BINDING STRIP FOR ARMHOLE

FRONT

SHOULDER LEVEL

BACK

ACTUAL SIZE OF 1·5MM (1/16") WIDE BLACK BRAID, THREE STRANDS OF SILK PLAITED OVER A TINY METAL STRIP, NOW TARNISHED. TWO LINES OF THIS BRAID, PLACED 6MM (¼") APART, ARE USED TO OUTLINE THE STYLIZED FLORAL MOTIFS ON THE BANDS OF BLACK AND WHITE SILK BOBBIN NET ROUND THE KIRTLE HEM. THE BASIC SHAPES OF THE MOTIFS ARE CUT IN BLACK TAFFETA AND STUCK IN POSITION WITH SOME KIND OF GUM, AS THEY HAVE NOT FRAYED AND ARE SLIGHTLY STIFF. SOME TRACES OF WHITE PAINT USED TO OUTLINE THE SHAPES OF THE MOTIFS STILL REMAIN ON THE TAFFETA.

IVORY SILK HEM LINING TO THIS LINE

PANEL OF IVORY SILK WITH SILVER THREADS IN THE WEFT, PROBABLY 'SILVER CHAMBLET', BACKED WITH LINEN AND WORKED AS ONE PIECE OF MATERIAL. THIS COVERS THE LOWER PART OF THE KIRTLE AT THE BACK.

GREEN STRIPED SELVEDGE MAY BE SEEN THROUGH ROTTEN AREAS OF SILK TAFFETA

PANEL OF IVORY SILK WITH SILVER THREADS IN THE WEFT, BACKED WITH LINEN AND WORKED AS ONE PIECE OF FABRIC, WHICH COVERS THE LOWER PART OF THIS KIRTLE AT THE FRONT BENEATH THE BANDS OF BLACK AND WHITE SILK BOBBIN NET WITH APPLIED SILK MOTIFS AND THE EMBROIDERED IVORY SILK PANEL.

CENTRE FRONT

IVORY SILK HEM LINING TO THIS LINE

IVORY SILK HEM LINING TO THIS LINE

TWO LINES OF BLACK TWISTED CORD 1·5MM (1/16") WIDE SEWN ON 6MM (¼") APART. THE CORD IS MADE OF TWO SILK THREADS, ONE VERY THIN AND ONE THICKER, BOTH WITH COTTON CORES. THESE ARE TWISTED TOGETHER TO GIVE A CURLY EFFECT. THIS CORD IS ALSO USED ON THE GOWN.

BANDS OF BLACK AND WHITE SILK BOBBIN NET

PANEL OF IVORY EMBROIDERED SILK TO MATCH THE SLEEVES MOUNTED OVER THE FRONT OF THE KIRTLE.

SELVEDGE AT EDGE OF HEM

THE CENTRE FRONT OF THE SKIRT IS INTERLINED WITH PINK LINEN TO APPROXIMATELY 38·1 CM (15") UP FROM THE HEMLINE. THE REST OF THE SKIRT IS INTERLINED IN THE SAME WAY FOR 11·4CM (4½"). THIS IS TO STIFFEN THE HEMLINE, TO HOLD IT OUT. THE LINEN CANNOT BE MEASURED ACCURATELY AS IT IS COMPLETELY CONCEALED BY THE IVORY SILK LINING. THE SKIRT IS LINED TO APPROXIMATELY 44·4 CM (17½") UP FROM THE HEMLINE WITH IVORY SILK TAFFETA.

1:1 INCH
1:1 CENTIMETRE

© 1984 JANET ARNOLD

45B. The black velvet loose gown is cut away in an inverted V-shape at the front and pieced on the right back. It is decorated with three stripes of black satin on both sides. Three rows of black silk cord with cotton cores are mounted on each strip, the centre one looped at intervals. The buttons and cord loops at the top of the gown may be fastened but those below are for decoration only. The standing collar is interlined with linen, probably two layers as it is quite stiff, and lined with black satin. The sleeves are made with a linen foundation padded with horsehair and a layer of coarse linen or buckram. This must have been stiffened with size, damped and moulded to shape. There are also at least six whalebones, bents or strips of osier running over the curved shape at its widest point and in struts down the arm. They can only be felt, not seen. The centre bone runs right up to the armhole. The padded sleeve foundation is covered with black velvet cut to shape and strips of black satin decorated with cord. The gown is embroidered with applied black satin motifs and couched black cords. Each motif is glued to a piece of paper to prevent fraying, cut out and mounted on the velvet, then outlined with black cord. The leaf shapes are made of rows of couched cord packed closely together.

45C. The gown is lined with fairly coarse black linen, now faded. Another layer of linen, cut to shape, is sewn round the armhole. The padded sleeve is assembled and the complete unit stitched into the gown. The raw edges are then covered with a black satin band cut on the straight grain. Linen stay strips are sewn across the shoulders and covered by the satin armhole and neck bindings. The buttons have wooden bases covered in black satin, with black and white cord (now discoloured) knotted in a net over the top.

45B

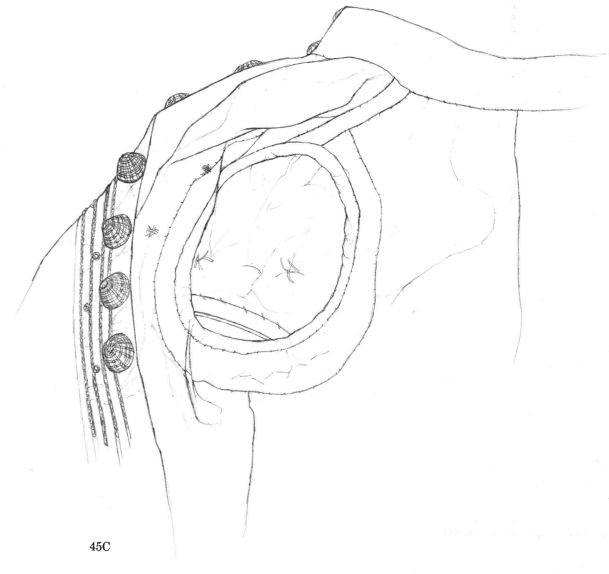

45C

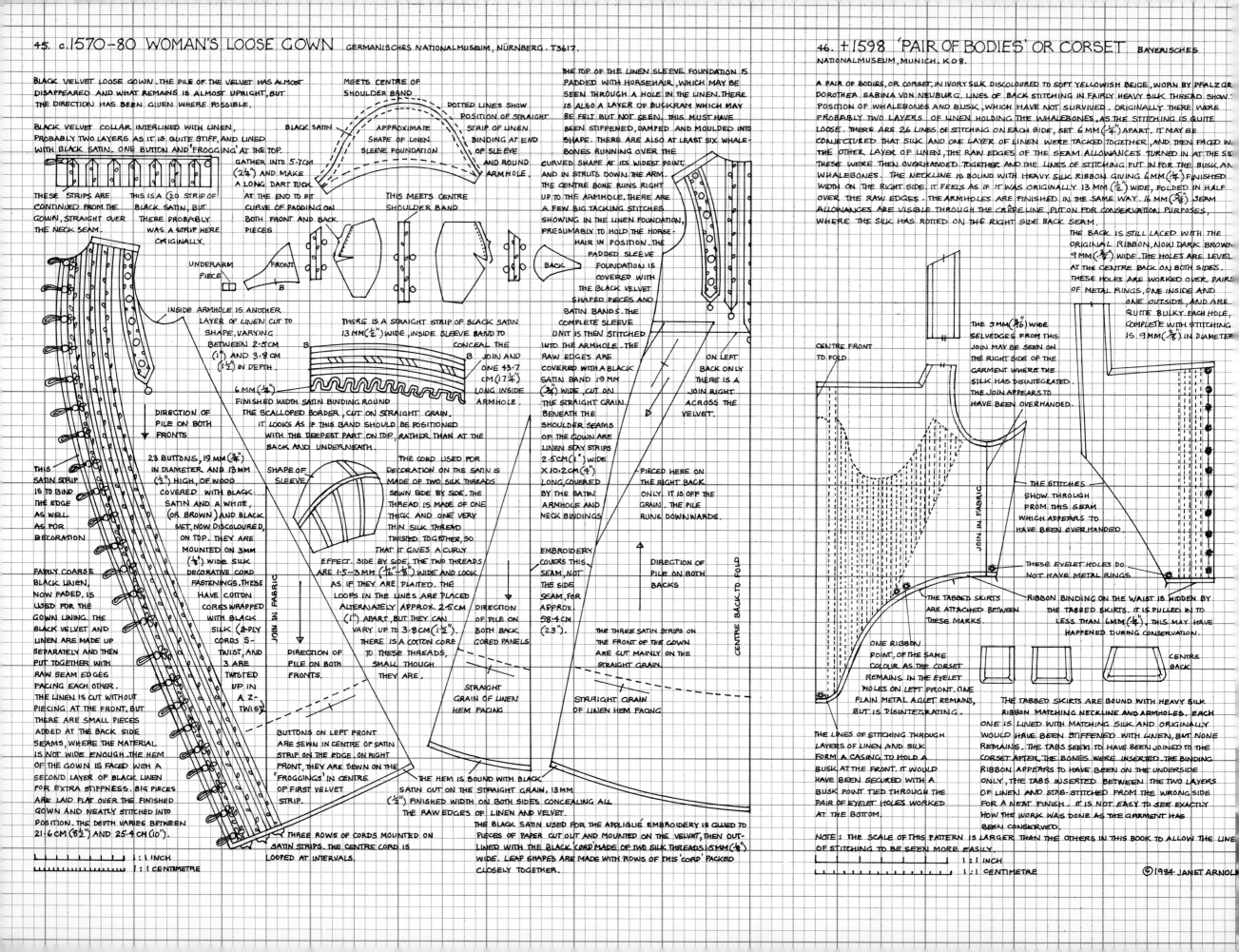

45. c.1570–80 WOMAN'S LOOSE GOWN GERMANISCHES NATIONALMUSEUM, NÜRNBERG. T3617.

BLACK VELVET LOOSE GOWN. THE PILE OF THE VELVET HAS ALMOST DISAPPEARED AND WHAT REMAINS IS ALMOST UPRIGHT, BUT THE DIRECTION HAS BEEN GIVEN WHERE POSSIBLE.

BLACK VELVET COLLAR INTERLINED WITH LINEN, PROBABLY TWO LAYERS AS IT IS QUITE STIFF, AND LINED WITH BLACK SATIN. ONE BUTTON AND 'FROGGING' AT THE TOP.

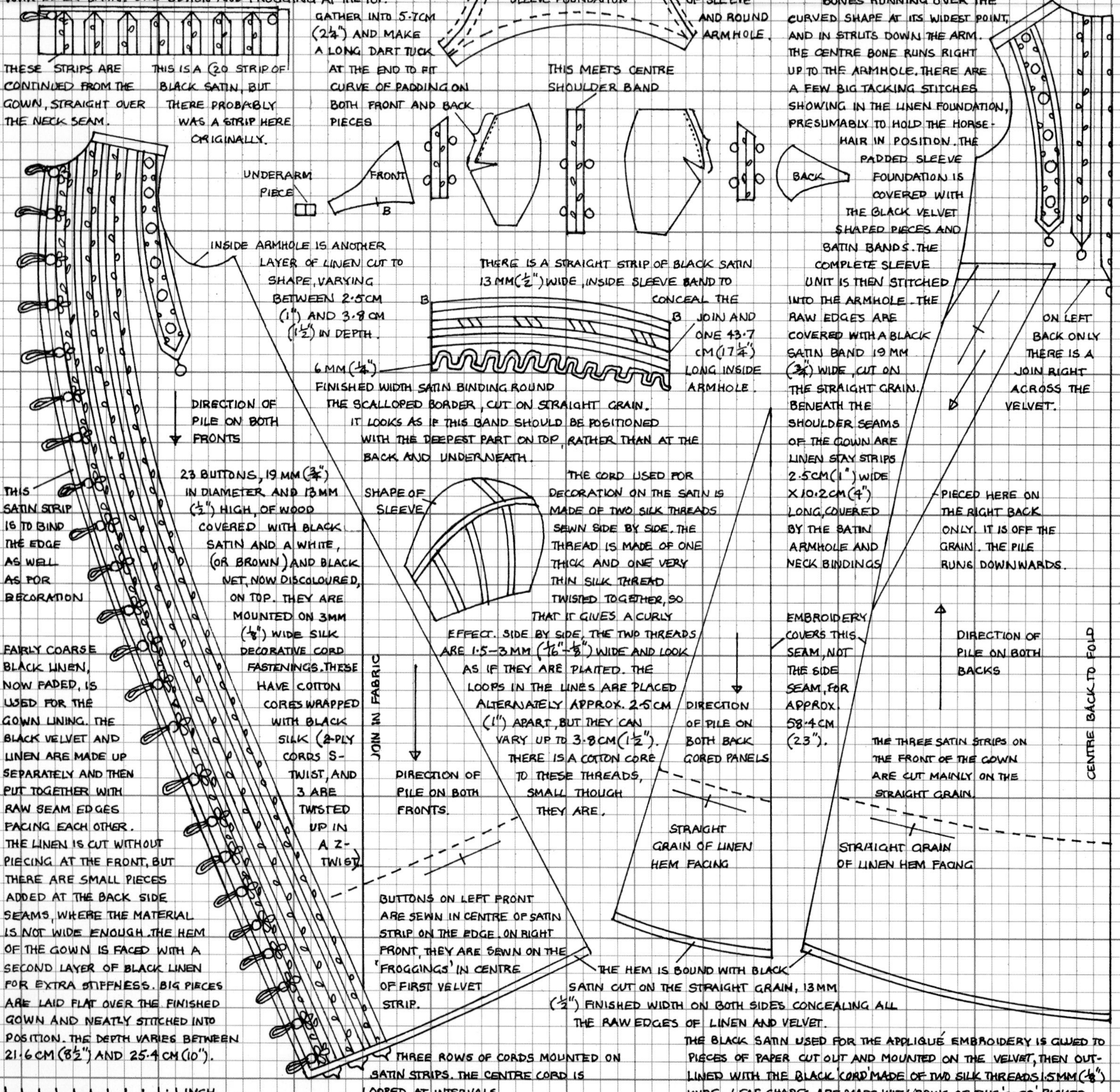

THESE STRIPS ARE CONTINUED FROM THE GOWN, STRAIGHT OVER THE NECK SEAM.
THIS IS A 20 STRIP OF BLACK SATIN, BUT THERE PROBABLY WAS A STRIP HERE ORIGINALLY.
GATHER INTO 5·7CM (2¼") AND MAKE A LONG DART TUCK AT THE END TO FIT CURVE OF PADDING ON BOTH FRONT AND BACK PIECES
MEETS CENTRE OF SHOULDER BAND
BLACK SATIN
APPROXIMATE SHAPE OF LINEN SLEEVE FOUNDATION
DOTTED LINES SHOW POSITION OF STRAIGHT STRIP OF LINEN BINDING AT END OF SLEEVE AND ROUND ARMHOLE.
THIS MEETS CENTRE SHOULDER BAND
UNDERARM PIECE
FRONT
B
BACK
INSIDE ARMHOLE IS ANOTHER LAYER OF LINEN CUT TO SHAPE, VARYING BETWEEN 2·5CM (1") AND 3·8 CM (1½") IN DEPTH.
THERE IS A STRAIGHT STRIP OF BLACK SATIN 13 MM (½") WIDE, INSIDE SLEEVE BAND TO CONCEAL THE JOIN AND ONE 43·7 CM (17¼") LONG INSIDE ARMHOLE.
B
B
6 MM (¼") FINISHED WIDTH SATIN BINDING ROUND THE SCALLOPED BORDER, CUT ON STRAIGHT GRAIN.
IT LOOKS AS IF THIS BAND SHOULD BE POSITIONED WITH THE DEEPEST PART ON TOP, RATHER THAN AT THE BACK AND UNDERNEATH.
DIRECTION OF PILE ON BOTH FRONTS
SHAPE OF SLEEVE
THIS SATIN STRIP IS TO BIND THE EDGE AS WELL AS FOR DECORATION
JOIN IN FABRIC
DIRECTION OF PILE ON BOTH FRONTS.
DIRECTION OF PILE ON BOTH BACK GORED PANELS
STRAIGHT GRAIN OF LINEN HEM FACING
STRAIGHT GRAIN OF LINEN HEM FACING
ON LEFT BACK ONLY THERE IS A JOIN RIGHT ACROSS THE VELVET.
PIECED HERE ON THE RIGHT BACK ONLY. IT IS OFF THE GRAIN. THE PILE RUNS DOWNWARDS.
EMBROIDERY COVERS THIS SEAM, NOT THE SIDE SEAM, FOR APPROX. 58·4CM (23").
DIRECTION OF PILE ON BOTH BACKS
CENTRE BACK TO FOLD
THE THREE SATIN STRIPS ON THE FRONT OF THE GOWN ARE CUT MAINLY ON THE STRAIGHT GRAIN.
THREE ROWS OF CORDS MOUNTED ON SATIN STRIPS. THE CENTRE CORD IS LOOPED AT INTERVALS.

THE TOP OF THE LINEN SLEEVE FOUNDATION IS PADDED WITH HORSEHAIR, WHICH MAY BE SEEN THROUGH A HOLE IN THE LINEN. THERE IS ALSO A LAYER OF BUCKRAM WHICH MAY BE FELT BUT NOT SEEN. THIS MUST HAVE BEEN STIFFENED, DAMPED AND MOULDED INTO SHAPE. THERE ARE ALSO AT LEAST SIX WHALEBONES RUNNING OVER THE CURVED SHAPE AT ITS WIDEST POINT, AND IN STRUTS DOWN THE ARM. THE CENTRE BONE RUNS RIGHT UP TO THE ARMHOLE. THERE ARE A FEW BIG TACKING STITCHES SHOWING IN THE LINEN FOUNDATION, PRESUMABLY TO HOLD THE HORSEHAIR IN POSITION. THE PADDED SLEEVE FOUNDATION IS COVERED WITH THE BLACK VELVET SHAPED PIECES AND SATIN BANDS. THE COMPLETE SLEEVE UNIT IS THEN STITCHED INTO THE ARMHOLE. THE RAW EDGES ARE COVERED WITH A BLACK SATIN BAND 19 MM (¾") WIDE, CUT ON THE STRAIGHT GRAIN. BENEATH THE SHOULDER SEAMS OF THE GOWN ARE LINEN STAY STRIPS 2·5CM (1") WIDE X 10·2CM (4") LONG, COVERED BY THE SATIN ARMHOLE AND NECK BINDINGS.

23 BUTTONS, 19 MM (¾") IN DIAMETER AND 13MM (½") HIGH, OF WOOD COVERED WITH BLACK SATIN AND A WHITE, (OR BROWN) AND BLACK NET, NOW DISCOLOURED, ON TOP. THEY ARE MOUNTED ON 3MM (⅛") WIDE SILK DECORATIVE CORD FASTENINGS. THESE HAVE COTTON CORES WRAPPED WITH BLACK SILK (2-PLY CORDS S-TWIST, AND 3 ARE TWISTED UP IN A Z-TWIST).

THE CORD USED FOR DECORATION ON THE SATIN IS MADE OF TWO SILK THREADS SEWN SIDE BY SIDE. THE THREAD IS MADE OF ONE THICK AND ONE VERY THIN SILK THREAD TWISTED TOGETHER, SO THAT IT GIVES A CURLY EFFECT. SIDE BY SIDE, THE TWO THREADS ARE 1·5–3MM ($\frac{1}{16}$"–⅛") WIDE AND LOOK AS IF THEY ARE PLAITED. THE LOOPS IN THE LINES ARE PLACED ALTERNATELY APPROX. 2·5CM (1") APART, BUT THEY CAN VARY UP TO 3·8CM (1½"). THERE IS A COTTON CORE TO THESE THREADS, SMALL THOUGH THEY ARE.

FAIRLY COARSE BLACK LINEN, NOW FADED, IS USED FOR THE GOWN LINING. THE BLACK VELVET AND LINEN ARE MADE UP SEPARATELY AND THEN PUT TOGETHER WITH RAW SEAM EDGES FACING EACH OTHER. THE LINEN IS CUT WITHOUT PIECING AT THE FRONT, BUT THERE ARE SMALL PIECES ADDED AT THE BACK SIDE SEAMS, WHERE THE MATERIAL IS NOT WIDE ENOUGH. THE HEM OF THE GOWN IS FACED WITH A SECOND LAYER OF BLACK LINEN FOR EXTRA STIFFNESS. BIG PIECES ARE LAID FLAT OVER THE FINISHED GOWN AND NEATLY STITCHED INTO POSITION. THE DEPTH VARIES BETWEEN 21·6 CM (8½") AND 25·4 CM (10").

BUTTONS ON LEFT FRONT ARE SEWN IN CENTRE OF SATIN STRIP ON THE EDGE. ON RIGHT FRONT, THEY ARE SEWN ON THE 'FROGGINGS' IN CENTRE OF FIRST VELVET STRIP.

THE HEM IS BOUND WITH BLACK SATIN CUT ON THE STRAIGHT GRAIN, 13MM (½") FINISHED WIDTH ON BOTH SIDES CONCEALING ALL THE RAW EDGES OF LINEN AND VELVET.

THE BLACK SATIN USED FOR THE APPLIQUÉ EMBROIDERY IS GLUED TO PIECES OF PAPER CUT OUT AND MOUNTED ON THE VELVET, THEN OUTLINED WITH THE BLACK 'CORD' MADE OF TWO SILK THREADS 1.5MM (⅛") WIDE. LEAF SHAPES ARE MADE WITH ROWS OF THIS 'CORD' PACKED CLOSELY TOGETHER.

1:1 INCH

1:1 CENTIMETRE

46. +1598 'PAIR OF BODIES' OR CORSET BAYERISCHES NATIONALMUSEUM, MUNICH. K08.

A PAIR OF BODIES, OR CORSET, IN IVORY SILK DISCOLOURED TO SOFT YELLOWISH BEIGE, WORN BY PFALZGR DOROTHEA SABINA VON NEUBURG. LINES OF BACK STITCHING IN FAIRLY HEAVY SILK THREAD SHOW POSITION OF WHALEBONES AND BUSK, WHICH HAVE NOT SURVIVED. ORIGINALLY THERE WERE PROBABLY TWO LAYERS OF LINEN HOLDING THE WHALEBONES, AS THE STITCHING IS QUITE LOOSE. THERE ARE 26 LINES OF STITCHING ON EACH SIDE, SET 6 MM (¼") APART. IT MAY BE CONJECTURED THAT SILK AND ONE LAYER OF LINEN WERE TACKED TOGETHER, AND THEN FACED W THE OTHER LAYER OF LINEN, THE RAW EDGES OF THE SEAM ALLOWANCES TURNED IN AT THE SIC THESE WERE THEN OVERHANDED TOGETHER AND THE LINES OF STITCHING PUT IN FOR THE BUSK AN WHALEBONES. THE NECKLINE IS BOUND WITH HEAVY SILK RIBBON GIVING 6MM (¼") FINISHED WIDTH ON THE RIGHT SIDE. IT FEELS AS IF IT WAS ORIGINALLY 13 MM (½") WIDE, FOLDED IN HALF OVER THE RAW EDGES. THE ARMHOLES ARE FINISHED IN THE SAME WAY. 16 MM (⅝") SEAM ALLOWANCES ARE VISIBLE THROUGH THE CRÊPELINE PUT ON FOR CONSERVATION PURPOSES, WHERE THE SILK HAS ROTTED ON THE RIGHT SIDE BACK SEAM.

THE BACK IS STILL LACED WITH THE ORIGINAL RIBBON, NOW DARK BROWN 9 MM (⅜") WIDE. THE HOLES ARE LEVEL AT THE CENTRE BACK ON BOTH SIDES. THESE HOLES ARE WORKED OVER PAIRS OF METAL RINGS, ONE INSIDE AND ONE OUTSIDE, AND ARE QUITE BULKY. EACH HOLE, COMPLETE WITH STITCHING IS 9MM (⅜") IN DIAMETER

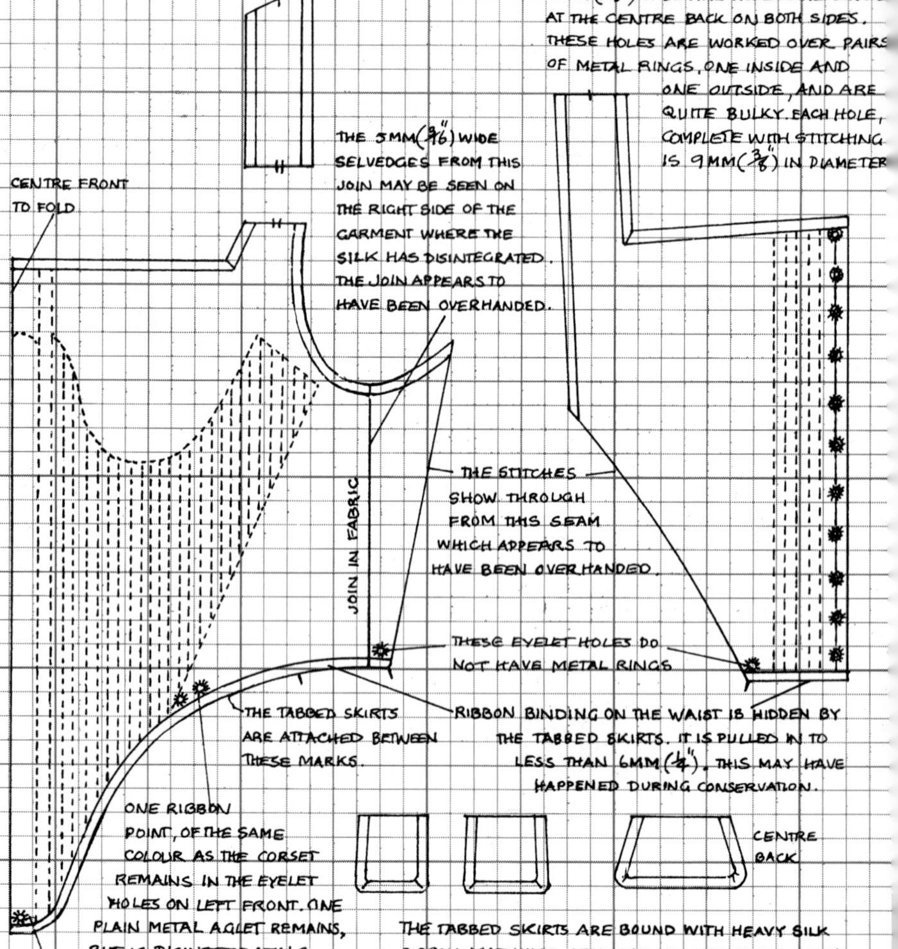

CENTRE FRONT TO FOLD
THE 5MM ($\frac{3}{16}$") WIDE SELVEDGES FROM THIS JOIN MAY BE SEEN ON THE RIGHT SIDE OF THE GARMENT WHERE THE SILK HAS DISINTEGRATED. THE JOIN APPEARS TO HAVE BEEN OVERHANDED.
JOIN IN FABRIC
THE STITCHES SHOW THROUGH FROM THIS SEAM WHICH APPEARS TO HAVE BEEN OVERHANDED.
THESE EYELET HOLES DO NOT HAVE METAL RINGS
THE TABBED SKIRTS ARE ATTACHED BETWEEN THESE MARKS.
RIBBON BINDING ON THE WAIST IS HIDDEN BY THE TABBED SKIRTS. IT IS PULLED IN TO LESS THAN 6MM (¼"). THIS MAY HAVE HAPPENED DURING CONSERVATION.
ONE RIBBON POINT, OF THE SAME COLOUR AS THE CORSET REMAINS IN THE EYELET HOLES ON LEFT FRONT. ONE PLAIN METAL AGLET REMAINS, BUT IS DISINTEGRATING.
CENTRE BACK

THE LINES OF STITCHING THROUGH LAYERS OF LINEN AND SILK FORM A CASING TO HOLD A BUSK AT THE FRONT. IT WOULD HAVE BEEN SECURED WITH A BUSK POINT TIED THROUGH THE PAIR OF EYELET HOLES WORKED AT THE BOTTOM.

THE TABBED SKIRTS ARE BOUND WITH HEAVY SILK RIBBON MATCHING NECKLINE AND ARMHOLES. EACH ONE IS LINED WITH MATCHING SILK AND ORIGINALLY WOULD HAVE BEEN STIFFENED WITH LINEN, BUT NONE REMAINS. THE TABS SEEM TO HAVE BEEN JOINED TO THE CORSET AFTER THE BONES WERE INSERTED. THE BINDING RIBBON APPEARS TO HAVE BEEN ON THE UNDERSIDE ONLY, THE TABS INSERTED BETWEEN THE TWO LAYERS OF LINEN AND STAB-STITCHED FROM THE WRONG SIDE FOR A NEAT FINISH. IT IS NOT EASY TO SEE EXACTLY HOW THE WORK WAS DONE AS THE GARMENT HAS BEEN CONSERVED.

NOTE: THE SCALE OF THIS PATTERN IS LARGER THAN THE OTHERS IN THIS BOOK TO ALLOW THE LINE OF STITCHING TO BE SEEN MORE EASILY.

1:1 INCH

1:1 CENTIMETRE

©1984 JANET ARNOL

46. A 'pair of bodies' or corset, made of lightweight, very finely corded silk, worn by Pfalzgräfin Dorothea Sabina von Neuburg when she was buried in the tomb at Lauingen in 1598, at the age of twenty-two. Originally the corset was probably ivory but has now discoloured to soft yellowish beige (Fig. 327). There would have been a linen lining and probably an interlining as well but this has all disappeared with the decomposing body. The lines of stitching which formed the casings for whalebones or bents (Fig. 330) are in silk thread and have survived. The wide casing at the centre front would have held a busk of wood or horn, tied in position with a busk point through the pair of eyelet holes. The corset laces up at the centre back through eyelet holes worked over metal rings on both inside and outside for reinforcement. The holes are placed evenly and when fastened the backs would lie unevenly at the waist. The tabbed skirts are bound with silk ribbon and were attached to the corset after it had been assembled. Originally the raw edges were probably hidden between the linen lining and the silk outer layer at the waist but the skirts are now stitched on top of the ribbon binding. The garment was too fragile to allow closer examination of the stitching. Pairs of eyelet holes worked at the sides and back waist were for points to attach a farthingale of the Spanish cone-shaped variety. One of the ribbon points remains on the left side with a single metal aglet or tag still attached to it.

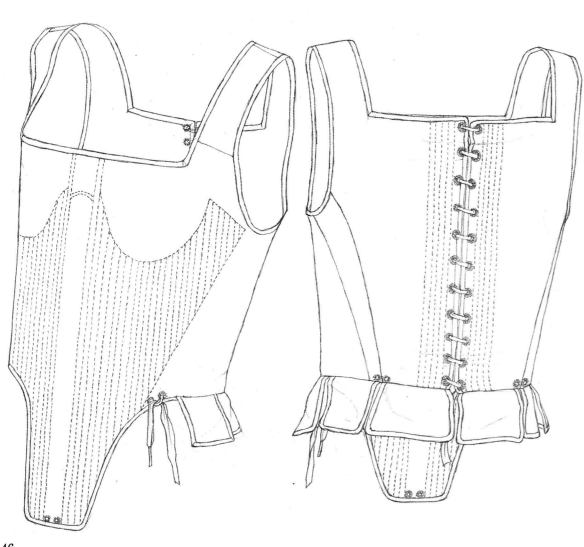

47. A rich russet velvet gown with a petticoat of soft green silk, worn by Pfalzgräfin Dorothea Sabina von Neuburg when she was buried in 1598. Much of the back of both gown and petticoat disintegrated with the decomposing corpse. The gown is trimmed with gold and silver metal bobbin lace. The undersleeves are in golden-yellow satin, cut and trimmed with rows of tarnished metal bobbin lace. The hanging sleeves are lined with scored and pinked golden-yellow satin. The upper left hanging sleeve was removed when the tomb was opened and is now in a private collection. The drawing shows the gown as it would have appeared originally.

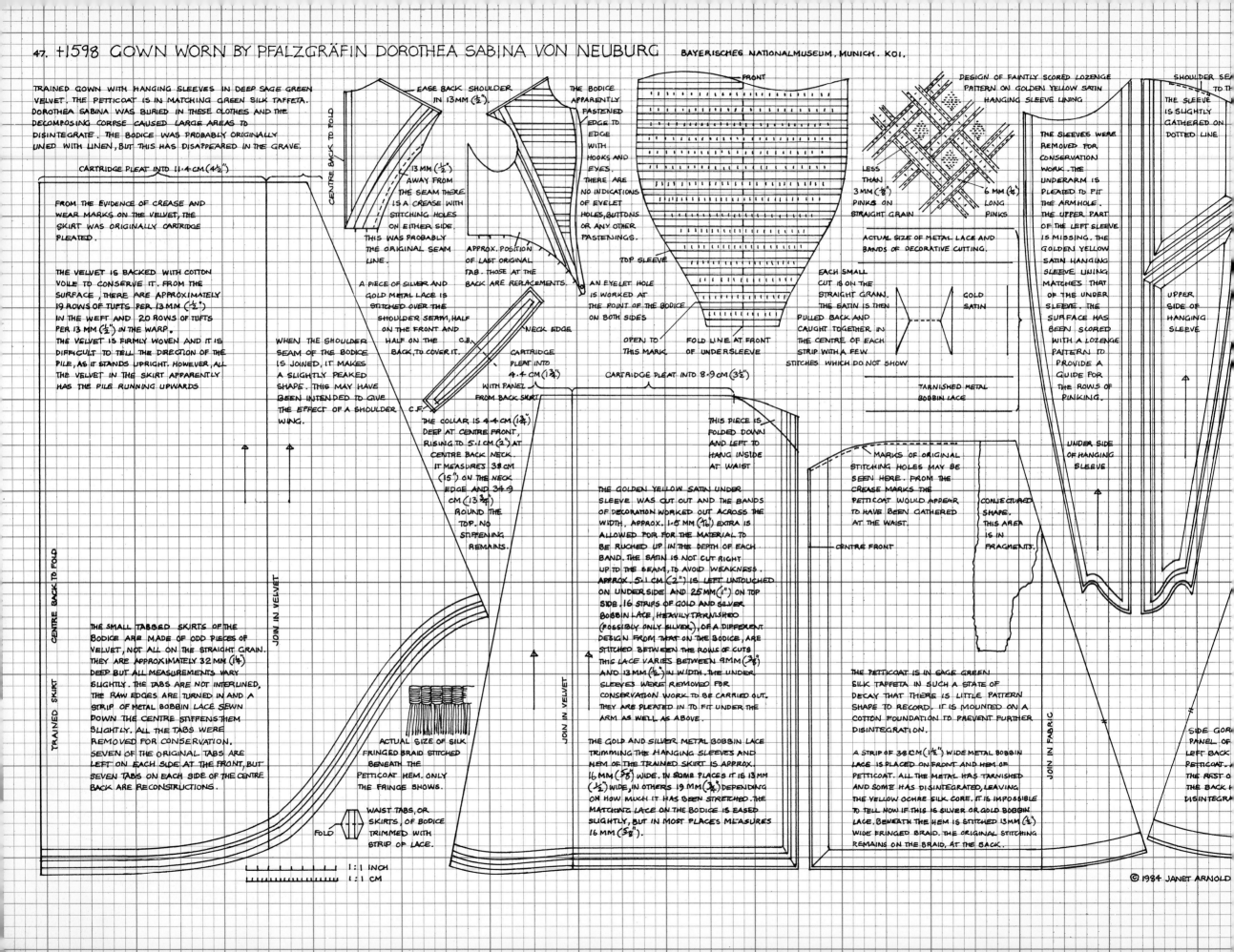

TRAINED GOWN WITH HANGING SLEEVES IN DEEP SAGE GREEN VELVET. THE PETTICOAT IS IN MATCHING GREEN SILK TAFFETA. DOROTHEA SABINA WAS BURIED IN THESE CLOTHES AND THE DECOMPOSING CORPSE CAUSED LARGE AREAS TO DISINTEGRATE. THE BODICE WAS PROBABLY ORIGINALLY LINED WITH LINEN, BUT THIS HAS DISAPPEARED IN THE GRAVE.

CARTRIDGE PLEAT INTO 11·4 CM (4½")

FROM THE EVIDENCE OF CREASE AND WEAR MARKS ON THE VELVET, THE SKIRT WAS ORIGINALLY CARTRIDGE PLEATED.

THE VELVET IS BACKED WITH COTTON VOILE TO CONSERVE IT. FROM THE SURFACE, THERE ARE APPROXIMATELY 19 ROWS OF TUFTS PER 13MM (½") IN THE WEFT AND 20 ROWS OF TUFTS PER 13 MM (½") IN THE WARP. THE VELVET IS FIRMLY WOVEN AND IT IS DIFFICULT TO TELL THE DIRECTION OF THE PILE, AS IT STANDS UPRIGHT. HOWEVER, ALL THE VELVET IN THE SKIRT APPARENTLY HAS THE PILE RUNNING UPWARDS

CENTRE BACK TO FOLD

TRAINED SKIRT

THE SMALL TABBED SKIRTS OF THE BODICE ARE MADE OF ODD PIECES OF VELVET, NOT ALL ON THE STRAIGHT GRAIN. THEY ARE APPROXIMATELY 32 MM (1¼") DEEP BUT ALL MEASUREMENTS VARY SLIGHTLY. THE TABS ARE NOT INTERLINED, THE RAW EDGES ARE TURNED IN AND A STRIP OF METAL BOBBIN LACE SEWN DOWN THE CENTRE STIFFENS THEM SLIGHTLY. ALL THE TABS WERE REMOVED FOR CONSERVATION. SEVEN OF THE ORIGINAL TABS ARE LEFT ON EACH SIDE AT THE FRONT, BUT SEVEN TABS ON EACH SIDE OF THE CENTRE BACK ARE RECONSTRUCTIONS.

JOIN IN VELVET

ACTUAL SIZE OF SILK FRINGED BRAID STITCHED BENEATH THE PETTICOAT HEM. ONLY THE FRINGE SHOWS.

WAIST TABS, OR SKIRTS, OF BODICE TRIMMED WITH STRIP OF LACE.

FOLD

EASE BACK SHOULDER IN 13MM (½")

CENTRE BACK TO FOLD

13 MM (½") AWAY FROM THE SEAM THERE IS A CREASE WITH STITCHING HOLES ON EITHER SIDE. THIS WAS PROBABLY THE ORIGINAL SEAM LINE.

A PIECE OF SILVER AND GOLD METAL LACE IS STITCHED OVER THE SHOULDER SEAM, HALF ON THE FRONT AND HALF ON THE BACK, TO COVER IT.

APPROX. POSITION OF LAST ORIGINAL TAB. THOSE AT THE BACK ARE REPLACEMENTS.

C.B.

NECK EDGE

CARTRIDGE PLEAT INTO 4·4 (1¾)

WITH PANEL FROM BACK SKIRT

C.F.

THE COLLAR IS 4·4 CM (1¾") DEEP AT CENTRE FRONT, RISING TO 5·1 CM (2") AT CENTRE BACK NECK. IT MEASURES 38 CM (15") ON THE NECK EDGE AND 34·9 CM (13¾") ROUND THE TOP. NO STIFFENING REMAINS.

WHEN THE SHOULDER SEAM OF THE BODICE IS JOINED, IT MAKES A SLIGHTLY PEAKED SHAPE. THIS MAY HAVE BEEN INTENDED TO GIVE THE EFFECT OF A SHOULDER WING.

JOIN IN VELVET

THE BODICE APPARENTLY FASTENED EDGE TO EDGE WITH HOOKS AND EYES. THERE ARE NO INDICATIONS OF EYELET HOLES, BUTTONS OR ANY OTHER FASTENINGS.

TOP SLEEVE

AN EYELET HOLE IS WORKED AT THE POINT OF THE BODICE ON BOTH SIDES

OPEN TO THIS MARK

FOLD LINE AT FRONT OF UNDERSLEEVE

CARTRIDGE PLEAT INTO 8·9 CM (3½")

FRONT

THE GOLDEN YELLOW SATIN UNDER SLEEVE WAS CUT OUT AND THE BANDS OF DECORATION WORKED OUT ACROSS THE WIDTH. APPROX. 1·5 MM (1/16") EXTRA IS ALLOWED FOR FOR THE MATERIAL TO BE RUCHED UP IN THE DEPTH OF EACH BAND. THE SATIN IS NOT CUT RIGHT UP TO THE SEAM, TO AVOID WEAKNESS. APPROX. 5·1 CM (2") IS LEFT UNTOUCHED ON UNDER SIDE AND 25MM (1") ON TOP SIDE. 16 STRIPS OF GOLD AND SILVER BOBBIN LACE, HEAVILY TARNISHED (POSSIBLY ONLY SILVER), OF A DIFFERENT DESIGN FROM THAT ON THE BODICE, ARE STITCHED BETWEEN THE ROWS OF CUTS THIS LACE VARIES BETWEEN 9MM (3/8") AND 13 MM (½") IN WIDTH. THE UNDER SLEEVES WERE REMOVED FOR CONSERVATION WORK TO BE CARRIED OUT. THEY ARE PLEATED IN TO FIT UNDER THE ARM AS WELL AS ABOVE.

THE GOLD AND SILVER METAL BOBBIN LACE TRIMMING THE HANGING SLEEVES AND HEM OF THE TRAINED SKIRT IS APPROX. 16 MM (5/8") WIDE. IN SOME PLACES IT IS 13 MM (½") WIDE, IN OTHERS 19 MM (3/4") DEPENDING ON HOW MUCH IT HAS BEEN STRETCHED. THE MATCHING LACE ON THE BODICE IS EASED SLIGHTLY, BUT IN MOST PLACES MEASURES 16 MM (5/8").

THIS PIECE IS FOLDED DOWN AND LEFT TO HANG INSIDE AT WAIST

JOIN IN VELVET

DESIGN OF FAINTLY SCORED LOZENGE PATTERN ON GOLDEN YELLOW SATIN HANGING SLEEVE LINING

LESS THAN 3MM (⅛") PINKS ON STRAIGHT GRAIN

6 MM (¼") LONG PINKS

ACTUAL SIZE OF METAL LACE AND BANDS OF DECORATIVE CUTTING.

EACH SMALL CUT IS ON THE STRAIGHT GRAIN. THE SATIN IS THEN PULLED BACK AND CAUGHT TOGETHER IN THE CENTRE OF EACH STRIP WITH A FEW STITCHES WHICH DO NOT SHOW

GOLD SATIN

TARNISHED METAL BOBBIN LACE

MARKS OF ORIGINAL STITCHING HOLES MAY BE SEEN HERE. FROM THE CREASE MARKS THE PETTICOAT WOULD APPEAR TO HAVE BEEN GATHERED AT THE WAIST.

CENTRE FRONT

CONJECTURED SHAPE. THIS AREA IS IN FRAGMENTS.

THE PETTICOAT IS IN SAGE GREEN SILK TAFFETA IN SUCH A STATE OF DECAY THAT THERE IS LITTLE PATTERN SHAPE TO RECORD. IT IS MOUNTED ON A COTTON FOUNDATION TO PREVENT FURTHER DISINTEGRATION.

A STRIP OF 38 CM (1½") WIDE METAL BOBBIN LACE IS PLACED ON FRONT AND HEM OF PETTICOAT. ALL THE METAL HAS TARNISHED AND SOME HAS DISINTEGRATED, LEAVING THE YELLOW OCHRE SILK CORE. IT IS IMPOSSIBLE TO TELL NOW IF THIS IS SILVER OR GOLD BOBBIN LACE. BENEATH THE HEM IS STITCHED 13MM (½") WIDE FRINGED BRAID. THE ORIGINAL STITCHING REMAINS ON THE BRAID, AT THE BACK.

SHOULDER SEA... TO TH...

THE SLEEVE IS SLIGHTLY GATHERED ON DOTTED LINE

THE SLEEVES WERE REMOVED FOR CONSERVATION WORK. THE UNDERARM IS PLEATED TO FIT THE ARMHOLE. THE UPPER PART OF THE LEFT SLEEVE IS MISSING. THE GOLDEN YELLOW SATIN HANGING SLEEVE LINING MATCHES THAT OF THE UNDER SLEEVE. THE SURFACE HAS BEEN SCORED WITH A LOZENGE PATTERN TO PROVIDE A GUIDE FOR THE ROWS OF PINKING.

UNDER SIDE OF HANGING SLEEVE

UPPER SIDE OF HANGING SLEEVE

JOIN IN FABRIC

SIDE GOR... PANEL OF LEFT BACK PETTICOAT... THE REST O... THE BACK... DISINTEGRA...

1:1 INCH
1:1 CM

...OWN IN ITALIAN CUT AND UNCUT VELVET IN AN INTERLACED DESIGN DATING FROM THE 1620S OR EARLY 1630S. IT WAS ...ABLY IN VERY POOR CONDITION WHEN TAKEN OUT OF THE TOMB AND RESTORATION WORK WAS CARRIED OUT IN c.1914. ...SKIRT SEEMS TO HAVE BEEN ARRANGED IN SMALL EVEN CARTRIDGE PLEATS AT THE WAIST, FROM THE ...ENCE OF WHAT CAN BE SEEN INSIDE THE FRONT BODICE, WHICH WAS STITCHED DOWN ...4. THE BODICE WOULD HAVE BEEN ...D WITH LINEN ORIGINALLY, BUT ...THIS HAS DISINTEGRATED IN THE ...VE, TOGETHER WITH HOOKS AND ...S FOR FASTENING THE FRONT EDGE ...DGE.

CENTRE BACK TO FOLD

NECK EDGE

THE COLLAR WOULD HAVE BEEN STIFFENED WITH LINEN ORIGINALLY, BUT ALL THIS HAS DISINTEGRATED IN THE TOMB.

SHOULDER WING TO THIS MARK

CENTRE BACK TO FOLD

THE OUTLINE OF THE INTERLACED SHAPES IS IN CUT VELVET. THE INNER PATTERN IS IN UNCUT VELVET, WITH A SMALL AREA OF CUT VELVET. THE SMALL SQUARES HAVE CUT AND UNCUT MOTIFS INSIDE. THE MATERIAL IS NOW REDDISH BROWN; THE ORIGINAL COLOUR IS UNCERTAIN.

BANDS OF BRAID

FOLD LINE

TOP OF WING

BACK

UNDERSIDE OF WING

THERE IS NO STIFFENING INSIDE THE SHOULDER WING BUT THERE WOULD ORIGINALLY HAVE BEEN LINEN WHICH HAS DISINTEGRATED IN THE TOMB. THE WING IS NOT CUT ON THE TRUE BIAS GRAIN AND PUCKERS SLIGHTLY. IT IS SHAPED IN SLIGHTLY AT THE FRONT, AND IS TRIMMED WITH BRAID.

THE SKIRT WAS ORIGINALLY GATHERED INTO SMALL CARTRIDGE PLEATS AND ATTACHED TO THE BODICE, FROM THE EVIDENCE OF CREASE MARKS.

THE SKIRT LIES FLAT AT THE FRONT TO THIS MARK

THE CENTRE FRONT APPEARS TO HAVE BEEN OPEN ORIGINALLY BUT IS NOW STITCHED DOWN.

JOIN IN FABRIC
JOIN IN FABRIC
JOIN IN FABRIC
JOIN IN FABRIC
CENTRE BACK JOIN IN FABRIC

DARK BROWN BRAID TRIMMING THE HEMLINE MAY ORIGINALLY HAVE BEEN BLACK. IT IS 16MM (5/8") WIDE.

1:1 INCH
1:1 CENTIMETRE

49. c.1600-10 PAIR OF SLEEVES GERMANISCHES NATIONALMUSEUM, NÜRNBERG. T2858/T2859.

PAIR OF SLEEVES IN SOFT GOLDEN BROWN SATIN LINED WITH MATCHING SILK. THE LINING IS ATTACHED TO THE FRONT SEAM INSIDE, AND THIS SEAM IS THEN OVERHANDED TOGETHER. THE LINING IS SLIPSTITCHED DOWN OVER ELBOW CURVE AFTER THE BACK SEAM HAS BEEN STITCHED UP, LEAVING A PLEAT FOR EASE. THERE ARE 38 ROWS OF EMBROIDERY ON THE UPPER SIDE OF THE LEFT SLEEVE AND 40 ON THE RIGHT, WITH 39 ROWS ON THE UNDERSIDE OF BOTH SLEEVES. THE EMBROIDERY IS CARRIED OUT IN FLAT SILVER STRIP STITCHED DOWN WITH SILK AND OUTLINED WITH SILVER METAL THREAD WITH A YELLOW SILK CORE. THE BUTTONS ARE 8 MM (5/16") IN DIAMETER, WORKED IN SILVER METAL THREAD WITH A SILK CORE.

ENLARGED DIAGRAM TO SHOW EMBROIDERY FOR STRAIGHT ROWS.

16 BUTTONS AND LOOPS OF BRAIDED SILVER METAL THREAD WITH SILK CORE, FOR OPENING AT FRONT OF SLEEVE.

ACTUAL SIZE OF EMBROIDERY

THE BANDS VARY SLIGHTLY IN WIDTH

SILVER THREAD

SIXTEEN WORKED BUTTONHOLES 13MM (1/2") LONG IN BROWN SILK WITH BANDS OF SILVER BETWEEN THEM.

50. c.1580-95 FOREPART MUSEO PARMIGIANINO, REGGIO EMILIA

FOREPART IN IVORY SATIN, STAMPED WITH HOT IRONS IN A GEOMETRIC DESIGN OF FLOWERS AND LEAVES. IT IS EMBROIDERED WITH AN INTERLOCKING LINEAR PATTERN IN COUCHED GOLD METAL THREAD ENCLOSING FLOWERS WORKED IN POLYCHROME SILKS. THE DESIGN IS SIMILAR TO THE LAYOUT OF AN ELIZABETHAN KNOT GARDEN. THE LEFT HALF OF THE FOREPART IS GIVEN. BOTH SIDES ARE PIECED IN A SIMILAR WAY. IT IS POSSIBLE THAT PIECES 1,2,3,4 WERE THE ORIGINAL FOREPART FOR A GOWN IN c.1580 WORN OVER A SPANISH FARTHINGALE. PIECES 5,6,7 MAY HAVE BEEN ADDED IN THE 1590S TO MAKE A FOREPART TO WEAR OVER A WIDE FRENCH FARTHINGALE.

PLAIN SILK PIECED TOGETHER

CENTRE FRONT TO FOLD

GUARD IN EMBROIDERED LINEN

FRONT PORTIONS 1,2,3,4 WERE JOINED ORIGINALLY AND THE EMBROIDERY WAS WORKED OVER THE JOINS. PIECES 5,6,7 WERE JOINED ON LATER AND ARE EMBROIDERED IN THE SAME WAY, BUT THE COUCHING IS CARRIED OUT IN YELLOW SILK. RED SILK IS USED FOR THE COUCHING ON PIECE 1, AT THE FRONT.

SMALL FLAT BITS OF SILVER FOIL ARE STITCHED TO THE BASE OF EACH MOTIF.

BLUE SILK AND GOLD METAL BRAID

GUARD IN IVORY LINEN EMBROIDERED WITH GOLD METAL THREAD AND POLYCHROME SILKS.

© 1984 JANET ARNOLD

+1639 Bayerisches Nationalmuseum, Munich

48. A gown in cut and uncut velvet woven to simulate strapwork, worn by Pfalzgräfin Dorothea Maria von Sulzbach when she was buried in the tomb at Lauingen in 1639, aged eighty. Natalie Rothstein dates the Italian velvet to the 1620s or early 1630s and the gown was probably made at that time. The interlaced pattern is in dark brown and sandy beige. No stiffening remains inside the deep shoulder wings but they were probably interlined with linen originally and the linen bodice has also disintegrated with the decomposing corpse. The gown was restored in 1914. The bodice would have fastened with hooks and eyes and the skirt

was originally attached at the waist with cartridge pleats, judging from traces of crease marks. The gown is trimmed with dark brown silk braid. No sleeves have been preserved with the gown but they may have been made of linen and so disintegrated at the same time as the linen lining. Patterns for gowns of this type are found in Burguen's *Geometria, y traça perteneciente al oficio de sastres* published in 1618 (Fig. 36). Like most elderly people Dorothea Maria probably continued to wear styles which she had worn in middle age and in which she felt comfortable.

c1615–20 Nationalmuseet, Copenhagen

51A. A black satin skirt or petticoat, pinked and embroidered with couched turquoise and coral-pink cord, French knots and black beads (Figs. 351–2) is similar in design to one worn by Lady Morton in her portrait (Fig. 349). It still retains four lines of holes in the rich coral-pink silk taffeta lining. These indicate the position of gathering threads and pins where the petticoat was ruched up over a farthingale, arranged in even pleats and carefully pinned (Fig. 350). Martha, wife of John Suckling, shows a deep flounce over a small farthingale in her effigy on their tomb in St Andrew's Church, Norwich, in 1613.

51B. Martha Suckling's skirt would have required only one row of gathering threads through a tuck in the material to produce this effect. Her doublet shows a pronounced curve in at the front waist. The hanging sleeves have scalloped edges.

51C. The effigy of one of John and Martha Suckling's daughters shows a flatter arrangement of the flounce. Here the tuck is simply stitched into position and pinned to the farthingale. The material is not gathered.

51D. Another of the Suckling daughters shows a gathered flounce and the tilt of the farthingale from the back.

48   51A   51B   51C   51D

c.1615-20 EMBROIDERED SKIRT OR PETTICOAT NATIONAL MUSEET, COPENHAGEN.

...CK SATIN PETTICOAT LINED WITH RICH CORAL PINK SILK TAFFETA. THE BLACK SATIN IS PINKED ALL OVER WITH 3MM ($\frac{1}{8}$) CUTS
...ROXIMATELY 9MM ($\frac{3}{8}$) APART. THIS PINKING, TOGETHER WITH THE BLACK DYE, HAS RESULTED IN THE SATIN DISINTEGRATING AND
...TS OF IT ARE NOW MOUNTED ON BLACK SILK. THE PETTICOAT IS COVERED WITH SILK CRÊPELINE, TO HOLD THE FRAGMENTS
...SILK TOGETHER.
...PETTICOAT WAS PROBABLY ORIGINALLY CARTRIDGE PLEATED TO FIT THE WAIST OF A BODICE. THE PINK SILK LINING STILL
...FOUR LINES OF HOLES, MARKED WITH A DOTTED LINE ······· FROM LINEN GATHERING THREADS AND PINS WHERE THE
...TICOAT WAS RUCHED UP OVER A FARTHINGALE. THIS ARRANGEMENT MAY BE SEEN IN MANY PORTRAITS. ORIGINALLY THE
...COAT WAS PROBABLY A LITTLE LONGER, THEN TRIMMED OFF AT THE WAIST TO USE FOR A LONG SKIRT FALLING FROM THE
...SED WAIST LEVEL UNDER THE BUST, WITHOUT A FARTHINGALE, IN ABOUT 1620.

THE LENGTHS OF BLACK SATIN ARE JOINED TOGETHER AND THE EMBROIDERY CARRIED OUT WHILE STRETCHED ON A FRAME.
THE PINK SILK TAFFETA IS JOINED AND THEN TURNED IN TOWARDS THE SATIN AT HEM AND CENTRE FRONTS. THE PLEATS
AT THE WAIST ARE UNEVENLY ARRANGED AND SEEM TO BE OF NINETEENTH CENTURY ORIGIN. MARKS OF FADING ON THE PINK
SILK LINING DO NOT MATCH THE PRESENT CREASES OR THE PLEATS. IT IS POSSIBLE THAT THE PETTICOAT WAS WORN AS A
DOMINO IN THE EIGHTEENTH CENTURY, WITH THE EMBROIDERED BLACK SATIN AS THE LINING.

FOLD LINE ···················· CENTRE BACK TO FOLD.

THE PLEATED EDGE IS BOUND WITH BLACK SATIN RIBBON FOLDED IN HALF LENGTHWISE,
PROBABLY DATING FROM THE 1880S. THIS FORMS A WAISTBAND MEASURING 118CM (46$\frac{1}{2}$).

SLIT FOR POCKET HOLE.
THERE IS NO POCKET BAG.

ENDS OF VERTICAL STRIPES OF
EMBROIDERY REACH THIS LINE

TIPS OF EMBROIDERED FLORAL
MOTIFS REACH THIS LINE

THIS IS FOLDED BACK TO
FORM A FACING

FIRST PANEL OF
EMBROIDERY FROM
THIS MARK

TOP BUTTON IS MISSING FROM
...TOP, SECOND, THIRD AND FIFTH
...OF BUTTONS. ALL THE OTHER
...TONS REMAIN

EDGE OF
EMBROIDERY AT
DOTTED LINE

LINES OF STITCHING HOLES
FOR FLOUNCE

...TUAL SIZE
...ACORN
...TON
...RKED OVER
...WOODEN CORE
...PINK AND
...RQUOISE
...K THREAD.
...BUTTON-
...LES ON THE
...T FRONT
...E MADE WITH
...PED CORD
...ONE
...TINUOUS
...NGTH. 13MM
...IS ALLOWED
...R EACH
...OP.

...TUAL SIZE
...LOOP.

TIPS OF EMBROIDERED MOTIFS, AT 12.7CM
(5") INTERVALS, REACH TO THIS DOTTED LINE.

THE BANDS OF EMBROIDERY IMITATING GUARDS
ARE IN ALTERNATING WIDTHS OF 19MM ($\frac{3}{4}$")
AND 5.1CM (2") WITH A SPACE OF 9MM ($\frac{3}{8}$")
BETWEEN EACH BAND. THE NARROW BAND
IS OUTLINED WITH COUCHED CORD ON
THE OUTER EDGES, CORAL PINK/
TURQUOISE/CORAL PINK. INSIDE IS A
CURVING DESIGN IN TURQUOISE/CORAL
PINK/TURQUOISE AND CURVING MOTIFS
OF PINK WITH TINY BLACK BEADS
INSIDE. THE TOTAL WIDTH OF THIS BAND
IS 19 MM ($\frac{3}{4}$").

THE WIDE BAND IS OUTLINED WITH COUCHED
CORD ON THE OUTER EDGES, TURQUOISE/
CORAL PINK/TURQUOISE WITH PINK FRENCH
KNOTS ON THE OUTSIDE. THE MOTIFS INSIDE
ARE CARRIED OUT IN TURQUOISE WITH
BLACK BEADS INSIDE, THEN PINK
WITH MORE BLACK BEADS. PINK AND
TURQUOISE FRENCH KNOTS AND SOME
PADDED STITCHES ARE ALSO USED.
THE TOTAL WIDTH OF THIS BAND IS
5.1CM (2").

THE CORD USED FOR BOTH NARROW AND
WIDE BANDS IS .8MM ($\frac{1}{32}$") IN DIAMETER.
THE BEADS ARE ALSO .8MM ($\frac{1}{32}$") IN
DIAMETER.
APPARENTLY TWO WIDTHS OF SATIN WERE
JOINED FOR THE EMBROIDERY TO BE
CARRIED OUT ON THE FRAME. THEN THE
PAIRS OF WIDTHS WERE STITCHED TOGETHER.
THESE JOINS ARE SO NEATLY DONE THAT
IT IS ALMOST IMPOSSIBLE TO SEE THEM.

BANDS OF EMBROIDERY FROM
HEM TO THIS LEVEL

JOIN IN BLACK SATIN

JOIN IN PINK TAFFETA LINING

JOIN IN PINK TAFFETA LINING

JOIN IN BLACK SATIN

JOIN IN BLACK SATIN

CENTRE BACK JOIN IN BLACK SATIN

CENTRE BACK PINK TAFFETA LINING TO FOLD

1:1 INCH   1:1 CENTIMETRE

© 1984 JANET ARNOLD

c1610–15   Victoria and Albert Museum, London

52A.   A loose gown of Italian silk dated to c1600 by Natalie Rothstein, which was acquired in 1900 from the heirlooms preserved by ancestors of Charles Isham, Lamport Hall, Northamptonshire. The silk is slashed diagonally between the woven motifs; although it was pieced carefully when the gown was remodelled in c1610–15, the slashes are arranged in different directions in each part of the gown. The silk is pleated down and stitched to a foundation yoke, hanging free below the shoulder blades.

52B.   The foundation yoke is made of ivory fustian, with linen warp and cotton weft, pad-stitched to a layer of saffron-yellow coarse linen. Tiny stitches may be seen in the fustian when looking into the gown. The silk is pleated up and stitched over the saffron-yellow linen. The stiffened collar has a pair of worked eyelet holes at the centre back for a ribbon point to attach a supportasse or underpropper to support a linen band or ruff.

52C.   The gown is trimmed with rich salmon-pink corded silk ribbon, now disintegrating and covered with pink silk crêpeline for conservation purposes. Over this was stitched narrow silver metal bobbin lace, worked with silver spangles. All this lace has been removed, probably to use on another gown, and only a few tiny fragments, with one spangle, remain.

52A

52B

52C

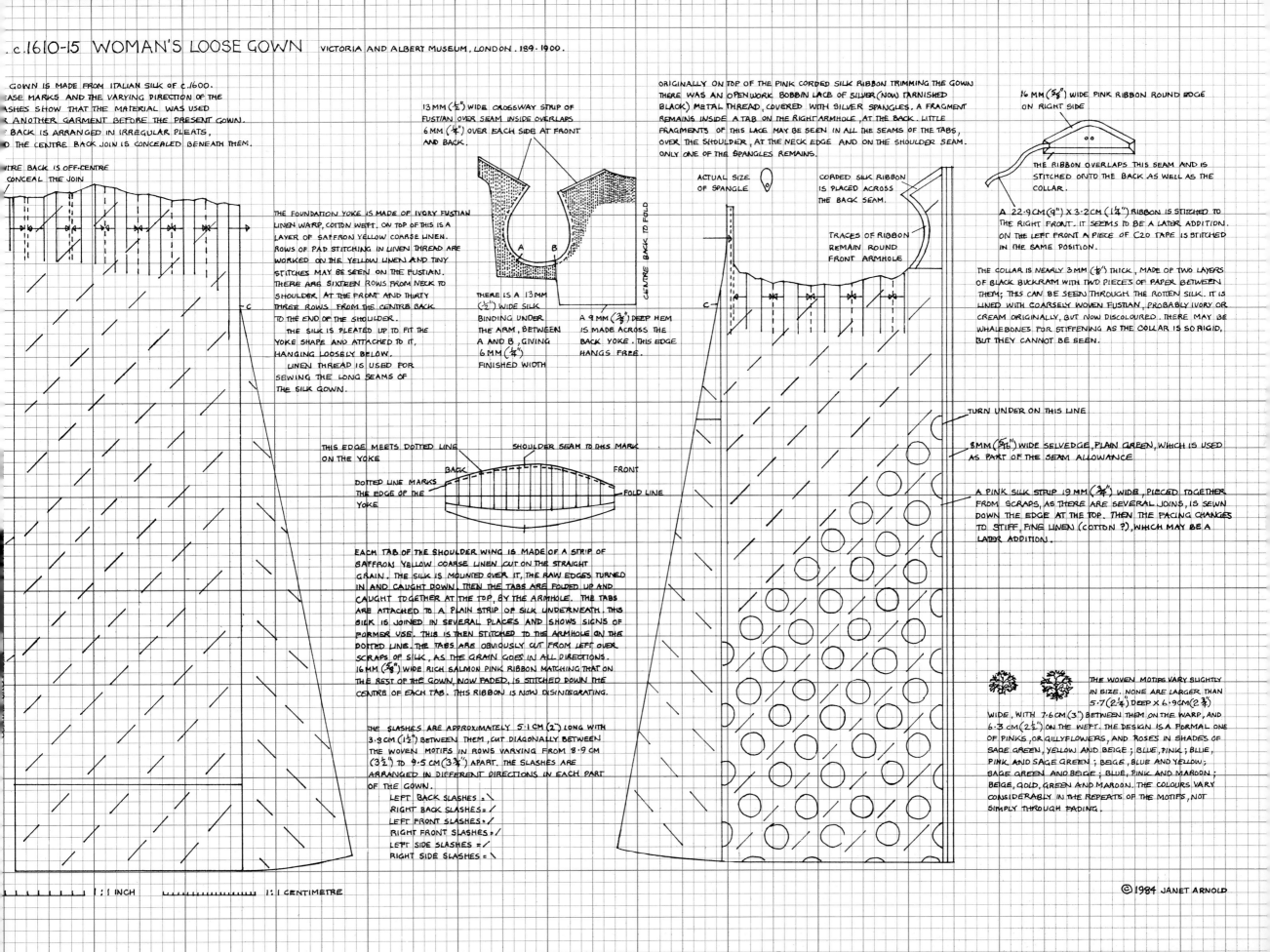

c.1610-15 WOMAN'S LOOSE GOWN   VICTORIA AND ALBERT MUSEUM, LONDON. 189-1900.

GOWN IS MADE FROM ITALIAN SILK OF c.1600.
EASE MARKS AND THE VARYING DIRECTION OF THE
SHES SHOW THAT THE MATERIAL WAS USED
ANOTHER GARMENT BEFORE THE PRESENT GOWN.
BACK IS ARRANGED IN IRREGULAR PLEATS,
THE CENTRE BACK JOIN IS CONCEALED BENEATH THEM.

TRE BACK IS OFF-CENTRE
CONCEAL THE JOIN

13MM (½") WIDE CROSSWAY STRIP OF
FUSTIAN OVER SEAM INSIDE OVERLAPS
6MM (¼") OVER EACH SIDE AT FRONT
AND BACK.

ORIGINALLY ON TOP OF THE PINK CORDED SILK RIBBON TRIMMING THE GOWN
THERE WAS AN OPENWORK BOBBIN LACE OF SILVER (NOW TARNISHED
BLACK) METAL THREAD, COVERED WITH SILVER SPANGLES. A FRAGMENT
REMAINS INSIDE A TAB ON THE RIGHT ARMHOLE, AT THE BACK. LITTLE
FRAGMENTS OF THIS LACE MAY BE SEEN IN ALL THE SEAMS OF THE TABS,
OVER THE SHOULDER, AT THE NECK EDGE AND ON THE SHOULDER SEAM.
ONLY ONE OF THE SPANGLES REMAINS.

16MM (⅝") WIDE PINK RIBBON ROUND EDGE
ON RIGHT SIDE

THE RIBBON OVERLAPS THIS SEAM AND IS
STITCHED ONTO THE BACK AS WELL AS THE
COLLAR.

A 22.9CM (9") X 3.2CM (1¼") RIBBON IS STITCHED TO
THE RIGHT FRONT. IT SEEMS TO BE A LATER ADDITION.
ON THE LEFT FRONT A PIECE OF C20 TAPE IS STITCHED
IN THE SAME POSITION.

THE COLLAR IS NEARLY 3MM (⅛") THICK, MADE OF TWO LAYERS
OF BLACK BUCKRAM WITH TWO PIECES OF PAPER BETWEEN
THEM; THIS CAN BE SEEN THROUGH THE ROTTEN SILK. IT IS
LINED WITH COARSELY WOVEN FUSTIAN, PROBABLY IVORY OR
CREAM ORIGINALLY, BUT NOW DISCOLOURED. THERE MAY BE
WHALEBONES FOR STIFFENING AS THE COLLAR IS SO RIGID,
BUT THEY CANNOT BE SEEN.

THE FOUNDATION YOKE IS MADE OF IVORY FUSTIAN
LINEN WARP, COTTON WEFT. ON TOP OF THIS IS A
LAYER OF SAFFRON YELLOW COARSE LINEN.
ROWS OF PAD STITCHING IN LINEN THREAD ARE
WORKED ON THE YELLOW LINEN AND TINY
STITCHES MAY BE SEEN ON THE FUSTIAN.
THERE ARE SIXTEEN ROWS FROM NECK TO
SHOULDER AT THE FRONT AND THIRTY
THREE ROWS FROM THE CENTRE BACK
TO THE END OF THE SHOULDER.
THE SILK IS PLEATED UP TO FIT THE
YOKE SHAPE AND ATTACHED TO IT,
HANGING LOOSELY BELOW.
LINEN THREAD IS USED FOR
SEWING THE LONG SEAMS OF
THE SILK GOWN.

ACTUAL SIZE
OF SPANGLE

CORDED SILK RIBBON
IS PLACED ACROSS
THE BACK SEAM.

TRACES OF RIBBON
REMAIN ROUND
FRONT ARMHOLE

CENTRE BACK TO FOLD

THERE IS A 13MM
(½") WIDE SILK
BINDING UNDER
THE ARM, BETWEEN
A AND B, GIVING
6MM (¼")
FINISHED WIDTH

A 9MM (⅜") DEEP HEM
IS MADE ACROSS THE
BACK YOKE. THIS EDGE
HANGS FREE.

TURN UNDER ON THIS LINE

8MM (⅝₁₆") WIDE SELVEDGE, PLAIN GREEN, WHICH IS USED
AS PART OF THE SEAM ALLOWANCE

A PINK SILK STRIP 19MM (¾") WIDE, PIECED TOGETHER
FROM SCRAPS, IS SEWN DOWN THE EDGE AT THE TOP. THEN THE FACING CHANGES
TO STIFF, FINE LINEN (COTTON ?), WHICH MAY BE A
LATER ADDITION.

THIS EDGE MEETS DOTTED LINE
ON THE YOKE

SHOULDER SEAM TO THIS MARK

BACK   FRONT

DOTTED LINE MARKS
THE EDGE OF THE
YOKE

FOLD LINE

EACH TAB OF THE SHOULDER WING IS MADE OF A STRIP OF
SAFFRON YELLOW COARSE LINEN CUT ON THE STRAIGHT
GRAIN. THE SILK IS MOUNTED OVER IT, THE RAW EDGES TURNED
IN AND CAUGHT DOWN. THEN THE TABS ARE FOLDED UP AND
CAUGHT TOGETHER AT THE TOP, BY THE ARMHOLE. THE TABS
ARE ATTACHED TO A PLAIN STRIP OF SILK UNDERNEATH. THIS
SILK IS JOINED IN SEVERAL PLACES AND SHOWS SIGNS OF
FORMER USE. THIS IS THEN STITCHED TO THE ARMHOLE ON THE
DOTTED LINE. THE TABS ARE OBVIOUSLY CUT FROM LEFT OVER
SCRAPS OF SILK, AS THE GRAIN GOES IN ALL DIRECTIONS.
16MM (⅝") WIDE RICH SALMON PINK RIBBON MATCHING THAT ON
THE REST OF THE GOWN, NOW FADED, IS STITCHED DOWN THE
CENTRE OF EACH TAB. THIS RIBBON IS NOW DISINTEGRATING.

THE SLASHES ARE APPROXIMATELY 5.1 CM (2") LONG WITH
3.8CM (1½") BETWEEN THEM, CUT DIAGONALLY BETWEEN
THE WOVEN MOTIFS IN ROWS VARYING FROM 8.9 CM
(3½") TO 9.5 CM (3¾") APART. THE SLASHES ARE
ARRANGED IN DIFFERENT DIRECTIONS IN EACH PART
OF THE GOWN.
LEFT BACK SLASHES = \
RIGHT BACK SLASHES = /
LEFT FRONT SLASHES = /
RIGHT FRONT SLASHES = /
LEFT SIDE SLASHES = /
RIGHT SIDE SLASHES = \

THE WOVEN MOTIFS VARY SLIGHTLY
IN SIZE. NONE ARE LARGER THAN
5.7 (2¼") DEEP X 6.9CM (2¾")
WIDE, WITH 7.6CM (3") BETWEEN THEM ON THE WARP, AND
6.3 CM (2½") ON THE WEFT. THE DESIGN IS A FORMAL ONE
OF PINKS, OR GILLYFLOWERS, AND ROSES IN SHADES OF
SAGE GREEN, YELLOW AND BEIGE; BLUE, PINK, BLUE;
PINK AND SAGE GREEN; BEIGE, BLUE AND YELLOW;
SAGE GREEN AND BEIGE; BLUE, PINK AND MAROON;
BEIGE, GOLD, GREEN AND MAROON. THE COLOURS VARY
CONSIDERABLY IN THE REPEATS OF THE MOTIFS, NOT
SIMPLY THROUGH FADING.

1:1 INCH   1:1 CENTIMETRE

© 1984 JANET ARNOLD

c1615–18 Burrell Collection, Glasgow

54. A white linen jacket, embroidered in vivid polychrome silks and gold metal thread, which shows a slightly raised waist level. The pattern shapes were drawn out on the linen and the embroidery worked within each shape while the length of material was stretched taut on a frame. The linen lining is stitched to the outer layer round the edges from the right side, raw edges turned in towards each other. The edges of the shoulder wings have been unpicked and it seems likely that originally they would have been trimmed with gold metal bobbin lace. Shaping is given by gussets set in at the waist. The jacket fastens edge to edge with hooks and eyes at the centre front. Here again there are signs of restitching and there may have been gold metal bobbin lace on both sides originally. Three pairs of hooks and eyes at the waist are heavier than the others, and are of dark grey metal; they seem to be original. The others are of brass wire and appear to be later replacements but the stitching is covered by the lining and cannot be examined. Jackets of this type appear in many early seventeenth-century portraits, some embroidered (Figs. 363 and 366) and others of woven silk (Figs. 353 and 361).

c1610–20 Victoria and Albert Museum, London

55. A young girl's loose gown in olive-green plush, a long-piled silk velvet, acquired in 1900 from the collection formed by an ancestor of Charles Isham, Lamport Hall, Northamptonshire. It was originally trimmed with silver metal braid but only a few fragments remain (Fig. 372). The plush is mounted on a foundation yoke of two layers of khaki-coloured linen, interlined with layers of linen buckram until the yoke is almost rigid over the shoulders, but slightly more pliable at back and front. The plush is too thick to arrange in gathers or large pleats. It is shaped at the back and stitched to the foundation yoke in long darts with small pleats under the arms. The wings are rigid extensions of the yoke (Fig. 370). The hanging sleeves are missing and the armholes are oversewn. The hem and vents at side and back seams are interlined with white linen and faced with olive-green wool with a diagonal weave, which covers the linen (Fig. 371). The latter is slightly motheaten. The front edges are stiffened with linen and faced with chartreuse silk. Much of the back has been cut away, probably for cushion covers in the nineteenth century, and the drawing shows the conjectured appearance of the gown in its original condition.

[WHI]TE LINEN JACKET EMBROIDERED WITH [POLY]CHROME SILKS AND GOLD METAL THREAD [LINE]D WITH RICH PINK SILK CUT TO THE SAME [SH]APE.

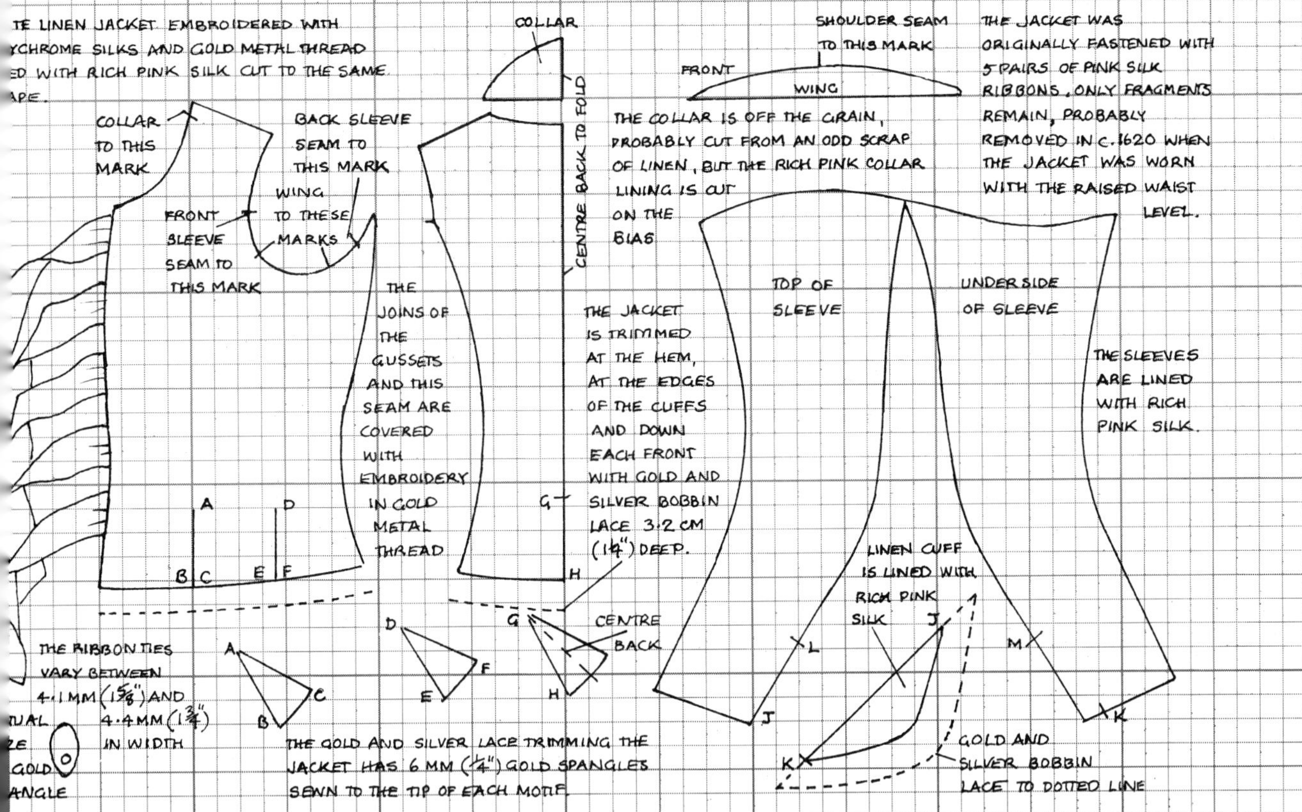

COLLAR TO THIS MARK

COLLAR

BACK SLEEVE SEAM TO THIS MARK

WING TO THESE MARKS

FRONT SLEEVE SEAM TO THIS MARK

FRONT

WING

CENTRE BACK TO FOLD

SHOULDER SEAM TO THIS MARK

THE JACKET WAS ORIGINALLY FASTENED WITH 5 PAIRS OF PINK SILK RIBBONS. ONLY FRAGMENTS REMAIN, PROBABLY REMOVED IN c.1620 WHEN THE JACKET WAS WORN WITH THE RAISED WAIST LEVEL.

THE COLLAR IS OFF THE GRAIN, PROBABLY CUT FROM AN ODD SCRAP OF LINEN, BUT THE RICH PINK COLLAR LINING IS CUT ON THE BIAS

TOP OF SLEEVE

UNDERSIDE OF SLEEVE

THE JOINS OF THE GUSSETS AND THIS SEAM ARE COVERED WITH EMBROIDERY IN GOLD METAL THREAD

THE JACKET IS TRIMMED AT THE HEM, AT THE EDGES OF THE CUFFS AND DOWN EACH FRONT WITH GOLD AND SILVER BOBBIN LACE 3·2 CM (1¼") DEEP.

THE SLEEVES ARE LINED WITH RICH PINK SILK.

A D
B C E F
G H
CENTRE BACK

LINEN CUFF IS LINED WITH RICH PINK SILK

THE RIBBON TIES VARY BETWEEN 4·1 MM (1⅝") AND [ACT]UAL 4·4 MM (1¾") [SIZE] IN WIDTH [GOLD] [SP]ANGLE

A
D G
E F H
B C
J

L K
M
GOLD AND SILVER BOBBIN LACE TO DOTTED LINE

THE GOLD AND SILVER LACE TRIMMING THE JACKET HAS 6 MM (¼") GOLD SPANGLES SEWN TO THE TIP OF EACH MOTIF.

c.1615-18 EMBROIDERED JACKET   BURRELL COLLECTION, GLASGOW

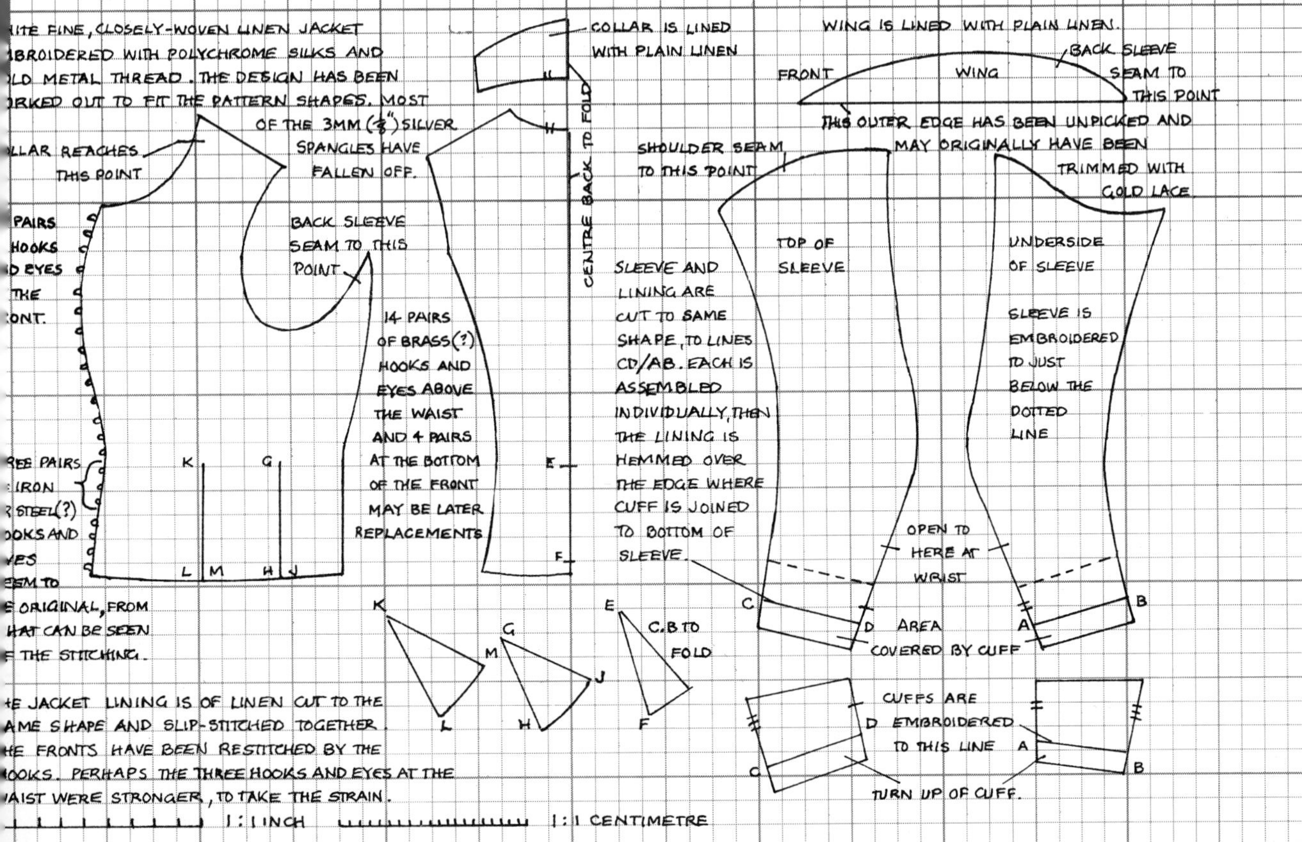

[WH]ITE FINE, CLOSELY-WOVEN LINEN JACKET [EM]BROIDERED WITH POLYCHROME SILKS AND [GO]LD METAL THREAD. THE DESIGN HAS BEEN [WO]RKED OUT TO FIT THE PATTERN SHAPES. MOST [OF THE] 3MM (⅛") SILVER SPANGLES HAVE FALLEN OFF.

[COL]LAR REACHES THIS POINT

COLLAR IS LINED WITH PLAIN LINEN

WING IS LINED WITH PLAIN LINEN.

FRONT

WING

BACK SLEEVE SEAM TO THIS POINT

SHOULDER SEAM TO THIS POINT

THIS OUTER EDGE HAS BEEN UNPICKED AND MAY ORIGINALLY HAVE BEEN TRIMMED WITH GOLD LACE

[..] PAIRS [..] HOOKS [AND] EYES [ABOVE] THE [..]ONT.

BACK SLEEVE SEAM TO THIS POINT

14 PAIRS OF BRASS(?) HOOKS AND EYES ABOVE THE WAIST AND 4 PAIRS AT THE BOTTOM OF THE FRONT MAY BE LATER REPLACEMENTS

CENTRE BACK TO FOLD

TOP OF SLEEVE

UNDERSIDE OF SLEEVE

SLEEVE AND LINING ARE CUT TO SAME SHAPE, TO LINES CD/AB. EACH IS ASSEMBLED INDIVIDUALLY, THEN THE LINING IS HEMMED OVER THE EDGE WHERE CUFF IS JOINED TO BOTTOM OF SLEEVE.

SLEEVE IS EMBROIDERED TO JUST BELOW THE DOTTED LINE

[TH]REE PAIRS [OF] IRON [OR] STEEL(?) [HO]OKS AND [EY]ES [SE]EM TO [BE] ORIGINAL, FROM [W]HAT CAN BE SEEN [OF] THE STITCHING.

K G J
L M H J

E
F
OPEN TO HERE AT WRIST

K M
G
E
J
L
F
C.B TO FOLD

C D AREA COVERED BY CUFF

D A B

[T]HE JACKET LINING IS OF LINEN CUT TO THE [S]AME SHAPE AND SLIP-STITCHED TOGETHER. [T]HE FRONTS HAVE BEEN RESTITCHED BY THE [H]OOKS. PERHAPS THE THREE HOOKS AND EYES AT THE [W]AIST WERE STRONGER, TO TAKE THE STRAIN.

CUFFS ARE EMBROIDERED TO THIS LINE A

TURN UP OF CUFF.

|████ 1:1 INCH |████ 1:1 CENTIMETRE

THE GOWN IS MADE OF OLIVE GREEN PLUSH, WITH A LONG PILE. THERE ARE TRACES OF SILVER METAL BRAID USED FOR TRIMMING. HALF THE BACK IS MISSING BUT THE RIGHT SIDE IS INTACT, ALTHOUGH THE BRAID TRIMMING HAS BEEN REMOVED. THERE IS NO LINING NOW, ALTHOUGH THERE MAY HAVE BEEN ONE ORIGINALLY.

THE 9 MM (⅜") WIDE GREEN AND YELLOW STRIPED SELVEDGES ARE USED AS SEAM TURNINGS AND CLIPPED AT INTERVALS TO AVOID PUCKERING. THE CUT EDGES ARE NOT NEATENED, BUT HAVE NOT FRAYED.

THE PLUSH IS DARTED TO FIT THE SHOULDERS OVER A YOKE PIECE. THIS IS MADE OF TWO LAYERS OF KHAKI-COLOURED LINEN INTERLINED WITH LAYERS OF LINEN BUCKRAM STIFFENED UNTIL ALMOST RIGID OVER THE SHOULDERS. THE YOKE IS A LITTLE MORE PLIABLE AT THE BACK AND FRONT.

THE SHOULDER WING IS MADE OF LAYERS OF STIFFENED LINEN OR PASTEBOARD AND LINED WITH PLUSH.

C.B. FOLD

STITCHES FROM SHOULDER WINGS

THERE IS NO INTERFACING IN THIS PART OF THE BACK

FRONT OF WING

STITCH TO GOWN ON THIS EDGE

B

BACK

A

CENTRE BACK SEAM IS SHAPED AT THE TOP. THERE IS AN EXTRA DART ON THE LEFT BACK.

THE SHOULDER WINGS ARE MOUNTED ON THIS LINE

A

THE ARROWS INDICATE THE DIRECTION OF THE PILE

THE RAW EDGES AT THE ARMHOLES ARE OVERSEWN TOGETHER. THERE WERE PROBABLY HANGING SLEEVES ORIGINALLY, BUT THESE ARE NOW MISSING.

LONG DARTS ARE PINCHED UP AT THE BACK AND STITCHED TO THE YOKE, THEN ALLOWED TO HANG FREE BELOW.

OPEN TO THIS MARK

JOIN IN FABRIC

STITCH MARKS INDICATE THAT ORIGINALLY THERE WAS 9MM (⅜") WIDE SILVER BRAID DOWN BOTH FRONT EDGES, SIDE SEAMS, CENTRE BACK SEAM, SHOULDER SEAMS AND ARMHOLES WHERE THE WINGS ARE ATTACHED. TINY FRAGMENTS OF THIS BRAID REMAIN.

CENTRE BACK JOIN

JOIN IN FABRIC

13MM (½") DEEP HEM FACING OF OLIVE GREEN WOOL WITH A DIAGONAL WEAVE.

3·2 CM (1¼") DEEP INTERFACING OF LINEN CANVAS TO STIFFEN THE HEMLINE.

DOTTED LINE INDICATES THE EDGE OF CHARTREUSE SILK STRIP DOWN FRONT EDGE WHICH RUNS OVER THE STIFFENED YOKE UNDER THE ARM.

INTERFACING AT THE FRONT IS APPROX 3·2 CM (1¼") WIDE, AND IS CONCEALED BENEATH THE 8·9 CM (3½") WIDE CHARTREUSE SILK STRIP. IT IS SLIGHTLY PUCKERED IN SOME PLACES.

OPEN TO THIS MARK AT CENTRE BACK

LINEN INTERFACING

LINES OF STITCHING REMAIN TO SHOW POSITION OF OLIVE GREEN WOOL FACING

SIDE SEAM OPEN BELOW THIS MARK

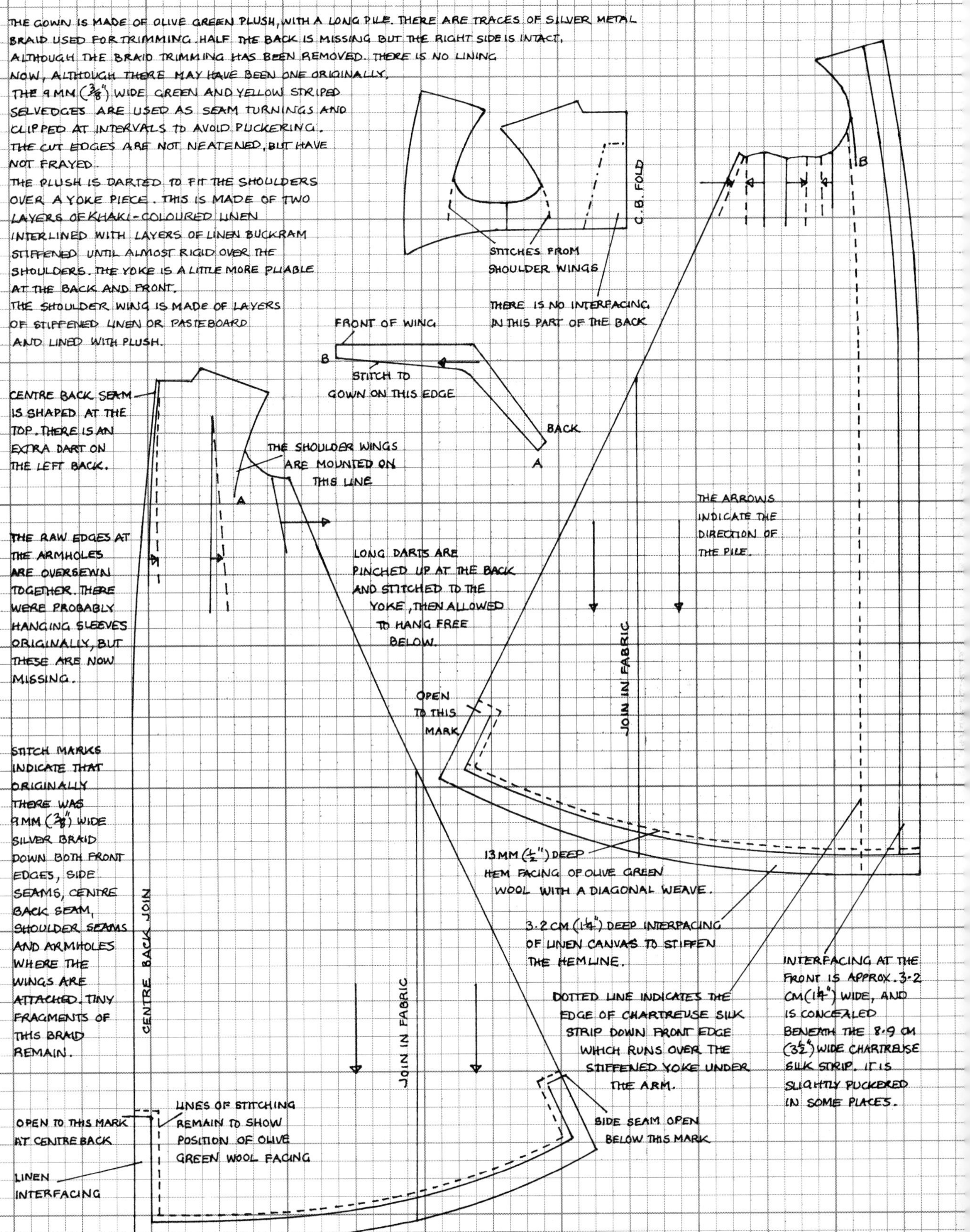

© 1984 JANET ARNOLD

56A.   A girl's loose gown in cut and uncut dark mulberry-coloured velvet, acquired in 1900 from the collection formed by an ancestor of Charles Isham, Lamport Hall, Northamptonshire. The hanging round, or Spanish, sleeves are lined with pink silk,

pinked for decoration (Fig. 378). Much of the back has been cut away, probably for furnishings in the nineteenth century, but enough remains to take a pattern. The gown was originally trimmed with bands of spangled silver bobbin lace, all of which has been removed. Its position is still marked by

tufts of yellow silk thread with an occasional spangle and fragment of silver metal strip, wrapped round a white silk core. It is extremely difficult to tell if the lace consisted of one wide band or two or three narrower ones, as the width between the dents in the velvet varies. The drawing shows the conjectured appearance of the gown in its original condition.

56B.   The velvet is mounted on a foundation yoke of pink silk interlined with stiff black buckram and lightly padded with a thin layer of wool, probably the same as that interlining the upper sides of the hanging sleeves. Rows of pad-stitching hold the layers together and tiny stitches may be seen in the silk when looking into the gown. A pair of eyelet holes is worked in the centre back of the stiffened standing collar for a ribbon point to attach a supportasse or underpropper to support a linen band or ruff.

56C.   Detail from the effigy of Joan, wife of Richard Alington, on their tomb of 1561, in the Rolls Chapel, London. Here the material, probably satin, is gathered into the front shoulder and back of the collar in the same way as Sir Francis Verney's gown (Fig. 271).

56C

56A

56B

c.1610-20 GIRL'S LOOSE GOWN   VICTORIA AND ALBERT MUSEUM, LONDON. 178-1900.

[MUL]BERRY CUT AND UNCUT VELVET GOWN, LARGE AREAS OF WHICH HAVE BEEN CUT AWAY.
[G]ROUND IS OF 2-PILE UNCUT VELVET. THE HIGHEST PILE IS AROUND THE AREAS OF CUT VELVET IN THE
[STYL]IZED DESIGN OF POMEGRANATES AND FLOWERS.
[THE] GOWN WAS ORIGINALLY TRIMMED WITH BANDS OF SPANGLED SILVER BOBBIN LACE, ALL OF
[WHI]CH HAVE BEEN REMOVED. TUFTS OF YELLOW SILK WITH WHICH THE LACE WAS SEWN
[ON] STILL REMAIN, WITH AN OCCASIONAL SPANGLE AND SILVER METAL THREAD
[WRA]PPED ROUND A WHITE SILK CORE TO SHOW THE POSITION.

14 LINES OF TINY PAD
STITCHES FROM C.B. NECK
TO END OF BUCKRAM

THESE ROWS OF STITCHES COME
THROUGH THE PINK SILK LINING.

THREE LINES OF LARGE STITCHES
ACROSS THE PLEATS INSIDE TO
HOLD THEM IN POSITION

A 3MM (⅛") WIDE STRIP
OF PINK SILK BINDING
IS STITCHED OVER THE
RAW EDGES OF THE
ARMHOLES, TO NEATEN
THEM.

MOST OF THE BACK IS
MISSING, CUT OFF BELOW
THIS DOTTED LINE.

A STRIP OF SILVER LACE
WITH SPANGLES WAS
ORIGINALLY STITCHED
RIGHT ACROSS THE
SHOULDERS TO CONCEAL
THE SEAM AND
THE LITTLE JOIN AT
THE FRONT.

DIRECTION
OF PILE

MISSING
AREA

A

THE SELVEDGES
ARE 13 MM (½")
WIDE, WITH
BRIGHT YELLOW
AND GREEN
STRIPES.

DIRECTION
OF PILE

SIDE SEAM   SELVEDGES LEFT HERE

DIRECTION
OF PILE

IT IS EXTREMELY DIFFICULT TO TELL IF
THERE WAS ONE WIDE BAND OF LACE, OR
TWO OR THREE NARROWER ONES, AS THE
WIDTH BETWEEN THE DENTS IN THE
VELVET VARIES.

PADDED TO THIS LINE OVER
SHOULDER, PROBABLY WITH
THIN WOOL, SAME AS
SLEEVE INTERLINING

INTERLINED WITH
BLACK BUCKRAM
TO THIS LINE

JOIN IN FABRIC

C.B. FOLD

DOTTED LINES
INDICATE LINES OF
STITCHING TO HOLD PLEATS
WHICH COME THROUGH
THE PINK SILK.

THE SMALL PINK SILK TAFFETA YOKE
WOULD PROBABLY HAVE BEEN MADE
FIRST, PADDED AND INTERLINED WITH
BLACK BUCKRAM, OR STIFFENED LINEN
CANVAS. THE VELVET WOULD THEN HAVE
BEEN PLEATED AND MOUNTED ON TOP.

THE SIDE GORES ON THE RIGHT SIDE OF THE
GOWN, WHICH ARE SHOWN HERE, WOULD
HAVE BEEN INTERCUT WITH THOSE ON THE
LEFT. THE PILE WOULD HAVE RUN
DOWNWARDS ON THE TWO SIDE GORES
AND UPWARDS ON THE SIDE FRONT GORE.
NOTHING REMAINS OF THE LEFT SIDE
GORES.

RUN AND FELL SEAM,
RATHER LUMPY, BUT
DOES NOT FRAY.

THE HEM IS DECORATED
WITH THREE ROWS OF
SILVER BOBBIN LACE 9MM
(⅜") WIDE. THE TOP ONE
SET 4.4CM (1¾") UP FROM
THE HEMLINE, AS FAR
AS CAN BE SEEN
FROM TUFTS OF
THREAD. ALL THE   DIRECTION
LACE HAS BEEN   OF PILE
REMOVED.

THE HEM IS LINED WITH 5.1CM (2") DEEP PINK SILK TAFFETA
TO HIDE THE 3.8CM (1½") DEEP BLACK BUCKRAM OR LINEN
STIFFENING. SOME OF THIS IS LEFT, BUT ONLY SMALL
FRAGMENTS OF THE PINK SILK REMAIN.

FRONT
YOKE PIECE
IS COMPLETELY
STIFFENED
WITH BLACK
BUCKRAM

JOIN IN
FABRIC

THE SHOULDER SEAM OF THE YOKE IS
COVERED WITH A STRAIGHT STRIP OF
SILK 9MM (⅜") WIDE.

PADDED TO THIS LINE FROM ARMHOLE
AND OVER SHOULDER, PROBABLY WITH
THIN WOOL.

UNDERARM
SEAM OF
SLEEVE TO
THIS POINT

WING TO THIS
POINT

A

THE PLEATS ARE CAUGHT
DOWN APPROXIMATELY
2.5 CM (1") FROM THE
ARMHOLE AND HANG FREE
FROM THERE. THE DOTTED
LINES INDICATE THE LINES
OF STITCHING.

THE FRONT IS STIFFENED WITH
A STRIP OF BLACK BUCKRAM,
HEAVILY COATED WITH SOME
STIFFENING AGENT, WHICH
REACHES FROM THE EDGE TO
THE DOTTED LINE.

A 5.1 CM (2") WIDE STRIP
OF PINK SILK TAFFETA
IS STITCHED INSIDE
THE EDGE TO CONCEAL
THE BUCKRAM STIFFENING.

THE FRONT AND HEM WERE
TRIMMED WITH THREE ROWS
OF SILVER BOBBIN LACE
9MM (⅜") WIDE. ALL OF THIS
HAS BEEN REMOVED.

AREAS WHERE THE VELVET HAS
BEEN CUT AWAY PROBABLY
TO USE THE SILVER LACE.

JOIN IN
FABRIC

FRONT SLEEVE
TO THESE POINTS

WING TO THIS
POINT

CENTRE BACK

NECK EDGE

THE COLLAR IS STIFFENED WITH VERY HEAVY
BUCKRAM AND LINED WITH PINK SILK, NOW
FADED. EYELET HOLES ARE WORKED AT THE
CENTRE BACK TO ATTACH A SUPPORTASSE.
TWO STRIPS OF 19MM (¾") WIDE RIBBON, 15.9 CM
(6¼") LONG ARE ATTACHED TO EACH SIDE OF THE
COLLAR. THESE ARE STITCHED ON WITH A
DIFFERENT TYPE OF SILK AND SEEM TO BE
LATER ADDITIONS.

THIS POINT MEETS
SHOULDER SEAM

BACK

THESE TWO TABS ARE ON THE CROSS GRAIN OF THE FABRIC
PRESUMABLY CUT OUT OF SCRAPS
FOR THE SHOULDER WING

THE SEAM IS
STITCHED TOGETHER
AT THE TOP FOR
3.8 CM (1½").

FRONT
LIES
BENEATH
ARM

TOP
AND
BACK

THE CURVED
EDGE OF THE
SLEEVE IS
CAUGHT
TOGETHER AT
THESE POINTS
WITH A FEW
STITCHES.
THERE IS NO
TRIMMING ON
THE UNDERSIDE
OF THE SLEEVE.

STRAIGHT EDGE OF LEFT
SLEEVE IS STIFFENED WITH
A STRIP OF BLACK BUCKRAM
3.8 CM (1½") WIDE ON
UNDERSIDE, AND RIGHT SLEEVE
WITH CREAM STIFFENED
HEAVY LINEN CANVAS STRIP.

WHOLE
TOP SIDE OF
SLEEVE IS
INTERLINED
WITH TWILL
WEAVE PALE
PINK WOOL.

THE HANGING SLEEVE IS OPEN ALL THE
WAY DOWN THESE STRAIGHT EDGES. EACH
HALF OF THE SLEEVE IS LINED WITH PALE PINK
SILK, PINKED WITH 1.5MM (1/16") CUTS FOR
DECORATION, APPROXIMATELY 6MM (¼") APART.
THE PINKING IS IRREGULAR
AND OFF THE GRAIN IN
SOME PLACES.

ACTUAL SIZE AND ARRANGEMENT
OF PINKING.

1:1 INCH
1:1 CENTIMETRE

© 1984 JANET ARNOLD

In 1975 the imperial system of measurement, based on the yard for length and the pound for weight, was officially replaced in the United Kingdom by the metric system, devised by the French during the Revolution. The Système International d'Unités (International System of Units) is the modern form of the metric system agreed in 1960 at an international conference. The international symbol for this system is SI and the linear measurements, with which we are concerned here, are expressed in millimetres and metres, using centimetres whenever this is more convenient.

The patterns in this book are based on a scale of $\frac{1}{8}$ inch:1 inch and printed on a grid designed to enable quick and easy enlargement, using an ordinary dressmaker's inch tape measure, when working from scale diagram to large sheet of pattern cutting paper. The scale of 1mm:1cm is too small for comfortable reading and scaling up with a metric tape measure. Tailors in the sixteenth century used inch, nail, yard and ell, which related to body measurements, and it seemed sensible to continue with the imperial system in this book. This decision was confirmed when I discovered that a special ruler for making quarter scale block patterns had been designed for pattern drafting classes at St Gorāns Gymnasium, 95 St Gorānsgaten, Stockholm, Sweden, in 1975, as the metric system was found to be inconvenient for this purpose. The units of measurement were almost $\frac{1}{8}$ inch.

Each pattern diagram is given with both imperial and metric scales. A scale rule is printed on page 125, each unit representing 1 cm. When using this the reader should simply ignore the grid on the pattern pages, except as a guide to the straight grain of the material. Neither conversion ruler nor tape can give absolutely accurate results, as the paper on which the pattern diagrams are printed may stretch slightly with variable humidity, but the patterns should be correct to within 12.7 mm ($\frac{1}{2}$ inch) when enlarged.

These conversion aids will enable the pattern diagrams on the $\frac{1}{8}$ inch:1 inch scale in this book to continue in use for quick comparison with other patterns taken on this scale before 1975. They will also familiarize students accustomed to metric measurements with the imperial system of measurement which has been used in England for centuries. The fascinating story of its development is told in 'English Linear Measures', the Stenton Lecture given by Professor Philip Grierson in 1971, published by the University of Reading. Widths and lengths of fabric were measured in inches, nails, feet, yards and ells and it is important for students of the history of textiles and costume to be familiar with them and to understand how they evolved and were standardized. They should also be aware that there were variations between the English measures and those of other countries. An undated note written by an anxious clerk in the office of the Great Wardrobe during the early years of Elizabeth I's reign makes this very plain:

'Memorandum that every Flemish ell is iij quarters of a yarde sterling, so that iiij elles Flemyshe is iij yards sterling, then viij [elles] makith vj yardes, xvj elles makith xij yardes, the xx elles makith xv yards, so that everie foure makith iij of that mesure, as iiij^{xx} [80] makith xxx score [60] and iiij^{c} [400] makith iij^{c} [300].

Memorandum that everie Flemyshe Elle is iij quarters of a yarde so that the Elle sterling hath v quarters of a yarde so that v elles Flemyshe makyth xv quarters whiche makith iij elles Sterling and x Elles Flemyshe makith vj Ells sterling & xx ells Flemyshe makith xij elles sterling so that every v makith iij as L Ells Flemyshe is xxx ells Sterling v skore is lx and so great numbres.'

Yet another set of measurements was used in Spain. Juan de Alcega describes the Castilian 'bara' in his *Libro de Geometria, pratica y traça*, printed in Madrid in 1589. Minsheu gives a reference to 'vara' from 'bara', in his *Dictionarie of Spanish and English* printed in 1599 and translates the word as 'a rod, a sticke, a yard, a cudgell, a twig', while *alna* is translated as 'a yard, an ell'. This dictionary is an enlarged version of Richard Percyvall's *Bibliotheca Hispanica* printed in 1591, where the same translations are given but the spelling of bara is not included. In neither dictionary is any mention made of the Castilian bara (or vara). It is not clear whether yard or ell is the best translation, although Stepney's *The Spanish Schoole-master*, printed in 1591, gives 'una vara' as a yard. Alcega does not mention the 'alna' in Castilian measures. The 1979 facsimile reprint of *Libro Geometria, pratica y traça* does not mention the two possible translations but simply gives bara as ell.

The Castilian bara, according to Alcega, was used for measuring all silks and woollen cloths. He describes its origin in an old Roman measure taken from the length of four grains of barley placed end to end, the 'dedo' or finger's breadth (the line printed in Alcega's book to show this measurement is 17.4 mm ($\frac{11}{16}$ inch) long). Four grains of barley were used to provide an average length. The ancient Roman foot measured sixteen times the dedo (i.e. 279 mm/11 inches) and this in turn equalled a third of the Castilian bara (i.e. 84 cm/33 inches). The bara was subdivided into twelfths, eighths, sixths, quarters, thirds and halves. Alcega points out that all these divisions are perfect fractions relative to the bara itself: he explains that divisions of fifths, sevenths and ninths are not used as, being uneven numbers, they will not divide into exact halves. From a practical point of view they are not divisions of a length of cloth either. The automatic folding of cloth will produce thirds, sixths and twelfths or halves, quarters and eighths, as any housewife folding towels or sheets will know.

In another part of the book Alcega describes merchants folding cloth in inches ('pulgadas') and says that for every 4 baras of the same cloth measured flat on the table by the tailor there would be $\frac{1}{6}$ bara short, so he should allow a little extra to make up the merchant's measure for his garment. Presumably the merchant did not allow for the material curving round on the folds, which would mount up to at least 6 inches over 4 yards. Alcega does not say how many inches there were in a Castilian bara but it will be seen that a bara, or yard, of 36 inches divides very neatly into twelfths (3 inches), sixths (6 inches) and thirds (12 inches) or eighths ($4\frac{1}{2}$ inches), quarters (9 inches) and halves (18 inches). The Castilian inch would then have been slightly shorter than the twentieth-century English inch if Alcega's line of $\frac{11}{16}$ inch for 4 grains of barley is correct. Burguen's *Geometria, y traça perteneciente al oficio de sastres*, printed in 1618, must have been warmly welcomed by tailors all over Spain as he explained the differences between the baras of Castile, Valencia and Aragon. The bara of Valencia was a twelfth longer than that of Castile. Twelve baras of Valencia made 13 baras of Castile and $13\frac{1}{2}$ baras of Aragon (Fig. 379).

In 1771 François Alexandre de Garsault described the French measures in *L'Art de la Lingere*, part of his *Descriptions des Arts et Métiers faites ou approuvées par Messieurs de l'Académie Royale des Sciences*. The linen draper used the ell to measure any quantity of linen for which she was asked and Garsault wrote that:

'Her terms of expression are the ell, or divisions of the ell [the ell used here is the Parisian ell (*l'aune de Paris*)] and are not understood by most people. On the other hand the King's foot (*le pied du Roi*), containing twelve inches, and its subdivision into twelfths of an inch (*lignes*) are familiar to almost everyone, and every measurement can be reduced to these terms.

The Parisian ell is fixed at 3 feet 7 inches and 8 twelfths [$43\frac{2}{3}$ inches]. The ell is generally marked on a wooden ruler one inch wide and half an inch thick. It is divided on both sides of its length, on one side into four quarters, the last quarter into two eighths, the last eighth into two sixteenths. On the opposite side it is divided into thirds, the last third into two sixths and the last sixth into two twelfths. The divisions are usually marked with golden nails. Both sides are edged with iron or copper to keep it permanently true.' These measurements may still have been very close to those in use during the sixteenth century in France.

F.W. Maitland pointed out in *Domesday Book and Beyond* that the English system of linear measures consisted of two basically independent groups of units, the large ones used for land and travelling distances contrasting with the small ones concerned primarily with cloth. The yard of 36 inches, divisible into 3 feet, was created in the twelfth century during the reign of Henry I and involved some revisions of the lengths of the foot and the inch. It can be roughly calculated from the nose to the fingertips when the arm is fully extended. In clothiers' hands the yard measure was divided by repeated halving through halves (18 inches), quarters (9 inches) and eighths ($4\frac{1}{2}$ inches) to sixteenths ($2\frac{1}{4}$ inches). As we have seen from Garsault's description, the divisions on the yardstick were marked with nails, which was no doubt why the sixteenth came to be called a 'nail' in England. This unit was still in common use during the first half of the nineteenth century but by the early twentieth century it was used only by old tailors and dressmakers. However, an eighth of a yard ($4\frac{1}{2}$ inches) could still be purchased in the fabric department of every large store in the country until the metric changeover was made in 1975.

The ell measure in England was at one time fixed by law at 2 yards, then $1\frac{1}{2}$ yards; finally in 1406 a group of weavers made a protest in favour of the ell of 5 quarters (45 inches) and by the sixteenth century this was accepted as the clothier's ell. This also continued in use during the nineteenth century. The width of 45 inches was shown on dressmakers' pattern layouts in the twentieth century as fabric was still made in it, although the word 'ell' was no longer used.

The smallest unit, the inch, is a borrowed word from the Latin 'uncia'. Grierson suggests that this is probably the same root as 'unguis', 'nail' originally referring to the breadth of the thumbnail, a carpenter's rather than a clothier's measure. The unit is called a thumb in Old Scots, Dutch and all the Scandinavian languages as well as 'pouce' in French. 'Uncia' is 'the twelfth part of the whole' and there are 12 inches in a foot. It is possible that 'uncia' or a word very similar to it, already referred to the small unit of a thumbnail and the length was then revised for the divisions of the foot measure. The top joint of the thumb is an approximate measure for one inch. This unit, like the yard, was eventually divided by repeated halving down to eighths of an inch, for the measurement of cloth used in dressmaking and tailoring. These are the units shown on tape measures, not tenths of an inch. Anyone who has folded cloth, if only in the form of a sheet or tablecloth, will know how automatically the halving and quartering takes place. As Professor Grierson points out, the history of both weights and measures has been governed by practical considerations rather than scientific ones.

Declaracion de las baras Castellana, Valenciana, y de Aragon.

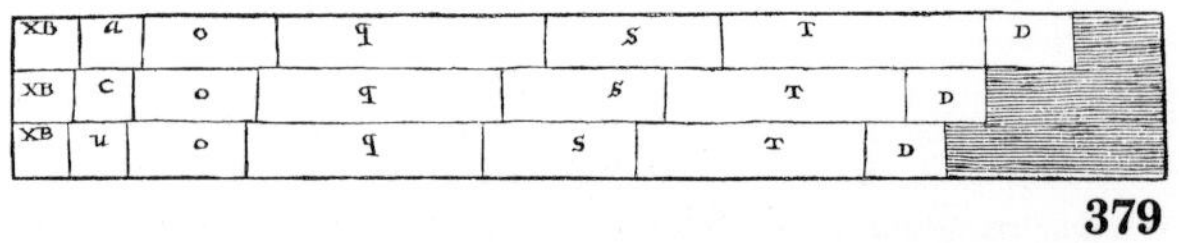

379

379. *'The bara of Valencia is a twelfth longer than the Castilian bara and it follows that twelve baras of Valencia are the same as thirteen Castilian baras and thirteen and a half baras of Aragon. The quarters, or divisions, shown here in the diagram are of Valencia, Castile and Aragon; those of Aragon are the same as those of Catalonia. So the tailor in any part of the kingdom will understand by how* much one bara differs from another, the most and the least. When he wishes to mark out a pattern he will prove the accuracy of the tables for the baras printed in this book. For those offering the excuse of ignorance, then I know it is made plain here.' This diagram shows the baras of Valencia (above), Castile (centre) and Aragon (below) with the divisions of 0 = an eighth, q = a quarter, s = a sixth and D = a twelfth. T is presumably a third, but only if D is included in the measurement. F. 214 from Geometria, y traça, by Francisco de la Rocha Burguen, 1618. Victoria and Albert Museum, London.

Metric and Imperial Conversion Table

1 ell = 45 inches = 1143 millimetres = 1·143 metres
1 yard = 36 inches = 914·4 millimetres = 0·9144 metre
1 foot = 12 inches = 304·8 millimetres = 0·3048 metre
1 nail = 2¼ inches = 57·15 millimetres
1 inch = 25·4 millimetres = 2·54 centimetres

Below top. *Metric conversion rule for use with the patterns in this book. This should be copied by photography for the most accurate results, as xeroxing is liable to distortion. Each unit represents 1cm and the reader should ignore the grid on the pattern pages, except as a guide to the straight grain of the material.*
Below centre. *Rule showing centimetres marked out in millimetres, and inches marked out in 1/64 inch, 1/32 inch and 1/16 inch divisions.*
Below bottom. *Rule showing inches marked out in 1/8 inch and 1/16 inch divisions.*

Table of Metric Equivalents

The following tables are based on British Standards (1 inch = 25·4 millimetres exactly). Copies of the complete standards may be obtained from the British Standards Institution, 2 Park Street, London W1Y 4AA.

inches	milli-metres	inches	milli-metres	inches	milli-metres	inches	milli-metres
1/64	0.3969	31/64	12.3031	61/64	24.2094	1 27/32	46.8313
1/32	0.7938	1/2	12.7000	31/32	24.6063	1 7/8	47.6250
3/64	1.1906	33/64	13.0969	63/64	25.0031	1 29/32	48.4188
1/16	1.5875	17/32	13.4938	1	25.4000	1 15/16	49.2125
5/64	1.9844	35/64	13.8906	1 1/32	26.1938	1 31/32	50.0063
3/32	2.3813	9/16	14.2875	1 1/16	26.9875	2	50.8000
7/64	2.7781	37/64	14.6844	1 3/32	27.7813	2 1/32	51.5938
1/8	3.1750	19/32	15.0813	1 1/8	28.5750	2 1/16	52.3875
9/64	3.5719	39/64	15.4781	1 5/32	29.3688	2 3/32	53.1813
5/32	3.9688	5/8	15.8750	1 3/16	30.1625	2 1/8	53.9750
11/64	4.3656	41/64	16.2719	1 7/32	30.9563	2 5/32	54.7688
3/16	4.7625	21/32	16.6688	1 1/4	31.7500	2 3/16	55.5625
13/64	5.1594	43/64	17.0656	1 9/32	32.5438	2 7/32	56.3563
7/32	5.5563	11/16	17.4625	1 5/16	33.3375	2 1/4	57.1500
15/64	5.9531	45/64	17.8594	1 11/32	34.1313	2 9/32	57.9438
1/4	6.3500	23/32	18.2563	1 3/8	34.9250	2 5/16	58.7375
17/64	6.7469	47/64	18.6531	1 13/32	35.7188	2 11/32	59.5313
9/32	7.1438	3/4	19.0500	1 7/16	36.5125	2 3/8	60.3250
19/64	7.5406	49/64	19.4469	1 15/32	37.3063	2 13/32	61.1188
5/16	7.9375	25/32	19.8438	1 1/2	38.1000	2 7/16	61.9125
21/64	8.3344	51/64	20.2406	1 17/32	38.8938	2 15/32	62.7063
11/32	8.7313	13/16	20.6375	1 9/16	39.6875	2 1/2	63.5000
23/64	9.1281	53/64	21.0344	1 19/32	40.4813	2 17/32	64.2938
3/8	9.5250	27/32	21.4313	1 5/8	41.2750	2 9/16	65.0875
25/64	9.9219	55/64	21.8281	1 21/32	42.0688	2 19/32	65.8813
13/32	10.3188	7/8	22.2250	1 11/16	42.8625	2 5/8	66.6750
27/64	10.7156	57/64	22.6219	1 23/32	43.6563	2 21/32	67.4688
7/16	11.1125	29/32	23.0188	1 3/4	44.4500	2 11/16	68.2625
29/64	11.5094	59/64	23.4156	1 25/32	45.2438	2 23/32	69.0563
15/32	11.9063	15/16	23.8125	1 13/16	46.0375	2 3/4	69.8500

inches	milli-metres	inches	milli-metres	inches	milli-metres	inches	milli-metres
2 25/32	70.6438	4 1/32	102.394	5 9/32	134.144	7 1/16	179.388
2 13/16	71.4375	4 1/16	103.188	5 5/16	134.938	7 1/8	180.975
2 27/32	72.2313	4 3/32	103.981	5 11/32	135.731	7 3/16	182.562
2 7/8	73.0250	4 1/8	104.775	5 3/8	136.525	7 1/4	184.150
2 29/32	73.8188	4 5/32	105.569	5 13/32	137.319	7 5/16	185.738
2 15/16	74.6125	4 3/16	106.362	5 7/16	138.112	7 3/8	187.325
2 31/32	75.4063	4 7/32	107.156	5 15/32	138.906	7 7/16	188.912
3	76.2000	4 1/4	107.950	5 1/2	139.700	7 1/2	190.500
3 1/32	76.9938	4 9/32	108.744	5 17/32	140.494	7 9/16	192.088
3 1/16	77.7875	4 5/16	109.538	5 9/16	141.288	7 5/8	193.675
3 3/32	78.5813	4 11/32	110.331	5 19/32	142.081	7 11/16	195.262
3 1/8	79.3750	4 3/8	111.125	5 5/8	142.875	7 3/4	196.850
3 5/32	80.1688	4 13/32	111.919	5 21/32	143.669	7 13/16	198.438
3 3/16	80.9625	4 7/16	112.712	5 11/16	144.462	7 7/8	200.025
3 7/32	81.7563	4 15/32	113.506	5 23/32	145.256	7 15/16	201.612
3 1/4	82.5500	4 1/2	114.300	5 3/4	146.050	8	203.200
3 9/32	83.3438	4 17/32	115.094	5 25/32	146.844	8 1/8	204.788
3 5/16	84.1375	4 9/16	115.888	5 13/16	147.638	8 1/8	206.375
3 11/32	84.9313	4 19/32	116.681	5 27/32	148.431	8 3/16	207.962
3 3/8	85.7250	4 5/8	117.475	5 7/8	149.225	8 1/4	209.550
3 13/32	86.5188	4 21/32	118.269	5 29/32	150.019	8 5/16	211.138
3 7/16	87.3125	4 11/16	119.062	5 15/16	150.812	8 3/8	212.725
3 15/32	88.1063	4 23/32	119.856	5 31/32	151.606	8 7/16	214.312
3 1/2	88.9000	4 3/4	120.650	6	152.400	8 1/2	215.900
3 17/32	89.6938	4 25/32	121.444	6 1/16	153.988	8 9/16	217.488
3 9/16	90.4875	4 13/16	122.238	6 1/8	155.575	8 5/8	219.075
3 19/32	91.2813	4 27/32	123.031	6 3/16	157.162	8 11/16	220.662
3 5/8	92.0750	4 7/8	123.825	6 1/4	158.750	8 3/4	222.250
3 21/32	92.8688	4 29/32	124.619	6 5/16	160.338	8 13/16	223.838
3 11/16	93.6625	4 15/16	125.412	6 3/8	161.925	8 7/8	225.425
3 23/32	94.4563	4 31/32	126.206	6 7/16	163.512	8 15/16	227.012
3 3/4	95.2500	5	127.000	6 1/2	165.100	9	228.600
3 25/32	96.0438	5 1/16	127.794	6 9/16	166.688	9 1/8	230.188
3 13/16	96.8375	5 1/8	128.588	6 5/8	168.275	9 1/8	231.775
3 27/32	97.6313	5 3/32	129.381	6 11/16	169.862	9 3/16	233.362
3 7/8	98.4250	5 1/8	130.175	6 3/4	171.450	9 1/4	234.950
3 29/32	99.2188	5 5/32	130.969	6 13/16	173.038	9 5/16	236.538
3 15/16	100.012	5 3/16	131.762	6 7/8	174.625	9 3/8	238.125
3 31/32	100.806	5 7/32	132.556	6 15/16	176.212	9 7/16	239.712
4	101.600	5 1/4	133.350	7	177.800	9 1/2	241.300

inches	milli-metres	inches	milli-metres	feet & inches	milli-metres	feet & inches	milli-metres
9 9/16	242.888	13	330.200	4 0	1219.20	7 4	2235.20
9 5/8	244.475	14	355.600	4 1	1244.60	7 5	2260.60
9 11/16	246.062	15	381.000	4 2	1270.00	7 6	2286.00
9 3/4	247.650	16	406.400	4 3	1295.40	7 7	2311.40
9 13/16	249.238	17	431.800	4 4	1320.80	7 8	2336.80
9 7/8	250.825	18	457.200	4 5	1346.20	7 9	2362.20
9 15/16	252.412	19	482.600	4 6	1371.60	7 10	2387.60
10	254.000	20	508.000	4 7	1397.00	7 11	2413.00
10 1/8	255.588	21	533.400	4 8	1422.40	8 0	2438.40
10 1/4	257.175	22	558.800	4 9	1447.80	8 1	2463.80
10 3/16	258.762	23	584.200	4 10	1473.20	8 2	2489.20
10 1/4	260.350	24	609.600	4 11	1498.60	8 3	2514.60
10 5/8	261.938	25	635.000	5 0	1524.00	8 4	2540.00
10 3/8	263.525	26	660.400	5 1	1549.40	8 5	2565.40
10 7/8	265.112	27	685.800	5 2	1574.80	8 6	2590.80
10 1/2	266.700	28	711.200	5 3	1600.20	8 7	2616.20
10 9/16	268.288	29	736.600	5 4	1625.60	8 8	2641.60
10 5/8	269.875	30	762.000	5 5	1651.00	8 9	2667.00
10 11/16	271.462	31	787.400	5 6	1676.40	8 10	2692.40
10 3/4	273.050	32	812.800	5 7	1701.80	8 11	2717.80
10 13/16	274.638	33	838.200	5 8	1727.20	9 0	2743.20
10 7/8	276.225	34	863.600	5 9	1752.60	9 1	2768.60
10 15/16	277.812	35	889.000	5 10	1778.00	9 2	2794.00
11	279.400	36	914.400	5 11	1803.40	9 3	2819.40
11 1/8	280.988	37	939.800	6 0	1828.80	9 4	2844.80
11 1/8	282.575	38	965.200	6 1	1854.20	9 5	2870.20
11 3/16	284.162	39	990.600	6 2	1879.60	9 6	2895.60
11 1/4	285.750	40	1016.00	6 3	1905.00	9 7	2921.00
11 5/16	287.338	41	1041.40	6 4	1930.40	9 8	2946.40
11 3/8	288.925	42	1066.80	6 5	1955.80	9 9	2971.80
11 7/16	290.512			6 6	1981.20	9 10	2997.20
11 1/2	292.100			6 7	2006.60	9 11	3022.60
11 9/16	293.688			6 8	2032.00	10 0	3048.00
11 5/8	295.275	feet & inches	milli-metres	6 9	2057.40	11 0	3352.80
11 11/16	296.862			6 10	2082.80	12 0	3657.60
11 3/4	298.450	3 7	1092.20	6 11	2108.20	13 0	3962.40
11 13/16	300.038	3 8	1117.60	7 0	2133.60	14 0	4267.20
11 7/8	301.625	3 9	1143.00	7 1	2159.00	15 0	4572.00
11 15/16	303.212	3 10	1168.40	7 2	2184.40	16 0	4876.80
12	304.800	3 11	1193.80	7 3	2209.80	17 0	5181.60

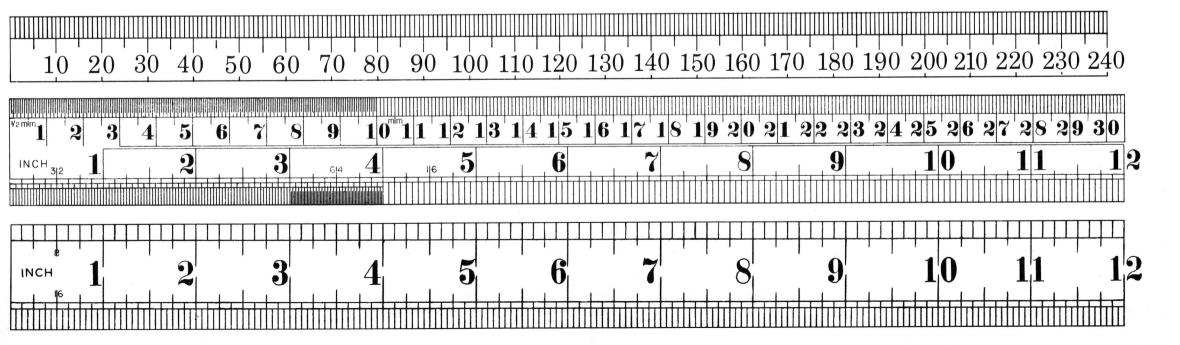

Although the clothes described and illustrated in this book cannot give a representative survey of the fashions between 1560 and 1620, since they are simply a large number of the surviving fragments from this period, the pattern diagrams can provide a useful guide when cutting theatrical costumes. They should be used in conjunction with the original tailors' patterns of the period on pages 3–13. All the clothes from which the patterns are taken were made for men, women and children of widely differing sizes. Approximate body measurements of the original wearers are given on page 127.

It is important to remember that a woman's figure was shaped by a 'pair of bodies' or corset consisting of two layers of closely woven linen or canvas with rows of stitching to form casings for bents (Fig. 329) or, after about 1580, whalebones. A wood or bone busk at the front kept her straight, while her rib cage was compressed and the bust flattened and pushed upwards by the shape of the corset (Figs. 326–7). The modern brassière must be discarded and the actress persuaded to wear the correct foundation garments (Figs. 380–1). The line of costume can be changed completely by the corset and by the stance adopted when wearing a wide-hooped Spanish or French farthingale (Fig. 382).

The pattern for the 'pair of bodies' on page 112 provides a basic shape which can be adapted for any figure. Good modern substitutes for linen are drill or coutil. The corset should be cut at least 5 cm (2″) smaller in circumference than the measurements of the wearer, so that it can be laced tightly to pull in the superfluous flesh. The material will stretch a little with the warmth of the body. Whalebone is now almost impossible to obtain and stiff plastic bones may be used instead. Mrs Jean Hunnisett uses Rigilene plastic boning, which she stitches directly to the corset by machine, rather than making casings for bones by machining two layers of material together. Both methods give good support but the casings allow the bones to move slightly, as they did in the sixteenth century.

A pattern for a Spanish farthingale is given in Fig. 27. It may be made a little wider at the hem by simply altering the angle of the gored seams. A calico toile should be made from the same width of material as that used originally to copy the exact dimensions of the farthingale. Any adjustments should be noted on the final full-size paper pattern together with the position of tucks forming casings for hoops. Originally the latter would have been made of osiers, bents or whalebone. Osiers may still be used but cane or steels are a good substitute. The silhouette of the 1580s was achieved by wearing a linen roll padded with cotton wool below the waist, usually over a Spanish farthingale. The roll gradually increased in size and by about 1590, when it became too heavy and cumbersome (Fig. 52), it was replaced by the drum-shaped farthingale (Fig. 53). No frame of this type appears to have survived. Fig. 383 gives a pattern diagram of one of moderate size, the shape conjectured from the details in Fig. 53. The casings would originally have held hoops of whalebone but cane is a good substitute. The farthingale may be made to open at the centre front or on both sides. The latter method, shown in Fig. 384 makes it possible to have the inner casing closed as well as the outer and the cane hoops are joined in complete circles. The waist is pleated into a band with a drawstring through it to allow the wearer to pull the frame up over her hips. Tabs with hooks or tapes to attach to rings at the bottom of the corset enable the farthingale to hang slightly below waist level. A padded roll is usually worn beneath the drum farthingale to support it and struts may be put between the hoops, although if the material is stretched taut it should support the weight of petticoat or gown, unless very heavy materials are used.

Men's doublets were often heavily padded or bombasted and the waist level varied considerably over the years. The breeches might be made with woollen interlinings as well as fustian linings to give extra fullness. Doublets were very tightly fitted and the weight of the breeches hooked on at the waist held them in position and stopped them riding up, as well as preventing the breeches from falling down. These points should all be borne in mind when enlarging the patterns for use today.

Various parts of a doublet might be made up individually, raw edges of silk and lining turned in to face each other and then assembled with overhanding on neat, folded edges. Tailors may have evolved this method to give journeymen and apprentices small units to work on but it has the additional advantage of avoiding bulky seams. In other examples the seams were back-stitched and the turnings folded back over the interlining and hemmed down to keep them flat (Fig. 197). When making a doublet today it is advisable to make the lining first and fit it, then arrange the padding on top and finally cut a toile for the outer layer in calico on a dress stand to make sure it will be large enough, before cutting out expensive material.

It is helpful to make reconstructions in calico to try out various techniques of cut and construction. The best method is to square the pattern up to full size on a large sheet of paper marked with 1″ squares (or 1 cm squares if using the metric conversion tables) and cut it out. No seams are allowed; the grain lines are indicated by the grid. It is unnecessary to draw the pattern of the skirt if it is very simple. It may be drawn directly on to the cloth with white chalk. The garment should be cut out in calico, or some other firmly woven cotton, and assembled with small tacking stitches according to the instructions given on the diagram. A dress stand padded to the size and shape of the figure, with suitable underpinnings for women's clothes, will be needed for fittings. A stand which is smaller than the finished measurements should be used to allow for padding to period shape. Non-woven materials like paper cloth are often used for cheapness, quick effect and ease of handling, as they do not fray. However, for a true reflection of the problems to be encountered in cutting, a woven fabric should be used, following the grain lines of the original pattern. Instructions for padding a stand are given in *Patterns of Fashion 1 c1660–1860* (1977 edition), page 74. Patterns of shirts, smocks and neckwear of c1550–1650 will be given in the next book in this series.

380. *Glenda Jackson wearing corset and padded roll of the 1580s, made by Jean Hunnisett for the BBC TV series* Elizabeth R, *designed by Elizabeth Waller in 1970.*

381. *Glenda Jackson wearing a drum-shaped farthingale of 1600 made by Jean Hunnisett for the BBC TV series* Elizabeth R, *designed by Elizabeth Waller in 1970.*

382. *Masque costumes for Iris and Ceres made by Norma Whittard for* The Tempest, *designed by Marina Bjornssen for the Royal Shakespeare Company in 1982.*

383 and 384. *Drum-shaped farthingale made from a straight strip of linen joined at the front, with two hoops inserted. Cotton may be used as a substitute.*

381

380

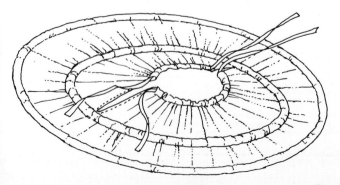

382

383

384

Table of Measurements

Men's clothes. Approximate body measurements are given +5cm(2") to 20.3cm(8") for ease and allowance for linings, padding and shirt worn beneath. Total measurements give final pattern size. At least 5cm(2") are needed for ease and a heavily padded garment takes up at least 10.1cm(4"). Waist measurements are given for breeches but leg lengths should be taken from patterns and adapted as required. Measurements for cloaks and hats are not given here.

Date	Description and pattern page	Chest	Waist	Front neck to waist	Back neck to waist
1. +1562	Doublet and trunk-hose worn by Don Garzia de'Medici, aged 15. Doublet waist points down slightly from natural waist level at front. Page 54	78.7cm(31") + 5cm(2")	60.9cm(24") + 5cm(2")	29.2cm(11½") + point of doublet below waist 6.3cm(2½")	36.7cm(14½")
3. +1574	Doublet worn by Cosimo de'Medici, aged 55. Doublet waist points down slightly from natural waist level at front. Page 56	101.6cm(40") + 7.6cm(3")	78.7cm(31") + 5cm(2")	38.1cm(15") + point of doublet below waist 7.6cm(3")	40.6cm(16")
4. +1567	Doublet and pluderhose worn by Svante Sture, aged 50. Natural waist level. Page 58	109.2cm(43") + 7.6cm(3")	86.3cm(34") + 5cm(2")	41.8cm(16½")	44.3cm(17½")
5. +1567	Doublet and pluderhose worn by Erik Sture, aged 21. Natural waist level. Page 61. See portrait, Fig. 94	81.2cm(32") + 5cm(2")	60.9cm(24") + 5cm(2")	34.2cm(13½")	41.8cm(16½")
6. +1567	Doublet and pluderhose worn by Nils Sture, aged 24. Natural waist level. Pages 64, 68	76.2cm(30") + 5cm(2")	66cm(26") + 5cm(2")	35.5cm(14")	43.1cm(17")
7. c1560	Youth's pinked and cut leather jerkin. Waist points down slightly at front. Page 68	81.2cm(32") + 5cm(2")	76.2cm(30") + 5cm(2")	31.6cm(12½") + point of doublet below waist 2.5cm(1")	40.6cm(16")
8. c1560	Lightly padded doublet, possibly an arming doublet, waist slightly short, curving down at centre front, probably for a short man. Page 71	86.3cm(34") + 10.1cm(4")	60.9cm(24") + 5cm(2")	31.6cm(12½") + point of doublet below waist 5cm(2")	38.1cm(15")
9. c1620	Jerkin intended to be worn open over a doublet. Page 71	83.8cm(33") + 12.7cm(5")	63.5cm(25") + 12.7cm(5")	38.1cm(15") + point of doublet below waist 7.6cm(3")	40.6cm(16")
10. c1595–1610	Embroidered leather doublet, lightly padded and stiffened with whalebones. Slightly raised waist level. Page 73	86.3cm(34") + 10.1cm(4")	88.9cm(35") + 5cm(2")	33cm(13") + point of doublet below waist 7.6cm(3")	35.5cm(14")
11. c1595–1605	Doublet for boy, probably about 12 years old, stiffened with whalebones. Page 73	73.6cm(29") + 7.6cm(3")	66cm(26") + 5cm(2")	30.4cm(12") + point of doublet below waist 3.8cm(1½")	34.2cm(13½")
12. c1600–1605	Heavily padded doublet and trunk-hose for tall middle-aged man, slightly old fashioned. Page 75	101.6cm(40") + 20.3cm(8")	96.5cm(38") + 20.3cm(8")	45.7cm(18") + point of doublet below waist 7.6cm(3")	50.8cm(20")
13. c1605–1610	Cut and pinked doublet with padded peascod belly. Raised waist level. Page 79	109.2cm(43") + 22.8cm(9")	93.9cm(37") + 22.8cm(9")	33cm(13") + point of doublet below waist 3.8cm(1½")	36.7cm(14½")
14. c1590–1600	Embroidered jerkin to be worn over a doublet, probably closed at the front. Page 79	83.8cm(33") + 12.7cm(5")	73.6cm(29") + 12.7cm(5")	38.1cm(15") + point of doublet below waist 8.8cm(3½")	41.8cm(16½")
15. c1610	Padded silk doublet. Raised waist level. Page 81	76.2cm(30") + 15.2cm(6")	60.9cm(24") + 15.2cm(6")	30.4cm(12")	43.1cm(17")
16. c1610	Youth's padded leather doublet. Raised waist level. Page 83	73.6cm(29") + 12.7cm(5")	53.3cm(21") + 15.2cm(6")	29.2cm(11½")	38.1cm(15")
17. c1610	Youth's padded leather doublet. Raised waist level. Page 83	60.9cm(24") + 12.7cm(5")	53.3cm(21") + 15.2cm(6")	28.5cm(11¼")	38.1cm(15")
18. c1615–1620	Pinked satin doublet. Raised waist level. Page 85	91.4cm(36") + 5cm(2")	81.2cm(32") + 5cm(2")	25.4cm(10") + point of doublet below raised waist level 6.3cm(2½")	38.1cm(15")
19. c1615–1625	Silk doublet. Raised waist level. Page 85	78.7cm(31") + 5cm(2")	53.3cm(21") + 5cm(2")	27.9cm(11") + point of doublet below raised waist level 12.7cm(5")	33cm(13")
20. c1615–1620	Pinked satin doublet. Raised waist level. Page 87	83.8cm(33") + 5cm(2")	71.1cm(28") + 5cm(2")	31.6cm(12½")	38.1cm(15")
21. c1615–1620	Breeches for man with large paunch. Page 87		134.6cm(53")		
22. 1618	Doublet and trunk-hose worn by Sir Richard (?) Cotton. Raised waist level. Page 89. See portrait, Fig. 190	93.9cm(37") + 7.6cm(3")	81.2cm(32") + 7.6cm(3")	27.9cm(11") + point of doublet below raised waist level 11.4cm(4½")	36.7cm(14½")
23. c1618–1620	Doublet and trunk-hose. Raised waist level. Page 91	88.9cm(35") + 5cm(2")	76.2cm(30") + 5cm(2")	30.4cm(12") + point of doublet below raised waist level 6.3cm(2½")	36.7cm(14½")

Date	Description and pattern page	Bust	Waist	Front neck to waist	Back neck to waist
36. c1600–1610	Loose gown for well-built person, to be worn over other clothes, about 182.8cm (6ft) in height. Page 99	121.9cm(48") + 40.6cm(16")		Front neck to ground 142.2cm(56")	Back neck to ground 147.3cm(58")
37. c1605–1615	Loose gown worn over other clothes, by tradition, by Sir Francis Verney. About 182.8cm (6ft) in height. Page 100	121.9cm(48") + 40.6cm(16")		Front neck to ground 151cm(59½")	Back neck to ground 152.4cm(60")

Women's clothes. Approximate body measurements are given +5cm(2") to 10.1cm(4") for ease and allowance for linings, smock and 'pair of bodies' worn beneath. Total measurements give final pattern size.

38. c1600–1610	Loose gown to be worn over kirtle by girl probably about 14 years old, to be worn over kirtle. Page 101	78.7cm(31") + 10.1cm(4")		Front neck to ground 119.3cm(47")	Back neck to ground 118.1cm(46½")
41. +1562	Gown worn over 'pair of 'bodies' by Eleanora of Toledo, wife of Cosimo I de'Medici, aged 40. She had 11 children, so her waist is large. Page 104	83.8cm(33") + 5cm(2")	73.6cm(29") + 5cm(2")	35.5cm(14") + point of bodice below waist level 11.4cm(4½"). Front waist to ground 97.7cm(38½")	38.1cm(15"). Back waist to ground with train 160cm (63")
42. +1600	Gown worn by Gräfin Katharina zur Lippe, aged 6. Page 106	50.8cm(20") + 5cm(2")	50.8cm(20") + 5cm(2")	17.7cm(7"). Front waist to ground 59.6cm(23½")	17.7cm(7"). Back waist to ground 72.3cm(28½")
43. c1585	Doublet worn by short slim woman or girl, stiffened with whalebones, probably worn without a 'pair of bodies' or corset. Page 106	78.7cm(31") + 5cm(2")	63.5cm(25") + 5cm(2")	33cm(13") + point of doublet below waist 2.5cm(1")	33.6cm(13¼")
44. c1570–1580	Kirtle worn under loose gown by a slim woman. Page 110	78.7cm(31") + 5cm(2")		Front neck to ground 137.1cm(54")	Back neck to ground 146.1cm(57½")
45. c1570–1580	Loose gown worn over kirtle by slim woman. Page 111	78.7cm(31") + 22.8cm(9")		Front neck to ground 137.1cm(54")	Back neck to ground 146.1cm(57½")
46. +1598	Silk 'pair of bodies' or corset worn by Pfalzgräfin Dorothea Sabina von Neuburg, aged 22. Page 111	71.1cm(28") No ease	50.8cm(20") No ease	30.4cm(12") + point of corset below waist 12.7cm(5")	30.4cm(12")
47. +1598	Trained gown worn by Pfalzgräfin Dorothea Sabina von Neuburg, aged 22, over a 'pair of bodies'. Page 114	71.1cm(28") + 7.6cm(3")	50.8cm(20") + 12.7cm(5")	30.4cm(12") + point of bodice below waist 10.1cm(4"). Front waist to ground (37")	30.4cm(12"). Back waist to ground with train 153.6cm(60½")
48. +1639	Gown worn by Pfalgräfin Dorothea Maria von Sulzbach, aged 80. Page 115	71.1cm(28") + 7.6cm(3")	58.4cm(23") + 7.6cm(3")	27.9cm(11") + point of bodice below waist 10.1cm(4")	33cm(13"). Back waist to ground with train 121.9cm(48")
52. c1600–1615	Loose gown, does not meet at centre front. Page 119	81.2cm(32")		139.7cm(55")	147.3cm(58")
53. c1610–1615	Embroidered jacket worn by Margaret Laton, with natural waist level, but worn in c1620 with raised waist level. Page 121. See Portrait Fig. 362	76.2cm(30") + 2.5cm(1")	63.5cm(25") + 5cm(2")	31.6cm(12½"). Front skirts below waist 8.2cm(3¼")	39.3cm(15½")
54. c1615–1618	Embroidered linen jacket. Raised waist level. Page 121	78.7cm(31") + 2.5cm(1")	63.5cm(25") + 2.5cm(1")	27.9cm(11"). Front skirts below raised waist level 11.4cm(4½")	35.5cm(14")
55. c1610–1620	Loose gown worn by girl aged about 12 over jacket and petticoat. Page 121	76.2cm(30")		Front neck to ground 111.7cm(44")	Back neck to ground 124.4cm(49")
56. c1610–1620	Loose gown worn by short slim young woman or girl, over jacket and petticoat. Page 123	81.2cm(32")		Front neck to ground 134.6cm(53")	Back neck to ground 137.1cm(54")

This table of measurements has been printed in very small type to save space. Anyone wishing to consult it frequently will find it more convenient to work from an enlargement.

Select Bibliography

This list of books and articles is intended as a brief guide for students and theatre designers embarking on sixteenth- and early seventeenth-century projects. Some of the items listed are foreign publications or are now out of print but may be borrowed through the National Central Library Service in Britain. *Costume*, the journal of the Costume Society (publications enquiries c/o Miss Helen Wood, Birtle Edge House, Bury, Lancashire BL9 6UW), *Dress*, the journal of the Costume Society of America (c/o The Costume Institute, The Metropolitan Museum, New York) and *Waffen-und Kostümkunde*, the journal of the Armour and Costume Society founded in Germany in 1896 (c/o Kunstbibliothek, Jebenstrasse 2, D–1000 Berlin 12), which contain many well-illustrated articles, are also available in some art college and polytechnic libraries. The last-named journal publishes articles in English as well as German. Titles marked with a dagger mention, or discuss fully, one or more of the items of clothing in this book.

Primary Sources

Reprints, some in facsimile, of books printed in the sixteenth and early seventeenth centuries. Printed transcripts of inventories, wills and similar material.

ALCEGA, J. DE *Tailor's Pattern Book 1589*, trans. J. Pain and C. Bainton, introduction and notes by J.L. Nevinson. Ruth Bean, Bedford, 1979. Facsimile of *Libro de Geometria, pratica y traça*, showing patterns laid out on various widths of material.

AMMAN, J. and SACHS, H. *The Book of Trades [Eygentliche Aller Stände auf Erden*, popularly known as *Ständebuch*, 1568]. Many facsimiles available, the most recent being Dover, New York, 1973. Clothes worn by craftsmen in Nürnberg.

AMMAN, J. *293 Renaissance Woodcuts for artists and illustrators [Künstbuchlin*, 1599]. Reprint, Dover, 1968. German soldiers, burghers and others, dating from 1578–91.

ARNOLD, J. 'Lost from Her Majesties Back', Costume Society Extra Publication, 7, 1980. Transcript of daybook kept in the Wardrobe of Robes recording clothes and jewels lost or given away by Queen Elizabeth I between 1561 and 1585.

BYRNE, M. ST CLARE. *The Elizabethan Home discovered in two dialogues by Claudius Hollyband and Peter Erondell* [printed as *The French Schoole maister* (1573, 1582) and *The French Garden* (1605)]. Methuen, 1949. Conversation manuals by two Huguenot refugees who taught French in London.

LEVEY, S.M. and PAYNE, P. *Le Pompe 1599: Patterns for Venetian bobbin lace*. Ruth Bean, Bedford, 1983. Pattern book of 1599 with modern examples worked from it.

NICHOLS, J. *The Progresses and Public Processions of Queen Elizabeth I*. 3 vols, 1823. Kraus Reprint Corporation, New York, 1973. Wide variety of contemporary documents.

NICHOLS, J. *The Progresses, Processions and Magnificent Festivities of King James I*. 4 vols, 1828. Kraus Reprint Corporation, New York, 1973. Wide variety of contemporary documents.

STUBBES, P. *The Anatomie of Abuses*, 1583. Facsimile, Theatrum Orbis Terrarum Ltd, Amsterdam, 1972. English fashions discussed by a Puritan.

VECELLIO, C. *Habiti Antichi et Moderni di tutto il Mondo*, 1598. Reprinted as *Vecellio's Renaissance Costume Book*, Dover, New York, 1977. 500 woodcuts of costume all over the known world of that time.

VINCIOLO, F. *Renaissance Patterns for Lace, Embroidery and Needlepoint [Singuliers et nouveaux pourtraicts*, 1587]. Facsimile, Dover, 1971. Numerous woodcut designs.

Secondary Sources

General works with chapters relating to sixteenth- and early seventeenth-century costume.

ARNOLD, J. *A Handbook of Costume*. Macmillan, 1973. 240 monochrome plates. A guide to the primary sources for costume study.

†BOUCHER, F. *A History of Costume in the West*. Thames and Hudson, 1967. 817 monochrome and 355 colour plates. Useful for quick visual reference.

DAVENPORT, M. *The Book of Costume*. Crown Publishers, New York, 1948. 3000 monochrome plates. A comprehensive history of costume up to 1860, covering dress, accessories, coiffure, etc. A standard work.

KELLY, F.M. and SCHWABE, R. *Historic Costume: a chronicle of fashion in Western Europe 1490–1790*. Batsford, 1925. Monochrome and colour plates, with many line drawings and some patterns. A standard work.

KELLY, F.M. and SCHWABE, R. *A Short History of Costume and Armour chiefly in England 1066–1800*. 1931, reprinted David & Charles, 1972. Monochrome and colour plates, with many line drawings. A standard work.

†KÖHLER, C. and SICHART, E. VON. *A History of Costume*, trans. A.K. Dallas. Harrap, 1928. Dover, New York, 1963. 600 monochrome and 16 colour plates.

KYBALOVA, L., HERBEYOVA, O. and LAMAROVA, M. *Pictorial Encyclopedia of Fashion*, trans. C. Rosoux. Hamlyn, 1968. Numerous useful monochrome and colour plates, unfortunately undated in some cases.

†VICTORIA AND ALBERT MUSEUM, *Four Hundred Years of Fashion*, ed. N. Rothstein. Collins, 1984. Catalogue of the items on display in 1984, with introductions to each area by M. Ginsburg, A. Hart and V. Mendes. Monochrome and colour plates.

†WAUGH, N. *Corsets and Crinolines*. Batsford 1954, reprinted 1972. 115 plates and 24 patterns of garments, a few of the sixteenth and early seventeenth centuries.

WAUGH, N. *The Cut of Men's Clothes, 1600–1900*. Faber, 1964. 29 pages of plates, 42 cutting diagrams, 27 tailors' patterns.

WAUGH, N. *The Cut of Women's Clothes, 1600–1930*, Faber, 1968. 71 monochrome plates, 75 cutting diagrams, 54 tailors' patterns.

Books and catalogues mainly or entirely devoted to costume and accessories of the sixteenth and early seventeenth centuries.

ANDERSON, R.M. *Hispanic Costume 1480–1530*. Hispanic Society of America, New York, 1979. Monochrome plates and 8 colour pages. Earlier period covering Spanish styles which developed and influenced all European fashions in the sixteenth century.

ARNOLD, J. *Queen Elizabeth's Wardrobe Unlock'd*. W.S. Maney and Son Ltd, Leeds, 1985. Over 500 plates of portraits and textiles. Includes Inventory of the Wardrobe of Robes in 1600.

BENTIVEGNA, F.C. *Abbigliamento e Costume nella pittura Italiana*. Carlo Bestetti, Rome. Vol. 1, *Rinascimento* (1962), covers the fifteenth and sixteenth centuries; vol. 2 *Baroco e Impero* (1964) covers the seventeenth and eighteenth centuries. Many monochrome and a few colour plates. Text in Italian.

BLUM, A. *The Last Valois, 1515–1590*. Costume of the Western World Series, Harrap, 1951. Monochrome and colour plates of French paintings and engravings.

BLUM, A. *Early Bourbon, 1590–1643*. Costume of the Western World Series, Harrap, 1951. Monochrome and colour plates of French paintings and engravings.

BOEHN, M. VON. *Modes and Manners*, trans. J. Joshua. Harrap, 1932–5, reprinted Arno, 1976. Vol. 2, *The Sixteenth Century*; vol. 3, *The Seventeenth Century*. Numerous monochrome and a few colour plates .

CHRISTENSEN, S.F. *De Danske Kongers Kronologiske Samling paa Rosenborg, Kongedragterne fra 17. og 18. aarhundrede*. 2 vols, Copenhagen, 1940. Danish monarchs' costumes from the seventeenth and eighteenth centuries.

CUMMING, V. *A Visual History of Costume: the Seventeenth Century*. Batsford, 1984. Monochrome plates.

†CUNNINGTON, C.W. and CUNNINGTON, P. *Handbook of English Costume in the Sixteenth Century*. Faber, 1954, revised edition 1970. Line drawings. A useful basic guide.

†CUNNINGTON, C.W. and CUNNINGTON, P. *Handbook of English Costume in the Seventeenth Century*. Faber, 1955, revised edition 1967. Line drawings. A useful basic guide.

†DIGBY, G.W. *Elizabethan Embroidery*. Faber, 1963. Monochrome and colour plates including some of costume.

HACKENBROCH, Y. *Renaissance Jewellery*. Sotheby Parke Bernet, 1980. Numerous monochrome and colour plates covering all types of jewellery from the late fifteenth to early seventeenth century.

KELLY, F.M. *Shakespearean Costume for Stage and Screen*. A. and C. Black, 1938. Revised edition 1970, which loses all the clear drawings by Leloir and Schwabe. Monochrome plates and line drawings. A useful basic guide.

LA MAR, V.A. *English Dress in the Age of Shakespeare*. Folger Shakespeare Library, Washington DC, 1958. 22 monochrome plates of paintings and engravings showing costume.

LAVER, J. *Early Tudor 1485–1558*. Costume of the Western World Series, Harrap, 1951. Monochrome and colour plates. Earlier period leading up to fashions of the mid- and late sixteenth century in England.

LELOIR, M. *Histoire du Costume de l'Antiquité à 1914*. Vol. 8, *1610–1643*. Ernst, 1933. Numerous plates with drawings and diagrams of cut.

LEVEY, S.M. *Lace: A History*. W.S. Maney and Son Ltd, Leeds, 1983. Comprehensive survey of European lace. Over 600 monochrome plates. A standard work.

LEVI-PISETZKY, R. *Storia del Costume in Italia*. Vol. 3, *Il Cinquecento Il Seicento*. Instituto Editoriale Italiano, Milan, 1966. Covers from c1500 to 1690. Numerous monochrome and colour plates.

LINTHICUM, M.C. *Costume in the Drama of Shakespeare and his Contemporaries*. Oxford, 1936, reprinted New York, 1963. Monochrome plates. A standard work with useful chapters on colours and textiles used for clothing during the sixteenth and early seventeenth centuries, with principal works cited.

MORSE, H.K. *Elizabethan Pageantry: a pictorial survey of costume and its commentators from 1560–1620*. Studio, 1934, reprinted 1976. Monochrome plates and useful descriptions of costume from contemporary sources.

NEWTON, S.M. *Renaissance Theatre Costume*. André Deutsch, 1973. Monochrome plates. A discussion of the sense of historic past in fifteenth- and sixteenth-century theatre costume.

†NIENHOLDT, E. *Kostüme des 16. und 17. Jahrhunderts*. Klinkhardt & Biermann, Braunschweig, 1962. 16 monochrome and 4 colour plates of surviving examples of costume in Europe. Text in German.

PETRASCHECK-HEIM, I. *Die Meisterstückbücher des Schneiderhandewerks in Innsbruck*. Sonderdruck ans Veröffentleichungen des Museum Ferdinandeum, Innsbruck, 1970. An account of the master tailors of Innsbruck and their pattern books from the sixteenth to eighteenth centuries, with numerous cutting diagrams. Text in German.

PROVINCIAAL MUSEUM STERCKSHOF, ANTWERP. *De Mode in Rubens' Tijd*. Antwerp, 1977. Monochrome plates. Catalogue of exhibition of fashions in the time of Rubens, with examples of early seventeenth-century costume and accessories.

PYLKKANEN, R. *Säätyläispuku Suomessa Vanhemmalla Waasaajalla, 1550–1620*. Helsinki, 1955. Monochrome plates. The costume of the nobility, clergy and burghers in the earlier Vasa period, 1550–1620. Text in Finnish with English summary.

READE, B. *The Dominance of Spain 1550–1660*. Costume of the Western World Series, Harrap, 1951. Monochrome and colour plates of engravings and portraits showing Spanish fashions.

REYNOLDS, G. *Elizabethan and Jacobean, 1558–1625*. Costume of the Western World Series, Harrap, 1951. Monochrome and colour plates of English costume.

STAATLICHE KUNSTSAMMLUNGEN, DRESDEN. *Historische Prunkleidung*. Dresden, 1963. Catalogue of costumes in the Dresden State Museum, c1550 to the early eighteenth century.

STADTMUSEUM, LINZ. *Figurinen nach alten Schnittbüchern*. Linz, 1968. Catalogue of exhibition showing tailors' patterns for men and women with clothes made from them, c1500–1724. Catalogue by Ingeborg Petrascheck-Heim, plates by Clara Hahmann.

†STOLLEIS, K. *Die Gewänder aus der Lauinger Furstengruft*. Deutscher Kunstverlag, Munich, 1977. Monochrome plates. Catalogue of costumes from the tombs of the Electors Palatine of the Wittelsbach line at Lauingen on the Danube. Includes a catalogue of the jewellery by Irmtraud Himmelheber. All items are now in the Bayerisches Nationalmuseum, Munich.

THIENEN, F. VAN. *The Great Age of Holland, 1600–50*. Costume of the Western World Series, Harrap, 1957. Monochrome and colour plates of engravings and paintings showing Dutch costume.

VICTORIA AND ALBERT MUSEUM. *Princely Magnificence*. Debrett's Peerage, 1980. Numerous colour and monochrome plates. Catalogue of Court jewels of the Renaissance 1500–1630, ed. Anna Somers Cocks.

WALTHER, A. *Das Hausbuch der Familie Melem. Ein Trachtenbuch des Frankfurter Patriziats aus dem 16. Jahrhundert*. Verlag für Wissenschaftliche Literatur, Frankfurt, 1968. Numerous colour plates. Shows clothes worn by members of the Melem family in the

sixteenth century.

WEIGERT, R.A. *Pourpoints et Vertugadins d'après les dessins de la collection Gaignières conservés au cabinet des Estampes de la Bibliothèque Nationale, 1515–1643*. Costumes et modes d'autrefois series, Rombaldi, Paris, 1958. Colour plates.

Books and catalogues not specifically on costume but useful for costume detail.

ANDERSSON, I. *Erik XIV. Livrustkammaren, Stockholm, 1964*. Monochrome plates of portraits and armour.

BELKIN, K.L. *The Costume Book: Corpus Rubenianum Ludwig Burchard, Part XXIV*. Harvey Miller-Heyden & Son, 1981. Illustrated catalogue raisonné in 26 parts of the work of Peter Paul Rubens. *The Costume Book*, a sketchbook by Rubens in the British Museum, contains drawings of figures in late fourteenth- and fifteenth-century Flemish and Burgundian Court fashions, early sixteeth-century German costume and late sixteenth-century Turkish, Persian and Arabic dress. Many are copies after earlier models.

BRAHAM, A. *Giovanni Battista Moroni*. National Gallery, London, 1978. Exhibition catalogue with monochrome plates of paintings.

RANGER'S HOUSE, BLACKHEATH *The Suffolk Collection*. GLC, 1975. Permanent exhibition catalogue with monochrome plates mainly of early seventeenth-century portraits.

REYNOLDS, G. *Nicholas Hilliard and Isaac Oliver*. HMSO, 1971. Over 200 monochrome and a few colour plates of miniatures. Catalogue of exhibition at the Victoria and Albert Museum in 1947, reissued with corrections.

STRONG, R. *The English Icon*. Routledge & Kegan Paul, 1969. Numerous monochrome and a few colour plates of Elizabethan and Jacobean portraits.

STRONG, R. *Tudor and Jacobean Portraits*. 2 vols, HMSO, 1969. Catalogue with monochrome and colour plates of the collection at the National Portrait Gallery, London.

STRONG, R. and MURRELL, J. *Artists of the Tudor Court: the Portrait Miniature Rediscovered 1520–1620*. Victoria and Albert Museum, 1983. Numerous monochrome and 8 pages of colour plates of miniatures and some large portraits.

STRONG, R. and ORGEL, O. *Inigo Jones: the Theatre of the Stuart Court*. 2 vols, Sotheby/Parke Bernet 1973. Numerous monochrome plates illustrating masque costume.

WILLIAMS, N. *All the Queen's Men*. Weidenfeld and Nicolson, 1972. Numerous monochrome and colour plates of Queen Elizabeth I and her courtiers.

Articles devoted to costume and accessories of the sixteenth and early seventeenth century.

ANTHONY, I. 'Clothing given to a Servant of the Late Sixteenth Century in Wales', *Costume*, 14 (1980), pp. 32–40. Transcript of list of clothing c1580–1610.

†ARNOLD, J. 'A study of three jerkins', *Costume*, 5 (1971), pp. 36–43, with notes by J.L. Nevinson and W. Rector. Includes discussion of fragments of a leather jerkin excavated in the City of London.

†ARNOLD, J. 'Sir Richard Cotton's suit', *The Burlington Magazine*, CXV (May 1973), pp. 326–9. Monochrome plates and pattern.

ARNOLD, J. 'Three examples of late sixteenth- and early seventeenth-century neckwear', *Waffen-und Kostümkunde*, Pt. 2 (1973), pp. 109–24. Monochrome plates and patterns of ruffs and supportasse.

†ARNOLD, J. 'Decorative Features: pinking, snipping and slashing', *Costume*, 9 (1975), pp. 22–6. Monochrome plates of sixteenth- and early seventeenth century pinking tools and pinked clothing.

ARNOLD, J. 'Elizabethan and Jacobean smocks and shirts', *Waffen-und Kostümkunde*, Pt. 2 (1977), pp. 89–110. The differences between smocks worn by women and shirts worn by men, with patterns.

†ARNOLD, J. 'Nils Sture's suit', *Costume*, 12 (1978), pp. 13–26. Detailed study of Swedish suit of 1567 with monochrome plates and pattern.

ARNOLD, J. 'The Coronation portrait of Queen Elizabeth I', *The Burlington Magazine*, CXX (November 1978), pp. 727–41. Includes transcript of materials and other items for the coronation of Queen Elizabeth I in 1559.

†ARNOLD J. 'Two Early Seventeenth-Century Fencing Doublets', *Waffen-und Kostümkunde*, Pt. 2 (1979), pp. 107–20. Padded leather doublets probably worn by pages, c1610, with monochrome plates and pattern.

ARNOLD, J. 'Jane Lambarde's Mantle', *Costume*, 14 (1980), pp. 56–72. Discusses Irish and lap mantles. Monochrome plates and pattern.

ARNOLD, J. 'The "Pictur" of Elizabeth I when Princess', *The Burlington Magazine*, CXXIII (May 1981), pp. 303–4. Portrait of 1547 linked to letter.

†ARNOLD, J. 'A woman's doublet of about 1585', *Waffen-und Kostümkunde*, Pt. 2 (1981), pp. 132–42. Detailed summary with monochrome plates and pattern.

BUCKLAND, K. 'The Monmouth Cap', *Costume*, 13 (1979), pp. 23–37. Knitted caps of the sixteenth and seventeenth centuries.

CUMMING, V. 'The trousseau of Princess Elizabeth Stuart', *Collectanea Londiniensa: Studies presented to Ralph Merrifield* (London and Middlesex Archaeological Society, 1978), pp. 315–28. Extracts from the Wardrobe Accounts for the trousseau of James I's daughter, Elizabeth of Bohemia, who was married in 1613.

EKSTRAND, G. 'Some Early Silk Stockings in Sweden', *Textile History*, 13, no. 2 (1982), pp. 165–82. Knitted silk stockings worn by various Swedish kings from 1592 to the mid-seventeenth century.

†FRIES, W. 'Die Kostümsammlung des Germanischen Nationalmuseums zu Nürnberg', *Anzeiger des Germanischen Nationalmuseums*, 1924–5 (1926), pp. 5–35. Descriptions and monochrome plates of sixteenth- and early seventeenth-century costumes at the Germanisches Nationalmuseum.

JAACKS, G. 'Hamburger "Mode" zu Beginn des Dreißigjahrigen Krieges', *Waffen-und Kostümkunde*, Pt. I (1983), pp. 2–16. Monochrome plates. Clothes worn by citizens of Hamburg in the late sixteenth and early seventeenth century.

†KING, D. 'Three Spanish cloaks', *Victoria and Albert Museum Bulletin*, IV, no. I (January 1968), pp. 26–30. Monochrome plates.

LEVEY, S.L. 'An Elizabethan Embroidered Cover', *Victoria and Albert Museum Year Book* (1972), pp. 76–86. The Grenville cover, late sixteenth century with designs for embroidery from Trevelyon's *Miscellany* of 1608.

LÖNNQVIST, B. 'Skinnkjorteln', *Finska Fornminnesföreningen* (Sartryck ur Finskt Museum, 1974) pp. 61–75. Discusses eighteenth-century kirtles made of lambskin, similar to kirtles in Amman's illustration of a furrier's workshop in Nürnberg in 1568.

MACTAGGART, P. and A. 'The Rich Wearing Apparel of Richard, 3rd Earl of Dorset', *Costume*, 14 (1980), pp. 41–55. Transcript of inventory of 1619 including the clothes he wears in Figs. 179 and 200 in this book.

†NEVINSON, J.L. 'New Material for the History of Seventeenth-Century Costume in England', *Apollo*, XX (1934), pp. 315–19. Monochrome plates of items in the collection at Claydon House, near Aylesbury.

NEVINSON, J.L. 'Men's Costume in the Isham Collection', *The Connoisseur*, XCIV (1934), pp. 313–20. Monochrome plates.

NEVINSON, J.L. 'English Embroidered Costume: Elizabeth and James I', *The Connoisseur* XCVII, Pts 1 and 2 (1936), pp. 25–9, 140–4. Monochrome plates.

NEVINSON, J.L. 'Peter Stent and John Overton, Publishers of Embroidery Designs', *Apollo* XXIV (1936), pp. 279–83. 9 monochrome plates.

NEVINSON, J.L. 'English Embroidered Costume in the Collection of Lord Middleton: Part II', *The Connoisseur*, CIII (1939), pp. 136–41. Monochrome plates.

NEVINSON, J.L. 'English Domestic Embroidery Patterns of the 16th and 17th Centuries', *The Walpole Society Annual*, XXVIII (1939–40), pp. 1–13. 8 monochrome plates.

NEVINSON, J.L. 'Shakespeare's Dress in his Portraits', *Shakespeare Quarterly*, XVIII, no. 2 (New York, 1967), pp. 101–16. 4 monochrome plates.

NEVINSON, J.L. 'The Embroidery Patterns of Thomas Trevelyon', *Walpole Society Annual*, XLI (1968), p. 38. Numerous designs and small motifs in 36 monochrome plates.

†NEVINSON, J.L. 'An early 17th-century Night Gown', *Waffen-und Kostümkunde*, Pt. I (1969), pp. 40–1. Monochrome plates.

NEVINSON, J.L. 'The Dress of the Citizens of London, 1540–1640',

Collectanea Londiniensia: Studies presented to Ralph Merrifield (London and Middlesex Archaeological Society, 1978), pp. 265–86. Monochrome plates.

NEVINSON, J.L. 'Illustrations of Costume in the "Alba Amicorum"', *Archaeologia*, CVI (1979), pp. 167–76. Autograph albums of the sixteenth and seventeenth centuries with costume illustrations. Monochrome and colour plates.

†NEVINSON, J.L. 'A Sixteenth-Century Doublet', *Documenta Textilia: Festschrift für S. Müller-Christensen*, ed. M. Flury-Lemberg and K. Stolleis (Deutscher Künstverlag, Munich, 1981), pp. 371–5. Satin doublet at Hever Castle, Kent.

NYLEN, A.M. 'Stureskjortorna', *Livrustkammaren*, IV, 8–9 (Journal of the Royal Armoury, Stockholm, 1948), pp. 217–76. Article on the Sture shirts of 1567 with monochrome plates and patterns. English summary. An English translation of this paper, obtained by Mrs Anne W. Murray, is on file in the archives of the Costume Division, Smithsonian Institute, Washington DC.

OLIAN, J.A. 'Sixteenth-Century Costume Books', *Dress*, no. 3 (1977), pp. 20–48. Useful account of twelve books by Amman, de Bruyn, Boissard, Vecellio and others. Monochrome plates.

PASOLD, E.W. 'In Search of William Lee', *Textile History*, vol. 6 (1975), pp. 7–17. Indenture made between Lee and George Brooke in 1600 about knitting frame invention.

PETRASCHECK-HEIM, I. 'Tailors' Masterpiece Books', *Costume*, 3 (1969), pp. 6–9. Monochrome plates of patterns.

PETRASCHECK-HEIM, I. 'Die Schweizer Leinenstickereien im Voralberger Landesmuseum', *Jahrbuch des Voralberger Landesmuseumsvereins* (Bregenz, 1979), pp. 243–77. Swiss linen embroidery, many dated pieces between 1563 and 1614.

ROHR, A. VON 'Kleidung eines Patriziers aus Einbeck von Ende des 16. Jahrhunderts', *Waffen-und Kostümkunde* (1976), pp 69–75. Examples of men's clothing surviving from the end of the sixteenth century.

ROHR, A. VON. 'Der Kleider-Nachlass des Herzogs Moritz von Sachsen-Lauenburg von 1612', *Waffen-und Kostümkunde* (1976), pp. 118–28. Items of clothing worn by Duke Moritz of Sachsen-Lauenburg who died in 1612, which are now in various museum collections.

SHOES: TRANSACTIONS OF MUSEUM ASSISTANTS GROUP NO 12 (1973), (Belfast, 1975). Record of seminar includes shoe fashions to 1600 by June Swann.

SPIERS, C.H. 'Deer skin leathers and their use for costume', *Costume*, 7 (1973), pp. 14–23. Useful sixteenth- and seventeenth-century material.

STERN, E. 'Peckover and Gallyard, Two Sixteenth-Century Norfolk Tailors', *Costume*, 15 (1981), pp. 13–23. Tailors' bills and purchases of materials from household accounts of the Stiffkey Bacons for 1587–97.

STOLLEIS, K. 'Die Kleidung des Octavian Secundus Fugger (1549–1600) aus dem Nachlassinventar von 1600/01', *Waffen-und Kostümkunde*, 23 (1981), pp. 113–31. Monochrome plates. Inventory of clothes owned by O.S. Fugger.

STOLLEIS, K. 'Die Kleider des Maria Jacobäa Fugger (1562–1588)', *Documenta Textilia: Festschrift für S. Müller-Christensen*, ed. M. Flury-Lemberg and K. Stolleis (Deutscher Kunstverlag, Munich, 1981). Inventory of clothes owned by M.J. Fugger.

THIENEN, F. VAN and BRAUN-RONSDORF, M. 'Ein Niederländische Silberschmeidearbeit des 17. Jahrhunderts', *Waffen-und Kostümkunde* (1970). Article on silver supportasse c1610–20.

TURNAU, I. 'Stockings from the coffins of the Pomeranian Princes preserved in the National Museum in Szczecin', *Textile History*, 8 (1977), pp. 167–9. Three stockings found in Polish tombs, dated to c1600, which may be machine-knitted.

WILCKENS, L. VON. 'Kleiderverzeichnisse aus zwei Jahrhunderten in den Nachlassinventaren wohlhabender Nürnbergerinnen', *Waffen-und Kostümkunde*, Pt. I (1979), pp. 25–41. Transcripts of lists of clothes from inventories of the estates of seven wealthy Nürnberg women of the sixteenth and seventeenth centuries. Monochrome plates.

WILCKENS, L. VON. 'Ein "Haarmantel" des 16. Jahrhunderts', *Waffen-und Kostümkunde*, Pt. I, (1980), pp. 39–44. Embroidered linen cape for spreading over shoulders while combing hair, thought to be Indo-Portuguese work, c1550–75.